The illustrated encyclopedia of the strategy, tactics and weapons of

RUSSIAN
MILITARY POWER

The illustrated encyclopedia of the strategy, tactics and weapons of

RUSSIAN
MILITARY POWER

Consultant:
Air Vice-Marshal Stewart Menaul, CB, CBE, DFC, AFC

BONANZA BOOKS
New York

A Salamander Book

1982 edition published by
Bonanza Books,
A division of Crown Publishers, Inc.,
One Park Avenue,
New York,
New York 10016,
United States of America.

© Salamander Books Ltd. 1980

ISBN 0-517-386968

All correspondence concerning the content of this volume should be addressed to Salamander Books Ltd., Salamander House, 27 Old Gloucester Street, London WC1N 3AF, United Kingdom.

Credits

Editor: Ray Bonds

Designer: Lloyd Martin

Color drawings:
  Aircraft: © Pilot Press Ltd.; Gordon Davies and Keith Fretwell.
  Armoured vehicles: John W. Wood & Associates, Gordon Davies and Terry Hadler.
  Missiles: Mike Badrocke and Wilf Hardy.
Line drawings:
  Aircraft: © Pilot Press Ltd.
  Warships: © Siegfried Breyer.

Filmset by SX Composing Ltd., and Modern Text Typesetting

Color reproduction: Bantam Litho Ltd.

Printed in Belgium by Henri Proost et Cie, Turnhout.

The Contributors

Consultant:
Air Vice-Marshal Stewart Menaul, CB, CBE, DFC, AFC, retired from the Royal Air Force in 1968 after a distinguished career in peace and war, and became Director-General of the Royal United Services Institute for Defence Studies, a post he held until 1976. He is Vice-President of the Military Commentators Circle, a member of the Consultative Council of the Foreign Affairs Research Institute, consultant to the Institute for the Study of Conflict, a member of the International Institute for Strategic Studies and consultant to a number of institutes in the United States. He is a contributor to many journals and magazines including *International Defense Review, Defence, NATO's Fifteen Nations, Flug Review, Flight International, Wehrtechnik, Strategic Review* and many others. He is a frequent broadcaster on defense and current affairs on radio and television in Britain and the United States. His most recent publication was *NATO in the Eighties — A War-Winning Strategy*, published by the Institute for the Study of Conflict.

Brigadier Shelford Bidwell is a military historian and student of contemporary defense affairs who has been an instructor at the British Army Staff College and the Royal School of Artillery, and editor and deputy director at the Royal United Services Institute for Defence Studies, London. He is a Fellow of the Royal Historical Society, and his books include *Modern Warfare, World War 3* (editor), *The Chindit War*, and Salamander's *The Illustrated Encyclopedia of Land Warfare in the 20th Century* (contributor).

Christopher N. Donnelly, BA, is Assistant Head of the Soviet Studies Centre, Royal Military Academy, Sandhurst. He is a frequent lecturer and a broadcaster on Soviet affairs, is a member of the Council of the Royal United Services Institute for Defence Studies, a member of the International Institute for Strategic Studies, and has contributed technical articles on Soviet tactics and weapons to international journals, including *International Defense Review, NATO's Fifteen Nations, Journal of the RUSI,* and *Soviet Armed Forces Yearbook.*

Dr. James E. Dornan, Jr. Before his death in 1979, the late Dr. Dornan was Associate Professor and Chairman, Department of Politics, Catholic University of America, and Senior Political Science Scientist at the Strategic Studies Center of Stanford Research Institute International.

Acknowledgements

Containing, as it does, such a wealth of hard technical data, fascinating and useful background information and, above all, such revealing photographs (many of which have never before been published in a book in the West), this book is unique. It represents the compilation of contributions from several institutions and individuals from many parts of the world. The publishers would like to thank all who have so contributed, and in particular give credit to the following: the late Dr James E. Dornan, Jr., whose chapter on the Soviet Strategic Rocket Forces has been updated and added to by the Salamander editorial team; the British Ministry of Defence and Soviet Studies Centre at RMA Sandhurst; various audio-visual agencies of the United States Department of Defense Office of Information; Harriet Fast Scott and *Air Force Magazine* who originally prepared the organisational charts on pages 54 and 62, and *Air Force Magazine* for also permitting us to use as a basis their map of Warsaw Pact and NATO air force bases in the preparation of the map shown on page 63; Novosti; E. and TV Films Ltd.

Ray Bonds

Professor John Erickson is Professor of Politics and the Director of Defence Studies, University of Edinburgh, Scotland; he is a frequent broadcaster on defense affairs on television and radio; the author of *The Soviet High Command*, and *The Road to Stalingrad*, and editor of *Soviet Military Power and Performance*; he is also consultant to the US Strategic Institute's *Strategic Review*.

Bill Gunston is a former World War II RAF pilot and flying instructor, and has spent most of his working life accumulating a wealth of information on the history of aviation and military technology. Since leaving the Service in 1948, he has acted as an adviser to several major aviation companies and become one of the most internationally respected authors on scientific and aviation subjects, and a frequent broadcaster. His numerous books include the Salamander titles *The Illustrated Encyclopedia of the World's Modern Military Aircraft*, *The Encyclopedia of the World's Combat Aircraft*, *Hitler's Luftwaffe* (with Tony Wood), *The Illustrated Encyclopedia of Combat Aircraft of World War II* and *Soviet Air Power* (with Bill Sweetman), and *The Illustrated Encyclopedia of the World's Rockets and Missiles*. A regular contributor to many leading international aviation and defense journals, he is a former technical editor of *Flight International* and technology editor of *Science Journal*. He is an assistant compiler of *Jane's All The World's Aircraft* and has contributed to *Brassey's Annual Defence Yearbook*.

Captain J.E. Moore, RN, FRGS, was born in Genoa, Italy, and educated in New Zealand and Sherborne School, Dorset, England. He entered the Royal Navy as a cadet on September 1 1939 and served in surface ships in the North Atlantic and Arctic, and as a hydrographer in the Far East before joining submarines in 1943. He continued in submarines after the war and was promoted to Commander in 1957. Following staff appointments in Turkey and the Plans Division of the Admiralty, he commanded the Seventh Submarines Squadron in Singapore. After promotion to Captain in 1967 he was Chief of Staff to CinC Naval Home Command, and was in charge of Soviet Naval Intelligence for the Royal Navy from 1969 to 1972. On voluntary retirement in 1972 Captain Moore became editor of *Jane's Fighting Ships.* He was consultant on Salamander's *The Encyclopedia of the World's Warships*, and his other books include *The Soviet Navy Today, Seapower and Politics* and *Warships of the Royal Navy*.

P.H. Vigor began his career in the field of Soviet studies when, during World War II, he was sent from Britain to get the Poles out of the USSR, and organise and train them as what was subsequently to become the 2nd Polish Corps under General Anders. He renewed his acquaintance with the Russians in 1945, when he was posted to Berlin. In 1948 he joined the staff at RMA Sandhurst, and took over as Head of the newly formed Soviet Studies Centre in 1973, a post he continued to hold until his retirement in 1979. He has broadcast a number of times on Soviet affairs, and is the author of numerous articles and books, among them *The Soviet View of War, Peace and Neutrality* and *A Guide to Marxism*. He is a regular contributor to the Journal of the Royal United Services Institute for Defence Studies.

Contents

Introduction

In the 1930s democratic people watched with growing incredulity as the world's political systems broke up: the Depression gave rise to disintegration, disintegration led to anarchy, and anarchy to war. Some eminent men, observing the pattern of events and foreseeing the consequences, tried to bring them to public notice. Sadly, the general reaction, especially in the Anglo-Saxon countries, was that those who warned of the dangers were 'prophets of doom' and 'alarmists'. Peace could be maintained, so the theory ran, by just one more minor concession; but each such surrender was never the last, but led inexorably towards bigger demands. This whole tragic story is epitomised in one word: 'Appeasement'. The extraordinary thing is that it all seems to have been forgotten and there is a strong possibility that the same bitter and costly lessons will have to be learnt all over again in the last two decades of the Twentieth Century. There are, however, two major differences: the first is that this time the destructive power that could be unleashed is of quite terrifying proportions, far greater than the worst horrors of all previous wars put together. The second is that the potential aggressor is far more powerful, and its armed forces and economy far more geared to war, than was Hitler's Germany.

The root cause of this situation and the principal threat to world peace is the Union of Soviet Socialist Republics, whose drive for dominance is based upon a military build-up without parallel in history.

The Soviet Union has acquired superpower status, and its voice is heeded in world affairs, because of, and *only* because of, its military might. The status is not in any way due to economic power, or trade, nor is it due to political or ideological leadership. The USSR has a front seat in the councils of the world only because of the size of its armed forces and their potential threatened or actual use as an instrument of Soviet policy. 'War', observed von Clausewitz, 'is a tool of policy . . . . the continuation of a nation's foreign policy by violent means'. The undoubted policy of the Communist Party of the Soviet Union (CPSU) is the establishment of (Russian-style) Communism, initially in the USSR, and subsequently its spread throughout the world. War will be used, therefore, to advance the cause of Communism on those occasions and in those places where it is considered to be the best tool for the job, *provided that* it does not involve undue risk to Mother Russia and the CPSU, and provided that victory is certain.

In those areas of the world where the use of armed force promises quick and effective results at little or no cost and minimum risk such force will be used to extend Soviet Communist influence, unrestrained by any bourgeois or Christian scruples over loss of life. Angola, Ethiopia and Afghanistan have all recently been 'communised' by force of arms. In no case did the Soviet Union risk confrontation with the USA; rather, it chose the timing with consummate skill, and in two cases even employed proxy forces, reducing the risk even further. Had any of the operations failed totally the Soviets could have withdrawn with little more than a temporary loss of face as they did, for example, in Cuba, Egypt and Somalia. High stakes, indeed, but at little cost and small risk!

The non-Communist world has only gradually been waking-up to the fact that the Soviet Union's unconcealed expansionism constitutes the gravest threat to peace the world has ever known. Further, the democracies are disunited as never before, and in early 1980, for example, could not even agree on measures to express their condemnation of the Soviet aggression in Afghanistan. The situation does, indeed, bear many similarities to the late 1930s, and then, too, those who warned of the dangers were branded as warmongers.

Every little patch of land, every additional little country whose allegiance is switched away from the Capitalist bloc to the Communist bloc is one extra weight on the Soviet scales in the 'balance of power'. Even this term is misleading, because it has different meanings in Moscow and Washington. In the West 'balance of power' implies a state of equilibrium between the world's greatest states, which guarantees stability and peace. In such a balance nobody would want war because they could not obtain the degree of superiority necessary to win. To the Soviet Union, however, peace can only be guaranteed if it and the Communist bloc can so tip the balance of power (or *correlation of forces*, as they term it) in their favour that the Capitalist bloc can never hope to challenge them. War would then cease to be an effective tool of Capitalist power, and overwhelming Communist military might would prevent Capitalism from lashing out desperately in its death throes. The more the 'correlation of forces' tips in Communism's favour, therefore, the less is the danger of global war; the stronger the Soviet armed forces, and the more they facilitate the spread of Soviet influence throughout the world, the greater is their contribution to a genuine and permanent *Pax Sovietica*.

The USSR does not seek parity; it seeks, in the long term, absolute military superiority—in other words, a permanent *imbalance* of power. If the Soviet Union were to state such a policy in public the West would obviously react by raising its guard and rearming properly, which would halt the imbalancing process which the Kremlin is aiming for. The deeds of the Soviet Union speak louder than any words, however, as this book clearly shows.

To this Marxist-Leninist view of the world must be added a traditional Russian view of great power status. The Russians have for a long time considered themselves to be the greatest European power, but they feel that an appropriate position in pan-European affairs has been denied them through a combination of accidents of fate and political obstruction by other countries. In recent years their elevation to superpower status, and their growing worldwide role, have given them a new self-confidence. This, when set against their traditional inferiority complex vis-à-vis the West in terms of wealth and standard-of-living, has resulted in an increase in their natural assertiveness. Just as any individual Russian in a position of authority will tend to become a bully and throw his weight about (as any Westerner who has clashed with Soviet bureaucracy can confirm) so will the whole country react when it is in a similar position among other nations. The Soviet attitude to their Warsaw Pact 'allies' bears this out in full, and in the Third World the Soviet Union has been accepted only for its aid or goods, never for love or admiration of its people or policies (indeed, these policies have caused some 'friendly' nations to turn away from the USSR toward the West).

The USSR has two major strategic aims. The first, and shorter-term, is the domination of Western Europe by the Soviet Union, and success in this will lead inevitably to achievement of the second, which is the elimination of the United States as an obstacle to Soviet progress. Western Europe is a major problem for the USSR as it is the antithesis of everything the Soviet system stands for and acts as an almost irresistible attraction for the peoples of Eastern Europe. Indeed, only by military power can the USSR manage to retain these satellites within its orbit, and the realities of that have been exhibited by the brutal suppression of uprisings in East Berlin, Hungary, Poland and Czechoslovakia. Perhaps the most telling comment of all, however, is the mute testimony of the border between East and West Germany, where hundreds of miles of barbed-wire, stone walls, minefields and electronic aids are needed to keep the people in. Most walls are built to keep intruders out; only prisons, mental homes and Communist countries need walls to keep the inmates from escaping.

Should a war in Europe start it will be essential for the USSR to win it *very quickly indeed*, achieving the military collapse of its opponents before the politicians can authorise nuclear release, and certainly before the USA decides on strategic nuclear retaliation. Speed in winning the war must, therefore, be all-important, and the Soviet armed forces' organisation, tactics and equipment reflect this. In modern terms, say the Soviet strategists, if the enemy is well-prepared and waiting there is little hope of winning a war quickly and without the use of nuclear weapons. No reasonably attainable level of conventional superiority can guarantee success *in a few days* unless the enemy is taken totally by suprise (which, taking into account satellite reconnaissance and other intelligence-gathering, is hardly possible today) and his deployment pre-empted or prevented. Then, with little opposition, the chances of a quick political victory are immeasurably increased. So, the next war, if the USSR can seize and retain the initiative, will not only be quick, but it will also be sudden. This requirement, too, is reflected in the organisation, equipment, tactics and training of the Soviet armed forces and constant readiness is always being stressed.

However, policies can misfire, and conflicts do break out when they have not been planned. A nation bullied by 'peaceful persuasion' may strike back by force; newly powerful nations or forceful leaders may emerge in a matter of a few years; wars may start by accident, or be triggered off by madmen, despite every reasonable precaution. Then, too, some of the local wars may escalate out of control. Also, the perceptions of the Soviet leaders may change and a new generation may come to believe that what was previously considered too risky is no longer so, especially in view of the military power now available to them. Regardless of the cause, however, if a war should start then the USSR would do its utmost to win it quickly and decisively.

In the present circumstances a war could involve either a strategic attack on the USA, or perhaps there would be an attempt to confine it to Europe. It is even possible, and certainly it is in the Soviet interest, that the war may start as a conventional conflict; after all, the Soviets would not wish to capture a nuclear-devastated wasteland.

The build-up of the Soviet armed forces would be a phenomenon of great academic interest were it not directed so powerfully against the West. That there are millions of Soviet people under arms is not news either. What is disquieting is that the vast forces of the Soviet Union are no longer simple peasants with simple weapons, but skilled and dedicated troops deploying equipment that is beating the West's in both quantity and, increasingly of late, in quality as well.

An even more fearsome menace is presented by what the Soviet military refer to as 'weapons of mass destruction'. We do not know much about their chemical and bacteriological weapons, beyond the announced fact that chemical weapons at least are regarded by the Soviet armed forces as routine options to be used whenever the tactical circumstances so dictate. But we do know quite a lot about the Soviet Strategic Rocket Forces and the ballistic missile submarines of Admiral Gorshkov's ever-expanding navy. Ordinary people are unfamiliar with the technicalities of 'throw-weights' and 'megatons', but if they study these forces they must inevitably conclude that with their planned overkill the Soviet Union could destroy the whole of animal life on this planet not just once, but ten or twenty times over.

There may be some who feel that this book is an anti-Soviet diatribe, concentrating on the sensational and ignoring factors favourable to the Eastern bloc. However, it is repeated that the deeds of the Soviet Union speak louder than any words, and perhaps the most telling comment of all is the well-documented conversion of President Carter. He entered the White House pledged to support détente, to cut military spending, to reduce arms sales, and to withdraw United States' forces from the Indian Ocean and South Korea. He clung tenaciously to these beliefs during his first three years in office; in 1977 he even proclaimed publicly that: '. . . . the US is now free of that inordinate fear of Communism which once led us to embrace any dictator who joined us in that fear'. The President extended a generous hand of friendship to the USSR, and strived to create a new atmosphere of trust and mutual understanding. The Soviet Union, however, has consistently failed to respond in kind, and has simply taken ever greater advantage of what it judged to be Carter's weakness. As a result President Carter has become almost as 'hawkish' as any post-War American leader, culminating in a totally unambiguous statement of his new stand:

'Let our position be absolutely clear; an attempt by any outside force to gain control of the Persian Gulf region will be regarded as an assault on the vital interests of the United States. And such an assault will be repelled by any means necessary, including military force.'

For those who refuse to believe the claims about the strength of the Soviet War Machine, let them heed the bitter lesson which President Carter has had to learn; let them read this book.

The Rise of Soviet Communism

The tasks of the Soviet armed forces are to defend the borders of the USSR, to maintain control over the satellites, or to prosecute an offensive war, whichever is dictated by the CPSU leadership. The Kremlin is still bitterly opposed to the Western form of society and reasserts this daily; the same applies, if for somewhat different reasons, to the Peoples' Republic of China. Such spiritual antagonisms would hardly be sufficient in themselves to provoke war in an era of nuclear weapons, but should the material and ideological interests coincide a war could be possible.

P. H. Vigor

The Soviet Union did not arise out of nothing in November 1917, a state newborn, devoid of roots with the past. On the contrary, it was an old state, a state which had been called Russia; and although as a result of the Revolution it admittedly became possessed of a new ideology, nevertheless it continued to be possessed of the old, old problems that had plagued the Russia of the tsars. For instance, it was too big a country to be administered easily and efficiently, and the Bolsheviks found the running of it as big a problem as the Romanov emperors had done. It was a country where the good farming land formed only a comparatively small proportion of the total surface area, and the Bolsheviks found it as difficult to feed the towns of Soviet

Lenin and a group of the Red Guards during the October Revolution. The Guards' task was to seize power for the Bolsheviks and they were the true precursors of the Red Army.

Russia as Nicholas II had found it difficult to feed those of Imperial Russia. More specifically related to our present purpose, Soviet Russia, like Imperial Russia, was bordered by a number of other countries which were sometimes friendly and sometimes hostile, but which could never be wholly ignored. In the military sense, therefore, just because she was Russia, and situated on the same spot on the globe where Russia had always been situated, the USSR, like Imperial Russia, was confronted by the need to possess armed forces that could guard those lengthy borders.

Nor was the purpose of the Soviet forces invariably defensive, any more than the purpose of those of the tsars had been. The one, like the other, resorted to the offensive on occasions, in order either to extend their existing dominions (Georgia in 1921, eastern Poland and Finland in 1939, Latvia, Lithuania and Estonia in 1940) or to chastise what their government considered to be intolerable provocation (China in 1929).

We therefore see that the Soviet Union needed, and so created, armies, navies and air forces for the same sort of reasons that other countries (what the average reader might mentally label 'ordinary' countries) needed and created theirs. On top of this, however, there was a further reason, derived from the Soviet Union's political and economic ideology, which increased the pressure on her Bolshevik rulers to create their military forces of a particular and unusual type, and to create them, moreover, on a very large scale indeed. Consequently, it is impossible to proceed any further with this discussion without examining, at least in outline, the nature of Soviet ideology; for

this provides an essential clue to the type of armed forces that materialised.

The ideology in question is Marxism–Leninism. This comprises those parts of Marx's theories which Lenin thought to be useful to him, coupled with his own views on politics and economics and, in particular, with his invention of a new type of political party (which is usually called a 'communist' party), whose function was to plan the seizure of power, to cling on to that power after its successful seizure and to make use of its grip on the various levers of government to force the population to evolve in particular directions towards a specific goal called 'communism'.

The ultimate goal of Marxism–Leninism, therefore, is the achievement of communism, a goal which the USSR, on its own admission, has not yet managed to reach. At the present moment, the USSR is a 'Union of Soviet *Socialist* Republics'; and it has advanced along the Leninist evolutionary chain only so far as the half-way house of socialism. Leninist-style socialism, unlike communism, permits the use of money; it also permits tremendous differentials in wages, as Soviet practice demonstrates. Thus in the Soviet Union today there are a great many people with a low standard of living and a great many others with one which, by comparison, must be rated extremely high. On the other hand, Leninist-style socialism concurs with communism in forbidding private enterprise, in the sense

Below: Red Guards pose for the camera during the October Revolution. Their actions put the Bolsheviks into power, but the conduct of government in the USSR and aspects of foreign policy are virtually the same today as under the Tsars.

Above: The famous Soviet aircraft designer A. N. Tupolev with one of his earliest designs, the ANT-1 'sport plane' of 1923. From these humble beginnings Tupolev went on to head the design bureau which was responsible for the Tu-2 attack bomber of World War II, the Tu-35 jet bomber, culminating in the Tu-144.

Below: Armed force as an ingredient for the seizure of power. A pro-Bolshevik mobile machine-gun detachment patrolling the streets of Moscow during the uprising. While the Russian character is in many ways resistant to change, the Soviet Army has always been quick to see how new ideas can be put to an effective and often novel military use.

sure that it would eventually happen.

Successive rulers in the communist countries have continued to share this belief.

Khrushchev proclaimed it in the course of a number of his speeches, such as those he made at the 22nd Party Congress; Brezhnev and his colleagues have continued to proclaim it in the days since Krushchev's overthrow. Thus, in the most recent party congress yet to have taken place, Brezhnev declared not merely that 'the total triumph of Socialism all over the world is inevitable', but also that it was the bounden duty of the Soviet Communist Party to speed up this process.

But as well as the actual date of this transformation being, even now, a matter of considerable uncertainty, a further degree of uncertainty hangs over the question concerning the means to be employed for bringing it about. A careful reading of Marx, Engels and Lenin, and indeed of such figures as Stalin, Khrushchev and Brezhnev, allows the reader to deduce from their works two answers, each of which, in its purest form, flatly contradicts the other. One answer says, or can be interpreted as saying, that time alone will be sufficient for its accomplishment; the other says that force will have to be used. The degree of force and the kind of force that will be necessary are, once again, enveloped in obscurity; but that a use of force of some kind is not only desirable but essential under certain circumstances has been asserted only quite recently by the newspaper *Pravda* in its issue of 6 August 1975.

Leaving aside the degree of force to be applied, the kind of force is relevant to our present purposes; for although some communist governments have indeed gained power by little more than an extension of civil violence (Kerala in India in 1957, for instance), others, including the Soviet Union itself, have required the application of a kind of force which must at least be called paramilitary throughout (Red Guards from the factories armed with rifles and machine-guns). Sometimes this has resulted in a purely professional military operation undertaken not by para-military, but by regular military units (the activities of the Petrograd Garrison and the Baltic Fleet in 1917 are an obvious example of this). Further down the scale come instances where the installation of a communist government in a country has been effected virtually single-handed by that country's regular armed forces. At the time of writing, it is not yet certain whether the 1975 revolution in Portugal is going to result in the coming to power of a communist government in that country; but if it is, it is both a recent and also a clear example of the use of force of this kind.

Finally, there are the instances where communist governments have been installed in countries as a result of invasion from without. In such cases, the Soviet Army has marched across their frontiers and forcibly 'bolshevised' them. (The armies of Communist China did the same thing in the case of Tibet, although a purist may object that the use of the word 'bolshevised' is inappropriate here.) Attempts are frequently made by the Soviet Communist Party to conceal from us this fact, generally by spouting the old quotation from Engels to the effect that one cannot thrust com-

of the private ownership of factories, farms and so on; and with the exception of the peasant's private plot, that is exactly the position in practice in the USSR today.

Moreover, Marxism-Leninism envisages this change-over from capitalism to communism as taking place eventually over the whole world. In other words, it will not just be Russia, together with the rest of what we often refer to as the 'Communist bloc' that will experience this transformation, but the United States, Great Britain, West Germany, France, Japan and all the capitalist countries as well. It is true that no actual date was set by either Marx or Lenin for the accomplishment of this worldwide transformation; but it is also true that they were

ВПЕРЕД! ПОБЕДА БЛИЗКА!

munism on people with a bayonet. Despite this quotation, the fact remains that on a number of occasions the Soviet armed forces have done precisely that.

This was done only when the circumstances were right, of course. And in this connection it is pertinent to remark that Soviet theory considers that circumstances are wrong for the undertaking of a military expedition unless its success can be virtually taken for granted. And, historically speaking,

there have been none too many occasions when an expedition undertaken by the Soviet armed forces was well-nigh bound to be successful: the Red Army and the Red Navy were weak both in respect of numbers and of quality of equipment until well into the late 1930s, and for a number of years after the end of World War II they had little hope of attacking successfully any but a primitive and poorly armed opponent, as a result of their tremendous losses in men and

Above: The Soviets have always made effective use of poster-art propaganda. This junior-lieutenant of a Guards unit (denoted by banner and star badge) is saying: 'Forward — victory is near.'

Below: Armed force as an instrument for the retention of power. This guard outside the Bolshevik headquarters in Petrograd in 1917 is composed of both uniformed soldiers and hastily armed civilian auxiliaries manning a heavy machine-gun.

material which they incurred on the Eastern Front.

Nevertheless, despite these qualifications, circumstances have been sufficiently favourable at various moments in the history of the Soviet armed forces for them to be employed on more than one occasion for the invasion of another country and its forcible 'bolshevisation'. Some of these occasions have already been mentioned above – Georgia in 1921, Latvia, Lithuania and Estonia in 1940 – but to these we must add the enforced 'communisation' of the countries of Eastern Europe at the end of World War II. Admittedly the entry of the Red Army into these latter countries was dictated by the need to pursue the forces of Nazi Germany; but once installed in them, it proceeded to make use of its presence to see that the governments brought to power in them should be communist in all but name. Of course it is virtually certain that if the peoples of those countries had had the chance of expressing their wishes, and expressing them freely and without constraint, they would not have wanted exactly that form of society that prevailed in them prior to the war. It is also certain, however, that the kind of society they wanted was not the sort they were forced to acquire as a result of the presence in their countries of the Soviet Army. In other words, in the case of the 'satellite' countries the Soviet armed forces produced, and were intended to produce, a 'communisation' of their societies and governments that can only be described as 'enforced'.

But the ideology of Marxism–Leninism has served not merely to equip the Soviet armed forces with a particular kind of offensive, in the sense that it has given them a motive to attack some other country which they might otherwise have left in peace; it has served also to equip them with a particular kind of defensive.

By this is meant that just as Marxism–Leninism indicated targets which might conceivably be suitable for military invasion but which Russian nationalism, if left to itself, would have rejected as unsuitable (Lenin's plan for the Red Army to march into Hungary in 1919 is a case in point), so it also created for Russia a number of enemies who, in the absence of any such ideological conflict, would probably never have been her enemies at all. The prime example undoubtedly is the United States of America.

The younger generation may be reasonably expected to imagine that the United States and the USSR have always been natural enemies; but a brief look at the history of these two countries will show that this view is wrong, or rather, to be accurate, that it is true only of the Russia of the Soviet period. It is not true of the Russia before the revolution.

Furthermore, it was no part of the classic Marxist tradition that the United States was to be regarded as particularly damnable by every good revolutionary. On the contrary, Marx and Engels themselves were, generally speaking, favourably inclined to the USA, holding that country to be a great deal more democratic and more progressive than the Britain, France, Germany, Austria, Italy, Spain and Russia of their time. Lenin before World War I was also of the same opinion,

and it was not until the American intervention in the Civil War of 1918–1920 that he altered his view of that country. But since that intervention was itself ideologically motivated, in the sense that its avowed purpose was to get rid of the communists from Russia; and since the American government's subsequent refusal to have diplomatic relations with the Soviet Union (a refusal with which it persisted until 1933) was also ideologically motivated, it is reasonable to say that it was the very existence of a communist government as such in control of Russia that led to the enmity between the latter and America which seems so natural today.

But although America is the most notable, it is not the only example of enmity between Russia and another country being mostly ideologically inspired. France must be counted another such, and so must Holland and Belgium. Admittedly France invaded Russia in the course of the Napoleonic wars, and repeated the experiment (although on a smaller scale) in the course of the Crimean War; but in the long sweep of the history of Franco–Russian relations these two incidents distinguish themselves as being very much of an exception. Relations between France and Russia were usually good, the huge distances separating the two countries being largely responsible for this. In addition, French civilization was traditionally very much admired by the educated classes of Russia; and the Russian aristocracy generally spoke French as fluently as they did Russian.

In the cases of Holland and Belgium, again it was the great distances which separated them from Russia that must be accounted chiefly responsible for their relations being so friendly. This situation held good so long as Imperial Russia continued in existence; it is only since the communists took power and threatened (or at any rate, seemed to threaten) the integrity of the whole of Western Europe that the Dutch and the Belgians joined an alliance that was aimed at resisting, militarily if necessary, the ambitions of the USSR.

Britain provides an example, however, of an old enmity having been merged and assimilated into a new one. For very many years, Britain was an opponent of Russia, fearing an advance eastwards by tsarist forces for the purpose of invading India. She was also afraid of the imbalance in Europe that would be created if Russia were to gain direct access to the Mediterranean Sea. That Britain now finds herself in the North Atlantic Treaty Organisation (NATO), with the object of blocking further Soviet advance in central, southern and western Europe, is merely to say that today she fears the invasion of her own homeland rather than that of any former colonial possessions, but that the traditional British suspicion of Russian intentions, and hence the traditional antagonism towards Russian policies, continues unchecked.

The case of Japan is similar. Japanese policies came into conflict with those of

It is a common Soviet practice to hold massive parades of military might. These not only show the primacy of Party over the military, but exhibit that power to both the Soviet people and foreigners alike.

ЗАЩИТИМ РОДНУЮ

МОСКВУ

Imperial Russia almost from the moment when Commodore Perry with his squadron of American warships in 1854 made the Japanese abandon their isolation and take their place in the world. The Russo–Japanese War of 1904–1905 was the first explosion between them; but the Japanese invasion of eastern Siberia during the Russian Civil War, the clashes in Mongolia between Soviet and Japanese forces in 1938 and 1939, and the Soviet attack on the Japanese army in Manchuria in 1945 are merely further examples of such explosions, which embrace both the tsarist and the communist periods. Nor, so long as the ownership of the Kuril Islands and the southern half of Sakhalin Island continues to be allotted as it is at present, can one truthfully say that Soviet–Japanese antagonism can possibly be regarded as dead.

Finally, there is China. Here is a country which, during the nineteenth century, was preyed on by tsarist Russia, just as she was preyed on by the Western European countries and by America and Japan. The predatory policies of Alexander III and Nicholas II naturally engendered hostility between China and Russia; but it was to be expected that, when the tsars were evicted and a confessedly anti-colonialist government took power in the Soviet Union, the causes of that hostility, essentially colonialist in their origin, should speedily be extinguished. This did not happen.

Nor did it happen later, which was even more remarkable, when China herself became subject to a communist government, and both the USSR and China were therefore ideologically akin. So far from that hostility being extinguished, it has, if anything grown. This is because the old traditional enmity has been reinforced by the new ideological enmity. The Soviet and Chinese versions of Marxism-Leninism, which in the years immediately following the Chinese Communist takeover were very much akin, have since that time evolved along divergent paths. The resulting differences between them have fuelled the traditional enmities between the Russian and the Chinese peoples, to such an extent that the two countries have fought each other on more than one occasion in areas around the frontier, as a result of which the Soviet Union now keeps a strong army of approximately 45 divisions along the Chinese border. Here, then, is another old enemy which is now also a new enemy; and the Soviet armed forces must therefore be designed and trained and equipped and deployed to cope with these different antagonisms. In addition, they must be able to suppress revolt within the 'satellite' countries and the USSR herself. Leaving aside the 'satellites', though, and concentrating on the Soviet Union's external enemies or potential enemies, it is clear that these forces must be able to implement, with regard to each single one of them, both

Above left: A poster dating from the early stages of the German invasion. Soldier, sailor and workers tell the people: "Let us defend our native Moscow".

Left: A typical example of the work of Soviet artists during World War II shows a tank unit in good spirits resting in a pine forest during a lull in the fighting.

Above: The modern Soviet Army holding a defensive position against Communist Chinese forces on the 'Kamennaya Ridge' in the Semipalatinsk region in 1969. The Soviets have an obsessive preoccupation with the threat from the East and frequent border incidents have led to a marked growth in the forces facing China.

Below: It will take many generations before the Soviet peoples forget the dreadful cost of the German attack on their country. During the years 1941 to 1945 some 7,500,000 Soviet soldiers and 3,000,000 civilians are believed to have died. This shattered house in Stalingrad carries a poster headed: 'Death to the Killers of Children'. Houses can be rebuilt but the mental scars remain.

an offensive and a defensive policy. If the Kremlin decides that the task of the Soviet armed forces is to confine themselves to preserving intact the present frontiers of Russia (i.e. to implementing a purely defensive policy), then the Russian generals and admirals must be able to achieve this.

If, on the other hand, the Kremlin decides on launching an offensive war on one or other of its neighbours, or on all of them, then this too the generals and admirals must be able to accomplish. As a third possibility, they may be required to defend one section of their frontiers, and attack in another.

The motive for this attack or this defence will, as has been seen, be partly due to the traditional sorts of causes that have sparked off warfare for centuries between one country and another (the desire to grab more territory or to prevent the loss of one's own territory, the wish to chastise an insult, the urge to gain access to markets or raw materials or to extend one's sphere of influence, and other factors). The USSR, like her tsarist predecessor, has on several occasions initiated wars of this sort, and has moreover suffered them at the hands of others. But another motive for attack or defence will be mainly ideological; and, once again, examples of each are to be met with in Soviet history.

Today, however, it is not very likely that either motive of itself would be sufficient to spark off actual hostilities. The USSR, even now, is bitterly opposed to our Western form of society, and asserts this almost hourly. But this kind of spiritual antagonism is hardly enough, in an age where both sides bristle with nuclear weapons, to spark off another war. The same sort of thing may be

said about the Russians' relations with China. In each case, it is only if the traditional (i.e. material) interest is strong, and coincides firmly with the ideological interest, so that both these interests point decisively in the same direction, that actual war is likely to break out; and this is true whether the putative aggressor is to be assumed to be the West or Communist China or the USSR herself.

On the other hand, in recent years the Russians have engaged in a number of experiments aimed at fighting their enemies by proxy. The Cubans in Angola and Mozambique are obvious examples of this. In Soviet terminology, these adventures are termed 'aid to the national liberation struggle'; and the struggle is not regarded in the Kremlin as being finally over until a Marxist-Leninist government (Moscow-orientated, not Peking-orientated) has been installed in the country in question. Such a government may reasonably be regarded as being reliably anti-Western and anti-Maoist; and the Western camp and the Maoist camp may consequently be thought to be weakened. In order to enable the Kremlin to provide this aid, the Soviet armed forces have had to acquire a number of new characteristics. These will be discussed at the end of the next chapter. In this chapter, however, which is concerned with the 'roots of discord' between the USSR and the rest of the world, it is sufficient to point out that this 'aid to the national liberation struggle', on which the Soviet leaders so frequently like to pride themselves, is planting the roots of a very great many new discords in parts of the world where they have never been heard before.

The Expansion of the Red Army

The lynch-pin of the Soviet armed forces is the **Red Army**, which is traditionally the senior service. This has grown in numbers and sophistication from a peasant horde to the modern, well-equipped army of today. The air force has always been regarded as an adjunct of the army and navy, but it, too, is now an ultra-modern force. The expansion of the Soviet Navy is probably best known in the West, but even here there is more than meets the eye. The great milestones in the development of the armed forces are the Civil War and World War II, since when there has been continual modernisation.

The famous 'Tachanka' —a machine-gun mounted on a horse-drawn cart— which was widely used by the Red Army in its early days.

P. H. Vigor

According to Soviet sources, the Red Army was born on what, according to the modern calendar, was 28 January 1918. Recruitment was originally intended to be voluntary; and the voluntary basis was successful enough to have attracted more than 100,000 recruits by the end of March 1918. This number was insufficient, however, and on 22 April 1918 the Bolsheviks were obliged to issue a decree making service in the Red Army compulsory.

The purpose of having a specifically 'Red' Army, instead of continuing with the old Imperial Russian Army, was to provide the Bolshevik government with an armed force which could be relied upon to use its weapons to keep that government in office. Lenin's view of the way a revolution would

develop caused him to expect the dispossessed propertied classes to attempt to stage a 'come-back' (or 'counter-revolution' as Marxist terminology would call it). Consequently, unless the army at the communists' disposal was in strong political sympathy with the aims of the Revolution, there was grave danger that it might not fight enthusiastically enough to prevent the come-back succeeding. In Lenin's opinion, therefore, it was essential that those who served in the Red Army should only be drawn from such sections of the old Russian society as might be expected to be revolutionary sympathisers; and it was for this reason that, right from the very beginning, the Red Army refused to accept in its ranks recruits drawn from those sections of the old Russian society which the communists considered 'reactionary'. Not that the old aristocracy or the old middle classes were prevented from making any contribution whatever to the military capacity of the communists: on the contrary, they too were conscripted. They were not, however, allowed to serve in any of the 'teeth' arms or technical services, but instead were recruited into so-called 'auxiliary units', generally labour battalions.

It is true that the exigencies of the Civil War compelled the Bolsheviks to admit into the ranks of their officer corps a considerable number of ex-tsarist officers, despite their 'bourgeois' background; but this was done only under the pressure of a most compelling necessity. Furthermore, the device

was discontinued as soon as circumstances permitted; and throughout the period of their service with the Red Army, the so-called 'military specialists' worked under the vigilant supervision of a body of men termed 'military commissars', whose job it was to see that the suspect 'military specialists' did not betray their employers.

There was thus implanted in the Soviet armed forces, right from the very beginning of their existence, the basic principle that in a communist state political reliability is of the first importance, to which all else, including professional ability, must be subordinated. Marx, Engels and Lenin, and all the other revolutionary leaders, had studied with care the part that was played by Napoleon in the history of the French Revolution; and they were all determined that no *Brumaire* coup (such as that which elevated Bonaparte to the office of 1st Consul in November 1799) should frustrate their own revolution. The armed forces of the USSR were then, and are now, the only body in the country that is physically capable of destroying the communist govern-

Below: Artillerymen of the Imperial Russian Army firing over open sights as an early observation aircraft flies overhead. The army suffered terribly during the war due to bad generalship, shocking planning and widespread ineptitude. At one crucial stage in 1915 artillery shells were in such short supply that each gun was rationed to three shells per day with a court martial for any officer who exceeded the limit!

ment; and the communist government was aware of it then, and is equally aware of it now. The institution of the political commissars, the authority vested in the Main Political Directorate of the Armed Forces and the political requirements demanded of Soviet officers are all symptoms of the profound influence which the ghost of Napoleon Bonaparte exerts, and has always exerted, on those in power in the Kremlin.

The needs of the Civil War (1918–1920) caused a rapid rise in the numbers of the Red Army. If in March 1918 its strength was only a little over 100,000, this had risen to over 306,000 by May of that same year, to over 1,000,000 by February 1919 and to over 3,000,000 by January 1920. At its peak in the Civil War years, the official strength of the Red Army was 5,498,000 (1 October 1920).

It must not be supposed that these enormous numbers were deployed *en masse*, like some titanic hammer, on a particular sector of the front. Nor were they ever deployed simultaneously over all the fronts together: official strengths were one thing, and reality another. Moreover, the nominal strength of the Red Army was much reduced by desertion. Furthermore, as Soviet generals testify, the nature of the Civil War was such that large numbers of so-called soldiers had to be employed by the communist leaders on very unsoldierly duties. When whole areas the size of Britain had been devastated by the continual fighting, the supply problem was appalling; thus soldiers were used to catch fish, to repair windmills, to provide firewood for railway engines, and even to operate match factories.

The Civil War was also an important milestone in the history of the Soviet armed forces from the point of view of strategy and tactics. So much emotion has entered into the study of this period, both on the side of the Reds and on that of the Whites, that it is important, when attempting an assessment of it, to try to be objective. And so far as the military aspects of this struggle are concerned, the objective facts are that although the numbers of the men involved in the war were vast, they were not nearly so vast as the territories over which they fought. Consequently, it was physically impossible for a static front to be formed, of the kind

which was formed across Western Europe between 1914 and 1918. The Civil War in Russia therefore inculcated in its participants a belief in the virtues of the offensive as opposed to the defensive, and of speed and manoeuvrability in the execution of it, which has remained to this day the hallmark of Soviet tactics.

The Civil War ended in a Red victory in December 1920; but in many ways the victory was Pyrrhic. The industry, the commerce, the agriculture of Soviet Russia were on the verge of collapse, and the armed forces had to be demobilised speedily in order to provide the manpower necessary for their reconstruction. Trotsky, the chief military architect of the Bolshevik victory, was in some disagreement with his colleagues as to how this should best be accomplished, but he too was emphatic that it had to be done. Consequently, whereas in 1920 the strength of the Soviet armed forces was over 5,000,000, by 1923 it had fallen to 610,000 and by 1924 had reached its nadir of 562,000. When it is remembered that this figure includes not only the army and navy but also the frontier guards, it will be apparent to what a degree of military impotence the Soviet Union had fallen.

But the Soviet leaders' Marxism constrained them to believe that the capitalist nations were always on the watch for an opportunity to make use of their military strength to invade Russia and put an end to communism. From which it followed that the above-mentioned military impotence could not be tolerated for a moment longer than was necessary, and that, so soon as the Soviet economy began to recover, the battle effectiveness of the Soviet armed forces should begin to recover too. The worsening of the international situation at the end of the 1920s and in the early 1930s gave added impetus to this train of thought, which was soon translated into action. Thus whereas, as has been said, the Soviet armed forces in 1924 numbered only 562,000, they had risen to a figure of 617,000 in 1928, of 885,000 in 1933 and of 1,513,000 by 1938.

This increase in strength of the Soviet armed forces took place simultaneously with an equally impressive increase in Soviet industrial production. The years 1928–1932 were the period of the first of the 5-year

plans upon the results of which depended the degree to which Soviet rearmament was possible. According to the published figures, this was considerable. Thus the total number of aircraft in service in 1928 is given as 1,394; by 1932 this had risen to 3,285; and by 1935 it had increased still further to 6,672. The figures for guns of a calibre of 76-mm or greater were 6,645 in 1928, 10,684 in 1932 and 13,837 in 1935. For tanks the corresponding figures were 92, 1,401 and 10,180 respectively.

The increased technological capability of the Red Army was backed by a military doctrine of corresponding efficacy. From its earliest days, it had been blessed with strategists and tacticians whose views of war were, if anything, in advance of their time. No doubt they had been assisted in their professional development by their contacts with the highly efficient German army officers which had been developed as a result of the Treaty of Rapallo (1922); but the fact remained that, as early as the middle 1920s, there were propounded in Soviet official circles views which were at least as advanced as any in Western Europe. The successes of the various 5-year plans allowed the Soviet leaders to put flesh on them. As a result, the USSR in 1932 produced the world's first mechanised corps, which included in its establishment more than 500 tanks. By 1936 the Soviet Union had a total of four mechanised corps, six independent mechanised brigades and six independent tank regiments. This approach to the use of armour contrasts strongly with that of some Western countries, whose conversion to the idea of using armour *en masse* was a very great deal more dilatory.

Soviet progress in this direction was brought to a halt, however, by Stalin's wrong evaluation of the Soviet experience of using tanks during the Spanish Civil War (1936–1939). As a result, the mechanised corps were disbanded, and their component tanks returned to their original task of fighting in penny packets in support of the infantry. It

was not until after the German invasion of Russia in 1941 that this decision was reversed.

Despite all this, however, the efficacy of the Red Army was clearly demonstrated when Soviet forces clashed with Japanese forces in Mongolia. The first clash, the Battle of Lake Khasan (July 1938), was a comparatively small-scale affair. But in the following year, in the Battle of Khalkin Gol, over 60 battalions of Soviet and Japanese infantry were embroiled in the fighting, together with appropriate supporting arms, including 600 tanks. The result was an undoubted victory for the USSR. It is an ironic comment on Stalin's Russia that the man who won the victory for the Soviet Union, Marshal Blyukher, was arrested and shot by the *NKVD* only a very short time after he had done so.

And, of course, the purge of the officer corps in 1937–1938 had a great effect on the battleworthiness of the Soviet armed forces. Its most famous victim was Marshal Tukhachevsky; but, according to Robert Conquest's *The Great Terror,* the Soviet Union lost, in addition, two more of the five marshals, 14 of the 16 army commanders, all eight of the full admirals, 60 of the 67 corps commanders, 136 of the 199 divisional commanders, 221 of the 397 brigade commanders and all 11 of the Vice-Commissars

Left: Red Army infantry on the march. Their rifles are the 7.62mm Mosin-Nagant, equipped with outmoded socket bayonet.

Below: A howitzer crew about to fire during the Civil War, with some interested villagers watching in the background.

for Defence, together with 75 of the 80 members of the Supreme Military Soviet. In all, according to Conquest, approximately 35,000 officers of all ranks were shot or imprisoned.

It can, of course, be argued (and has been argued) that the removal from office of many of these was of direct benefit to the Soviet armed forces, in that a considerable number of the victims were elderly men, 'dead wood', whose savage pruning did much to rejuvenate the Red Army. On the other hand, it can hardly be denied that the command and control of the Red Army during the early stages of the Russo–Finnish War of 1939–1940 left much to be desired; and that, although the rank-and-file fought sturdily and in the best traditions of the Russian army, the generalship and the logistics were extremely defective. Other causes for the initial Russian disasters include the unusual severity of the weather during that winter, the lack of proper skiing equipment among

the Soviet forces and the great heroism and military ability displayed by the Finns.

Nevertheless, despite its initial setbacks, the Red Army did ultimately win the war, which came to an end in March 1940. As things turned out, this gave the Soviet leaders a breathing space of approximately 15 months in which to prepare for their forthcoming struggle with Germany. Events, however, proved that this was not really long enough. The numbers of planes, tanks and other equipment available to the Soviet armed forces looked very formidable on paper; but much of the stuff was obsolescent, and incapable of meeting their Nazi counterparts on anything like equal terms. That admirable tank, the T-34, had admittedly come off the drawing-board and gone into production by the time of Hitler's invasion in 1941, but the numbers actually available were extremely small. A similar comment applies to Soviet aircraft.

The part played by the Soviet armed forces

Top: BT-7 Fast Tanks accompany infantry in an attack against the Japanese in the Khalkin-Gol area, during the brief Russo-Japanese war in Manchuria/Mongolia in 1939.

Above: Perhaps the most successful tank of World War II, the T-34/85 entered service in 1943. These tanks are supporting an attack near Odessa in the Ukrainian Front in 1944.

Above right: The 1940 parade through Red Square, with mobile anti-aircraft guns passing Lenin's tomb. This particular parade failed to deter the Germans from attacking.

Right: These Klim Voroshilov (KV-1) heavy tanks are being presented to soldiers of the Red Army by a group of patriotic donors, farmers from the Moscow area.

in helping to win World War II is so well known that, in an outline history, there seems not much point in doing more than sketch in its salient features. An important cause of Hitler's failure in Russia was his underestimation of the size of the forces necessary to allow him to achieve victory. Including the troops of his allies, he had less than 190 divisions available for the purpose; and these proved far too few. If just his occupation policies had been less barbarous, his troops might have sufficed; but the treatment meted out to Russian civilians in the areas occupied by Hitler's armies was so cruel as to drive into armed opposition the bulk of the inhabitants of those regions. Consequently, the holding down of the occupied territories was an important military task for the Nazi generals, and troops which might otherwise have been used for fighting against the Red Army were pinned down in garrison duties in the rear.

The milestones of the war on the Eastern Front were the appalling losses of the Soviet armed forces in the first few weeks of the war there, due to the strategic and tactical surprise which the Nazi generals were able to achieve (itself due largely to Stalin's lunatic policies); the success of the Red Army in preventing the fall of Moscow in the winter of 1941; the defence of Leningrad; the heroic resistance of the Russian soldiers to the German attacks on Stalingrad in the autumn of 1942, and their subsequent going over to that offensive which resulted in the encirclement and total destruction of Paulus' 6th Army in February 1943; the Battle of Kursk in the same year, which has been authoritatively described as the real turning-point of the war on the Eastern Front; the Red Army's offensive in the summer of 1944, which drove the Nazis back across Central Europe to the borders of Germany itself; and finally, in 1945, the Soviet invasion of Germany, culminating in the capture of Berlin. Nor, when speaking of the Soviet armed forces' contribution to the winning of World War II, should we forget their campaign in the Far East against the Japanese Kwantung Army in the summer of 1945 (militarily irrelevant though that campaign may have been so far as the attainment of victory over Imperial Japan was concerned).

But although World War II had been won, the cost to the Russians had been appalling. The destruction of towns and villages in European Russia had been horrific; and the toll in Soviet lives, according to Molotov, was of the order of 20,000,000. Recent demographic studies suggest that this figure may be even higher. Fortunately for the Soviet Union, however, there was no enemy left on this earth who wanted to go to war with her. Although there were undoubtedly voices to be heard in the West, declaring that a preventive war on Russia was highly desirable, the major Western powers, so far from preparing for it, began to demobilise their armies and navies as soon as Germany and Japan had been decisively beaten.

The history of the Soviet armed forces since 1945 is therefore one of very little fighting, but at the same time one of continual modernisation, of continual pondering over the lessons of the 'Great Patriotic War',

Above: A B-25 Mitchell bomber supplied to the Soviet Union by the United States during World War II. The USA and Great Britain supplied large amounts of aid to the USSR during the war, but received little thanks or public acknowledgement for their efforts. Total US aid came to 17,150,000 tons.

and of an unremitting determination to prevent a repetition of a capitalist invasion of the 'Socialist Motherland'. This determination has found its practical expression in the size of the forces kept under arms by the Kremlin since the end of World War II and in the number and quality of the weapons with which these forces have been equipped. In addition, the period 1945–1953 saw the Soviet armed forces being used by Stalin to support his expansionist foreign policy; as a result of their help, a considerable area of Europe fell under the sway of the USSR for the first time.

The end of World War II saw the first use of atomic weapons, which subsequently evolved into nuclear ones. The Soviet attitude towards these weapons was strongly influenced by the fact that the West possessed them, a circumstance which made the Kremlin devote great energy to producing Soviet versions of them as soon as it could. The first Soviet atomic device was tested in 1949, and the first Soviet nuclear device in 1953. At the same time, as Soviet industry recovered from the ravages of World War II, a good deal of the output of its more sophisticated branches was directed towards the production of modern equipment for the use of the Soviet armed forces. Ever newer tanks, ever more formidable artillery, ever more effective aircraft poured out of the Soviet factories; while in the means of delivering a missile on to a very far distant target the Russian technicians succeeded in outstripping the West. The year 1957 was

a milestone in the history of the Soviet armed forces, for in that year the USSR successfully tested a missile which, launched from Soviet territory, was capable of hitting the territory of the United States. In that year, therefore, the total immunity to destruction by Soviet weapons which the USA had enjoyed since the dawn of time, was brought to an end, and the world's strategic balance significantly altered. It was this policy which allowed Khrushchev to seek to adopt a policy of relying almost exclusively upon nuclear weapons for the defence of the Soviet Union, and thereby make it possible to effect drastic reductions in the conventional forces. That this policy was unpopular with the Soviet military goes without saying; and after the fall of Khrushchev in 1964 the conventional forces of the USSR were restored to their traditional importance.

The postwar years were also those of the growth of the Soviet Navy, which moved

ever farther away from those coastal waters which had been its customary playground, and went out on to the high seas after the fashion of the British and American navies, and began to sail the oceans of the world. Prior to World War II, it had consisted of little more than large numbers of small ships and small, short-range submarines designed for coastal defence. In 1970, however, the great naval manoeuvres, code-named 'Okean', proved to even the most sceptical Western observer that the Soviet Navy had made great progress since the end of World War II. Since that date, the steady growth in

Below: A Soviet admiral visits the Chinese Navy at the high noon of Soviet-Sino fraternal relations in 1956. On 24 May the previous year the Soviet Navy had finally vacated Port Arthur (now Lushun) the occupation of which had long been an affront to Chinese dignity. The great split came in 1960 and is now wider than ever.

the numbers of nuclear submarines, the building of the series of helicopter/VTOL carriers, and the impressive total of modern surface vessels of every conceivable kind available to Soviet admirals are further evidence of the Soviet Navy's ever increasing power. How it will use that power has not yet been satisfactorily assessed by Western observers; but many of the latter, who once assumed that the motive behind the growth of the Soviet Navy was essentially defensive, are now beginning to have second thoughts on the matter.

As for the air forces, the Soviet leaders traditionally refused to regard them as a separate service. Before World War II, therefore, their function was to co-operate either with the army or else with the navy; and their machines were designed for the purpose of fulfilling those functions and nothing else. Consequently, the planes allotted to the army were designed for reconnaissance and ground support, and heavy bombers simply were not made in significant quantities. Similarly, those intended for the navy naturally had to conform to the navy's strategic and tactical doctrines of the time. Since these were concerned exclusively with the prevention of an enemy seaborne landing on Soviet territory, and since the Soviet economy of the 1920s and 1930s would not allow of the construction of a modern fleet, the aim of the Soviet admirals was to have very large numbers of light forces which could engage the enemy like a cloud of mosquitoes, but (like mosquitoes) only near their base. The aircraft allotted to the support of the Soviet Navy had therefore also only a very short range, which proved a serious handicap in World War II, as Admiral Gorshkov has testified.

Today, however, the picture looks very different. Although, once again, the Soviet Air Force as such can hardly be said to exist, the aircraft available to the Russian leaders form an impressive 'mix'. Apart from those allotted to the support of the ground forces and of the navy, there are first-class machines to be found in the ranks of Air Defence Command (*PVO Strany*) and Air Transport Command. Nor is the long-range bomber now omitted from the inventory of Soviet aircraft. The Long-Range Air Force now has a total of over 800 long-range and medium-range machines. Unlike the air forces of the West, the Soviet capability in long-range strategic aircraft is not weakening but growing.

But equally as important as the history of the armed forces themselves is the history of the evolution of their military doctrine. This aimed originally merely at defending the frontiers of Soviet Russia, as has already been explained above: there was no question in those days of projecting Soviet power across the world; yet in the 1970s that sort of projection of power has become quite common (Cuba, Angola, Mozambique and the Horn of Africa, are all examples of this). Furthermore, in the early 1970s it came to be considered necessary for the Soviet forces stationed in Central Europe to be able to fight, and win, a conventional war or a mixed conventional/nuclear war, as well as a purely nuclear one. This requirement inevitably demanded a far broader and more sophisticated 'mix' of weapons than had been deemed necessary under the old 'purely nuclear' doctrine; and the present array of the Group of Soviet Forces in Germany is a direct reflection of that fact. Moreover, Soviet military thinking gives pride of place to the offensive; so whatever kind of war is fought in Europe has got to be fought offensively. This fact, too, has had its effect upon the 'mix' of Soviet weaponry.

Finally, this concern with the projection of power has had very important consequences. The Russians, of course, do not speak of 'the projection of power'; they speak instead of 'support for the national liberation struggle'. When the USSR was militarily weak, the support for that struggle was very small, and consisted of little more than gifts to the 'national liberation fighters' of a few Kalashnikovs and the appropriate ammunition. It could not consist of much more than that because, until the mid 1970s, the USSR was without the capability of projecting armed force across seas and oceans. Clearly, however, she had seen that she would need to acquire that capability, if the 'national liberation struggle' was to be properly supported, and Soviet influence was to be expanded across the globe, and not confined to the Euro-Asian land mass. The new sorts of ships and aircraft necessary for providing that capability are now seen to be entering the Soviet inventory; and future generations may well conclude that the Kremlin's decision to acquire that capability was a major milestone in the history of the evolution of the armed forces of the USSR.

Above: Soviet T-54 tanks seen near a modern housing estate in the suburbs of Prague during the Soviet invasion of Czechoslovakia in September 1968, a savage assertion of the 'Brezhnev doctrine' which aroused world-wide protest. The policy of the Soviet Union towards neighbouring states is indistinguishable from that of Imperial Russia which expanded steadily over the centuries. The great growth in military strength of the Soviet armed forces, allied to the apparent lack of firm resolve in the West, has enabled the Soviets to feel they can once again assert themselves, as has been shown in Afghanistan. This Soviet intervensionist policy is seen as a most dangerous threat to the Free World.

The Organisation of Soviet Forces

The CPSU realises only too well that Party control over the Soviet armed forces is essential, and elaborate mechanisms exist to ensure that this shall be so. Further, there is constant political education at all levels to make certain that officers and men understand the home and foreign policies of the CPSU and the tasks which are expected to devolve upon them as a result. More difficult for a Westerner to comprehend is the fact that the Soviet armed forces are not so much an instrument of the State but rather the instruments of Communist Party policy – a significant difference.

Christopher Donnelly

It is the role of the Communist Party of the Soviet Union (CPSU) to guide and direct Soviet society along the road to communism. In fulfilment of this (its historic mission, as it believes), the Communist Party feels that it is obliged to exert its control over every aspect of human behaviour.

Every branch of that organism which is Soviet society is subject to the direction and supervision of the CPSU, and the armed forces are no exception. Indeed, because they constitute the party's main instrument for controlling Soviet society as a whole, yet are at the same time the only organisation within that society which could ever succeed in overthrowing the dictatorship of the party, the armed forces are singled out for especially thorough control and supervision by the party.

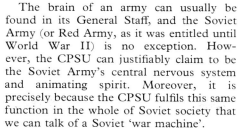

The massive military parades held annually in Moscow and elsewhere in the USSR serve to emphasise that Soviet super power status is based not on economic strength or ideological influence, but on raw military might backed by firm political resolve.

The brain of an army can usually be found in its General Staff, and the Soviet Army (or Red Army, as it was entitled until World War II) is no exception. However, the CPSU can justifiably claim to be the Soviet Army's central nervous system and animating spirit. Moreover, it is precisely because the CPSU fulfils this same function in the whole of Soviet society that we can talk of a Soviet 'war machine'.

By inserting party members into every social institution at all levels, and by ensuring that professional promotion relies on party approval, the CPSU contrives to achieve, however enforced, a unity of aim and purpose in Soviet society which is rarely to be found in a Western country.

Because Marxist ideology insists that the hostile capitalist West will seek to destroy the Soviet state and end the rule of the Communist Party (and the history of the USSR over the past 50 years tends to reinforce this belief in the minds of Soviet citizens), it is hardly surprising that the party has made use of its position of power during this time to prepare the Soviet economy and the Soviet people for war. While it is difficult to reach a precise figure, many Western specialists would agree that a good third of all public expenditure and resources in the Soviet Union is earmarked for arms. What is more, the characteristics of the Soviet system mean that it is far easier to divert effort into defence projects than it would be in a Western society.

The secret lies in total centralisation allied with close control and supervision. The Soviet economy is a planned economy. That is to say that the production of every item down to, for instance, every cup and saucer or every rifle bullet, is done according to a master plan produced by *Gosplan* – the State Planning Ministry – in Moscow. A revised plan is produced every five years or so to take account of changes in requirements and conditions. The market influences of supply and demand which control capitalist economy are not allowed to operate, and state control of the mass media and all means of public expression make it very difficult for individuals to make their complaints heard. The net result is that public opinion has little or no effect on the plan.

The function of the various economic ministries of the Soviet government is to see to the implementation of that part of the plan which concerns them, and to advise the planners as to what could be expected to be achieved. Decisions concerning the economic developments of the country are made by the ruling bodies of the Communist Party, particularly by the *Politburo*, headed at the moment by Brezhnev. In the same way, the other ministries, such as the Ministry of Education, the Ministry of Health and the Ministry of Defence, to name but a few, simply exist to put into practice the decisions of the party leaders, and advise them in their own special field when requested to do so. The Minister of Defence, for example, was co-opted into the *Politburo* in 1973 because at that time the Party chiefs felt the

Below: The fear of yet another invasion is very real to Soviet citizens, however much the West may disclaim any such intent. This fear binds people together and encourages defence training by workers like these.

The Command Structure of the Soviet Armed Forces

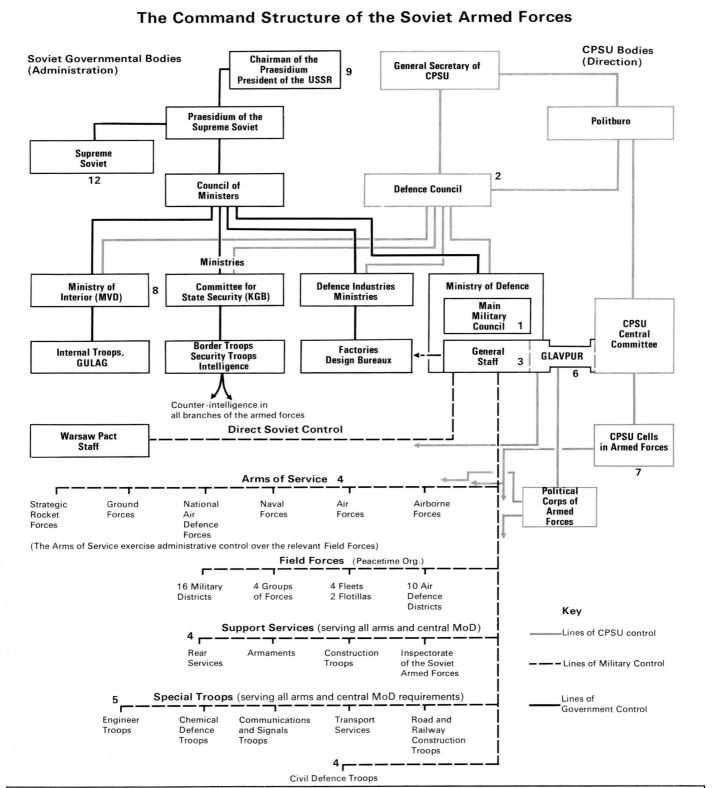

Soviet Governmental Bodies (Administration)

CPSU Bodies (Direction)

Chairman of the Praesidium President of the USSR **9**

General Secretary of CPSU

Praesidium of the Supreme Soviet

Politburo

Supreme Soviet **12**

Council of Ministers

Defence Council **2**

Ministries

Ministry of Interior (MVD) **8**

Committee for State Security (KGB)

Defence Industries Ministries

Ministry of Defence

Main Military Council **1**

CPSU Central Committee

Internal Troops, GULAG

Border Troops Security Troops Intelligence

Factories Design Bureaux

General Staff **3**

GLAVPUR **6**

Counter-intelligence in all branches of the armed forces

Direct Soviet Control

Warsaw Pact Staff

CPSU Cells in Armed Forces **7**

Arms of Service 4

Political Corps of Armed Forces

Strategic Rocket Forces | Ground Forces | National Air Defence Forces | Naval Forces | Air Forces | Airborne Forces

(The Arms of Service exercise administrative control over the relevant Field Forces)

Field Forces (Peacetime Org.)

16 Military Districts | 4 Groups of Forces | 4 Fleets 2 Flotillas | 10 Air Defence Districts

4 Support Services (serving all arms and central MoD)

Rear Services | Armaments | Construction Troops | Inspectorate of the Soviet Armed Forces

5 Special Troops (serving all arms and central MoD requirements)

Engineer Troops | Chemical Defence Troops | Communications and Signals Troops | Transport Services | Road and Railway Construction Troops

4 Civil Defence Troops

Key

——— Lines of CPSU control

– – – Lines of Military Control

—— Lines of Government Control

Key to Diagram

1. The Main Military Council (which becomes the Stavka in wartime) is responsible for the implementation of the broad policy decisions of the Defence Council. In wartime it wields the operational command of the Armed Forces. **2.** The Defence Council formulates all Soviet Military Policy. Its members include the General Secretary of the CPSU and Soviet President, the Minister of Defence, the Chief of the General Staff, and the heads of the KGB and MVD. **3.** The General Staff includes several First Deputy Ministers of Defence including the C-in-C of the Warsaw Pact, the Chief of the General Staff, the Chief of the Main Political Directorate and others. It is organised into several Directorates. Operations; Intelligence; Warsaw Pact; Procurement etc. **4.** Each commanded by a Deputy Minister of Defence. **5.** Each branch of the Special troops is commanded by a senior officer responsible for his given functions throughout the Armed Forces. There is therefore no overall commander of Special Troops as such. **6.** The Main Political Directorate (GLAVPUR) fulfills the functions of both the Political Directorate of the Ministry of Defence and the Military Section of the CPSU Central Committee,

with dual subordination. **7.** Over 90 per cent of officers are CPSU or Komsomol members. There is a CPSU cell in every service unit, HQ or establishment, and Party or Komsomol cells in every sub-unit. These work in close co-ordination with GLAVPUR staffs at every level. **8.** Note that the MVD and KGB troops, whilst organised and administered on Army lines, are in no way subordinated to or responsible to the Ministry of Defence. Note also that the heads of these Ministries sit on the Defence Council. **9.** As at April 1980 also Chief Marshal of the Soviet Armed Forces, L. I. Brezhnev. **10.** There are political officers or teams in *every* service unit down to company level or equivalent and in every HQ and control element. **11.** The 8 Divisions of the Airborne Forces, whilst administratively part of the Ground Forces are operationally held as strategic reserve of the High Command. **12.** The Supreme Soviet is the Titular Governing body or 'Parliament'. It meets for two weeks each year and has little influence on policy.
One of the main features of the Command Structure of the Soviet Armed Forces is the complete integration of Military and Political in the Central System, and the Political representation in every unit and sub-unit and at every level of command, right down to army company.

need of specialised and competent advice when entering into such important negotiations as the SALT (Strategic Arms Limitation Talks) and MBFR (Mutual Balanced Force Reductions) discussions. When the party no longer feels the need for such close collaboration with the military, no doubt the Minister of Defence will lose his seat on the party's ruling body.

Should, then, the party decide that it needs a larger army and more tanks, it will simply instruct *Gosplan* to allot a larger slice of the economic cake to tank production in the next plan, building new factories or converting existing ones to cope with the increased demand.

This, then, is the first practical step to the creation of a single-minded war machine. It has an important and useful spin-off in that, with such centralised direction on such a large scale, standardisation of military equipment is far easier than in capitalist economies where each firm involved in defence industries is likely to produce equipment to its own specifications.

At the present time, as indeed since the economy was first effectively industrialised in the 1930s, the CPSU allots a very high priority to the defence industry. Factories controlled by one of the ministries in the defence sector are assured better supplies of raw materials and, for their workforce, higher wages and bonuses than factories working for a purely civilian ministry. It is into the ministries of the defence sector that the latest technology is introduced as a priority.

Defence production

The nine Ministries at at present constitute the Soviet defence sector (see Table 1; the exact numbers and functions of the ministries change every now and then to accommodate technological developments and administrative requirements) all produce not only military goods, but also related civilian goods and also goods for purely civilian purposes. Thus, with any technology transfer from the West, it is not possible to ensure that it will be employed only in the civilian sector. Such an arrangement also creates a situation where a plant of the defence industry, with production split between, say, tanks and tractors, can by virtue of its arrangement of assembly lines easily convert its entire output to tanks. In this way, the directives of the party (via GOSPLAN) can be more speedily fulfilled.

The nine defence ministries are subordinate to the Military Industrial Commission of the Council of Ministers. The present Minister of Defence, D. F. Ustinov, headed this organisation until his promotion in 1976. Party direction is provided by the Defence Industries Department of the Central Committee. The Deputy Minister of Defence for Armaments probably represents military interests on these organisations, co-ordinating military weapons and equipment requirements with the ministries that will be responsible for production, and with the design bureaux.

Soviet military equipment is designed by permanent design bureaux, and production is assigned to the factory most capable of producing it. In practice, factories tend to a certain extent to become 'tied' to bureaux. Trials are done by the bureaux in co-opera-

tion with the producer and the military. Military officers are posted to serve both in design bureaux and factories, and are responsible both for conveying to the designers and producers details of practical military requirements, and also for stringent quality control to ensure that the finished product meets military requirements.

The result of the remarkable level of integration, coupled with the fact that all parties to the process have been educated within the narrow confines of the Soviet system, of Soviet military doctrine, is that Soviet military equipment is of a very high standard indeed in marked contrast to much of the produce of the civilian sector.

The Soviet principles of military art apply not only to the battlefield, but also to the drawing office, and tactical weapons reflect tactical requirements. The permanence of bureaux makes for continuity in 'families' of weapons systems and works to avoid lost expertise. The Russians also have an impressive record of producing highly effective weapons systems from old fashioned technology by means of very skilful design practice. The PKM machine gun, the ZSU-23-4 AA system, and the MiG-25 Foxbat all display this feature. Soviet aircraft are

Above: Representatives of the armed forces publicly demonstrate their loyalty to the Party at the 25th CPSU Congress.

designated not after their makers but their design bureaux, e.g. the Tu-144 is the design of the Tupolev bureau.

The militarization of Soviet society

The second step towards establishing a functioning war machine is the psychological preparation of the population. The state makes good use of its total control of the educational system and the information networks to keep the spirit of war alive in the population. This takes two forms: firstly, the propaganda line in schools and in the mass media emphasises the military threat which capitalist nations and blocs pose to the Soviet Union, and glorifies the feats of the Soviet Army, widely publicising exercises, holding public parades and celebrating anniversaries of glorious victories; secondly, the civilian economy is run in military fashion with periodic 'storming' of the economic targets, and decorating 'Heroes of Labour' for victories achieved in the struggle to build socialism. Indeed, in its whole atmosphere the Soviet Union strikes

Table 1 : Ministries of the defence sector of Soviet industry

Title	Military equipment	Civilian production
1. Ministry of the Defence Industry	Tanks, artillery, small arms.	Optical equipment, chemicals, rail rolling stock, tractors, motorcycles
2. Ministry of Machine Building	Munitions	Chemicals, fertilizers.
3. Ministry of General Machine Building	Large missiles and rockets	Space rockets.
4. Ministry of Medium Machine Building	Nuclear weapons, reactors, and fuels	Nuclear reactors and fuels.
5. Ministry of the Aviation Industry	Military aircraft and helicopters	Civilian aircraft, domestic aluminium products, domestic machinery (washing machines, etc.).
6. Ministry of the Shipbuilding Industry	Warships	Merchant ships, trawlers, ships' equipment, oil storage equipment.
7. Ministry of the Radio Industry	Radios, radars, computers, etc.	Computers, televisions, radios, tape recorders.
8. Ministry of the Industry of Communications Equipment	Advanced electronics	Advanced electronics.
9. Ministry of the Electronics Industry	Electronic components for the above ministries.	

the casual visitor as a nation at war, and the patriotic posters with their calls to work harder and the general scarcity of consumer goods tend to accentuate this feeling. The above must not be construed as meaning that the Soviet people want a war. They most definitely do not. However, they are kept aware that they might have to fight a war if capitalism, that most evil of social systems, attempts to destroy socialism; and they are told that by whatever means that war would be fought, the Soviet Union would be bound to win.

The third step to the creation of an effective war machine is to ensure the total integration of civilians and the military within society. The idea of a 'nation in arms' is dear to the Marxist's heart; and although the Soviet system may fall some way short of that ideal, it does nevertheless go a good way towards it. Militarization begins early. Most young children at primary school are members of the 'Pioneers', the most junior Communist Party Organisation. No form of young peoples' organisations are allowed at all, other than those actually sponsored by the CPSU. At the age of 14 a very high proportion of young people pass automatically into the 'Komsomol', or Communist Youth League. These organisations are not part of their appeal. Many of the activities of these organisations are specifically military. For example, the basis of the Pioneers' Summer Camp Programme, entitled 'Zarnitsa' – 'Summer Lightning' – is a series of war games. In this, the youngsters operate as 'Detachments' and 'Battalions', have appointed 'Commanders' who issue stylized 'orders' with 'combat tasks'. The young boys and girls train as 'riflemen' with mock rifles; study to identify real Soviet weapons; learn fieldcraft, map-reading, minor tactics; and practise grenade throwing. 'Recce Personnel' make a speciality of climbing obstacles, observation, concealment, mapreading etc. 'Signallers' learn simple semaphore and the operation of field telephones. 'Medics' learn basic first aid and casevac. 'Clerks' and 'Cooks' are other specialisations.

The war games are a combination of military exercise, adventure training, and sports competitions. Similar war games are held for teenage members of the Komsomol, entitled 'Orlyonok' ('little eagle'). Pioneer and Komsomol members are also mobilized for Civil Defence exercises, and, along with

Examples of civil-military integration. Above: Each year tens of thousands of troops, even from front line units, are employed on harvesting duties. Without military transport and manpower to draw on, the Soviet agricultural system would be unable to cope.

Above right: As part of the compulsory military training in their last years at school, these young Russians are being introduced to Air Force electronic equipment.

the armed services, for assisting with the harvest.

Normal school sports are done as part of the school curriculum, but under the banner of 'Be ready for labour and defence'. The sporting 'norms' which must be achieved by all able bodied 16 to 17 year olds wishing to graduate from high school include such activities as the ability (for boys) to throw a 500 gramme hand grenade 25 metres.

In his last three years at school, the young man in the USSR must by law do 140 hours of basic military training to prepare himself for military service. Military departments have been set up to serve all schools, factories and on some farms with over 10 young men in the 15 to 18 year age group. The young man, for two hours each week, learns basic military skills at the hands of serving or retired officers or NCOs, or Komsomol enthusiasts, who have been employed by or posted to the school for that purpose. The system reaches about three out of four potential conscripts.

There have also existed in the Soviet Union, almost since the days of the revolution, sports organisations under party control which provide excellent facilities for any youth or girl wishing to take up such para-military sports as shooting, gliding, parachuting or skiing. The current organisation with this function is called 'DOSAAF' (voluntary society for co-operation with the army, the air force and the fleets). Through over 300,000 establishments, DOSAAF provides, for minimum cost to the user, an excellent range of sporting facilities. As well as basic sports, the society offers specialised sports having a military value (swimming, skiing, shooting, flying, orienteering, etc.) and since the mid 1970s, DOSAAF has held a large share of the responsibility for carrying out the pre-service military training for 15 to 18 year olds in schools, factories and on farms. For those of all ages interested in sport,

DOSAAF provides excellent facilities, particularly near large towns. The young man showing an aptitude for parachuting or skin-diving should, on conscription, be steered towards a military career where his speciality can be well utilized, although in actual fact the conscription system is often not too efficient in achieving this.

The integration of serving officers into the defence industries has been referred to above. However, the military are very active in prominent posts throughout Soviet society. To take one example, the senior military commander in any city or district is automatically appointed to a seat on the local government body at that level, e.g. the commandant of a garrison located in a town would have a seat on the town council; the commander in chief of a military district would be appointed as a Deputy to the Supreme Soviet of the republic in which the district was situated, and also probably to the Supreme Soviet of the USSR.

It must also be borne in mind that the army in Russia traditionally fulfilled the function of bringing the members of the different races of the empire into close contact with each other, subjecting them to a single unifying discipline and programme of education. The Soviet Army continues to fulfil this useful function, and thus contributes greatly to increasing the cohesion of the Soviet Union.

The organisation of the Soviet Armed Forces

There are three significant areas in which the Soviet Armed Forces differ most radically in their organisation from the Armed Forces of NATO countries. These are:

(a) The enormous extent of direct political control and the existence of political representation right down to the lowest command levels.

(b) The subordination of different branches of the Armed Forces to different ministries.

(c) The division of the arms of service of the Soviet forces according to function rather than environment.

The USSR is run not by the Soviet Government, but by the Politburo and the General Secretary of the CPSU. It is in the Politburo, supported by the CPSU Central Committee, that all policy decisions are taken. The function of the Soviet Government is merely to carry out the orders of the

Party leadership. It is to the CPSU General Secretary, therefore, that the Soviet armed forces are really answerable, through the offices of the military representatives on the Politburo and the Central Committee of the CPSU. In law, however, the Soviet Armed Forces, through their various ministries, are subordinate to the Praesidium of the Supreme Soviet of the USSR. It is the Chairman of that Praesidium, the Soviet President, who is legally responsible for the Armed Forces. However, at the moment, L. I. Brezhnev holds the positions of both General Secretary of the CPSU and Soviet President. Moreover he has assumed the title of Marshal of the Soviet Union and Head of Armed Forces, so there is little doubt as to where the power really lies.

To increase the effectiveness of Party control, and to provide a safeguard against any elements of the Military usurping the power of the Party leadership, administrative control of the Soviet Armed Forces is exercised by three distinct and separate ministries. The Ministry of Defence controls the bulk of Soviet combat and support forces (about 3,700,000 men) and also the Civil Defence network (over 25,000 regular personnel); the Ministry of the Interior (MVD) controls internal security troops (260,000) including the labour camp network GULAG; and the Committee for State Security (KGB) has over 200,000 men under arms as border guards and internal security guards on special duties.

The heads of all three Ministries also sit on the Politburo, thus emphasising the solidity of Party control in this vital area of Government.

Defence policy would appear to be formulated in the Defence Council, probably composed of the appropriate members of the Politburo (the General Secretary, Ministers of Defence, State Security and Internal Affairs), the Chief of the Warsaw Pact Forces, and the heads of the military defence industries. Temporary members are likely to be co-opted onto the Council to provide specific specialist advice as necessary.

**Below: Three of the most powerful men in the Soviet Military—Marshals Ustinov (Minister of Defence), Yepishev (head of Glavpur), and Ogarkov (CGS)—on the joint WP exercise 'shield-76'. All are firm friends and supporters of Brezhnev.
Below right: As Soviet President, CPSU General Secretary, and Commander-in-Chief of the armed forces, Brezhnev holds all the reins of real power in the USSR.**

The Ministry of Defence and the Military branches of the MVD and KGB are the Governmental organs responsible for implementing plans made in the Defence Council. Because of the internal security nature of the task of the MVD and KGB, we shall concern ourselves here mainly with the organisation of the Ministry of Defence and the forces under its control.

Within the Ministry of Defence, the main Military Council is the senior controlling body. It is responsible for planning and supervising the implementation of the broad policy decisions of the Defence Council. In wartime it assumes the operational command of the armed forces as the 'Stavka'. It is composed of the minister and all deputy ministers of defence, the CGS and other senior general staff officers. The detailed running of the armed forces (along the lines laid down by the Military Council) is done by the General Staff, and the post of Chief of the General Staff is the senior professional military appointment in the Soviet armed forces, senior in fact, if not on paper, to the Chief of the Warsaw Pact Forces.

The considerable amount of intermingling of functions, the high incidence of senior Party or Military personnel holding important posts on several key organisations makes for a considerable degree of coordination and integration not only of military with political, but also of these elements with other Ministries having a military function, such as the Ministry for Industry, or the Ministry of Health, Ministry of Foreign Affairs, etc.

Due to the special traditions of the Soviet armed forces, the General Staff is dominated by Army officers despite the recent rise to prominence of the Navy. Through the C-in-C of the Warsaw Pact, the Soviet General Staff would control the Warsaw Pact armies in war. Even in peacetime the Soviet General Staff has an overwhelming influence on the other Warsaw Pact armies in all major matters.

As outlined above, direct political control within the armed forces is exercised by the Main Political Directorate of the Ministry of Defence—*GLAVPUR*. This organisation fulfils at the same time the function of Military Section of the CPSU Central Committee. Staff of the Political Directorate are present in every military institution and unit and at *every* command level down to the political deputy in a company. In practice, the Political Directorate directs the work of the Communist Party cells which exist in

each army unit as they exist in every institution in Soviet society.

The organisation of the Soviet Armed Forces according to function causes the Internal Security troops and the Border troops to be controlled each by their own separate ministry. However, within the Ministry of Defence itself, arms of service are formed according to function, too. Whereas Nato armed forces are invariably divided into Army, Navy and Air Force, the five arms of service of the Soviety Ministry of Defence troops cut across traditional environmental grouping. These arms of service, which come under the direct operational control of the General Staff, are:
1. The Strategic Rocket Forces.
2. The Ground Forces.
3. The National Air Defence Forces.
4. The Air Forces.
5. The Navy.

The Strategic Rocket Forces constitute the senior arm of service. Their commander controls about 1,400 ICBMs and 700 IRBMs and MRBMs (land based), and probably also directs the deployment both of the SLBMs held by the Navy and the long range aviation bombers when carrying strategic nuclear weapons.

The Ground Forces Commander is responsible for about 165 divisions (Tank, Motor-Rifle or Airborne) which are under the operational command of the General Staff either through the 16 Military Districts and 4 Groups of Forces or, as in the case of the Airborne Forces, directly as strategic troops. The teeth-arm branches which make up the Ground Forces command are the Tank Troops, the Motor-Rifle Troops, the Rocket and Artillery Troops (with tactical operational nuclear missiles), and the Ground Forces Air Defence Troops.

The National Air Defence Force comprises all anti-aircraft and ABM systems, fighter interception, ground based and airborne early warning. This command administers its men, missiles and aircraft through two main Air Defence Districts centred on Moscow and Baku, and a large number of lesser Air Defence Districts based on regions within Military Districts.

The Admiral of the Fleet controls his ships and submarines, coastal defences and Naval Air Force through the administrative mechanism of four fleets. It is unlikely that he has full control over his nuclear missile boats.

There are five branches of the Soviet Air Forces: the Tactical Aviation; Long Range

Aviation; Fighter Aviation of the National Air Defence; Naval Aviation; and Military Transport Aviation. The Commander in Chief of the Air Forces exercises administrative control over all but the Naval Air Force; however, in wartime he actually commands only the Air Transport (including Aeroflot, the civil airline). The other branches are subordinated to different commands: the Tactical Aviation to *Armies* or *Fronts*; the long range aviation to the Strategic Rocket Forces or Theatre Commands; and the Fighter Aviation of the Air Defence Troops to the National Air Defence command.

Rear Service Troops, Construction Troops and Civil Defence Troops are not subordinate to any one of the above service branches, but are each separate commands, the former two with responsibilities to support the five arms of service under direct Ministry of Defence control. An armaments (procurement) branch holds a similar status, coordinating its effort with the relevant civilian industries. 'Specialist' troops, which in Soviet terminology mean Engineers, Chemical troops, Signals troops, Transport, and Road and Railway troops, also have the status of distinct services, but sub-units of these branches are normally held organic to teeth arm units (e.g., a signals company will be an organic part of a motor-rifle unit).

For the purpose of defence organisation, the USSR is divided territorially into 16 Military Districts and four Fleet Areas, and Soviet forces in East Europe are divided into four Groups of Forces, each having the status of a Military District.

A Military District is in effect a large administrative framework for the support of military units and the organisation and supply of military formations in a given territorial area. The Fleet fulfils the same function for a sea area. In peacetime the district is responsible for the garrisoning, training, and rear supply of forces; and also for military integration with the civil population, including Civil Defence organisations, pre-service training, conscription, military farms, etc. In wartime, the Military District is responsible for moving formations on to a war footing, transporting them to the battlefront, supplying them and eventually replacing them with fresh forces. A *Group of Forces* is in effect a Military District already on a wartime footing. The importance of individual Military Districts and Group of Forces depends mainly on their geographical location, which itself largely determines the level of forces maintained within them.

In the event of war, the formations of a Military District will be formed into groups of Armies (Russian (FRONTY')). Several 'FRONTY' in a given geographical area would constitute a Theatre of Combat Action (TVD). A Soviet TVD would be roughly comparable to, say, 'AFCENT' or 'AFNORTH' in Nato. Two or more TVD, and associated Fleet(s) where appropriate, in a given geographical area, would constitute a

Theatre of War (eg, the 'European Theatre').

A Soviet *Front* can have any number of *Armies*, but in practice four or five would be about average. An *Army* is likewise comprised of any number of *Divisions*, but similarly, four would appear to be the norm nowadays. Armies with a preponderance of tank formations are known as Tank Armies. Armies with a greater balance of tank and motor rifle formations, or composed of a preponderance of motor rifle formations, are called Combined Arms Armies. The term 'Shock Army' is traditional title maintained for historical reasons. Military activity at *Front* or *Army* level is termed 'operational', and the Russian word '*operatsiya*' (operation) usually means specifically activity on the scale of *Army* or *Front*.

The Soviet armed forces have never had a truly independent air force. The air arm has always been considered as a 'third dimension' in a land (or sea) battle. This has led not to a neglect of air power, but to its development in a specific fashion, always subordinate to a specific function. For example, the tactical aviation employed in a Military District or Group of Forces—that is, in war—in a *Front*, is completely subordinate to the *Front* (Ground Forces) Commander, and will be used according to his directions, *not* according to the directions of the senior airman.

The weapons of the Strategic Rocket Forces are employed for strategic (i.e., TVD or National) aims, but may on occasion be employed in support of a major operation, to supplement the tactical and operational muscles of the *Front* Commanders. Although the airborne forces are organisationally part of the Ground Forces, in practice they too are strategic troops maintained under direct control of the Stavka. They can, of course, be subordinated to the TVD or *Front* Commander if necessary.

Leading role of the Communist Party
It is the Communist Party, whose direction and control of Soviet society (and particularly of the armed forces) which provides that essential motivation which makes the Soviet war machine what it is. The first and most obvious means of control available to the party is that which is available to any government up to a point – the party, by controlling the economy, controls the purse which pays the men and provides the equipment and the expensive exercises. The Soviet military press is daily filled with acclamations about how concerned the party is for the well-being of the armed forces, and how the armed forces owe their all to the party. Such a level of control is, however, far from sufficient. There are three further means of control – firstly there is the *KGB*. The Committee for State Security, as its title means, is the latest name for the paramilitary security and intelligence organisation which is in fact the Communist Party's own private army; some of its earlier titles were the *Cheka*, the *OGPU* and the *NKVD*. It is the senior of all Soviet police organisations and has a special branch which deals with the security and reliability of the armed forces. *KGB* agents and informers are to be found at all levels and in all branches of the Soviet armed forces.

Important though it is, the *KGB* is interested mainly in seeing that the normal

Above: Green epaulettes identify these KGB Border Guards. Patrolling on foot or horseback, in tanks or planes, these troops keep intruders out—and Soviet citizens in.

means of political direction in the armed forces are functioning properly. These normal means are, firstly, the Communist Party organisation which exists at all levels within the armed forces, as it does within any branch of Soviet society and, secondly, the Main Political Directorate of the Soviet Army and Navy (its Russian title is abbreviated to *GLAVPUR*). This latter is a large, separate and extremely influential corps in the armed forces, and is responsible for the political reliability of those forces at all times.

The Communist Party organisation in the armed forces exists primarily to ensure that the personnel, particularly the regular cadre of officers, ensigns and extended service NCOs, identify their own interests with those of the party. A great deal of pressure is exerted, most of all on the officers, to encourage them to become members of the party or, if under 25 years of age, members of the Young Communist League (*Komsomol*). In fact, of junior officers, probably about two-thirds are Communist Party or active *Komsomol* members; for senior captains and majors, the figure is about three out of every four; while membership of the party is more or less obligatory for senior officers, or any post of especial responsibility.

Party or *Komsomol* meetings are held regularly at company level or equivalent; but rarely, if ever, will the company commander be the senior party member. On principle, political and military control is separated at all levels except the very highest, in order to provide an extra means of control. The senior party official, the secretary, is responsible for party affairs to his immediate party boss at battalion level and not to the company commander, and so on up the entire organisation.

The responsibility for the functioning of any unit, including the political education of the men, their discipline, morale and

spiritual well-being belongs entirely to the unit commander himself. In the ground forces, for example, for the normal unit, i.e. a regiment of three or four battalions, this will be a lieutenant-colonel or colonel. To assist him in running the unit, the commander has on his staff several deputies, each with a special area of responsibility, e.g. the Deputy Regimental Commander for Rear Services, who normally hold the rank of major. One of these deputies will invariably be the Deputy Commander for Political Affairs, or '*Zampolit*'. His job, as a member of the Political Directorate, is to remove the burden of political education from the shoulders of the unit commander and organise, co-ordinate or run all unit political activities.

The *Zampolit*'s task is to assist the commander to maintain discipline and morale and thus keep the men fighting and obeying orders. The political activities are in fact merely the means by which this is done, ensuring at the same time, of course, that loyalties are strictly in favour of the party. To help him in his duties, the *Zampolit* has several assistants in each battalion and company of the regiment: these may be officers or ensigns. He can also call on the Communist Party organisation in the unit to assist him in his programme; indeed, he will normally work in close co-ordination with the party at all times.

The latest party regulations insist that each soldier in the armed forces is to receive the following political instruction as a basic minimum: two two-hour classes in Marxist–Leninist theory per week; one hour per week of Marxist interpretation of current events, either as two 30-minute classes or as one 10-minute talk six days out of seven; and special talks in the field lasting up to three hours during major exercises. There are also to be permanent propaganda displays in all barracks, clubhouses and messes, troops are to participate in rallies and parades on communist 'feast-days' and the weekly or fortnightly unit news bulletin is to carry political instruction.

In addition to sharing the burden of organising the above, all officers must attend at least 50 hours of political instruction per year. This normally takes the form of attendance at a week-long course on a specific theme (such as how best to engender a true hatred of imperialism in the men under one's command), plus attendance at rallies or classes in current affairs.

It must be remembered that, in addition, most officers will be involved in sparetime work for the Communist Party or *Komsomol,* or studying for promotion or staff academy entrance exams, of which political studies are an obligatory part.

The only cultural organisations and activities countenanced in the USSR are those sponsored or approved by the party. This means that activities which in the armed forces of a Western state would be considered amusement or recreational activities will inevitably bear a communist message if performed in the Soviet armed forces. Popular Soviet examples are: 'brains trusts', when the men may quiz a panel of experts; the contents of libraries, and library displays; unit film shows, concerts or amateur dramatics; and, of course, all programmes on the services radio stations.

The job of the political deputy of a unit is not merely to co-ordinate and supervise all this activity – a mammoth task in itself – but he must also do the jobs that the education officer and padre do in a British unit. He must organise and supervise all education classes, arranging, for example, Russian classes for non-Russian speakers. (In the belief that military units comprised principally of one nationality, e.g. Ukrainians or Armenians, pose a threat of nationalist dissent to party rule, the Soviet leaders take great care nowadays to split up all national groups right down to section level, despite the linguistic problem this presents to those given the task of training conscripts, 20 per cent of whom may have only the faintest grasp of Russian.) Soldiers are encouraged to take all their welfare problems to the political deputy when the unit commander is busy; and should the Soviet high command have any urgent message for the troops, the political deputy is made responsible for conveying it. As an example of this last point, one might quote the campaigns organised to prevent wastage of

bread in those years when the Soviet grain harvest has been abnormally low.

This enforced political involvement is in direct contrast with most Western armies, which forbid political involvement on the part of their officers and men; and it constitutes what is certainly the most striking difference between the armed forces of a communist-style state and those of a Western country.

The Soviet serviceman

The brief description that follows of the purely military side of the personnel structure of the Soviet armed forces is designed to show the career structure and conditions for the Soviet military; but the reader is warned to remember at all times that, in the Soviet view, the military and political spheres are totally indivisible.

The personnel structure of the army is based on a large corps of regular volunteer officers, assisted by a somewhat lesser number of regular NCOs, who together make up approximately one-third of the army's manpower. The other two-thirds are conscripts, inducted for two or three years. Because the regular element are more numerous in the HQ's and technical posts, in a teeth arms unit, about 80 per cent of the manpower is made up of conscripts.

From earliest infancy, the young Soviet citizen learns to accept that he must do national service, and he learns to respect and honour the armed forces as the means of defending 'Socialism' and the 'Soviet Homeland' from the capitalists who would love to destroy them.

From his first schooldays, he is brought into regular contact with the armed forces, through his participation in Pioneer and Komsomol activities, through his preconscription training, and through constant exposure to military affairs. This exposure is accomplished by regular parades in all major cities or garrison towns, organised visits to war memorials, or by the constant media coverage of exercises and weekly TV programmes such as 'I serve the Soviet Union', which show (idealized) aspects of life in the Soviet armed forces.

At the age of 17, every young Soviet man must register for conscription. He can apply

for exemption or deferment on health grounds, for certain family reasons (e.g., if he is working, and the only supporter of aged parents), or if he is enrolled for certain university courses of particular value to the state. Exemption on educational grounds is no longer automatic, but is facilitated if the parents hold influential party or governmental positions. Many of those who obtain deferment or exemption on educational grounds do a reserve officer training course while at University, and on graduation receive the rank of Junior Lieutenant of the Reserve. Conscripts with higher education serve for 18 months; all others serve for two years. An exception are those taken into the sea-going Navy who do three years because of the higher technical training requirement for sailors on ships.

The staff of the local Military Commissariat of the Military District, where the young man registers for conscription, are responsible for allocating him to serve in one of the various branches of the armed forces. This includes not just the five combat arms of service (the Air Force, Navy, etc.) but also the Civil Defence, the Construction Troops, the Special Troops (Signals, Engineers), Rear Services, or the KGB or the MVD.

Conscription takes place twice yearly, in May and June and in November and December, and the young man becomes liable for call up just before his eighteenth birthday. If his deferments take him past the age of 27 he is no longer liable. Units compute their conscript requirements in advance and inform an appointed Military District accordingly. Which unit the conscript will be posted to depends largely on the luck of the draw. Consideration is taken of any special skills or interest, although not as much as should be the case. The most important consideration is that of security.

Below left: Political indoctrination of sailors has received special attention in the Baltic Fleet since the mutiny of 1975.

Below: A conscript of the KGB coastguard service on watch. His badges denote proficiency in military and political training. KGB forces are totally independent of MOD control.

balled in dumps is no longer modern. However, a T-54 tank and a M-30 gun are still not weapons to be ignored, particularly if one has just expended the last anti-tank round on the last T-72.

Para-military forces: KGB and MVD

The Committee for State Security (KGB) and the Ministry of the Interior (MVD) are the latest in a long line of organisations by means of which the ruler of Russia has controlled his people. The role of the Oprichnina of Ivan the Terrible, of the 'Third Section' of Tsars Nicholas and Alexander, of Lenin's Che Ka and Stalin's NKVD is carried on today by these two ministries. The KGB is well-known for its foreign espionage and subversive activities, the MVD for its string of concentration camps, 'GULAG'. However, these are only parts of the organisations.

The MVD is concerned with all internal law and order, and controls the Militia (the normal Civil Police), the GAI (State Transport Police) and the Fire Service. In addition, the MVD controls about 260,000 Internal Troops, and it is these which are considered as part of the Soviet armed forces. Internal Troops guard important state installations—even in peacetime—such as major bridges, railway stations, power stations, etc. They run the labour camps and special railway lines serving them. They are well equipped with armoured vehicles and tanks. In war or crisis, they support the police in ensuring internal security and, along with troops of the KGB, they would have the task of securing the rear of field armies and running PoW camps.

The KGB has wide-ranging responsibilities, not just as an intelligence organisation spying abroad, but also as an internal security force. It is responsible only to the very highest echelons of the Party leadership. It is the senior 'policing force', and its officers carry influence disproportionate to their ranks. The KGB infiltrates all echelons of Soviet life—even the CPSU. In the armed forces it provides a counterintelligence cell in every formation (during the 1941–45 war this was known as 'smersh'). It has a security element in every establishment (factory or university) engaged in military work—known as the 'First Department'. Covertly, the KGB recruits officers as collaborators within the armed forces and defence establishment who 'keep an eye' on the loyalty of the armed forces. Normal military intelligence duties are carried out by the Soviet Army's Main Intelligence Directorate—the GRU. The GRU also runs its own spy network abroad, to rival that of the KGB, but it is a much less powerful organisation and it too must be infiltrated by the KGB.

Those parts of the KGB which form part of the Soviet armed forces (although like the Internal Troops, they are in no way subordinate to the Ministry of Defence) are the Border Guard Troops and Security Troops, totalling some 200,000. The Border Guards, as their title suggests, provide strong guards along the whole Soviet border and at every entry point. All customs and immigration are the responsibility of this command. Like Internal Troops, they are run on army lines, with uniforms identical, save for the colour of epaulettes and piping (maroon for Internal Troops, green for Border Guards, blue for Security Troops). They are largely conscript forces with regular officers and SNCOs. The KGB Border Troops have a complete range of AFVs, and also aircraft and artillery. The coastguard element have fast missile-armed patrol boats. Border clashes with the Chinese on the Ussuri River and in Central Asia involved KGB troops, not MoD troops.

Like the MVD troops, in wartime the Border Guards would have security responsibilities in the rear of field armies. In the 1941–45 war, the functions of the MVD and KGB were united in NKVD. Every army had an NKVD regiment in its rear to ensure security of both the Soviet troops and the civilian population. When the Red Army crossed into Eastern Europe in 1944 this number was increased to two or even three regiments per Army. On occasion, the NKVD regiments were committed to battle as army units, but unlike the Waffen SS they were not an elite combat force.

Security Troops of the KGB guard key governmental installations throughout the USSR. In Moscow they guard the Kremlin, and have elements close to all large army barracks. They provide guards at all nuclear plants and Strategic Rocket Forces installations. Theirs is the responsibility for handling nuclear warheads in the armed forces, even on the battlefield. They also provide a secure high-level communications net for the armed forces and for ruling elements of the Party.

The Military Construction Troops

There are over a quarter of a million troops serving in the Ministry of Defence Construction Units in the USSR. These are organised as conventional military units with a regular officer corps and about 85 per cent conscripts serving for the usual two years. However, they are not usually armed. They are employed in important military and civilian construction projects throughout the USSR, building not only barracks and military installations and bases, but also such things as facilities for the 1980 Olympic Games in Moscow. Large numbers of them are employed on the back-up construction for the BAM—the Baykalo-Amur-Main Line Railway. This strategic railway will provide a more secure land link to the Soviet Far East. The present Trans-Siberian Railway runs along the Chinese border, whereas the BAM runs 300–500 miles further north. It will also serve to open up the mineral-rich wastelands of Eastern Siberia.

Because of their non-combatant status, the construction troops are a common recipient of the less reliable elements of Soviet society. Active national minorities, religious believers and dissidents are likely to end up in a construction unit along with the educationally backward.

Road and Railway Troops

These two branches of the Ministry of Defence function like the Construction Troops. Their specific task is the construction and maintenance of roads and railways and bridges, not just for military purposes but for the civilian economy as well. It is

Military construction troops are employed on major state projects. Above left: the Baikal-Amut railway is pushed through inhospitable country to carry the strategic Trans-Siberia line well north of the Chinese border.

Left: Army labour and Western technology help Soviet engineers to reduce the national oil shortage. This strategic pipeline brings oil from Siberia westwards to supply European Russia and Eastern Europe.

the railway troops who are principally responsible for laying the line on the BAM.

The importance of Railway Troops in wartime is obvious in view of the USSR's reliance on railways for its strategic mobilization and deployment. It is on this type of task that prisoners of war are likely to be employed. The Road Troops construct and maintain supply routes behind advancing armies in war, in cooperation with combat engineers.

The Military Communications Directorate (VOSO)

This organisation is responsible for planning and directing strategic movement by all means of transport. It establishes major traffic control centres, cooperates with the Civil Railway control and with Aeroflot to move men, supplies and equipment as efficiently as possible over civilian and military transport nets. In wartime it hands over its control responsibility in the rear area of higher formations to the army's Commandants Service, who plan and organise traffic control in the combat zone, right up to the battle area. It is the Commandants Service who provide the white-helmeted traffic regulators to direct troop movements on the march and into battle.

The Civil Defence Organisation

The Communist Party itself, with members in every town and village, every school, factory, and farm in the USSR, is the most important of the country's tools for war survival. The Party provides the leadership, direction and discipline that the Russian nature needs, and it controls even in peacetime every social activity in the USSR. The means of control it employs in peacetime will be those it relies on for post-strike recovery. The prime means of control are: the armed forces; the police and MVD forces, the KGB, and regular Ministry of Defence troops; the central and local government system, with its almost total centralized control of: (a) food and food distribution, (b) the construction industry, (c) production facilities and the labour force, (d) all national finance, and (e) the national communications networks; and the mass media and educational systems, both entirely in government hands.

The chief functions of the Soviet Civil Defence are: firstly, to co-ordinate under Party control the relevant Civil Defence functions of all these agencies; secondly, to provide comprehensive studies and plans, and the framework for exercises, so that Civil Defence procedures can be perfected; thirdly, to provide an organisational and personnel structure to enable the mass of population to be educated in and mobilized for effective Civil Defence work.

Structure of the Civil Defence network

The hub of the Soviet Civil Defence network is the central HQ and control apparatus which forms part of the Soviet Ministry of Defence. This HQ directs all national and local civilian and military Civil Defence programmes, and commands the regular military Civil Defence personnel. Previously, Civil Defence had been a responsibility of the Ministry of Internal Affairs, but the present organisation, which dates from 1971, indicates its increased status. From about 1973 onwards, Civil Defence has had a greatly increased budget and allocation of manpower resources.

The regular officers and conscripts (estimates vary between 20 and 50,000 in all) of the army's regular Civil Defence Troops form the basis of the Civil Defence network. They are trained not only in basic soldiering, but also in Civil Defence

skills—operating engineering machinery, fire fighting, traffic control, first aid, etc. In addition, the Ministry of Defence's Construction Troops, Railway and Road (Construction) Troops, and VOSO (the Transport Organisation Service) are also called up to fulfil Civil Defence tasks, particularly in the construction of shelter facilities.

Probably equal in number to the Military Civil Defence Troops (again estimates vary as to actual numbers) is a corps of full time civilian Civil Defence personnel, occupying posts in central and local government and industrial enterprises. They are subordinate to the local Republican Councils of Ministers and receive their orders from the Deputy Minister of Defence in charge of the Civil Defence network via local governmental channels. The co-ordination of Military and Civilian Civil Defence effort is one of the chief tasks—and problems—of Army General Altunin, who at present holds the appointment of Deputy Minister of Defence and Chief of Civil Defence. The full time civilian Civil Defence staff are responsible for preparing Civil Defence plans for their respective organisations (e.g., towns or factory emergency evacuation plans, rescue drills, etc.); for preparing the universal Civil Defence training programme, which should embrace all personnel in their town, farm or factory; and for recruiting, organising and training the large number of part time Civil Defence personnel on whom the system depends—not just the voluntary Civil Defence helpers, rescue teams and so on, but the drivers of bulldozers,

Above: Regular Civil Defence exercises test both the Army's CD Corps and the Civilian CD organisation.
Top: Soviet army bowsers in East Germany carry fuel from Comecon pipeline terminals to field units. All major WP exercises assume the likelihood of escalation to nuclear war.

etc., whose civilian skills are so valuable in emergency.

To these ends, not only does each town or large factory have full time and part time Civil Defence staff, but the directors of the various municipal services have official responsibility, as de facto Civil Defence officers, for the Civil Defence preparations of their own branch or organisation. For example, the head of a town's medical services is ultimately responsible for the ability of his organisation to function in a post-strike environment.

The attached diagram shows the Civil Defence structure in a town. This is *not* a separate organisation, but shows onto whose shoulders in local government the responsibilities for organizing Civil Defence fall. Most of the organisational and planning work would fall to one of the Deputies of the Chairman of the Town Executive Committee, who would have one or two full time Civil Defence staff officers under him.

All personnel in municipal departments are expected to have done a 20 hour basic course in Civil Defence knowledge, and managers and

Civil Defence Organisation in a Soviet Town (Local Government Organisation)

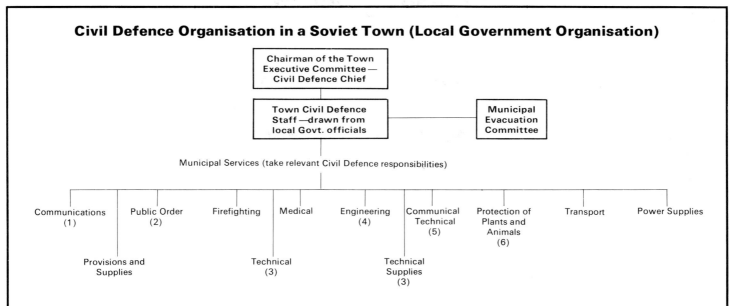

This structure is paralleled in regional and 'oblast' (district) level local Government organisation, and a similar, although more basic, system operates in a large industrial enterprise or on a State Farm.

Key to diagram
1. Local Post Office Staff. 2. The local Militia and their volunteer "People's Squad". 3. Drawn from municipal maintenance, planning and supply departments responsible for the supply and maintenance of all equipment, and establishing water supplies. 4. Drawn from local building and construction agencies. Tasks are shelter construction, repair, route and rubble clearance and rescue. 5. Involves local laundry, shower baths and street cleansing departments, responsible for decontamination. 6. Local veterinary and agricultural services, responsible for decontamination of plants and animals and checking basic food stocks for contamination.

senior officials are expected to be fully conversant with the Civil Defence functions of their department. Enthusiasts and those so ordered can attend a course at the Civil Defence Academy in Leningrad, or at one of several Civil Defence colleges elsewhere. (The Military Civil Defence college provides officers for the Army's Civil Defence Troops.)

The official aims of the Soviet Civil Defence organisation are as follows:

(a) Protection of the population from weapons of mass destruction.
(b) To prepare economic facilities (factories, farms, administrative organisations) for stability of operation in the face of attack.
(c) To perform rescue and emergency restoration work at sites of destruction in order to establish national recovery.

Protection of the population is to be achieved by the following measures:

(a) Effective early warning.
(b) Effective training in early warning drills.
(c) Dispersal of essential work force from large towns to surrounding villages.
(d) Evacuation of non-essential populations deep into the countryside; evacuation and concealment of essential R and D establishments.
(e) Providing essential individual means of protection.
(f) Providing blast shelters for key governmental personnel and industrial work force in urban areas, and fallout shelters for the population in evacuation and dispersal areas.
(g) Creation of food and water reserves.
(h) Effective training in decontamination and protection.
(i) Providing a contamination monitoring and recce service.
(j) Implementing anti-epidemic measures.
(k) Organising search and rescue operations.

The efficiency of the Soviet Civil Defence system is admitted to be patchy. A simple rule of thumb is that the more important a town, factory or similar site is to the function of (a) the military and (b) the governmental systems, the better will be the level of Civil Defence preparations. For example, in major naval dock areas or towns with important army installations, in factories producing vital defence material, or in areas close to the key Party and governmental control centres, the number of Civil Defence shelters and the level of popular training will be far higher than in a town or installation without any such important facility.

There is available a comprehensive, though not entirely accurate, Civil Defence handbook for all personnel, and over the past few years, there have been an increasing number of combined Military and Civilian exercises involving towns or certain factories in a given area. The fact that these have to date been on a limited scale should not be taken to indicate a lack of serious effort in this regard. The programme of integrated exercises is in its infancy, and what we are seeing is a very gradual development of effective Civil Defence capability within a limited budget. There can be little doubt that the system has been much improved over the last ten years, and that continued improvement can be expected.

Little progress has apparently been made in the field of planning mass evacuation, and no really large scale exercises have yet been reported. In the provision of shelters, a recent construction programme has gone some way to providing protection facilities for key personnel in important areas, but there is little evidence that any mass shelters are in existence, and even obvious shelters such as underground railways do not yet appear to have been adequately equipped for the task. Whilst stockpiles of food and fuel reserves exist, and stocks of protective masks and clothing may also exist, there is little evidence of exercises in the distribution of these, such as were common in European countries before 1939.

Consequently, one is forced to conclude that some of the more enthusiastic claims made for the Soviet Civil Defence system, particularly in some US circles, are unsubstantiated. We see no evidence that the USSR could at the moment hope to provide adequate protection to ensure beyond doubt the survival of its social system with minimal damage. However, this is not to say that the Soviet Civil Defence effort is to be derided, or that it is not worthwhile. The following points must be considered:

(a) Despite a long history and tradition of Civil Defence, the achievements of the present Civil Defence system should really be measured from 1971, when it was rejuvenated. Since then it has made great strides and will probably continue to do so in the foreseeable future.
(b) The system has achieved an increased level of awareness among the public and appears to be overcoming public apathy, particularly in those key areas where a lot of time and money is put into Civil Defence effort.
(c) There is now an established shelter network for key personnel that would ensure at least the survival of a governmental command structure.
(d) There is in existence a comprehensive framework of a Civil Defence system which could be activated fairly quickly, were the Party to make it a priority.
(e) The Civil Defence system is part of an overall system of social control which has proven its ability to function in adversity.
(f) The high level of armed services in the USSR provides a powerful disciplinary force in the country, to which the Civil Defence system could harness much of the civilian organisation in emergency. To this end, Civil Defence is one of the most unifying elements of the Soviet war machine.
(g) The Russian's natural character is to respond very positively to coercion. Force has always been a most effective means of rule and, in an emergency, these last three points would combine to counteract the post-strike chaos.

Soviet Global Policy in Peace and War

The Soviet attitude to war is clear: Marxist-Leninist theory dictates that war with Capitalism is inevitable so the Soviet armed forces must be ready to win. The first aim of the armed forces is to make the USSR impregnable against attack; the second is to reduce the power of the Western capitalist bloc; and the third is to support wars of national liberation wherever they may occur. One thing is certain: the primary Soviet objective is to succeed in disrupting the Western alliance under cover of détente, Mutual Balanced Force Reduction (MBFR) and political subversion.

Brigadier Shelford Bidwell

If we are to understand Soviet strategy it is important to realise that the Soviet viewpoint, Soviet terms of reference and Soviet modes of thought differ fundamentally from those which we regard as normal in non-Marxist society in the West. The Western view of defence and international relationships is that military arrangements should be geared to security, not to impose policy by force, and that peace, in an absolute sense, is an overriding goal, for bitter experience in this century has proved that armed conflict is unprofitable. By contrast the Soviet view is apocalyptic. Marx-Leninism teaches that the world as we know it is doomed to irreconcilable conflict between the capitalist and socialist systems, and that there can be no peace until the socialist system has pre-

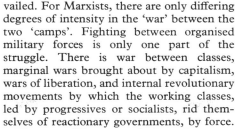

Typifying an alarming new phase in Soviet expansionism is this T-62 main battle tank in a hull-down position among the rocks overlooking the road from Jellalabad to Kabul during the 1979-80 invasion of Afghanistan. Note the extra long-range fuel tanks piled on the rear decking, and the infra-red night sight above the mantlet.

vailed. For Marxists, there are only differing degrees of intensity in the 'war' between the two 'camps'. Fighting between organised military forces is only one part of the struggle. There is war between classes, marginal wars brought about by capitalism, wars of liberation, and internal revolutionary movements by which the working classes, led by progressives or socialists, rid themselves of reactionary governments, by force.

There are Western apologists who argue, not unconvincingly, that Soviet behaviour is no more than what is normal in any great power. They see a historical resemblance between the empire of the Tsars and the Soviet empire. All great powers seek to increase their sphere of influence, to make favourable alliances, to secure their frontiers and, if they indulge in peaceful exercises, such as arms control, to extract as much political advantage from them as possible. No nation suffered more in 1939–1945 than the Russians. Small wonder that they have built up their armed forces to a level at which they can never again be threatened. The same historical imperatives that caused imperial Britain to build up a great fleet have caused the Soviet Union to do exactly the same thing. If the Soviet Union seeks to bring smaller countries into her orbit, or establish overseas bases, that is all part of the 'great game'. As for global war, or nuclear war, or 'World War III', the Soviet leaders (it can be argued) are not maniacs. They are as aware as anyone else that all that would result would be universal ruin and the destruction of both political systems. It can also be argued, with some force, that except for the suppression of dissidence inside the Soviet empire (Hungary, Czechoslovakia) the Soviet Union has been at peace, as compared with the incessant wars in which the rest of the world has been engaged: Korea,

the Middle East, Vietnam, India-Pakistan and so on.

Such a view is naive. Nothing is more mistaken than to believe that Soviet foreign policy, Soviet military strategy, the Soviet attitude towards 'peace' and 'détente' are mirror-images of our own, arise from the same assumption and follow the same logic. The Soviet, or Marxist, world-view has been analysed in the first chapter of this book, but before discussing purely military strategy it will be convenient to remind the reader that: 'The illusion about Soviet pragmatism dies hard, as does wishful thinking about the Soviet approach to détente. After Yalta there was disenchantment in the West when it finally dawned that Stalin's use of the word "democracy" did not coincide with Western usage. Now there has been another painful discovery of the obvious—Brezhnev's concept of détente differs from the Western one . . . It is still assumed by many that the Soviet leaders follow the Western "rules of the game" . . .',[1] something forcibly brought to Western attention in 1980 by the Soviet occupation of Afghanistan.

We know, from literature that is available to all students, that according to Marx-Leninism the socialist and capitalist systems are not only bound to collide, but in a real sense are already in collision. It is an article of faith that wars in general arise because of the class struggle. The imperialist-capitalist

Below: The high-tide of President Carter's efforts to achieve a permanent change in US relations with the USSR came at the SALT-II talks in mid-1979. Behind the two smiling presidents stand Kosygin and the uniformed figures of Marshals Ustinov (Minister of Defence) and Ogarkov (First Deputy Defence Minister and CinC WP). Seven months later the USSR's invasion of Afghanistan disillusioned Carter.

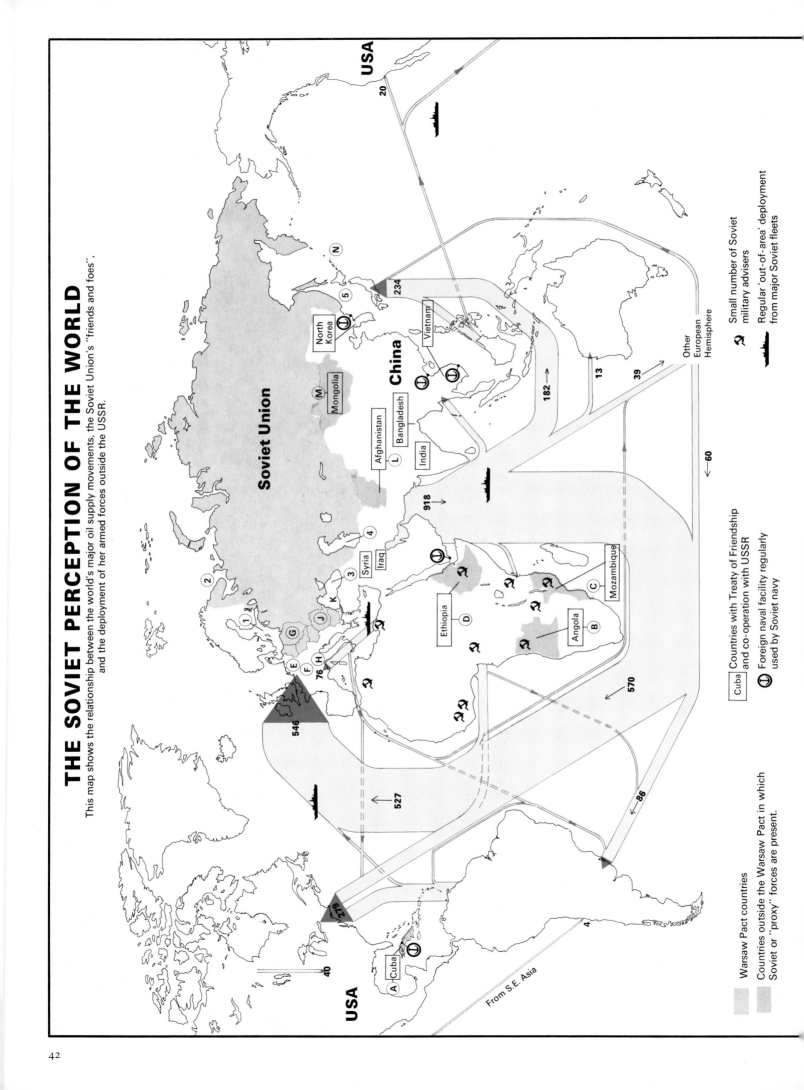

THE SOVIET PERCEPTION OF THE WORLD

This map shows the relationship between the world's major oil supply movements, the Soviet Union's "friends and foes", and the deployment of her armed forces outside the USSR.

USA

20

Soviet Union

China

N

5

234

North Korea

Vietnam

M

Mongolia

Afghanistan

L

Bangladesh

India

182

13

39

Other European Hemisphere

60

918

4

2

3

Syria

Iraq

Ethiopia

D

Angola

B

C

Mozambique

570

1

G

J

K

E

F

76 H

546

527

86

219

40

A Cuba

USA

4

From S.E. Asia

Warsaw Pact countries

Countries outside the Warsaw Pact in which Soviet or "proxy" forces are present.

Cuba Countries with Treaty of Friendship and co-operation with USSR

Foreign naval facility regularly used by Soviet navy

Small number of Soviet military advisers

Regular 'out-of-area' deployment from major Soviet fleets

USSR – the world's largest state

The USSR is the largest political unit in the world, stretching from Europe across 6,100 miles to the Pacific, and from the Arctic 2,800 miles southwards to Iran and Afghanistan. The USSR is 8.5 million square miles in area, has 9,950 miles of coastline and 9,800 miles of frontier, and borders on no less than 12 countries.

The first Russian state was set up at Kiev but was destroyed by the Mongols in 13th Century. A new Russia developed, centred on Moscow and began an unceasing expansion under the Romanov Tsars. The Pacific was reached in 1639 and the first Baltic town was founded in 1702. The process started by the Tsars has continued under the Communists, with the Baltic states of Latvia, Estonia and Lithuania assimilated in 1940, while after World War II areas traditionally Polish and Japanese were annexed. In such an historical context the recent Soviet move into Afghanistan can be seen as the next logical step in a process which has been going on for some 600 years. The deeds and dispositions of the Soviet armed forces speak louder than any words, as shown here:

treaties and deployments set up to safeguard the USSR. At the core of Soviet defence philosophy is the domination of Eastern Europe through the Warsaw Pact, supported to a lesser degree by the 'special relationship' with Finland. The Pact area (light grey on the map) serves two purposes: it is both a shield against another invasion, and it is a potential springboard for the launching of a Soviet invasion of Western Europe. It must always be remembered that the Pact is not like the NATO Alliance, and, as is made clear in the chapter on the Warsaw Pact in this book, Soviet domination is absolute.

Since the end of World War II the USSR has been establishing a series of treaties of 'friendship and cooperation' with the apparent design of forming a protective arc around its southern periphery. This policy has had some successes, but it has also had some spectacular failures, eg. Egypt, Somalia.

A most significant factor shown on the map is the major oil supply movements (expressed in millions of tonnes) in 1979, and it is quite clear how the USSR is now approaching the sources of the world's oil, the very life-blood of Western economies.

The Soviet Perception of the Threat

This map has been drawn with the USSR at the centre to illustrate how the world appears to the leaders in the Kremlin. They feel threatened from three directions: from the West, the East and from the North over the polar region. Perhaps the most immediate threat is felt to be from Western Europe. No Russian forgets that his country has been invaded five times in the past 160 years (1814 Napoleon; 1855 England and France; 1914 Germany; 1919 England, France and the USA; 1941 Germany). The eastern threat is also taken very seriously; the USSR is very wary of the resurgence of Japan as a military power, and of the Chinese assumption of world power status. Greatest of all, however, is the threat from the United States, either in concert with NATO, or, in the strategic nuclear context, possibly alone. Finally, the USSR is so huge and embraces so many disparate races, that the ruling Russians can never afford to overlook the possibility of an internal explosion by one (or more) of the minority groups.

The map shows the current (1980) network of alliances,

Key	Country	Motor Rifle Div.	Tank Div.	Air Army	Others
A	Cuba	—	—	¼	300 men
B	Angola	—	—	—	1,130
C	Mozambique	—	—	—	300 men
D	Ethiopia	—	—	—	—
E	Germany (DDR)	10	10	1	—
F	Czechoslovakia	3	2	1	—
G	Poland	—	2	1	—
H	Hungary	2	2	1	—
J	Romania	—	—	—	—
K	Bulgaria	—	—	—	—
L	Afghanistan	6	1	½	1 AB div.
M	Mongolia	2	1	—	—
N	Kuriles	1	—	—	—

Naval Forces

Key	Fleet	Subs	Maj. Surface	Min. Surface	LSTs
①	Baltic	60	75	332	37
②	Northern	149	83	136	14
③	Black Sea }	42	91	277	60
④	Caspian }				
⑤	Pacific	110	94	269	55

system, because of the fear that the proletariat, through the example of the socialist states already in existence, may throw off their chains, will seek to destroy its enemy. The third world war will arise, says a distinguished Russian strategist, when the capitalist leaders, in desperation '. . . strive for the utter defeat of the armed forces of the socialist states and the liquidation of their political system, establishing instead capitalist systems and the enslavement of these countries'.[2]

So there can be no doubt. What confuses the Western student is that if Marxian dialectic presupposes the success of the class struggle why is it necessary to adopt an aggressive, offensive forward policy, as everything will come right in the end? The answer is that the Marxist view is that it is not enough to be passive. The inevitable process of history must be helped and accelerated. Force, according to the creed, is the only midwife of the new world society that has yet to be born.

Next, there is the Soviet view of warfare itself; of a global war between the two camps. In such a war there can be no question of any limited objectives, a partial success, an armistice and a peace conference followed by compromise and accommodation by both sides. Soviet strategists do not believe in such procedures. All that happens, in capitalist wars, is that one side or the other, when it feels strong enough, goes to war again in quest of the objectives it had not secured on a previous occasion. The Soviet military philosophy is that an opponent must be crushed beyond the point of recovery and for ever. We can see this in action in purely revolutionary situations, when the overthrown class is 'liquidated', a term which means, as it is seen in the awful example of Kampuchea, physical elimination. The Soviet strategists are as aware as their Western counterparts of the immense destructive power of nuclear weapons, but this does not mean that they see them as purely deterrent. On the contrary, they believe that they can be used to eliminate the class enemy, in short order.

Here it is worth commenting on NATO strategy. NATO relies on a 'graduated response' to defeat a physical invasion of its territory; a defensive operation by conventional forces, the release of small 'battlefield' nuclear weapons, then the use of 'theatre' nuclear weapons, with the awful threat of strategic nuclear bombardment directed at the Soviet homeland itself as the final threat. There is no evidence whatever that the Soviet Union would respond to such a progressive 'arm-twisting', any more than the Vietnamese did when subjected to escalation of conventional force by the United States. It is more a defence doctrine designed for political consumption in NATO states than based on military reality. Marxist or not, the lesson of previous wars is that aggressors do not launch them unless they believe that they have a high probability of success, and are unlikely to be deterred until they have been decisively defeated.

We do not know, of course, what Soviet tactical thinking will be, or how the Soviet leaders would react in any specific set of circumstances. To that extent they are pragmatic. We do, however, know what their principles are. The best guides to

Soviet actions and intentions are to be found in their own military literature, the evidence of the size and structure of their armed forces, and their current actions. From these it is clear that Soviet strategists are guided by three principles.

First, the Soviet Union must be so strong in every department, nuclear missiles, the army, the air force, air defence and the navy, that it is impregnable.

Second, if it has to fight a global war it must defeat its opponent in the shortest possible time.

Third, peace is simply a time for preparation for this final struggle, and must be spent in improving the Soviet strategic posture worldwide, by taking the part of all the progressive states outside the present Soviet orbit and drawing them into the socialist camp, and by assisting in the class struggle to overthrow imperialist or reactionary governments wherever they may be found.

Soviet foreign policy—with all its tactical shifts and its outward opportunism, however much it may seek détente, talk about 'peace', initiate conferences about strategic arms limitation and force reductions—is a war policy, aimed at extending the size and increasing the strength of the Soviet Union in every respect: economic, military, and political.

We can, therefore, conveniently consider a global nuclear war and the ongoing revolutionary struggle, as separate phases, and begin by examining nuclear strategy.

The Western view of nuclear warfare resolves around deterrence, and therefore the assessment by each side of the other's intentions: an elaborate poker game, in which the hints or clues given by one side may leave the other so uncertain that it will hesitate to be the first to unleash the terrible weapon. It is by no means certain that the Soviet leaders' perceptions and those of Western analysts actually coincide. There is good reason to believe that their doctrine is to wage war à outrance with every weapon available, and it is possible that so far all that has deterred them is the belief that they are weaker in this arm. As is well known even to non-specialists, there are two alternative nuclear strategies. One is of wholesale destruction. The other is of 'counter-force', i.e., an attack on the opponent's nuclear weapon systems. To guard against a totally successful surprise attack both sides possess three kinds of delivery systems, land, air and sea-based, so that sufficient will always remain for retaliation. No complete defence system can be set up, however many resources may be devoted to it, which can guard effectively against nuclear attack. The best hope is counter-force, and it is believed that this is the Soviet policy.

The nuclear equation is too complex to be dealt with in a few short paragraphs, but roughly it looks like this. The United States has some 2,270 delivery vehicles of all kinds, capable of delivering 11,000 nuclear warheads. Their yield (power) is smaller than the biggest Soviet warheads, some of which are as large as 25 MT (25,000,000 tons of equivalent high explosive) but they are very accurate. The Soviet nuclear force has some 2,500 delivery vehicles with only some 5,000 very large warheads, but the situation is not static. The Americans are converting their silo-based system to a mobile one, so reducing the chances of their being located exactly, and thereby the danger of a successful Soviet first strike. They also have up their sleeve, but not fully deployed, the cruise missile, a sort of fast, small pilotless aircraft capable of evading normal early warning systems and delivering its warhead with very great accuracy. On the Soviet side there is a change under way to multiple warheads and much improved accuracy. The American view is that in the 1980s the Soviet strategic force will overtake the United States in both numerical strength and also accuracy, which will change the whole Western concept of deterrence.

This is not the only use for nuclear weapons, or the only area where there is an imbalance disadvantageous to NATO. Both sides deploy 'theatre' nuclear weapons, whose task in the event of war is to attack targets deep in the rear of the opposing armies, such as bases, airfields and centres of communication; what would have been called 'strategic' targets in the days of conventional, pre-nuclear air power. There is no sharp boundary between the targets in either category. We can safely assume that some 'theatre' targets are deep in Soviet territory, and some in the United Kingdom. There are also 'battlefield' nuclear weapons, on which NATO relies to counterbalance the substantial superiority in conventional troops enjoyed by the Warsaw Pact forces. NATO is at a great disadvantage because its plans are entirely defensive, and therefore if it is forced to use these 'tactical', or 'battlefield', nuclear weapons it will be, perforce, on its own soil, with the inevitable destruction of its own towns and casualties to its civil population that such a defence entails. Now, for a number of years American nuclear scientists have been aware of the possibility of designing a warhead whose emission of short range but penetrating neutrons is intensified but whose blast effect is greatly reduced. This is the so-called 'neutron bomb', more correctly the 'enhanced radiation' weapon. The advantage this offers to an army fighting a defensive battle on its own territory against an aggressor whose troops are all protected by armour, is that the neutron flux is exceptionally effective against tanks and armoured vehicles, but the area affected is correspondingly small, so that the danger to friendly troops and civilians is reduced. It is no exaggeration to say that the neutron weapon is a tactical breakthrough.[3]

The tactics of nuclear warfare and a description of nuclear weapons in general lie outside the scope of this chapter. What is relevant is that Soviet strategy in peace is to build up their own nuclear armoury while working on the natural fear and dislike of nuclear weapons in the West to inhibit the introduction of new designs of weapon. The 'neutron bomb' was the successful target of a propaganda campaign which led to the President of the United States deciding that, for the time at least, this vital and relatively humane weapon would not be introduced. At the time of writing the Soviet Union is affecting a great show of indignation over the proposal to deploy another nuclear weapon of radical design, the cruise missile. (The cruise missile can be designed to fit varying roles and methods of launch, and could be

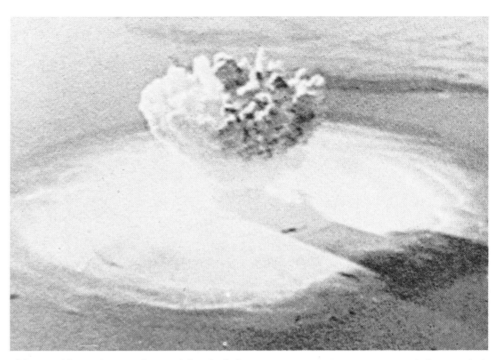

either a 'theatre' or a 'strategic' missile.) Political pressure for détente and arms control are not, in Soviet eyes, in any way incompatible with strengthening the armed forces of the Soviet Union, including its huge nuclear armoury and rocket forces. Opinions on the relative advantages to the United States and the Soviet Union of the SALT-II agreement differ, but we can be certain that Soviet leaders would not have entered into it had it not improved their position and it is significant that they succeeded in excluding two powerful intermediate range allegedly 'theatre' weapons—the SS-20 missile (3,000 to 4,000 miles range) and the Tu-22 'Backfire' bomber (5,500 miles)—from its provisions.

The NATO nations began proportionately to reduce their conventional forces, partly because at first the, now discarded, NATO plan was to rely on nuclear retaliation from the first, the 'trip-wire' strategy, and partly because to crowd the battlefield with conventional troops was only to provide nuclear targets. The Soviet planners have never subscribed to this view. In the first place they have always been great believers in the use of mass. They are good practical tacticians, but their approach to war has never been to rely on some fancy plan of manoeuvre. Soviet planners begin by calculating the amount of guns, tanks and aircraft required to crush the enemy, *for certain*. They believe in superiority of numbers and superiority of fire-power. Their divisions as organised are wholly armoured, because armoured troops have a ten-to-one advantage over ordinary infantry and artillerymen in the open when under nuclear attack. Above all they are influenced by the tactics of the German *blitzkrieg* which carved into Russia in 1941. The *blitzkrieg* was designed to knock out a superior opponent before he had a chance to organise his defences and bring his full industrial and man-power potential into play, and so avoid a long war of attrition. The Soviet planners, being Marxists, believe that the balance of military power is with the belligerent possessing the largest and most efficient industrial base, but they estimate that, at the moment, the

Soviet Union cannot match the United States and western Europe in this respect. They have accordingly themselves adopted a *blitzkrieg* doctrine, as opposed to the older and slower tactics of 'the Russian steam-roller'.

Until a few years ago the Soviet Army planned its offensives very much in the style of 1943–1944, using divisions by the score supported by massed artillery and hundreds of tanks advancing according to a rigid plan and a rigid schedule. To produce the vast numbers of weapons required the models were effective, but crude and simple as compared with the sophisticated weaponry of the West. NATO has hitherto relied on its technical superiority and a faster, more flexible command system, to stop a mass attack of this kind. Especially, it relies on the superiority of its aircraft in the ground-attack role. This advantage is, however, being gradually whittled away. Soviet military theory still emphasises the importance of numbers. For instance, in the central-north sector of the Warsaw Pact forces oppose some 7,000 NATO tanks with no fewer than 20,500; some 2,350 combat aircraft with 4,200, and 27 assorted divisions with 47 tank and mechanised divisions, each one stronger in artillery and armour than their opponents. At the same time the new models of all types of weapon arriving in the Soviet army approach or equal the NATO models in technical excellence. Aware of NATO reliance on air-delivered tactical weapons a whole inventory of surface-to-air missiles have been introduced for deployment on the battlefield, which has freed the Soviet air force from the role of interception to concentrate, like NATO, on ground attack.[4]

Blitzkriegs cannot be carried out by commanders who can do no more than follow dully the paragraphs of an operation order. Quick wits and initiative are required to seize the fleeting opportunities of an

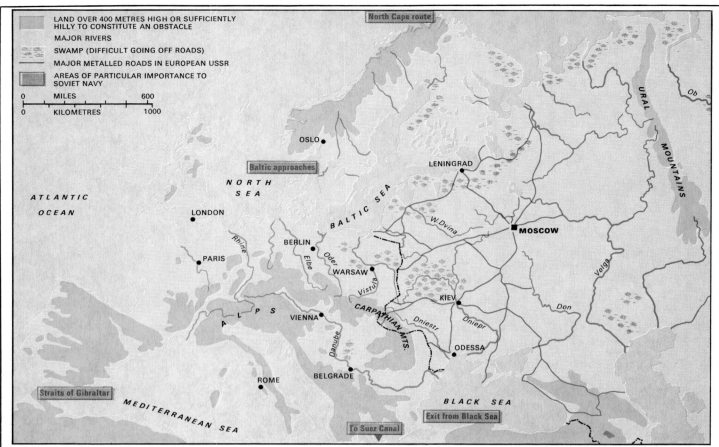

Legend:
- LAND OVER 400 METRES HIGH OR SUFFICIENTLY HILLY TO CONSTITUTE AN OBSTACLE
- MAJOR RIVERS
- SWAMP (DIFFICULT GOING OFF ROADS)
- MAJOR METALLED ROADS IN EUROPEAN USSR
- AREAS OF PARTICULAR IMPORTANCE TO SOVIET NAVY

0 — MILES — 600
0 — KILOMETRES — 1000

North Cape route

OSLO

Baltic approaches

LENINGRAD

NORTH SEA

BALTIC SEA

LONDON

W.Dvina

MOSCOW

Rhine

BERLIN

Elbe

Oder

WARSAW

PARIS

Vistula

KIEV

ATLANTIC OCEAN

A L P S

VIENNA

CARPATHIAN MTS.

Dniestr

Dniepr

Don

Volga

URAL MOUNTAINS

Ob

Danube

ODESSA

Straits of Gibraltar

ROME

BELGRADE

MEDITERRANEAN SEA

BLACK SEA

Exit from Black Sea

To Suez Canal

European geographic features of strategic importance to USSR

When seen from Moscow, the strategic geography of the USSR is not at all attractive from the point of view of defence. Almost the whole of the European USSR is an enormous plain which stretches unbroken from the Ural mountains to the English Channel, and from the Black Sea to the Arctic Ocean. The major natural obstacles to any invader are the very size of the country, its lack of all-weather roads, and the frequent large rivers and areas of marshland. To the south and east of Moscow, the plain stretches to the Pamirs and Tien Shan mountains, where the border with China runs. The only strategic land link with the Soviet Far East is the Trans Siberian railway, whose tortuous route runs south of Lake Baikal and along the Chinese border for some 1,500 miles. The urgency with which the Soviet authorities are at present constructing a second railway several hundred miles further north is proof of the importance they attach to reducing this strategic vulnerability.

Major road network in European USSR

Although the USSR has an extensive road network, less than 8% is metalled, the remainder being graded or simply compacted earth. There are no metalled roads linking European USSR with Asiatic USSR, and there are large tracts of country with no all-weather roads between towns at all, especially east of the Ural mountains. Indeed, there are only six, through, all-weather roads linking the Soviet industrial regions with Eastern Europe. These are: along the coast of the Baltic; from Moscow via Minsk to Warsaw; from Kiev to Poland, Hungary and Czechoslovakia; and from Odessa via Kishinev into Romania. These roads are, in the main, 20 to 24 feet wide and made of concrete or tar-macadam. Travel on such roads is virtually impossible in Spring, Autumn and in a wet Summer. A particular obstacle is the Pripet Marsh in Byellorussia, which covers an area the size of Wales astride the main route from Moscow to Warsaw.

Many towns and villages, even in European Russia just cannot be reached except by river or by air, even in the 1980s.

Ninety-eight per cent of Soviet freight is moved by rail or by river and long-distance passenger movement is almost entirely by rail or by air. Military resupply to Soviet forces in Europe relies on rail transport, with small amounts being moved by road. A rapidly increasing proportion of personnel movement is by air, using military and civil aircraft, and the entire changeover of annual drafts is now done by air. This is quick and cheap, and practises the rapid reinforcement plans as well.

---

armoured battle. Much attention therefore has been given in Soviet training to producing the right sort of leader, down to the grade of warrant officer. Such qualities may seem incompatible with a rigidly authoritarian society demanding unquestioning obedience, but this was a problem the army of the Third Reich was able to solve and there is no reason to believe that the Soviet Army will not be equally successful. It is largely a question of intelligence and educational levels, which have been steadily rising in the Soviet Union. The Soviet forces are, therefore, equipped and poised to launch a *blitzkrieg* regardless of whether nuclear weapons are used or not. Such an attack would take the classical form of a multiple penetration of the NATO defences by armoured columns, all tasked to break through without regard for flank or rear penetration and with the NATO airfields, headquarters and short range nuclear delivery systems as objectives, while a second wave of tanks and mechanized divisions follows on to mop up and complete the destruction of the NATO defences.

If all the evidence is that in the eyes of Soviet strategists a global war must take the form of a nuclear exchange on the largest scale plus a *blitzkrieg* whose objectives are to remove all military resistance in the shortest possible time, the existence of a new and growing Soviet ocean-going navy seems irrelevant. Navies, with their roles of guarding sea routes, blockade and transporting military forces to distant theatres are more appropriate to protracted war. The basic reason for the Soviet navy is that the whole vast Soviet war machine is so constructed that it can deal with war *on any level*. The army, for instance, has no fewer than eight airborne divisions, whose use would not be confined to global war, and five brigades of marines capable of amphibious operation, which hardly fits in with the concept of *blitzkrieg*. The navy has three functions. In the event of a nuclear war some fleets will remain in being and, con-trary to the popular idea, large parts of the northern hemisphere and the whole of the southern will be unscathed (excluding, of course, very unpleasant long-term environmental effects). The navy will then be a powerful means of asserting Soviet hegemony over the Third World in the wake of the nuclear destruction of the West. Second, and this depends on the extent to which the Soviet Union can consider itself free from the ultimate threat of nuclear retaliation, the navy would be of the greatest use in a 'half-war' or limited war situation.

The West lives by its maritime trade, and on oil imported by sea. The Soviet navy has the largest fleet of attack submarines in the world, and it is being constantly increased. For instance, the Northern Fleet, whose role is to throw a net around the whole of NATO's sea-ward left flank, has 120 submarines. This figure speaks for itself. It is, however, the third and peace-time role of the navy which justifies the enormous expense of its creation. The Soviet strategists have correctly read the British and United States experience. A navy is a most effective instrument for conveying the impression of political and military power without actually firing a shot. (The role of United States sea-power in the Cuban missile crisis was not lost on them.) In the world-wide struggle predicated by Marxism-Leninism the navy plays an essential role. Conversely, the Soviet pattern of intervention, although it is opportunist, never misses a chance to establish in its client states a naval base, or base facilities, in areas of strategic interest.

The other instrument used to further the Soviet penetration of uncommitted states and their capture for the socialist camp is the arms trade. The Soviet Union is, after the United States, the second greatest exporter of arms, being responsible for some 30 to 40 per cent of the world total. With arms go advisers, who, if the circumstances are appropriate, are followed by political advisers and experts in police-work. Exact figures are not known, as they are in the case of the arms exports of Western countries, but some idea of the scale on which the Soviet Union operates when the stake is worth while is given by the example of Egypt. In the 1967 war Egypt lost some 90 per cent of her Soviet supplied artillery and 800 tanks, all of which were promptly replaced, with more besides. By 1970 there were, reputedly as instructors, 200 Soviet pilots, 12,000 artillerymen (assisting in the operation of the huge batteries of SAMs in the Canal Zone) and some 4,000 instructors for tank, infantry and field artillery units.

Afghanistan, Algeria, Angola, Ethiopia, Iraw, Libya, Mozambique, South Yemen and Vietnam are almost entirely equipped with Soviet equipment in the three vital fields of tanks, artillery and combat aircraft. In the client states around the Mediterranean alone the total holding of Soviet battle tanks is some 7,300, although by no means all are of the latest marks. Tiny Libya, with a population of barely 3,000,000, has no fewer than 2,000. (We can compare Britain's complement, a mere 900 Chieftains.) In addition Soviet small arms and infantry heavy weapons are found in the hands of guerrilla or liberation movements around the world. Supply on this scale is a heavy burden for a country comparatively poor by Western standards and whose economy is already distorted by the immense industrial effort required to support its own expanding armed forces and space projects. The benefits might well be questioned, especially in view of the poor return from the Middle East.

This is not the Soviet view. In Soviet eyes both the risk and expense are worth while, and rebuffs or failures something to be expected from time to time. The only limiting consideration is the risk of precipitating a global war. The Soviet leaders are both shrewd and cautious. They know when to probe and press, and when to withdraw. It is worth noting that over the questions of access to Berlin, the stationing of nuclear missile systems in Cuba, and their threat of armed support of the defeated Egyptians in 1973 the Soviet leaders withdrew in the face of firm action. It is also worth noting that they refrained from any overt action when President Sadat firmly disengaged Egypt

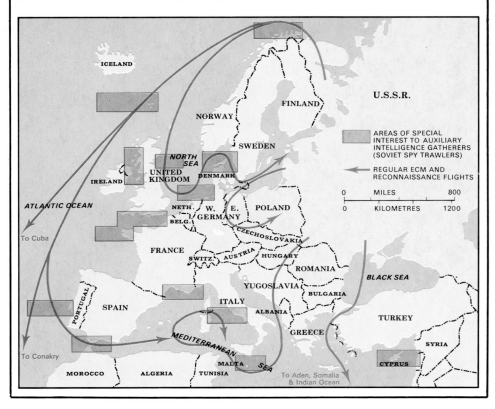

Soviet ECM and reconnaissance aircraft routes over Europe, and regular patrol areas of Soviet intelligence-gathering "trawlers"

from Soviet plans and Soviet tutelage and sought a unilateral peace settlement with Israel, leaving the Soviet policy in the Levant in ruins.

Soviet intervention is based on the strict letter of bilateral agreements. For instance, even though the pretext is bogus the Soviet leaders insist that their 'invasion' of Afghanistan was only by the invitation of the legitimate government under the terms of a treaty allowing for mutual assistance.

Afghanistan is a particularly interesting example of the Soviet method, because at first sight it would appear to offer little return for a large expenditure of effort, and also to have offended much liberal, Third World and Muslim opinion, jeopardised the ratification of SALT-II and, possibly,

hardened the attitude of the NATO states. Control of Afghanistan would offer none of the solid and immediate benefits offered by, for instance, the alliance with Cuba, or with the Soviet-dominated or orientated states on the seaboard of the Eastern Mediterranean and the mouth of the Red Sea. The Afghan peoples are warlike, turbulent, difficult to govern and notoriously hostile to foreigners. To be sure, the occupation of Afghanistan in so ruthless, prompt and efficient a manner may have been calculated to daunt Iran and Pakistan and increase Soviet prestige, power counting for more than good intentions in Eastern politics.

It is easy to write scenarios of similar interventions in the affairs of Afghanistan's neighbours, with the ultimate aim of ob-

Left: Two BTR-60PB APCs supplied by the invading Soviet Army pause at a cross-roads on the Kabul-Jellalabad highway, Afghanistan. General Grigorenko, now in exile in the USA, has warned that the lack of response in the West could encourage the USSR to attack W. Europe in 1980.

Below left: The Soviet Union carries out an unremitting programme of surveillance, visual, photographic and electronic. Most newsworthy are the ''spyships'', usually converted trawlers, and there has been one of these vessels off the coast of Northern Ireland for the past ten years, carefully monitoring British Army communications. The campaign also involves aircraft, surface ships and submarines.

Right: A Soviet exercise in Turkestan Military District, currently commanded by Colonel-General Yu. Maximov. This Military District was awarded the Order of the Red Banner in 1968 for ''its outstanding contribution to the defence capacity of the Soviet state'' and it was from here that the invasion of Afghanistan was launched in 1979-80, over the hills in the background of this picture.

Below: Infantrymen of the Turkestan Military District charge across barren land near the Afghan border. These Soviet foot-soldiers are tough, well-trained and well-motivated for a war in the West, but it will be interesting to see how their morale stands up to an aggressive war against wily, cunning and ruthless Muslim soldiers, who repeatedly repulsed the British Raj at the height of its power, and for whom the Soviets will be just another foreign invader to be taught a lesson.

taining access to the Arabian Sea through a port on the coast of the Pakistan province of Baluchistan. Of these the most plausible is the notion of an independent, Soviet-orientated republic of Baluchi-speaking peoples created by dissidents out of the predominantly Baluchi provinces of Iran and Pakistan, which could then be absorbed into the Soviet bloc using the same pretexts and the same tactics as in Afghanistan. Such developments are not impossible, but we can only surmise—what soldiers call 'appreciate'—the *tactical* intentions of the Soviet leaders. We can be more certain about their long-term political strategic aims. They on their side have carefully 'appreciated' the Western position: the United States entering the year of a presidential election and ridiculously entangled in Iran; the United Nations impotent, as usual; the NATO alliance with its waverers (in this context France and the German Federal Republic); the victim a country remote from Western experience and Western interests. As in the case of Czechoslovakia the Soviet leaders may have considered that the cries of indignation would die down, the search for détente and for Soviet markets for Western exports be resumed and the Sovietisation of Afghanistan be gradually, but finally accepted as an accomplished fact. In short, the rape of Afghanistan was undertaken because it was safe to do it, and it conformed with the ultimate Soviet aim.

This is a general rule but, it must be emphasised, it is a very broad one. Each Soviet goal or possible target is assessed on its merits, and the means to achieve it fashioned in the light of that assessment. Each is different. Cuba required no coercion and little persuasion to join the Soviet bloc. (Except for those unfortunate Cubans liquidated in the process.) A Sovietised Cuba shows the world that the Russians have a reliable ally within 200 miles of the continental United States, on whose soil it can even station a Soviet combat unit with impunity. As seen from Latin America the Soviet Union is far away across the Pacific or, looking eastwards, a remote part of a remote Europe, but the Soviet presence in Cuba is both close and visible. Cuba's greatest value, however, is as a Soviet proxy. Until they invaded Afghanistan the Soviet leaders had abstained from using Soviet troops outside their own acknowledged sphere of influence, in eastern Europe. Cuban troops employed in Africa have the double advantage of relieving the Russians from the odium of an actual military presence, and can also appear as the Third World in its Sovietised, liberated, and freedom loving guise, coming to the assistance of other peoples of the Third World still engaged in their liberation struggle.

In Africa Soviet strategy has progressed favourably, but here again the combination of opportunity and solid gain varies from territory to territory. The advantages of Soviet-orientated Angola and Mozambique, offering fleet base facilities in Capricorn Africa commanding the Cape route by which the oil products of the Persian Gulf states reach western Europe require no explanation. To this can be added the long term prospects of bringing sufficient pressure against South Africa first to neutralise it as an African power and, perhaps, later to bring it down.

The usefulness of Ethiopia is less obvious (except, as said, that every accretion to the Soviet camp is a gain), but it has access to the Red Sea through Eritrea, which explains the long, hard fight to suppress the as yet undefeated Eritrean insurgents who wish to break away from Ethiopia. Soviet advisers may have miscalculated the strong antipathy to Ethiopia of her near neighbours. The Somali Republic has broken loose from the Soviet grouping and for a short time the world saw the odd spectacle of two Soviet client states fighting each other with Soviet weapons, but as said, set-backs of this nature are one of the accepted risks of the Soviet method of operation. The game is always worth the candle, and the soundness of the principle of probing everywhere for a possible soft spot is proved in this case by the fact that Soviet plans in the Horn of Africa and Ethiopia are, so far, effectively covered by the Soviet foothold across the sea, in Aden and South Yemen. If all goes well (it must be borne in mind that these complicated manoeuvres are by no means complete, and some only in their early stages) the Soviet navy will eventually control the Red Sea route and also have a haven, or havens, at the north-east corner of the Indian Ocean. What we can observe in fact is a reconstruction of the former British Imperial network of communications, with Benguela and Beira instead of Simonstown, but Suez still a missing link, owing to Egypt's refusal to be caught in the Soviet web.

In the continuing confrontation between the two super-powers, after the central sector of NATO, which is the keystone of the whole European defensive system, the most important area is the Middle East: both for purely geographical reasons as well as Marxist theory. There is the same emphasis, for instance, on the old British Imperial route through the Mediterranean, to Suez, Aden and points east, except that it now begins, for the Soviet 'empire', in the Black Sea. The Middle East is important because: (1) it commands the most convenient air and sea routes between Europe and Asia; (2) a navy operating in the Indian Ocean could be based on friendly ports on its southern seaboard (similarly, Soviet squadrons threatening the Mediterranean flank of NATO require base facilities which can only be provided by the Soviet orientated Mediterranean Arab states); (3) pressure on Turkey can be applied from both north and south if Syria and Iraq were to be fully integrated into the Soviet camp; (4) a large part of the oil on which the West relies for its industries is supplied by the Arab states of the Middle East and Iran; (5) the Arab states, though divided over many questions, are becoming increasingly conscious of their identity as Arabs and brothers in the Islamic religion, a process begun as long ago as World War I, and have now emerged as a world political force.

So far Russian plans there have miscarried for two reasons. The military adventure, or arming the Egyptian and Syrians to attack and crush Israel, has been foiled by Israeli valour and military skill. More significant even than that, however, and of the consequent refusal of the Egyptians to continue to shed their blood in what is for them an unnecessary and costly war, is that the Arabs are a subtle and intelligent race, whose rulers are conscious of their new power, well able to perceive when they are being manipulated, likely to pursue their own especial interests and too independent to attach themselves to either superpower, except so far as it is to their clear advantage. This does not mean that the Soviet leaders will give up, for they never do that. They are extremely patient, and they will persist in the Middle East, but slowly and relying on diplomacy and with it, their undoubted skill in subversion. The weak point of the oil-rich states, of which Iran offers a glaring example, is the discrepancy between the vast income in 'petrodollars' and the poverty of the working people. As long as this remains unbridged there will always be discontent, especially among the younger and better educated members of the middle classes, and therefore no lack of recruits, first to socialist theories, and then for revolutionary practice: both readily provided by the Russians. Many of the leaders both of liberation movements and of successfully established pro-Soviet regimes have received their grounding in Marxist ideology in the Soviet Union, and also their instruction in the tactics of guerrilla warfare.

Broadly speaking, this is also the policy followed by the Soviet leaders with regard to all the Third World countries, but this is more a question of Soviet foreign policy and international relations rather than strategic aims, although these cannot be separated.

There remains the great question of Soviet relations with China. This is funda-

Below: A MiG-23U (NATO Reporting Name: Flogger-C) of the Libyan Air Force taxis past a civil Caravelle airliner. The Flogger swing-wing interceptor has been exported widely.

mentally different from those with the Western capitalist-imperialist nations, if for no other reason than that there is nothing in Marx-Leninism that would have made it possible to forecast that so bitter a schism in the Socialist camp could take place. The quarrel derives both from ideological differences, and the rigid, authoritarian attitude of the Soviet interpreters of Marxist dogma that, as the Russians were the leaders of the revolution, all other adherents to the Socialist camp must accept that they are subordinate and in a state of tutelage. The Chinese find this attitude intolerable, as they consider that they are in every way the intellectual superiors of the Russians, and that under their own leader, Mao-Tse Tung, they achieved their own revolution unaided by Moscow in the world's most populous country. An analysis of this fraught and complex relationship is for experts, and lies outside the scope of this chapter, but its effect on Soviet strategy is simple and clear. China is regarded as an enemy, and in line with their strategic principles Soviet defensive posture is offensive. The Chinese armed forces, although they are numerically very strong (man-power 4,360,000, combat aircraft 5,500, tanks some 11,000), their equipment, except perhaps their artillery, is obsolete, their strategic nuclear force, although in being, is undeveloped and no match for that of the Soviet Union and their navy suitable only for use in coastal waters. The Chinese army is designed for and only capable of territorial defence. According to some accounts its punitive raid into Vietnam in 1979 revealed that it had some serious weaknesses in deployment and tactics.

A detached observer would not consider that China constitutes a great military threat to the Soviet Union but, characteristically, a powerful detachment of the Soviet army is deployed along the Sino-Soviet frontier: nearly 40 per cent of its total, approximately six tank and 40 motor rifle divisions, together with supporting aircraft and a share of the rocket forces. (To give some impression of what these bald figures mean the Soviet forces facing China are roughly of the same order as those of the United States concentrated against Germany in 1944–1945, although of course their deployment covers a vastly greater frontage.) It is worth noting that the Soviet planners are able to do this without prejudice to the overwhelming strength of their conventional forces facing NATO. It is quite sufficient either to repel any local Chinese aggression, unlikely as this may be, or to undertake a localised offensive should this be necessary.

Soviet moves against China do not stop there. Vietnam is now firmly in the Soviet camp, and the Vietnamese invasion of Kampuchea (Cambodia) serves the double purpose of lowering China's prestige by demonstrating that she is powerless to prevent the liquidation of the regime of Pol Pot, a Chinese client, and also of establishing an extensive strategic foothold on China's south-western border. The Soviet navy also gains fleet base facilities in the South China Seas; one more link in the chain of bases that it hopes one day to extend from ocean to ocean.

It would be unwise to try and forecast how any of the current Soviet manoeuvres are likely to turn out, or what fresh initiatives the Soviet leaders might attempt in, say, such crucial areas as the Arab Middle East, in Iran, or towards India and Pakistan, all areas of keen Soviet interest, or towards the West, whose economic aids and skills the Soviet Union badly requires. All that can

Top left: Where once only British sailors trod in Aden, now these Soviet sailors from the Kashin-class destroyer *Steregushchy* (right) enjoy their shore-leave in the Red Sea heat.

Above left: The Soviet Union has been the paymaster and quartermaster to many guerrilla movements; their simple, rugged and well-made infantry weapons have been both popular and effective. These MPLA soldiers in Angola are armed with the RPG-7 rocket launcher.
Above: Soviet infantrymen in the desert on the Russo-Afghan border. They are armed with the 7·62mm AKM assault rifle, an excellent weapon which is used in many countries.

be prophesied is that Soviet policy, regardless of tactical pauses or even local withdrawals or wider attempts to reestablish détente, will remain entirely consistent, and its aim the simple one of strengthening the Soviet military position in every part of the globe.

Notes:
1. P. H. Vigor. His book *The Soviet View of War, Peace and Neutrality* (Routledge & Kegan Paul) London, 1975 is essential reading for anyone wishing to acquire a deeper understanding of the subject of this brief chapter.
2. Marshal V. D. Sokolovsky, author of a standard Soviet work, *Military Strategy*.
3. See *The Neutron Bomb Political, Technological and Military Issues*, S. T. Cohen, Institute for Foreign Policy Analysis Inc., Cambridge, Mass., USA Special Report, November, 1978.
4. All troop levels mentioned in this chapter are acknowledged to the International Institute for Strategic Studies' *The Military Balance 1979-1980*.

The Defence of Soviet Airspace

Throughout the 1950s and 1960s the USSR felt itself under threat from the long-range bombers of the West. As a result vast resources were poured into the development of the Air Defence Forces (PVO-Strany). This force now embraces all known modern methods of air defence, and despite the now minimal threat from manned aircraft the Soviets show no sign of reducing its size or efficiency. An interesting example of the monolithic, centralised control occurred in 1968 when a Korean airliner strayed into Soviet airspace: every single decision had to be referred to Moscow.

A dramatic salvo launch of SA-1 (Guild) surface-to-air guided missiles. This was the first SAM to be operationally deployed in the USSR, and is now being replaced.

Air Vice-Marshal S. W. B. Menaul

The Russians have been obsessed with the defence and security of their homeland since Napoleonic times – and with good reason. It is hardly surprising therefore that those who direct the affairs of the Soviet Union today are sparing no effort to provide their people with the most effective defence possible, both passive and active, against air attack by aircraft or missiles. The forces assigned to the task of defending the Soviet homeland and their Eastern European empire are known as the troops of the National Air Defence Command (*PVO Strany*). This force ranks third in order of precedence after the Strategic Rocket Forces and the Ground Forces, and became an independent arm of the Soviet armed forces in 1954, with its own commander-in-

chief responsible through the Services of the Armed Forces (Deputy Ministers of Defence) to the Ministry of Defence in Moscow.

At the end of World War II the Russians lacked a comprehensive air defence organisation. They had no effective radar early warning or tracking system and only a rudimentary fighter control organisation operating along their western front. The rapid development of United States Strategic Air Command (SAC), armed with atomic and thermo-nuclear weapons, and the British Bomber Command's nuclear V-bomber force posed a threat to the Soviet Union in the 1950s that its government could not ignore. It would have been possible even as late as 1957 to penetrate into Soviet territory with manned aircraft almost anywhere along the 1,300-mile frontier from Murmansk to Odessa and attack industrial targets deep inside the Soviet Union in the knowledge that there would be only light opposition – despite the advanced technology in air defence which fell into Soviet hands in Germany in 1945 and which should have been put to better use in the decade that followed.

In 1955 the most effective interceptor aircraft deployed by the Soviet Air Force was the MiG-15. Although produced in large numbers, the type was beginning to be replaced by the more advanced MiG-17 and MiG-19. But none of these simple aircraft were all-weather fighters, and they posed only a modest threat to SAC and Bomber Command. The interceptor fighter force was, however, being augmented by the first of the surface-to-air missile systems, the SA-1, which posed a formidable threat to all types of aircraft as the destruction of a Lockheed U-2 reconnaissance aircraft over central Russia demonstrated in 1960. Between 1956 and 1960 American U-2 reconnaissance aircraft had roamed at will over the entire Soviet Union from bases in Norway, Turkey, Germany and Japan, but on 1 May 1960 Gary Powers in a U-2 was shot down at 65,000 feet by a surface-to-air missile (SAM). By the late

1950s the entire system of air defence including aircraft, radars, surface-to-air missiles and anti-aircraft guns had developed into a cohesive organisation centrally directed from Moscow through a single command structure. The aircraft element was provided by the Soviet Air Force and administered by it, but came under the operational control of the Commander-in-Chief of the Air Defence Command. The organisation for the air defence of the Soviet homeland and Warsaw Pact countries could be said to have been completed in 1966 by the addition of the first anti-ballistic missile (ABM) defences, the Galosh system, deployed around Moscow. SALT-1 and subsequent agreements, however, have limited the deployment of ABM systems by both the 'superpowers' and imposed certain limitations on the future deployment of radars. But research and development into ABM systems continues, and improved versions of the standard Galosh missile are entering service. A new short range interceptor missile and radars are also reported to be under development.

The Warsaw Pact nations are of course included in the current *PVO Strany* organisation, and collectively they provide a formidable additional forward air defence system against manned aircraft attempting to penetrate to targets deep in the Soviet Union. But the advent of long-range, stand-off missiles launched from aircraft would largely nullify the air defence interceptor capability currently deployed. The ABM system around Moscow would give some, but by no means total, protection to the citizens of the Soviet capital against strategic nuclear missile attack, and a degree of area protection beyond the limits of the city of Moscow itself, but cruise missiles, if fully developed by the United

Below: The air defence force (PVO-Strany) possesses some 7,000 radar stations, 2,600 interceptor aircraft, 64 anti-ballistic missiles (ABMs) (all around Moscow), and an estimated 10,000 SAM launchers. The SA-2 (Guideline) seen here remains in wide-scale service.

States, will further complicate the Soviet defence problem.

The manpower strength of the national Air Defence Command is over 500,000 Soviet troops, to which must be added about 100,000 Warsaw Pact forces. Western observers might well ask if such an elaborate air defence system is necessary, since the manned aircraft threat posed by the West is less than 1,000 aircraft, of which only about 500 are categorised as strategic nuclear bombers. But the Soviets have a vast air space to protect against attack from almost any direction, and their 2,600 first-line interceptor aircraft and 11,000 surface-to-air missile launchers must be deployed over a wide area. Soviet concepts of air defence, although similar to those in the West, must take account of attacks from high and low altitude and by nearly every type of weapon in the strategic inventory and some in the tactical forces of the West as well. The missile is currently the predominant strategic nuclear threat to the Soviet Union, both from the West and in due course from China, and active defence against strategic missile attack, in view of the ABM Treaty, is little more than symbolic.

PVO Strany organisation

PVO Strany, which became independent in 1954, is one of the five major elements of the Soviet armed forces. These are, in order of precedence: the Strategic Rocket Forces, the Ground Forces, the National Air Defence Command (*PVO Strany*), the Air Forces and the Naval Forces. The Commander-in-Chief of the National Air Defence Command is Marshal of Aviation A. Koldunov. He operates directly under the Ministry of Defence in Moscow and controls his command through subsidiary headquarters, which in turn control the main elements of his command. These are:

(a) Radar Troops (*Radiotekhnicheskie Voiska*)
(b) Anti-Aircraft Artillery Troops (*Zenitnaya Artilleriya*)
(c) Anti-Aircraft Missile Troops (*Zenitno-Raketmye Voiska*)
(d) Fighter Aviation of the Air Force (*Istrebitel'naya Aviatsiya*)

As its name implies, *PVO Strany* is concerned primarily with the air defence of the Soviet homeland, but since aircraft of similar types operate to provide air defence for ground forces (*PVO Voisk*) in the Frontal Aviation forces, they work in close co-operation with the *PVO Strany* but are under the operational control of the C-in-C Ground Forces. They too could be employed in the air defence of the Soviet homeland if required, and inter-operability is a recognised procedure. There is an additional element of *PVO* not much heard of in the West. It is known as *Protivokozmicheskaya Oborona* (*PKO*) and is charged with the defence of the homeland against space weapons, nuclear or conventional, and with monitoring the activities of intelligence and reconnaissance space vehicles. With the conclusion in 1965 of the space agreement which prohibited the use of vehicles with bombs in space, the *PKO* is currently maintained at a low profile, although it has certainly not been abandoned. It all sounds complicated, but in a centralised, rigidly controlled system where every policy decision emanates from one central organisation in Moscow,

it appears to work efficiently. It is debatable if it would function smoothly in war, however.

The operational direction and control of the Air Defence Command, exercised from Moscow through the commander-in-chief, extends to 16 air defence districts, of which six are in the Warsaw Pact countries and the remainder in the Soviet Union. Early warning and interceptor control organisations within each district are linked to a central controlling authority and to Soviet air defence units. There is a similar chain of command to WP air defence units.

Radar Troops

Radar early warning and control systems cover the entire Soviet land mass and include the Warsaw Pact countries. More than 5,000 surveillance radars are currently deployed and are increasing in number and complexity as the Soviets strive to maintain effective early warning and interception systems against attack from both East and West and in the face of increased jamming capabilities by potential enemies. This is a never-ending process in the battle of measure, counter-measure and counter-counter-measure. The radar troops' task is to provide early warning of approaching enemy aircraft or missiles, identify and track them, and direct missiles or aircraft to intercept and destroy them.

Coming late into the field of advanced technology in radar, early warning, control and interception, the Soviet Union has made strenuous efforts to catch up with the West and in one respect at least has succeeded. In airborne early warning and control the Soviet Union moved ahead of the West with the deployment in 1973 of airborne early warning and control systems (AWACS) using the Tu-126 Moss aircraft. The techniques employed are similar in concept to the US system, which deploys the Boeing E-3A, but the radar and control equipments are almost certainly inferior to US equipments, particularly in overland tracking and control capability. NATO is deploying the E-3A in Europe, and the Royal Air Force is developing the Nimrod AEW for use in the UK Air Defence Region.

Early warning and acquisition of incoming enemy targets in the Warsaw Pact area are provided by Tall King radars with associated range-, azimuth- and height-finding radars feeding into a command and control centre in the area where the decision to intercept by surface-to-air missiles or interceptor aircraft is taken. In mid-1977 a new early-warning system intended to counter small, low-flying targets such as cruise

Above centre: Just visible over the crest-line is a P-50 ground-controlled interception radar (NATO code name: Bar Lock). It is used to guide interceptor aircraft, such as MiG-23.

Far left: The elderly SA-2 (Guideline) surface-to-air missile is still in large-scale service with the Soviet forces. SA-2 was used by the North Vietnamese, but was usually avoided by American aircraft so its value today is small.

Left: A captain supervising the operations of a mobile radar station. The techniques being used to track the targets manually are quite outmoded by Western standards, but these Soviet sets may have been replaced by now.

missiles was said to be under development. In the case of missiles, data are transmitted to a 'Fansong' radar at an SA-2 missile site which combines target-tracking and missile-guidance in the same unit, or Low Blow in the case of SA-3s and Long Track for SA-4s and SA-6s, both of which have Pat Hand radars for direction and launch control. Although lagging behind the United States and the West in electronic techniques, the Soviets are increasingly deploying the more modern phased array radars to replace the older manually-controlled equipments. The anti-ballistic missile system deployed around Moscow has modern radars, the three major components of which are a long-range early warning radar (Hen House) believed to be capable of locating targets at ranges of 3,000 miles, a second radar (Dog House) capable of identifying and discriminating between war-heads and decoys at ranges of 1,500 miles, the information filtered and assessed being fed to the third element, the Try Add radars, for launch control of the Galosh ABM missiles of which there are 64 launchers in a ring around Moscow.

AA Artillery Troops

Although the Soviet Union earned something of a reputation for its proficiency in all aspects of artillery before and during World War II, it did not produce efficient anti-aircraft defences either during that war or immediately after it. The threat of atomic attack by strategic bombers did, however, galvanise Soviet planners into action in the 1950s and the advent of surface-to-air missiles as defence against high-flying aircraft rapidly replaced anti-aircraft artillery in the late 1950s and early 1960s. The destruction of a United States U-2 aircraft by a Soviet surface-to-air missile in May 1960

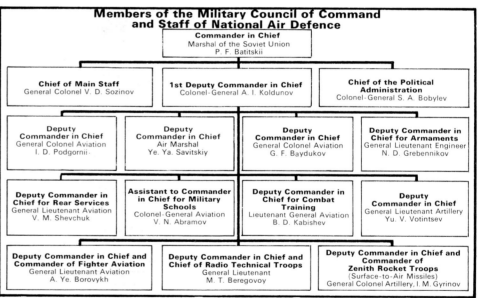

Members of the Military Council of Command and Staff of National Air Defence

Commander in Chief
Marshal of the Soviet Union
P. F. Batitskii

Chief of Main Staff	1st Deputy Commander in Chief	Chief of the Political Administration
General Colonel V. D. Sozinov	Colonel-General A. I. Koldunov	Colonel-General S. A. Bobylev

Deputy Commander in Chief	Deputy Commander in Chief	Deputy Commander in Chief	Deputy Commander in Chief for Armaments
General Colonel Aviation I. D. Podgornii	Air Marshal Ye. Ya. Savitskiy	General Colonel Aviation G. F. Baydukov	General Lieutenant Engineer N. D. Grebennikov

Deputy Commander in Chief for Rear Services	Assistant to Commander in Chief for Military Schools	Deputy Commander in Chief for Combat Training	Deputy Commander in Chief
General Lieutenant Aviation V. M. Shevchuk	Colonel-General Aviation V. N. Abramov	Lieutenant General Aviation B. D. Kabishev	General Lieutenant Artillery Yu. V. Votintsev

Deputy Commander in Chief and Commander of Fighter Aviation	Deputy Commander in Chief and Chief of Radio Technical Troops	Deputy Commander in Chief and Commander of Zenith Rocket Troops
General Lieutenant Aviation A. Ye. Borovykh	General Lieutenant M. T. Beregovoy	(Surface-to-Air Missiles) General Colonel Artillery, I. M. Gyrinov

compelled those concerned with the operation of strategic bomber forces in the West to reassess the chances of survival of high-flying aircraft penetrating the new Soviet air defence system, which was rapidly developing into a missile and interceptor aircraft organisation with a high degree of effectiveness against such high-flying aircraft.

Eventually, strategic bomber forces in the West were compelled to adopt low-level tactics, which in turn demanded changes in the air defence weapons systems of the Soviet Union. The counter to low-flying aircraft in the form of missiles and guns has now been deployed and was shown to be effective in the Yom Kippur War of 1973. In the Vietnam war, US tactics and the use of electronic counter-measures (ECM) did

much to nullify the effectiveness of SAM systems and enabled US Boeing B-52 bombers to operate with acceptable losses at high level. But such relative immunity would be unlikely over the Soviet Union or Eastern Europe, and changes in tactics from high- to low-level must be expected as the measure/counter-measure war in the ether develops.

Modern Soviet anti-aircraft guns range from 14.5 mm to 130 mm in calibre. The most effective weapons against low-flying aircraft in the Yom Kippur War were the ZSU-23-4 23-mm four-barrelled system and the ZSU-57-2 57-mm twin-barrel systems, with their accompanying radar code-named Gun Dish.

Of the larger calibre anti-aircraft gun

systems, the 130-mm gun served by Flap Wheel radar was prominent in the Vietnam war. The smaller calibre guns, mounted in pairs or fours on self-propelled vehicles, are now widely deployed not only for the air defence of the homeland, but as part of the mobile air defence capability of ground troops.

AA Missile Troops

The first surface-to-air missile (SAM) defences were deployed around Moscow in 1956 and the first missile, the SA-1, although obsolete, is still deployed today. But the mainstay of the surface-to-air system is the SA-2 Guideline widely deployed throughout the Soviet Union as part of the extensive defence system estimated at more than

Left: The air defence of the Soviet Union starts with airborne early-warning using aircraft such as this Tu-126 (NATO code name: Moss).

Below: ZU-23 twin automatic anti-aircraft cannon at range practice. The "four-in-line" is the archetypical Soviet gun deployment, followed since the days of the Tsars.

Bottom: An S-60 anti-aircraft gunner sighting an aircraft. Alone among the major powers, the USSR retains a massive number of guns and these are regarded with respect by pilots who might have to fly against them.

Below right: SA-4 (NATO code name: Ganef) surface-to-air missiles ready to fire from their mobile, tracked launchers.

11,000 missiles on 1,650 sites. It is also widely deployed in satellite countries, the Middle East, the Far East and some African countries. The SA-2 has a slant range (the distance between two points of different altitude) of 25 miles and is effective at altitudes of 2,000–80,000 feet. It has a conventional war-head of about 300 lbs of high explosive. There are six launchers surrounding a central fire-control unit. Guidance is automatic radio-command with radar target-tracking. The SA-3 Goa is a low-altitude missile with a slant range of 15 miles and is twin-mounted on a tracked chassis. It too is widely used inside and outside the Soviet Union. It complements the SA-2 and is radio-command guided with radar terminal homing. It has a conventional HE war-head. The SA-5 Gammon, the most advanced Soviet missile, is deployed in the Moscow–Leningrad complex for long range, high-altitude interception and has a possible anti-ballistic missile capability. It has a slant range approaching 100 miles, an effective ceiling of 95,000 feet and an intercept speed of Mach 5. Its guidance system is radar-homing. The SA-4 Ganef, twin-mounted on tracked carriers, and the SA-6 Gainful, triple-mounted on tracked carriers, have ramjet propulsion, and are designed to counter battlefield air threats at medium- and low-level and to protect rear areas of the military districts providing support to the forward forces in Soviet military districts and in the Warsaw Pact countries.

Between them, these two missiles also provide the major elements of SAM support to advancing troops on the battlefield and were noticeably successful against Israeli aircraft in the Yom Kippur War. But like all radio/radar-directed systems they are vulnerable to jamming, and an ECM counter based on examination of a captured system has already been developed in the United States. Although primarily for use on the battlefield, the man-portable SA-7 *Strela* shoulder-fired missile, which has passive infra-red homing for guidance, has been produced in enormous quantities and is widely used for defence against low-flying aircraft. It has a maximum range of about two miles and can engage targets between 150 and 4,000 feet. SA-8 and SA-9 are mobile self-contained air defence systems covering altitudes of 150–30,000 feet. SA-10, which covers 1,000–15,000 feet, has active terminal radar guidance and a speed of Mach 6, is now being deployed.

Under the terms of the ABM Treaty of 1972, modified in 1973, the two superpowers are permitted to deploy only one ABM system each. The system is limited to 100 launchers and 100 missiles, which may be deployed either around the national capital or around an inter-continental ballistic missile (ICBM) complex. The Soviet ABM system was already deployed around Moscow when the ABM Treaty was agreed and it remains the only system so far deployed by the Soviet Union. A further 36 launchers

and Try Add engagement radars are in process of construction to bring the Galosh system up to the maximum of 100 launchers and missiles with associated radars permitted under the ABM Treaty. The SA-5 Gammon may have an ABM capability, and research and development into new ABM systems continues. At least one new missile has been tested in recent months. The SH-4 improved Galosh is now entering service, and there are reports of a hypersonic SAM intended to intercept US SRAM missiles.

Fighter Aviation

The defences against manned aircraft in the Soviet Union have made enormous progress in recent years from the original Tallinn line system deployed along the western boundary of the Soviet Union in the late 1950s and early 1960s. Today the air defence system has been improved in quality and quantity of the radars and interceptors deployed along the entire western border from Murmansk in the north to the Turkish frontier, and in depth, with particular emphasis on the Leningrad/Moscow area and Baku. More than 2,600 interceptor fighters are deployed in the *IA-PVO*, many of which have all-

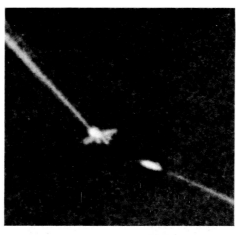

Above: A Soviet surface-to-air missile heading for an interception of an unmanned drone target. Most Soviet SAMs have high-explosive warheads with both proximity and impact fuzes but some may also have command fuzes.

Below: The famous ZSU-23-4 mounts four 23mm cannon and a simple radar on a tracked chassis and proved itself to be extremely effective in Arab hands during the 1973 Yom Kippur War.

Above left: An SA-6 (Gainful) SAM
battery at readiness to fire. This system
comprises two vehicles: the missile
launcher and a similar tracked chassis
carrying a large acquisition and tracking
radar.

Above: SA-9 (Gaskin) is a vehicle-mounted
version of the SA-7 (Grail) missile and is
used for close air defence at division level.

weather capability. The most important type is the Sukhoi Su-15 Flagon, which is steadily replacing earlier interceptors such as MiG-21 Fishbeds, Su-9/11 Fishpots, and transonic Yak-28P Firebars. A specialised long-range interception task is carried out by the big Tu-28P Fiddler. MiG-25 Foxbat A interceptors are being joined in service by the much improved MiG-25M Foxbat E. Fighter Aviation is currently commanded by General-Lieutenant A. Borovykh who is responsible to the C-in-C of the *PVO*, Marshal Koldunov.

To this force must be added aircraft of the Warsaw Pact countries, particularly those of the Polish, Czech and East German air forces, which together have over 1,000 interceptors, mostly MiG-21s. Nearly all are armed with air-to-air missiles (Alkali, Anab, Ash, Atoll and Acrid, either radar or infra-red homing, or a combination of both. The aircraft are also fitted with guns of various calibres and rockets.

The weapons

The MiG-21 Fishbed, of which there are something like 20 different versions, is the most widely deployed fighter interceptor in the world. In keeping with Soviet aviation practice, each succeeding version of an aircraft already deployed operationally has some improvement incorporated to enhance its performance: sometimes increased engine power, modifications to the airframe or the introduction of new weapons systems or avionics. The MiG-21F Fishbed-C is a straightforward, clear-weather, single-seat fighter armed with one 30-mm NR-30

cannon and two Atoll air-to-air missiles (AAMs) or rocket packs for ground attack. It is still in service.

The MiG-21PF Fishbed-D was the first of a new series with search/track radar to improve all-weather capability. It has an uprated engine and rocket-assisted take-off. A further development, the MiG-21PFM Fishbed-F, was soon superseded by the MiG-21PFMA Fishbed-J which is a multi-role aircraft with four underwing pylons and a GSh-23 twin-barrel cannon of 23-mm calibre. It also carries four radar-homing Atoll air-to-air missiles. Other versions are the Fishbed-K and L which have modifications to the airframe of the basic MF type. Performance characteristics are similar and a typical war load for all versions would be one twin-barrel 23-mm GSh gun with 200 rounds of ammunition and, on the underwing pylons, two K-13A Atoll (infra-red homing) and two Advanced Atoll (radar-homing) air-to-air missiles or two pods of 16 57-mm rockets or two drop-tanks. Alternative loads would be rockets or bombs on the pylons instead of air-to-air missiles.

The MiG-25 Foxbat was flown in 1964 and was initially intended as a defence against the North American B-70 Mach 3 bomber. Although the B-70 was cancelled the MiG-25 entered fairly small scale service in 1971. It is fitted with two Tumansky R-266 turbojets of 27,000 lb thrust with reheat, and has a maximum speed 'clean' of at least Mach 3 at 75,000 feet. The MiG-25 serves with the PVO-Strany as an interceptor, and with Frontal Aviation as a reconnaissance aircraft. Now entering service is a much improved interceptor version, the MiG-25M Foxbat E. Unlike earlier versions it may have a look-down, shoot-down capability against low-flying targets. It is likely to operate in close co-operation with the airborne early warning and control (AWACS) Moss aircraft against low-flying enemy aircraft. The reconnaissance version, fitted with cameras, radar and infra-red equipment, is already operational and

operated over the Mediterranean during and after the Yom Kippur War.

The Sukhoi family of interceptors makes a substantial contribution to the *PVO Strany*'s interceptor force of nearly 3,500 aircraft. The Su-9 Fishpot is the longest serving variant, having entered operational service in 1959. It is a single-engined, single-seat fighter carrying four 'Alkali' air-to-air missiles under the wings but usually no cannon. The Su-11 Fishpot-C is an improved version of the Su-9 with a more powerful engine, the Lyulka AL-7F turbojet of 22,000 lbs thrust with afterburner. It has a maximum speed of Mach 1.8 at 36,000 feet and carries two 'Anab' air-to-air missiles, one radar-homing and one infrared. These earlier types are likely to be replaced by the Sukhoi Su-15 Flagon, which is of similar tailed-delta layout but is larger, with two engines and a much bigger radar. The initial Flagon A, which entered service in 1968, was very much a low-risk system, combining the AL-7F turbojet fitted to the Su-11 with the radar and AA-3-2 Advanced Anab missiles of the Yak-28P. The Flagon E, in production since 1973, is more powerful and heavier, with uprated engines, AA-6 Acrid missiles and an internal GSh-23 cannon.

The Tupolev Tu-28P Fiddler is a long-range interceptor deployed mainly in the north of the Soviet Union and is armed with four air-to-air 'Ash' missiles. It is a twin-jet, two-seater aircraft with a maximum speed of Mach 1.75. About 200 are in service.

The Yakovlev Yak-28P Firebar is a two-seater transonic all-weather twin-jet interceptor with a maximum speed of Mach 1.1 at 35,000 feet and a service ceiling of 55,000 feet. It is armed with two air-to-air 'Anab' missiles on pylons under the outer wings.

Up to 1970 Soviet air defence with manned aircraft, guns and surface-to-air missiles and associated radars followed patterns already well established in the West, particularly in the United States. Research and development to improve the performance of ground-based radars in range and discrimination was a continuous process in most advanced industrialised countries, and one of the major problems facing technologists was to find effective means of acquiring and tracking aircraft at low level over land and sea. The answer appeared to lie in deploying airborne radar for search and tracking and for the direction of controlled interception, either by manned fighters or missiles.

The Tu-126 Moss was the first Soviet system to be deployed operationally and is still the only Soviet airborne warning and control system. About 12 aircraft are currently operational and have been in service since 1970. The object of any AWACS aircraft is to provide detection and tracking of approaching enemy aircraft at any altitude over land or sea, but particularly at low level where detection, acquisition and tracking by ground-based radars is difficult, and often impossible, because of interference by radar returns from ground objects (clutter). Having detected enemy aircraft the AWACS must have a communications system with which to alert, control and direct fighters or missiles to intercept the enemy either from land bases or from on board ship. Detection and subsequent tracking is achieved by means of a large, rotating scanner operating a surveillance radar, information from which is fed to radar receivers, electronic processing equipment and display consoles in the fuselage of the aircraft, which also houses computers and a data-link system to transmit information to intercept systems which can use the information either for direct interception or as further directed by the AWACS aircraft. Not enough is known of the individual equipments in the 'Moss' system to establish how efficient they are, but it is known that these aircraft were deployed operationally in the Indo-Pakistan War of 1971, apparently with considerable success.

The Tu-126 Moss aircraft carries a crew of 12. It is powered by four NK-12MV turboprop engines and has a range of 7,700 miles at a cruise speed of 380–485 mph. The endurance at cruising speed for a 1,250-mile radius is six hours, which with flight refuelling can be extended to 17 hours.

Above: The MiG-21 (NATO code name: Fishbed) has served the Soviet air force well. This is the main version in service with IA-PVO, being examined here by Swedish officers during a Soviet goodwill visit to that country.

Above right: Ground engineers of the IA-PVO at work on MiG-23 (Flogger) aircraft. The large radome houses "High Lark" radar.

Right: The MiG-25 (Foxbat) interceptor can carry four AA-6 missiles which, at 20ft. in length, are still the largest AAMs in service. Although 20 years old, the MiG-25 is treated with great respect in the West.

Below right: A Tupolev Tu-28P (Fiddler) interceptor carrying two AA-5 (Ash) air-to-air missiles on the inner pylons. Four AAMs can be mounted: two radar guided and two with infrared warheads.

AWACS aircraft can be deployed in air defence systems such as the *PVO Strany* or in the battlefield area in the role of surveillance, control of friendly aircraft and the direction of interceptors or missiles, or they can equally well be deployed in maritime operations in similar roles. They are highly mobile and flexible systems, but like any other aircraft the Tu-126 is vulnerable to interception by aircraft, missiles or AA guns, which to some extent limits its deployment even where ECM and other forms of protection are provided. But the risk of destruction is not as high as might be supposed, and the value of the AWACS will almost certainly outweigh the risks of destruction in time of war. The airborne radar itself can, of course, be jammed, but measures to overcome this deficiency can also be taken, even to the extent of locating and destroying the offending jammer.

The Soviet air defence of the homeland, the *PVO Strany*, now embraces all known modern methods of air defence and follows doctrines similar to those adopted in the West, although the strategy for implementing these doctrines often differs. Despite the limited threat from manned aircraft the

Soviets show no sign of down-grading the size or efficiency of their air defence system. Among the advantages which could be claimed for the *PVO Strany* over Western systems are total standardisation of doctrine, organisation and equipment, common logistic supply, and inter-operability between units deployed in widely differing areas. All these come under one central controlling authority, and yet by its very nature such a monolithic system could, and sometimes does, create problems of inflexibility in deployment and decision-making. In war, major decisions would be made by the central staffs, with little initiative permitted to the commanders on the spot.

In air warfare conditions change more rapidly than in any other environment, and rigidity in command and control could produce fatal weaknesses in defence, however good the weapons and equipment might be. But it must be said that despite advances which Soviet technology has made in the last decade, their weapons systems (including aircraft, avionics and missiles) are still inferior to those available to the West. As described in another section, the Soviets have had ample opportunity to test their equipment under operational conditions in Vietnam and in the 1973 Middle East war. They found many deficiencies in their aircraft and weapons, and have no doubt renewed their efforts in research and development to improve the quality of their equipment.

It is vital that the West should maintain research and development in the field of aeronautics, avionics and weapons systems at a high level, to ensure that the present lead which they undoubtedly enjoy is not surrendered to the Soviet Union. The air-launched ballistic missile, the supersonic bomber with stand-off missiles, new guidance systems to reduce inaccuracies in delivery, penetration aids and total all-weather capability must be the goal in future developments of air power as part of the strategic threat of retaliation against the Soviet Union implicit in the West's strategy of deterrence, defence and *détente* in that order.

The Modern Soviet Air Force

The Soviet Union has poured vast amounts of capital and resources into the development of a thoroughly modern air force, to be the equal of anything in the West. The result has been some redoubtable aircraft, with the lack of quality in some areas being more than compensated for by sheer quantity. Aircraft like the MiG-27, Backfire and the Hind-D helicopter are, however, world leaders in performance and role-suitability and are making Western designers look to their laurels. A particular area of weakness is that of avionics, in which the Soviet Union is way behind the West.

Mikoyan MiG-25 (Foxbat) at low altitude. When it first appeared in the mid-1960s this remarkable aircraft outclassed anything in the NATO inventory and the United States developed the F-15 Eagle specifically to counter it.

Air Vice-Marshal S. W. B. Menaul

The Russians are rightly included among the pioneers of aviation, but their claim to have preceded the Wright brothers in the achievement of powered flight is treated with a certain amount of scepticism by most Western nations. Even if it is conceded that Alexander Mozhaisky may have designed and built an aircraft powered by a steam engine in 1884, the claim that he also flew it taxes the imagination too far. There were, however, many pioneer aircraft designers in Russia at the turn of the century, and the name of Igor Sikorsky is too well known in aviation history to question the authenticity of Soviet claims that he was designing and building aircraft of various types as early as 1908.

During World War I the Russo–Baltic

Wagon Works produced at least 80 great four-engined bombers of the Ilya Mourometz type, based on the *Russian Knight,* and these equipped the world's first strategic bomber force, the EVK or Squadron of Flying Ships. Many hundreds of other Russian aircraft, built by many factories led by the Anatra, Shchetinin, Lebed' and Mosca groups, played a significant part in the mighty campaigns on the Eastern Front in 1914–17. As today, tsarist airpower was deployed by the Imperial Navy as well as by the army air force.

But in 1917 the Revolution interrupted Soviet developments in aeronautical engineering as indeed it interrupted and retarded progress in many other fields of engineering activity. In the aftermath of the Revolution many Russian aviation engineers were to disappear for ever, while others escaped to Europe or America. Sikorsky settled in the United States, where today his name is synonymous with the design and production of helicopters. From 1917, for a period of about 10 years, Soviet aviation was virtually at a standstill while the industrialised nations of Europe and the United States were advancing the science of aeronautics for civil and military application. There was neither the will on the part of the new rulers of the Soviet Union nor the brain power and engineering skills on the part of the designers to develop aviation on a par with the West; and to some extent the gap is still evident even today, though great progress has been made by the Soviets in the last 20 years.

One name which has become a household word, not only in the Soviet Union but in aviation circles throughout the world, is that of Andrei Tupolev, who as a young man trained as an engineer and then decided to make a career in aviation, which he believed held the key to the future development of the vast land mass of the Soviet Union. He was a founder, together with Professor Zhukovski, of the Central Aero-Dynamics and Hydro-Dynamics Research Institute (*TsAGI*) in Moscow in 1918. In 1922 Tupolev designed his ANT-1, pictured on page 12. But such was the scarcity of aeronautical engineering talent in the early 1920s that the Soviet Union not only imported foreign aircraft and engines, but foreign engineers and mechanics, especially from France and Germany. Nevertheless, throughout the 1920s Soviet engineers produced a variety of aircraft, most of which relied on engines of foreign origin either directly imported or made under licence – chiefly British, French and German.

Among the more enlightened and progressive of the new generation of Soviet designers was Sergei Ilyushin, who as a youth had served as a mechanic in the Russian air force in World War I. After graduating from the Air Academy he went to the *TsAGI*, where he was much influenced by Tupolev. His first design was unambitious – a glider – but in subsequent designs he established a reputation for thoroughness and simplicity which exists to this day. He was one of a number of dedicated individualists involved in the new science of aeronautics whose enthusiasm was not shared by officialdom, so that at the end of the communists' much vaunted first 5-year plan, introduced in 1928, Soviet aviation had made only modest progress. Most of the

home-produced aircraft were light, single-engined types used mainly for communications purposes and as fighters.

Tupolev's contribution during this period was the ANT-6, a four-engined aircraft suitable for use as a bomber or transport, but unfortunately Soviet engine designers could not produce sufficiently powerful and reliable engines to meet the specifications of Tupolev's design. The ANT-6 entered service as a bomber in 1932 and subsequently as a transport aircraft for use with the rapidly expanding Soviet parachute force, for which the Russians were to become famous just before World War II.

The second 5-year plan coincided with Hitler's rise to power in Germany in the early 1930s, and since the Soviet Union had depended to a large extent on German technology and manpower in the development of her aviation industry, she now had to seek assistance elsewhere. By 1939, with help from the United States, the Soviet Union was producing about 4,500 aircraft a year, of which something less than 2,000 were fighters, about 1,000 bombers (of which about 200 were four-engined) and the rest transport and training types of various designs. The quality of Soviet aviation products, however, did not compare favourably with those being manufactured in Britain, the United States or Germany, and Soviet doctrine for the employment of air power in the event of war was different from that currently being advocated in the West.

While air strategists in the West, led by Douhet, Mitchell and Trenchard, were advocating independent air operations based on the concept of strategic bombing, the Soviets decided on a policy of subordinating air power to the role of army support, and to a lesser extent support of naval operations. They drew lessons from the Spanish Civil War which were not accepted by the USA, Britain, France or Germany. The four-engined bombers designed by Tupolev were not, therefore, destined to provide a strategic bomber force comparable with the US 8th Air Force or RAF Bomber Command. Had they done so, the course of World War II so far as the Russo–German front was concerned might have taken a different turn. Soviet emphasis in World War II was almost entirely on interception and tactical air support for the armies. The best Russian aircraft at the beginning of World War II were the Lavochkin LaGG-1 and 3 single-engined monoplane fighters and the Petlyakov Pe-2 light bomber, both of which were produced in large numbers.

Among the outstanding designers of World War II who has since achieved a lasting reputation was Artem Mikoyan who, with Mikhail Gurevich, was to produce a long and distinguished line of MiG fighters. The first design, the MiG-1, produced in 1940, was a single-engined fighter whose performance on test was disappointing. It was quickly superseded by a modified version, the MiG-3, which had a more powerful engine. This was followed by the MiG-5, a radial-engined progressive development of the MiG-3. The type saw limited service in 1943, but further work on the variant was halted in favour of the generally superior Lavochkin La-5 mentioned later.

Before World War II few Soviet aircraft

had the performance of contemporary US, British or German aircraft, except for the outstanding Polikarpov I-16 fighter. But the traumatic experiences in the early days of the German assault on the Soviet Union in 1941 acted as a stimulus to the design and production of higher-performance aircraft and encouraged new designers. During the 1930s the name of Aleksandir Yakovlev began to be heard with increasing frequency among Soviet designers. He served his apprenticeship under Tupolev, designed a long and successful series of Yak single-engined fighters, and eventually became a chief designer in the Soviet Union.

By 1941 Soviet factories were producing approximately 1,000 aircraft a month, an increasing percentage of them Ilyushin Il-2 *Shturmovik* ground-attack machines. This was an excellent type, and was destined to play a very considerable part in Russia's final defeat of Nazi Germany. Other designs in major production were the LaGG, MiG and Yak single-engined fighters, and the Petlyakov Pe-2, Tupolev SB-2 and Ilyushin Il-4 twin-engined bombers. As the German invasion of the Soviet Union in 1941 gathered momentum it became apparent that the Soviet Air Force was no match for the German *Luftwaffe*. More than 5,000 Soviet aircraft were destroyed in the first few months of the war. The only Soviet aircraft that appeared to contribute anything to the support of the ground forces in those desperate days was the Il-2, which was specially suited to attacks against tanks. Of wood and metal construction with considerable armour plating, it survived heavy ground-to-air defences, but was vulnerable to air attack from the rear. A two-seat version was therefore introduced with a rear gunner operating a 12.7-mm machine-gun.

The almost total rout of the Soviet armies and the rapid advance of the German land forces compelled the Soviet authorities to move their aircraft factories eastwards to the Urals and beyond for safety, an operation conducted under great difficulty and one which was bound to interrupt the pro-

Below: Among the many features of the MiG-21 'bis' (Fishbed-N) are an enlarged dorsal spine fairing and a fat pitot boom carrying air-data transducers. Many thousands of MiG-21s are in service with some thirty air forces.

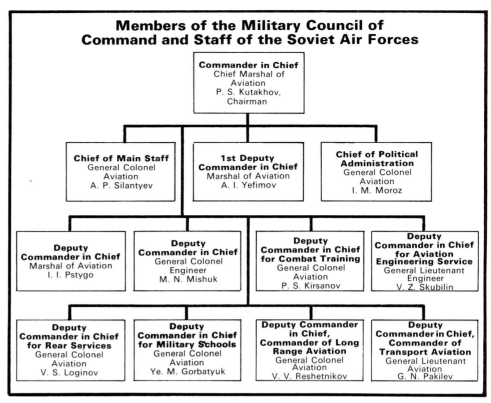

Members of the Military Council of Command and Staff of the Soviet Air Forces

Commander in Chief
Chief Marshal of Aviation
P. S. Kutakhov, Chairman

Chief of Main Staff
General Colonel Aviation
A. P. Silantyev

1st Deputy Commander in Chief
Marshal of Aviation
A. I. Yefimov

Chief of Political Administration
General Colonel Aviation
I. M. Moroz

Deputy Commander in Chief
Marshal of Aviation
I. I. Pstygo

Deputy Commander in Chief
General Colonel Engineer
M. N. Mishuk

Deputy Commander in Chief for Combat Training
General Colonel Aviation
P. S. Kirsanov

Deputy Commander in Chief for Aviation Engineering Service
General Lieutenant Engineer
V. Z. Skubilin

Deputy Commander in Chief for Rear Services
General Colonel Aviation
V. S. Loginov

Deputy Commander in Chief for Military Schools
General Colonel Aviation
Ye. M. Gorbatyuk

Deputy Commander in Chief, Commander of Long Range Aviation
General Colonel Aviation
V. V. Reshetnikov

Deputy Commander in Chief, Commander of Transport Aviation
General Lieutenant Aviation
G. N. Pakilev

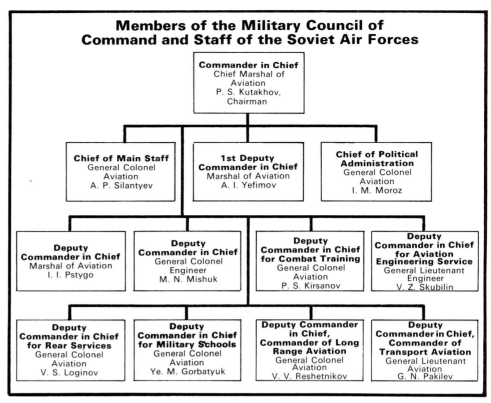

Command and Staff of Naval Aviation

Commander
General Colonel Aviation
A. A. Mironenko

Chief of Staff
General Colonel Aviation
G. A. Kuznetsov

Deputy Commander
General Colonel Aviation
A. N. Tomashevskiy

Chief of Political Department
General Major Aviation
P. V. Mordashenkov

Senior Aviation Engineer
General Lieutenant Engineer
M. M. Kruglov

Commander Naval Aviation Northern Fleet
(not identified)

Commander Naval Aviation Baltic Fleet
General Colonel Aviation
S. A. Gulyayev

Commander Naval Aviation Black Sea Fleet
General Lieutenant Aviation
V. I. Voronov

Commander Naval Aviation Pacific Fleet
General Lieutenant Aviation
A. I. Pavlovskiy

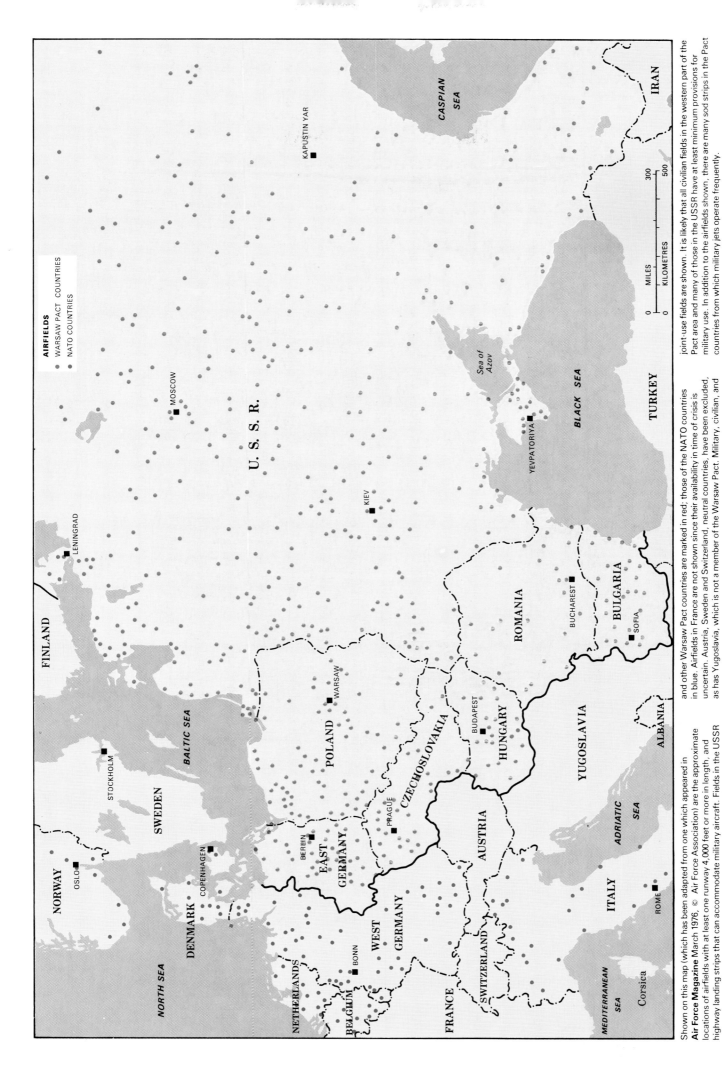

Shown on this map (which has been adapted from one which appeared in **Air Force Magazine** March 1976, © Air Force Association) are the approximate locations of airfields with at least one runway 4,000 feet or more in length, and highway landing strips that can accommodate military aircraft. Fields in the USSR

and other Warsaw Pact countries are marked in red; those of the NATO countries in blue. Airfields in France are not shown since their availability in time of crisis is uncertain. Austria, Sweden and Switzerland, neutral countries, have been excluded, as has Yugoslavia, which is not a member of the Warsaw Pact. Military, civilian, and

joint-use fields are shown. It is likely that all civilian fields in the western part of the Pact area and many of those in the USSR have at least minimum provisions for military use. In addition to the airfields shown, there are many sod strips in the Pact countries from which military jets operate frequently.

AIRFIELDS

■ WARSAW PACT COUNTRIES

● NATO COUNTRIES

duction of aircraft urgently needed for air defence and support of the ground forces. The first production aircraft from the new factories was the Lavochkin La-5, whose sturdy wooden construction was well suited to the available materials and skills. Its performance kept up with German progress, and right to the end of the war Lavochkin fighters were able to take on German fighters at the low to medium altitudes favoured by the Russians with every chance of success.

By the time the tide turned in the Russians' favour in 1943, with considerable help from the United States and Britain, the Russians were producing about 3,000 aircraft a month, the majority of them designed for interception and close army support. But in 1942 it had been decided to establish a long-range force, whose main role was to be supply dropping to partisans behind the enemy lines. The force was equipped with Petlyakov Pe-8 four engined aircraft, which had been designed for long-range bombing missions, though few were used in this role.

When eventually the Russians entered Berlin, their armies were supported by over 20,000 aircraft and production was running at over 40,000 machines a year. They did not, however, possess an effective long-range bomber force except for the Pe-8s and a few North American B-25 Mitchells which were given to the Soviet Air Force in late 1943. They had no jet interceptor aircraft and no radar early warning or controlled interception system. It was not until after the German surrender that the Russian political and military leaders, including Stalin, were able to witness at first hand the effects of the British and US strategic bomber offensive, which impressed them deeply and from which they learned the right lessons, even if they were slow to act on them.

The destruction of Hiroshima and Nagasaki by strategic air power and the atomic bomb also contributed to the Soviet decision to revise its concepts for the use of air power in war. A great mass of German high-technology equipment and documents captured by the Russian armies was transported back to the Soviet Union, together with a considerable number of scientists, engineers and technicians, enabling the Russians from 1945 onwards to develop modern concepts of air power. This included the development of an elaborate air defence system and strategic bomber forces, which in the early 1950s were to be the only means of delivery of their atomic and thermo-nuclear weapons, the first of which was tested in 1949, much to the surprise of the West. But one aspect of air power which the Soviets had neglected in World War II was strategic bombing. Although they had a large bomber force at the beginning of the war, they had very few four-engined bomber aircraft and no modern blind bombing equipment equivalent to the British H2S or United States H2X radar aids to navigation and bombing. So the Soviets had to embark on the creation of a bomber force entirely from their own resources. They were fortunate in acquiring three American Boeing B-29s that had force-landed in Soviet territory late in World War II. These they copied under the direction of Tupolev and produced in quantity as the Tu-4, NATO code-named Bull. By

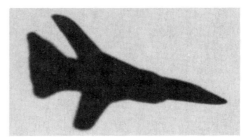

1954 more than 1,400 of them had been produced as the forerunners of the Myasishchev Mya-4 Bison, Tupolev Tu-16 Badger and Tupolev Tu-95 Bear strategic turbojet and turboprop bomber and reconnaissance aircraft that form the principal elements of the long-range air force today.

Although captured German engines included the German Junkers Jumo 004 and BMW 003 turbojets, the real boost to Soviet jet engine design came with the transfer of British Rolls-Royce Nene and Derwent centrifugal flow turbojet engines provided by a benevolent British Labour Government in 1946. The Soviet version of the Nene engine, the RD-45, produced 5,000 lb thrust which, when installed in the MiG-15, enabled this aircraft to achieve speeds of 660 miles per hour. Eventually more than 15,000 MiG-15s were produced and found their way into many air forces throughout the world, being particularly conspicuous in the Chinese and North Korean air forces during the Korean War.

The Soviet Air Force
(*Voenno-Vozdushnye Sily, V-VS*)
The modern Soviet Air Force is one of five major elements of the Soviet armed forces and ranks fourth in the Soviet order of precedence. It is commanded by Marshal of Aviation P. S. Kutakhov, and has over 400,000 men and 12,000 combat aircraft. The Soviet Air Force consists of three major commands and a further two which, although part of the Soviet Air Force for administrative, research and supply purposes, do not come under the operational command and control of the air force commander-in-chief. The three primary arms are Frontal Aviation (*Frontovaya Aviatsiya*),

Top: The first available photograph of the long-range interdiction (attack) aircraft formerly designated Su-19 Fencer.

Above: In early 1980 these photographs became available, by which time it was known that the correct designation is Su-24. They show the aircraft has a broad flattish nose like that of the MiG-27.

Long-Range Aviation (*Dal'naya Aviatsiya*) and Air Transport (*Voenno-Transportnaya Aviatsiya*). The two other elements are Fighter Aviation/Air Defence Command (*Istrebitel'naya Aviatsiya*) which forms part of the National Air Defence Command (*Protivo-Vozdushnaya Oborona Strany* or *PVO Strany*) and Naval Aviation (*Aviatsiya Voenno-Morskogo Flota*) which provides air support for Soviet naval operations. The Commander-in-Chief of the Soviet Air Force exercises administrative control over the first three elements, all of which have a certain amount of operational independence in peacetime, but operational control of the Air Defence Fighter Command units (*IA-PVO*) is vested in the Commander-in-Chief, Air Defence Command, while Naval Aviation is under the operational command and control of the Commander-in-Chief, Naval Forces. Both these forces use common facilities with the Soviet Air Force e.g. airfields.

Frontal Aviation
With a strength of more than 5,000 aircraft, of which 4,000 are deployed in support of Warsaw Pact forces opposing NATO in the European theatre, Frontal Aviation, the Russian version of the West's tactical air forces, is by far the largest element of the Soviet Air Forces. The primary role of this

command is the air support of the Ground Forces, for which it is equipped with fighters to provide counter air operations (to gain and maintain local air superiority); ground-attack aircraft for close air support of ground troops; strike aircraft for inter-diction missions; photographic- and radar-reconnaissance aircraft; tactical transports and helicopters to provide air mobility for the Ground Forces; armed helicopters for employment in the anti-tank role; and elec-tronic counter-measures (ECM) aircraft for operations in the battle zone. The size of the Frontal Aviation forces, together with their equipment and the command struc-ture under which they operate, are indicative of the importance which the Soviet High Command attaches to close co-operation between air and ground forces in the land battle, and emphasises the Soviet doctrinal principle of 'all arms co-ordination' as the key to success in modern warfare.

Frontal Aviation is organised in 16 Tactical Air Armies, more than half of which are deployed in the western USSR and Warsaw Pact countries. Each military district in the European Soviet Union has its own Frontal Aviation Army. In addition, there are four 'groups of forces' in the Warsaw Pact area, pride of place being awarded to the 16th Frontal Aviation Army supporting the elite Group of Soviet Forces in (East) Germany (GSFG). Each military district has its own commander and under him the air and land forces of that district form 'groups of forces', the most important being the European groups designated Northern, Central, Southern and GSFG. Overall command and control is exercised by the General Staff, and in war *STAVKA* (the Supreme High Command) would

Above: A Mikoyan-Gurevich MiG-23S (Flogger-B) being readied for a flight. Note the large, circular-section radome and the perforated splitter-plate in the engine air-intake.

Top right: A Sukhoi Su-17 (Fitter-C), the swing-wing attack and close-support aircraft which was developed from the much less effective Su-7. Maximum speed at optimum operating height is 1,432mph.

Above right: Mikoyan-Gurevich MiG-27 (Flogger-D), the tactical attack development of the MiG-23. The variable-geometry wings can be swept from a minimum of 16° to a maximum of 72°.

Right: The large vertical tail surfaces of the MiG-25 are required for directional control at high speed; NATO radars have tracked MiG-25s at Mach 2.8.

control the battle or the redeployment of forces through the commander-in-chief according to the requirements of a par-ticular front at any given time. Air armies or elements of them could be redeployed from one group to another as required.

An Air Army is subdivided into divisions, assigned to a specific role; each division comprises three regiments, each operating a single type of aircraft, and three squadrons of 12 aircraft make up each regiment. Air Armies vary in size from the 750 aircraft of the mighty 16th in East Germany to the 200 of rear-area Air Armies. From the MiG-15s and 17s of the Korean War (some of which are still in service) the modern air army has been expanded and re-equipped with MiG-21 Fishbed, Sukhoi Su-7 Fitter, Yakovlev Yak-28 Brewer, and more recently with the MiG-23/27 Flogger, Su-24 (former-

ly Su-19) Fencer and Su-17 Fitter-C. There are also a few Ilyushin Il-28 Beagle and some Yak-28 and Antonov An-12 Cub electronic warfare aircraft. The MiG-17 Fresco, of which there are about 700, is employed mainly in close air support mis-sions but has been almost entirely re-placed by the MiG-23 Flogger. But the reluctance of the Soviet Union to withdraw weapons systems from operational service is seen in the extremely long life of the MiG-17 in the same way as tanks, armoured personnel carriers (APCs) and guns are re-tained long after they have ceased to be capable of fulfilling their primary role. Soviet emphasis on numbers obviously in-fluences this attitude to obsolete equipment, and the high attrition rates in the Yom Kippur War of October 1973 tend to con-firm the Soviet view that however unso-

phisticated aircraft may be, there comes a time when numbers matter.

The MiG-21 variants (J, K and L) are employed in the interceptor air superiority role in combat zones, with counter air and battlefield interdiction as secondary roles. Although the later MiG-21 variants are multi-role fighter-bombers, they are hampered by their short range and small payload. They normally carry a twin 23-mm cannon pack and four air-to-air Atoll infra-red or radar missiles. They can also carry four 240-mm rockets or two 1,102-lb bombs.

The Su-24 Fencer is one of three new, advanced aircraft lately introduced into Frontal Aviation squadrons of the Soviet Air Force. It is a variable-geometry, two-seater aircraft designed specifically as a fighter-bomber and bears a striking resemblance to the US General Dynamics F-111, but is smaller and lighter. Its warload is 10,000 lb and includes nuclear weapons and air-to-surface missiles. Performance characteristics include interdiction on targets anywhere in Europe in a variety of modes, e.g., hi-lo-hi or lo-lo-lo. Radius of action and weapons load depend on operational tactics adopted but aircraft have supersonic dash at low level and maximum speed is Mach 2.3 at 36,000 feet.

The Su-17 Fitter-C is a variable-geometry version of the well established ground-attack aircraft, the Su-7 Fitter, the major design improvements being a large portion of each wing (about 13 feet) pivoted to improve take-off and landing and range performance over the Su-7. The Su-17 has the more powerful Lyulka AL-21F engine and has a greater warload than the Su-7. It has additional under-fuselage pylons for bombs, rockets and fuel tanks. It retains the wing-root NR-30 cannon and the weapon-aiming systems of the later Su-7BMK. Maximum speed is about Mach 1.6 at 36,000 feet. Export models are designated Su-20.

The Su-7 ground-attack aircraft has been in operational service for nearly two decades and has seen active operations in the Middle East wars and in the 1971 Indo/Pakistan war. It is a single-engined, single-seat aircraft with a maximum speed of Mach 1.6 at high level. It carries two 30-mm cannon in the wing roots and has underwing attachments for bombs or rockets up to a total weight of about 5,500 lb. Its primary role is close air support.

The most important new type, however, is the Mikoyan MiG-23/27 Flogger family of closely related variable-sweep combat aircraft, armed with a variety of completely new guided weapons. Fully comparable with its Western contemporaries, the Flogger has been introduced rapidly into service with Soviet Frontal Aviation units and has been exported in large numbers, although in mid-1977 none of the Soviet Union's Warsaw Pact neighbours had been issued with the type. The philosophy of basing two very different combat types on a single basic wing, centre section and tail unit has facilitated speedy production, estimated at nearly 300 aircraft a year.

Flogger variants are deployed in the air-superiority and strike roles. The first to be put into service, reaching East Germany in Mid-1971, was the MiG-23S Flogger B fighter with a laser gunsight, an internal GSh-23 cannon and a quartet of new air-to-air missiles – the medium-range AA-7 Apex and the AA-8 Aphid dogfighter missile. It is fitted with a new-type intercept radar known as High Lark to NATO. In 1975 the MiG-23S was followed into service by the Flogger D, so different from the fighter that the Soviet Air Forces redesignated it MiG-27. Optimised for the strike role, the MiG-27 is slower than the Mach 2.2 Flogger B but has a longer range, with provision for drop tanks under the outer wings. It carries advanced AS-7 and AS-10 air-to-surface missiles with laser and TV guidance.

The Yak-28 is used in the reconnaissance role, and the Brewer E has recently been identified in the ECM role. There is also evidence that additional reconnaissance is provided to units in the Warsaw Pact countries and particularly to the 16th Frontal Aviation Army stationed in the German Democratic Republic, by the Mach 3 high-flying MiG-25 Foxbat operating from airfields in Poland. A new capability was added to Frontal Aviation in 1973 with the arrival of the first Mil Mi-24 Hind gunship helicopters. Progressive development has now produced the Hind D, a very capable all-weather and night attack

Top: One of the most famous flights by a MiG-25 was that by a disaffected Soviet pilot who avoided Japanese air defences and landed at Hakodate on 6 September 1976. The aircraft was handed back after detailed examination.

Above: A Sukhoi Su-15 (Flagon) climbing on an interception mission. The two large missiles are AA-3s (Anab) with infra-red homing heads.

Right: A Tupolev Tu-20 (Bear-D) on a recconaissance flight over the Atlantic. This large turboprop machine has been in service for 24 years and is used for surveillance, direction of anti-ship missiles, and launching missiles.

helicopter armed with a multi-barrel machine gun, anti-tank missiles and unguided rockets, with a cabin for 8–10 fully armed troops or reloads for the missile rails. Tu-26 Backfire bombers (referred to by the Soviets as Tu22M) have been excluded from the SALT II treaty and are classed as medium bombers, not strategic. They will now be deployed in attacks on European targets rather than against strategic targets in the United States.

Long-Range Aviation

The Long-Range Aviation force consists of three air components, two deployed in European Russia and one in the East. It is commanded by Colonel-General V. V. Reshetnikov and is a subordinate command of the Soviet Air Force, although it has a fair measure of operational independence. The strength in aircraft has remained comparatively constant in recent years and until the introduction of the new Tupolev Backfire supersonic variable-geometry bomber, the older Bears and Badgers, with a few Bisons, formed the major strategic bombing capability for a decade and are still in service. For medium-range targets the Badgers are augmented by the supersonic Tupolev Tu-22 Blinder.

The total strength of the force today is

about 900 combat aircraft, made up of 100 Tu-95 Bears, 450 Tu-16 Badgers, 180 Tu-22 Blinders and about 80 of the new supersonic Backfires. Approximately 85 Mya-4 Bison aircraft operate in the tanker role and occasionally Bears are employed for in-flight refuelling simply by transferring fuel from one bomber to another. The tankers serve both the long-range bomber aircraft and the reconnaissance force of Naval Aviation, of which there are about 100 Tu-95 Bear-B reconnaissance and ECM aircraft, augmented by variants of the Mya-4 and Tu-16.

The principal role of the Bear and other heavy aircraft which make up the force of 130 long-range nuclear strike aircraft is nuclear (or conventional) weapon delivery by free-fall bombs and air-to-surface missiles (AS-3 Kangaroo and AS-2 Kipper). The Tu-22 Blinder carries the more modern AS-4 Kitchen missile, which has a range of 465 miles. Priority targets for attack would be nuclear delivery systems in the United States and Europe, and industrial complexes, transportation and supply depots.

The SALT II agreement excluded the Tu-26 Backfire on the assurance of President Brezhnev that it will not be deployed to attack the United States and that production will not exceed 30 aircraft a year. The Backfire will now be deployed either in Long-Range Aviation or Frontal Aviation or both and targeted on Europe. But the Soviets are determined to maintain a triad of strategic nuclear delivery systems, i.e., silo-based missiles, submarine-launched missiles and manned bombers. A new four-engined supersonic bomber, the Tu-160(?), with a range of 7,300 nautical miles, is at the test stage and a new cruise missile for carriage on the aircraft has already been tested.

Backfire is a twin-engined aircraft with variable geometry on its outer wings. Like the B-1 it is designed to cruise economically at altitude with wings spread and yet to fly fast and smoothly with wings swept at low level. A technical analysis carried out in the United States by the Advanced Concepts Division of McDonnell Douglas estimated a weight of around 245,000 lb for a fully loaded Backfire, lower than first estimates. Unrefuelled radius of action is about 2,800 miles at medium altitude and subsonic speed, but this is reduced very sharply if, for instance, the last 100 miles to the target and back has to be covered at low level and high speed. At low level the radius of action is about 900 miles. Maximum speed at high altitude is around Mach 2.

Backfire is reported to carry one AS-6 Kingfish missile under each wing glove, with inertial guidance, radar homing and a 400-mile range. It is likely to be some years before the Soviet Union develops an attack missile which can be carried in the relatively small internal weapon bays, which have a total capacity of some 17,500 lb of nuclear or conventional free-fall or retarded bombs. A single cannon in the tail barbette is aimed by a Fan Tail radar. Backfire is likely to be fitted with terrain-following radar and Doppler/inertial navigation systems.

The long-range air units are deployed throughout the Soviet Union, with many staging bases in the Arctic region and the Leningrad Military District from which

they carry out their roles of armed reconnaissance over the Atlantic in peacetime, and from which they would operate in the reconnaissance and attack roles against targets in the United States and Europe and in support of maritime operations in war.

But the majority of the Soviet long-range aircraft (Bears, Badgers and Bisons) are getting old and would be highly vulnerable to modern interceptor aircraft and surface-to-air missiles despite the ECM capability with which they are now equipped. It is questionable, therefore, in view of the enormous build-up of Soviet inter-continental missiles, both silo-based and submarine-launched, whether any of these subsonic ECM/tankers would be employed in strategic nuclear attack deep into the United States or even over Western Europe. They would almost certainly be confined to peripheral targets and to attacks at sea. Certainly the reduction in the United States Continental Air Defence System (CONAD), particularly in manned interceptors, gives the impression that the United States does not consider Soviet long-range nuclear bombers as a serious threat. All the strategic Nike-Hercules surface-to-air missiles deployed in the United States are being phased out except for two areas, one in Alaska and the other in Florida, and interceptor aircraft are to be further reduced to less than 150 – nearly 5,000 fewer than in the Warsaw Pact forces!

Military Air Transport

The Military Air Transport force is commanded by Lieutenant-General G. N. Pakilev. It has always been an important

Top: East meets West above the North Sea as a USN F-4 Phantom tracks a Tupolev Tu-20 (Bear-D) long-range reconnaissance aircraft.

Above: Two flight crews stand in front of a Tupolev Tu-22 (Blinder). The main shortcoming of the Tu-22 has been its limited range.

Above right: The bomber known to NATO as 'Backfire' was thought to be designated Tupolev Tu-26 by the Soviets until President Brezhnev referred to it as 'Tu-22M' during SALT-II talks in 1979.

Right: The mighty Tupolev Tu-24 (Moss) airborne warning and control system (AWACS). Note the large rotating radome and the multiplicity of antennas and detectors on the fuselage sides and bottom; even elevator tips carry sensors.

element in Soviet aviation since Tupolev, in 1918, first propounded his theory that aviation held the key to the development of the Soviet land mass. In more recent years Military Air Transport has played an important role in extending Soviet influence beyond national frontiers. In the Yom Kippur War, the Soviet Union gave an impressive demonstration of the importance of Military Air Transport not only in re-supplying Egypt and Syria with much needed replacement weapons of war, but also in its ability to mobilise large airborne forces for deployment by air outside Soviet frontiers. It is possible that if conditions in this Middle East war had deteriorated to the disadvantage of the Arabs, to the extent that Cairo would have been threatened by Israeli

Recently there has been a considerable increase in helicopter production and deployment to equip new helicopter assault forces currently being deployed on both western and eastern fronts. The Mi-4 helicopter is used primarily for troop-transport in assault attacks while the Mi-6, also suitable for troop-transport, has been adapted for the carriage of light 57-mm self-propelled guns and their crews, which provide anti-aircraft support to troops deployed in flank manoeuvres. The Mi-8 is the primary vehicle for assault troops and also carries rockets to supply supporting fire to disembarking troops. The Mi-24 Hind is the latest addition to the Soviet 'heliborne' forces. The Mi-12 is probably designed to lift heavy equipment such as tanks and missiles, but few have so far been observed in operational units.

Naval Aviation

Soviet Naval Aviation, though under the operational control of the navy and commanded by Colonel-General Mironenko, comes under the Soviet Air Force for supply of aircraft and other administrative functions. It often uses air force bases and command facilities, and the aircraft flown by Naval Aviation are similar to those operated by other arms of the air force but with modifications to meet the particular requirements of a maritime role. Naval Aviation supports the four Soviet fleets – the Northern, Baltic, Black Sea and Far Eastern Fleets. The aircraft front-line strength is currently about 1,200. This includes 50 Tu-95 Bear aircraft for long-range reconnaissance, 400 Tu-16 Badger bombers, about 50 Tu-22

armoured columns, the threat of Soviet intervention to save Egypt would have been very real. But the threat met with a prompt response from the United States, which culminated in a general alert of US forces. Fortunately, wiser counsels prevailed and a cease-fire was agreed with the approval of both the superpowers.

In addition to purely military transport aircraft there is of course a very large reserve backing provided by the Civil Air Fleet (*Aeroflot*) which is by far the largest civil air organisation in the world. It is directed by P. B. Bugayev, who holds the rank of Marshal of Aviation in the Soviet Air Force. The Air Transport forces at present consist of about 1,600 aircraft made up of 600 An-24 light transports; 900 An-12 and Il-18

medium transports; and about 100 An-22 heavy-lift aircraft. The superb Il-76 heavy turbofan-engined freighter is coming into large-scale use, replacing the An-12. There are also some smaller tactical transport/communications aircraft and a very large complement of some 2,000 helicopters varying in size from the small communications and troop-carrying Mil Mi-2, through the medium Mi-4, Mi-6, Mi-8 and Mi-10, to the enormous Mi-12, the largest heavy-lift helicopter in service anywhere in the world. The Soviets are acutely conscious of the strategic and tactical advantages which air mobility can confer on ground forces, and they have also recognised the utility of the helicopter in many other roles including anti-tank, casualty evacuation and re-supply.

Blinder medium bombers and Tu-26 Back-fire bombers, and a few Su-17 strike fighters. The Badger bombers carry AS-5 Kelt or AS-2 Kipper long-range air-to-surface missiles and are also capable of carrying free-fall bombs, both conventional and nuclear. The Tu-22 Blinders, of which there are four versions, are employed mainly on medium-range strike/reconnaissance missions and carry the more effective AS-4 Kitchen air-to-surface missile. There are also approximately 50 Il-38 May anti-submarine warfare and reconnaissance aircraft.

The navy has its own force of approximately 250 helicopters, mostly Mi-4 Hound and Ka-25 Hormone anti-submarine warfare aircraft. The Mi-4s are being supplemented by a new type, the Mil Mi-14 Haze amphibious ASW helicopter, developed from the Mi-8 and in the same class as the Sikorsky SH-3. Two anti-submarine helicopter cruisers (the *Moskva* and the *Leningrad*) carry their own force of helicopters.

The strength of Soviet naval aviation was boosted in 1976 by deployment of the aircraft-carrier *Kiev* and in 1978 by her sister ship *Minsk* both of which carry Yak 36 Forger V/TOL aircraft and Ka-25 Hormone helicopters. The *Minsk* has recently joined the Far East fleet. In war the main role of Naval Aviation will be the attack of enemy naval forces, particularly the US carrier task forces in the Atlantic and Mediterranean.

Improvements in Soviet equipment and technology

The Soviet Union took every opportunity to test its military equipment in the Vietnamese War and in the Yom Kippur War of October 1973. All kinds of modern arms were supplied to the North Vietnamese together with Soviet advisers, who helped to operate them and to train the North Vietnamese to operate some of the more sophisticated equipments. But so far as the air was concerned, the major emphasis in Vietnam was on air defence of North Vietnam against formidable US and South Vietnamese air attack. The North Viet-

nam air force was small, poorly trained and not very efficient. It had no bombing or strike capability against the South Vietnam forces and only rarely did North Vietnam aircraft venture across the demilitarised zone into South Vietnam air space, and then only in the closing stages of the war, when the North Vietnamese communist ground forces swept rapidly south through South Vietnam to occupy Saigon and force the surrender of

Above: The Soviet ability to deliver ground combat forces by air is second to none, and is exemplified by the Antonov An-12s (Cub) lined up on the ground and the larger Antonov An-22 (Cock) coming into land. Vehicles are ASU-85s.

Below: The Mil Mi-24 (Hind-D) is probably the most versatile and effective attack helicopter in service today. It has been used extensively in Afghanistan.

Above: Now active all over the world's oceans is the Ilyushin Il-38 (May) seen here with its weapons-bay door open, having just dropped a sonobuoy.

Below: The flight-deck of the Soviet aircraft carrier *Kiev*, with a Yakovlev Yak-36 (Forger-A) being serviced. This aircraft is only the second fixed-wing VTOL machine to enter service and represents a fine technical achievement.

Soviet Naval Aviation

several	Tu-16	Badger-A	bomber-trainer
290	Tu-16	Badger-C/G	bomber (ASM)
50	Tu-22	Blinder-A	bomber
few		Backfire	bomber (ASM)
few	Su-17	Fitter-C	strike
50	Tu-16	Badger-D	reconnaissance
50	Tu-95	Bear-D	reconnaissance
few	An-12	Cub-C	reconnaissance (ECM)
75	Be-12	Mail	maritime patrol/ASW
55	Il-38	May	maritime patrol/ASW
few	Tu-95	Bear-F	maritime patrol
several	Tu-16	Badger	ECM
75+	Tu-16	Badger	tankers
160 {	Ka-25	Hormone-A	helicopter-reconnaissance
	Ka-25	Hormone-B	helicopter-ASW
50	Mi-14	Haze	helicopter-ASW
few	Mi-8	Hip	helicopter-minesweeper

Approximately 300 transport, training, and utility aircraft also are operated by Soviet Naval Aviation.

the South Vietnam government. The air defence of Hanoi, Haiphong and industrial areas of the north against the massive air assault by United States strategic and tactical bombers required a vast arsenal of over 6,000 anti-aircraft guns of all calibres and 200 surface-to-air missiles, mostly SA-2 'Guidelines'. Despite the proliferation of defences, however, US strategic air attacks against targets in the North were conducted with relatively small losses except in 1972, during the resumed bomber onslaught against the North, when US bombers met the heaviest concentration of missile and gun air defences ever encountered. In the period between 18 and 30 December 1972 the United States lost 15 B-52s, which represented a loss rate of just over 2 per cent. This was certainly tolerable, and could have been sustained for much longer if the war had not ended in early 1973. Countermeasures, both evasive action and ECM, did much to keep the losses down and to nullify the effectiveness of the Soviet SA-2 missiles, and escorting US fighters were able to deal effectively with the small number of MiG interceptors which the North Vietnamese deployed against the US bomber forces. But the Vietnam War, despite the intensity of operations and the losses sustained by US strategic and tactical air units, particularly in helicopters, provided relatively few lessons that would be applicable to a war in central Europe, but it did provide the Soviet Union with the opportunity to use its defensive equipment in a sophisticated air environment.

The Yom Kippur War of October 1973 provided a much more realistic scenario from which to assess the effectiveness of Soviet and US air weapons systems, both offensive and defensive. Most of the Arab air forces were supplied with Soviet aircraft and equipment, while the majority of Israeli squadrons had US or French aircraft. The Egyptians had a massive SAM defence system deployed along the Suez Canal, under cover of which the Egyptian army made its initial assault across the canal into Sinai. The Israelis had no similar SAM defence system, although they did have

anti-aircraft guns and some missiles. The war lasted only 18 days, however, and although attrition rates in sophisticated and expensive weapons systems were high, the cease-fire prevented an accurate assessment of how the air weapons systems deployed by both sides would have influenced the course of the war had it not ended abruptly because of the intervention of the superpowers. What is clear is that after the initial Egyptian offensive across the canal, during which the SAM defences provided a very effective umbrella and took a heavy toll of Israeli aircraft, the Egyptian army lost the initiative to the Israelis and thereafter fought defensive actions against qualitatively superior Israeli forces employing better tactics and imbued with the offensive spirit. Israeli aircraft on the whole were shown to be superior to the MiG-21s and Su-7s, but the Egyptian SAM systems proved highly successful in the opening phases of the war though were later shown to be susceptible to ECM and anti-radiation suppression weapons. The Israelis had no answer to the SA-6 and their ECM system against the SA-3s was limited. The capture of Soviet equipment has, however, provided the United States with all the information it required to develop electronic countermeasures against most of the currently deployed Soviet SAM systems.

Despite prodigious efforts in research and development, and the acquisition of advanced technology from the West by various means, it is generally conceded that the standard of Soviet arms and equipment in all three elements – land, sea and air – is generally inferior to that of the West, although in certain categories of technology the Soviets may have a slight lead. But the Soviets are indulging in research and development projects that far exceed the efforts of the United States and Western Europe, and despite the disadvantages of lower efficiency in a totally state-controlled system the Soviets are prepared to seek parity with the West in modern weapons technology whatever the cost; moreover, what they lack in quality they make up for abundantly in numbers.

Soviet Aircraft

Bill Gunston

On the following 24 pages are details and illustrations of all the chief types of aircraft known to be in the Soviet inventory. Some, such as that immediately below, are far from new but are serving in such numbers they cannot be omitted. Others, such as the tantalizing new fighter, attack aircraft and strategic bomber(s) were in mid-1980 so little known in the West that their entries are little more than a distillation of unconfirmed reports emanating mostly from Washington. This section emphasises the fitness-for-purpose characteristic of aircraft available to the Warsaw Pact.

Antonov (WSK) An-2

An-2 (many variants) and WSK-Mielec An-2; ("Colt")

Origin: The bureau of Oleg K. Antonov, Soviet Union; today made only by WSK-Mielec, Poland, and State Industry of China.
Type: STOL transport.
Engine: One 1,000hp Shvetsov ASh-62IR nine-cylinder radial; (since 1960) one 1,000hp WSK-Kalisz ASz-62IR.
Dimensions: Span 59ft 8½in (18·18m) (lower wing 46ft 8½in, 14·24m); length 41ft 9½in (12·74m); height 13ft 1½in (4·00m).
Weights: (2P): Empty 7,605lb (3450kg); maximum loaded 12,125lb (5500kg).
Performance: Maximum speed (P, 11,574lb, 5250kg) 160mph (258km/h); typical cruise 115mph (185km/h), min safe speed 56mph (90km/h); service ceiling 14,425ft (4400m); typical takeoff or landing over 35ft (10·7m) on grass 1,050ft (320m); range with 1,102lb (500kg) payload 560 miles (900km).
History: First flight 31 August 1947; service delivery (An-2) July 1948, (Fong Chou) December 1957, (WSK) 1960.
Development: When this bulky biplane appeared in 1947 it appeared to be an obsolete mistake. So un-

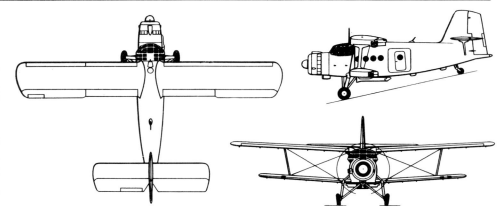

Above: Three-view of An-2M agricultural version of An-2, made only in USSR.

mistaken was it that it has been manufactured in larger quantities than any other single type of aircraft since World War II: Soviet production had topped 5,000 when responsibility was passed to Poland in 1960, and a few hundred additional aircraft with angular tails were made in the Soviet Union in 1964–70; Polish output was continuing in 1977 with the nation's total well over 7,500, and the Chinese Fong Chou output is thought to exceed 5,000, making a combined figure of something over 18,000. Of these perhaps one-quarter are military, and many serve in para-military roles. Versions are numerous, and have different designations in the Soviet Union and Poland, but the chief military roles are paratroop and aircrew training, supply of frontier posts and general transport/casevac duties.

Antonov An-12

An-12; NATO code name "Cub"

Origin: Design bureau of Oleg K. Antonov, Kiev, Soviet Union.
Type: "Cub-A", paratroop and cargo transport; "Cub-B", Elint (electronic-intelligence) platform; "Cub-C", ECM platform.
Engines: Four 4,000ehp Ivchenko AI-20K single-shaft turboprops.
Dimensions: Span 124ft 8in (38m); length 121ft 4½in (37m); height 32ft 3in (9·83m).
Weights: Empty 61,730lb (28,000kg); loaded 121,475lb (55,100kg).
Performance: Maximum speed 482mph (777km/h); maximum cruising speed 416mph (670km/h); maximum rate of climb 1,970ft (600m)/min; service ceiling 33,500ft (10,200m); range with full payload 2,236 miles (3600km).
Armament: Powered tail turret with two 23mm NR-23 cannon.
History: First flight (civil An-10) 1957; (An-12) believed 1958.
Development: In 1958 Antonov flew a large twin-turboprop which owed something to German designs of World War II and the C-130. From this evolved the An-10 airliner and the An-12, which since 1960 has been a standard transport with many air forces. Fully pressurised, the An-12 has an exceptionally high performance yet can operate from unpaved surfaces. At least one was fitted with large skis with shallow V planing surfaces equipped with heating (to prevent sticking to ice or snow) and brakes. Nearly all have the tail turret, and under the transparent nose is a weather and mapping radar, which in most Soviet Air Force An-12s has been changed to a more powerful and larger design. The rear ramp door is made in left and right halves which can be folded upwards inside the

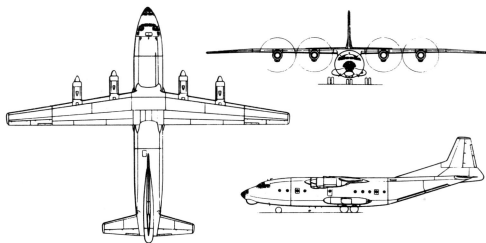

fuselage, either for loading heavy freight with the aid of a built-in gantry or for the dispatch of 100 paratroops in less than one minute. Typical freight load is 44,090lb (20,000kg), and the An-12 can carry all Soviet APCs, the ASU-85 SP-gun and such anti-aircraft vehicles as the ZSU-23-4 and SA-6 missile carrier. In manoeuvres of Warsaw Pact forces as many as 30 of these capable aircraft have landed at one airstrip in simulated battle conditions.

Below: An An-12BP transport (called Cub-A by NATO) with armament fitted. The turret is retained in the Cub-B EW/ECM version, but removed from Cub-C.

Above: Three-view of An-12 without turret.

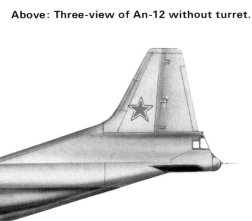

Antonov An-22

An-22 Antei (Antheus) (NATO name "Cock")
Origin: The design bureau of Oleg K. Antonov, Soviet Union.
Type: Heavy logistic transport.
Engines: Four 15,000shp Kuznetsov NK-12MA single-shaft turboprops.
Dimensions: Span 211ft 4in (64·40m); length overall (prototype) 189ft 7in (57·80m); height overall 41ft 1½in (12·53m).
Weights: Empty, equipped 251,325lb (114.000kg); maximum loaded 551,160lb (250,000kg).
Performance: Maximum cruise 422mph (679km/h); range with max payload of 176,350lb (80,000kg) 3,100 miles (5000km), range with max fuel and payload of 99,200lb (45,000kg) 6,800 miles (10,950km).
History: First flight 27 February 1965; final delivery, believed 1974.
Development: Largest aircraft in the world apart from the 747 and C-5A, the An-22 is the result of a surprisingly late decision to mate the great NK-12M engine/propeller combination with a capacious freight fuselage. As early as July 1967 three Soviet air force Anteis took part in an air display in the assault role, and since then an unknown number have operated with both the civil operator, Aeroflot, and the air force. Anteis carried almost all the war material supplied to the MPLA in Angola, and have made many other long overseas flights besides setting various world records for payload/height and speed/payload, the speeds all being in the region of 370mph (596km/h). The nose

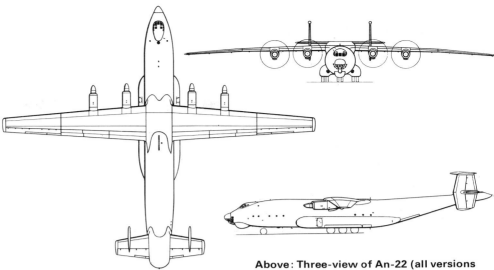

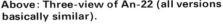

Above: Three-view of An-22 (all versions basically similar).

does not open but houses two large radars, for navigation, mapping, weather and airdropping, as well as several other avionic aids. There are seats for about 29 passengers aft of the flight deck, while at the lower level is a hold 14ft 5in (4·40m) square in section, with beaver-tail rear doors.

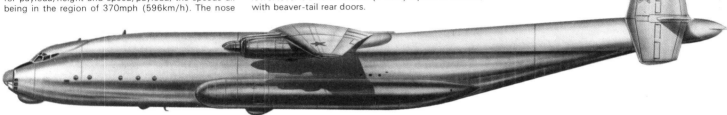

Above: An-22 of the V-TA, the Soviet Air Force transport force. Few military Antei have been seen, though about 50 were delivered in 1967-74.

Right: A V-TA An-22 coming in to land during a major exercise during which T-62 battle tanks were airlifted.

Below: Close-up of the nose, showing the remarkable combination of nose weather radar, ground mapping and air-delivery radar and visual observer station.

Antonov An-26

An-24V, 24RV, 24T, 26, 30 and 32 (NATO names: 24, "Coke"; 26, "Curl"; 30, "Clank"; 32, "Cline".

Origin: The design bureau of Oleg K. Antonov, Soviet Union.

Type: (24V and RV) passenger and troop transport, (24T and 26) freight transport, (30) aerial survey and mapping.

Engines: (24V and T) two Ivchenko AI-24A single-shaft turboprops, shaft power not disclosed but 2,550ehp; (24RV) same, plus one 1,985lb (900kg) thrust RU-19-300 auxiliary turbojet in right nacelle; (26 and 30) two AI-24T each rated at 2,820ehp plus (26) one RU-19-300, or (30) one 1,765lb thrust (800kg) RU-19A-300; (32) two 5,180ehp Ivchenko AI-20M turboprops.

Dimensions: Span 95ft 9½in (29·20m); length overall (24) 77ft 2½in (23·53m), (26) 78ft 1in (23·80m), (30) 79ft 7in (24·26m); height (24, 30) 27ft 3½in (8·32m), (26) 28ft 1½in (8.575m).

Weights: Empty (24) 29,320lb (13,300kg), (26) 33,113lb (15,020kg); maximum loaded (24V, T) 46,300lb (21,000kg), (24RV) 48,060lb (21,800kg), (26) 52,911lb (24,000kg), (30) 50,706lb (23,000kg).

Performance: Typical cruising speed 267mph (430 km/h); range with max payload of 12,125lb (5500kg), no reserves, (24V) 341 miles (550km), (24T) 397 miles (640km), (26) about 400 miles (645km).

History: First flight (24) April 1960, (26) late 1960s.

Development: One of the world's most numerous turboprop transports, the An 24 is primarily civil but small numbers of several versions have been supplied to the air forces listed above. The more powerful An-26 has a beaver-tail rear door for loading or airdropping bulky loads; it serves with Bangladesh, Cuba, Hungary, Jugoslavia, Peru, Poland, Romania and Somalia. The An-30 can carry IR, magnetic and other sensors. The An-32 has much greater power, and an enlarged tail with slotted tailplane, for operation from airfields in extreme hot/high-altitude conditions. It is intended to carry loads of 3000kg (6,614lb) over sectors of 1100km (683 miles) operating from rough strips at heights up to 4500m (14,750ft) in 25°C temperatures.

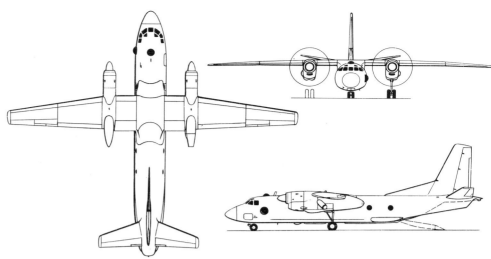

Above: Three-view of An-26 (note right engine nacelle).

Below: Side elevation of an An-26 exported to the Somalian Aeronautical Corps.

Foot of page: One of the fleet of An-26 short-haul transports supplied to Jugoslavia to replace C-47s.

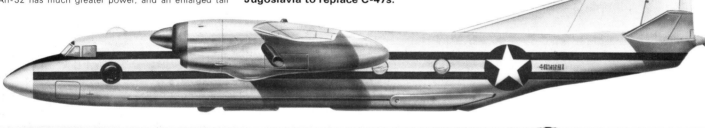

Beriev M-12

Be-12 Tchaika; NATO code-name "Mail"

Origin: Design bureau of Georgi Mikhailovich Beriev, Taganrog, Soviet Union.

Type: Ocean reconnaissance and utility amphibian.

Engines: Two 4,190ehp Ivchenko AI-20D single-shaft turboprops.

Dimensions: Span 97ft 6in (29·7m); length overall 99ft (30·2m); height on land 22ft 11½in (7m).

Weights: Empty approximately 48,000lb (21,772kg); maximum approximately 66,140lb (30,000kg).

Performance: Maximum speed about 380mph (612 km/h); cruising speed 199mph (320km/h); service ceiling 38,000ft (11,582m); range with full equipment 2,485 miles (4000km).

Armament: At least 6,600lb (3000kg) sonobuoys and AS bombs in internal weapon bay; one to three external hard points for stores under each outer wing.

History: First flight 1960 or earlier; combat service probably about 1962; set many world records in 1964, 1968, 1972 and 1973.

Development: The bureau of Georgi M. Beriev, at Taganrog on the Azov Sea, is the centre for Soviet marine aircraft. The Be-6, powered by two 2,300hp Ash-73TK radial engines and in the class of the Martin PBM or P5M, served as the standard long-range ocean patrol flying boat from 1949 until about 1967. In 1961 Beriev flew a remarkable large flying boat, the Be-10, powered by two Lyulka AL-7PB turbojets, but though this set world records it never entered major operational service. Instead a more pedestrian turboprop aircraft, first seen at the 1961 Moscow Aviation Day at the same time as the swept-wing Be-10, has fast become the Soviet Union's standard large marine aircraft. The Be-12 Tchaika (Seagull) is an amphibian, with retractable tailwheel-type landing gear. Its twin fins are unusual on modern aircraft, and the gull wing, which puts the engines high above the spray, gives an air of gracefulness. The Be-12 is extremely versatile. The search and mapping radar projects far ahead of the glazed nose, and a MAD (magnetic anomaly detector) extends 15ft behind the tail. Much of the hull is filled with equipment and there is a weapon and sonobuoy bay aft of the wing with watertight doors in the bottom aft of the step. Be-12s, known as M-12s in service with the Soviet naval air fleets, have set many class records for speed, height and load-carrying. They are based all around the Soviet shores, mainly with the Northern and Black Sea fleets.

Below: This extremely useful and versatile aircraft has given good service, but may be showing signs of fatigue or salt-water corrosion. Producing a successor might not be judged a cost effective exercise—at least, not in the West.

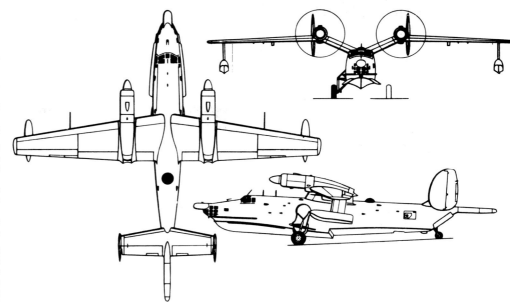

Above: Three-view of M-12 Tchaika; all examples appear to be generally similar though EW equipment is now appearing.

Below: An M-12 photographed by an aircraft of the US Navy. The wing floats and MAD "stinger" are not retractable.

Ilyushin IL-18 and IL-38

Il-18 ('Coot') and Il-38 ('May')

Origin: Bureau named for Sergei Ilyushin, Moscow Khodinka.

Type: Il-18, passenger transport; "Coot-A" version, electronic warfare; Il-38, maritime patrol and ASW (data for latter).

Engines: Four Ivchenko AI-20 single-shaft turboprops, probably rated at about 5,000shp each.

Dimensions: Span 122ft 8½in (37·4m); length 129ft 10in (39·6m); height about 35ft (10·7m).

Weights: Empty, approximately 90,000lb (40,820kg); maximum loaded, approximately 180,000lb (81,650kg).

Performance: Maximum speed, about 450mph (724km/h); maximum cruising speed about 400mph (644km/h); range with typical mission load, about 4,500 miles (7240km); endurance, about 15hr.

Armament: Internal weapon bay ahead of and behind wing accommodating full range of anti-submarine torpedoes, bombs, mines and other stores; possibly external racks for stores such as guided missiles between weapon-bay doors under wing and beneath outer wings.

History: First flight (IL-18 transport) July 1957; first disclosure of IL-38, 1974, by which time it was well established in operational service.

Development: Following the example of the US Navy and Lockheed with the Electra/P-3 Orion transformation, the Soviet Naval Air Arm (AV-MF) used the IL-18 transport as the basis of the `considerably changed IL-38, known to NATO by the code-name of "May". Compared with the transport it has a wing moved forward and a considerably longer rear fuselage, showing the gross shift in centre of gravity resulting from the changed role. Whereas in the transport the payload is distributed evenly ahead of and behind the wing, the rear fuselage of the IL-38 contains only sensors, sonobuoy launchers of several kinds and a galley, with the main tactical compartment just behind and above the wing, with a probable tactical crew of eight. Most of the heavy stores and consoles are ahead of the wing, together with the search radar. The only added item at the rear is the MAD (magnetic anomaly detector) stinger, not a heavy item. So far little is known of the IL-38 and photographs show few of the items one would expect to see. There is no weapon bay below the wing and pressurized fuselage, as in the Nimrod and P-3, no major sensor outlets and aerials

and no apparent external stores pylons. On the other hand the IL-38 is potentially as good as a P-3, though probably not up to the sensor and computer standard of the P-3C. Few Il-18 transports are in military service, but in 1978 a complete rebuild was photographed by the RAF, covered with electronics aerials. From stem to stern the "Coot-A" version bristles with sensors and aerials, including a pod under the forward fuselage well over 10m (33ft) long. Equipment is considered to include SLAR (side-looking airborne radar), IR (infrared) linescan and a vast array of passive recording and analysis systems.

Below: Unlike almost all other maritime patrol and ASW aircraft the IL-38 has a low-mounted wing, which causes the weapon bay to be split into front and rear parts by the wing box. The great length of the rear fuselage (3·7m, 146in longer than that of the IL-18) may simply balance mass and side area of the radar.

Above: Three-view of standard IL-38; the IL-18 variants have a shorter fuselage.

Foot of page: A fine photograph of an IL-38 with forward weapon-bay doors open (for dropping drogue-stabilized sonobuoys) during exercises over international waters. It was taken from a Nimrod of No 120 Sqn, RAF Kinloss, which accompanied the Soviet aircraft for an extended period. Colour was greyish white.

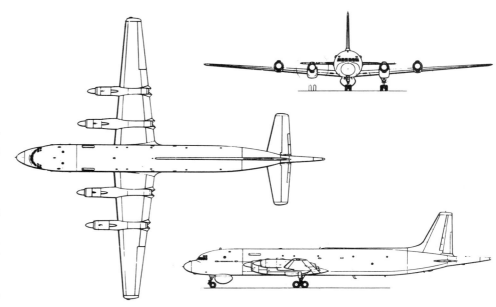

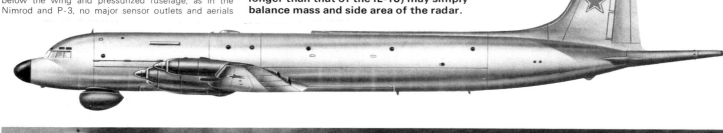

Ilyushin IL-76

IL-76 ("Candid")
Origin: Bureau named for Ilyushin, Soviet Union.
Type: Heavy freight transport.
Engines: Four 26,455lb (12,000kg) thrust Soloviev D-30KP two-shaft turbofans.
Dimensions: Span 165ft 8in (50·5m); length 152ft 10½in (46·59m); height 48ft 5in (14·76m).
Weights: Empty, about 159,000lb (72,000kg); maximum loaded 346,125lb (157,000kg).
Performance: Maximum speed, about 560mph (900km/h); maximum cruising speed 528mph (850km/h); normal long-range cruising height 42,650ft (13,000m); range with maximum payload of 88,185lb (40,000kg) 3,100 miles (5000km).
Armament: Military version has rear turret (twin NR-23?).
History: First flight 25 March 1971; production deliveries 1973.
Development: First seen in the West at the 1971 Paris Salon, the IL-76 created a most favourable impression. Though superficially seeming to be another Ilyushin copy of a Lockheed design, in this case the C-141, in fact the resemblance is coincidental. The design was prepared to meet a basic need in the Soviet Union for a really capable freighter which, while carrying large indivisible loads, with a high cruising speed and intercontinental range, could operate from relatively poor airstrips. The result is a very useful aircraft which, though initially being used by Aeroflot in the 1971–75 and 1976–80 plans for opening up Siberia, the far north and far east of the Soviet Union, is obviously a first-class strategic and tactical transport for military use. It has very powerful engines, all fitted with reversers, a high-lift wing for good STOL performance and a high-flotation landing gear with 20 wheels. The nose is typical of modern Soviet aircraft for "outback" operation, and closely resembles that of the An-22. The big fuselage, usefully larger in cross-section than that of the C-141, is fully pressurized and incorporates a powerful auxiliary power unit and freight handling systems. There seems no reason why

the rear clamshell doors should not be opened in flight to permit heavy dropping. In 1977 deliveries appeared to have swung in favour of the military and though publicity continues to feature only the Aeroflot version the military V-TA has been steadily receiving these excellent aircraft as replacements for the AN-12, the total in use by early 1980 being estimated at 150. In 1978 export deliveries were made to Iraq, and a few are believed to be serving in some Warsaw Pact air forces. In the same year a tanker version was believed to have entered service to support the Tu-26 "Backfires" of the DA and AV-MF, but this had not been revealed by 1980.

Below: Side elevation of an IL-76 of the military V-TA. As in the case of the An-22, few military IL-76s have been seen.

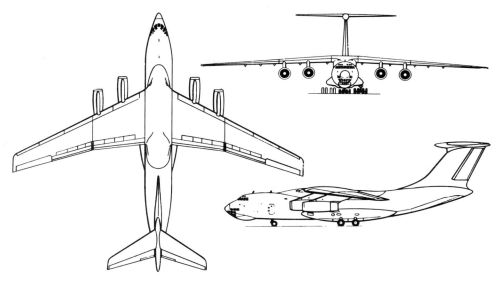

Above: Three-view of standard IL-76.

Foot of page: One of the ongoing tasks allotted to civil IL-76 freighters has been assisting the exploitation of natural resources in Siberia. This photograph was taken at Tyumen, in a big oil/gas field region.

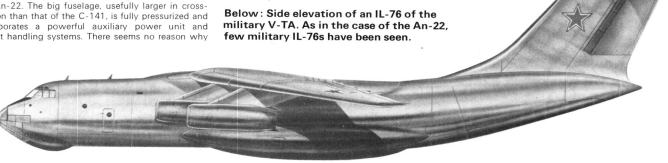

Kamov Ka-25

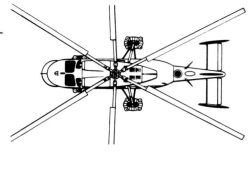

Ka-25
(several versions, designations unknown)
Origin: Design bureau named for Nikolai I. Kamov, Soviet Union.
Type: Ship-based ASW, search/rescue and utility helicopter.
Engines: Two 900hp Glushenkov GTD-3 free-turbine turboshaft.
Dimensions: Main rotor diameter (both) 51ft 8in (15·75m); fuselage length about 34ft (10·36m); height 17ft 8in (5·4m).
Weights: Empty about 11,023lb (5000kg); maximum loaded 16,535lb (7500kg).
Performance: Maximum speed 120mph (193km/h); service ceiling, about 11,000ft (3350m); range, about 400 miles (650km).
Armament: One or two 400mm AS torpedoes, nuclear or conventional depth charges or other stores, carried in internal weapon bay.
History: First flight (Ka-20) probably 1960; service delivery of initial production version, probably 1965.
Development: Nikolai Kamov, who died in 1973, was one of the leaders of rotorcraft in the Soviet Union, a characteristic of nearly all his designs being the use of superimposed co-axial rotors to give greater lift in a vehicle of smaller overall size. Large numbers of Ka-15 and -18 piston-engined machines were used by Soviet armed forces, but in 1961 the Aviation Day fly-past at Tushino included a completely new machine designated a Ka-20 and carrying a guided

missile on each side. It was allotted the NATO code-name of "Harp". Clearly powered by gas turbines, it looked formidable. Later in the 1960s it became clear that from this helicopter Kamov's bureau, under chief engineer Barshevsky, had developed the standard ship-based machine of the Soviet fleets, replacing the Mi-4. Designated the Ka-25 and allotted the new Western code name of "Hormone", it is in service in at least five major versions, with numerous subtypes. Whereas the "missiles" displayed in 1961 have never been seen since, and are thought to have been dummies, the

Ka-25 is extremely fully equipped with all-weather anti-submarine sensing and attack equipment. The four landing wheels are each surrounded by a buoyancy bag ring which can be swiftly inflated by the gas bottles just above it. Ka-25s are used aboard the carriers (ASW cruisers) *Minsk, Kiev, Moskva* and *Leningrad, Kresta* and *Kara* class cruisers and from shore bases.

Above: Three-view of Ka-25 of the so-called Hormone-A sub-type, with emergency flotation bags on landing gear.

Below: Stern of the *Admiral Isachenkov*, a Kresta II class cruiser, showing the Ka-25 and its open hangar.

Mikoyan/Gurevich MiG-15 UTI

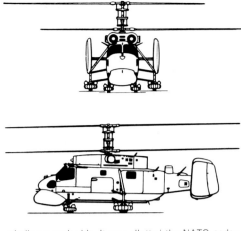

MiG-15UTI (SBLim-1, CS-102, F-2)
Origin: Design, the Mikoyan/Gurevich bureau, Soviet Union; licence production as described in text.
Type: dual-control trainer.
Engine: (most -15UTI) one 5,952lb (2700kg) VK-1 of same layout.
Dimensions: Span 33ft 0¾in (10·08m); length 32ft 11¼in (10·04m); height 12ft 1½in (3·7m).
Weights: Empty close to 8,820lb (4000kg); maximum loaded 11,905lb (5400kg), (10,692lb clean).
Performance: Maximum speed 630mph (1015km/h); initial climb 10,500ft (3200m)/min; service ceiling 47,980ft (14,625m); range (at height, with slipper tanks) 885 miles (1424km).
Armament: single 23mm with 80 rounds or 12·7mm UBK-E with 150 rounds under left side, with two underwing hardpoints for slipper tanks or stores of up to 1,102lb (500kg).
History: First flight 1948.
Development: No combat aircraft in history has had a bigger impact than the MiG-15 which — thanks to the British government which supplied the engines — was developed with remarkable speed in 1948-9 and was in action in Korea soon afterwards. The MiG bureau were equally swift to rectify fundamental deficiencies

Three-view of MiG-15UTI (some have underwing drop-tanks).

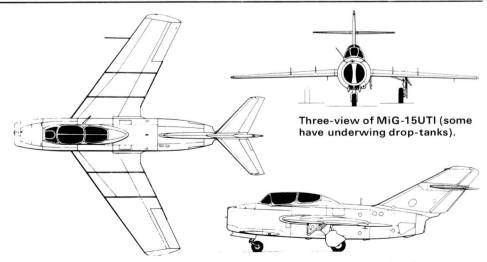

in the basic design (with the MiG-17) but the MiG-15 was nevertheless satisfactory as a trainer and since 1955 has probably been the most widely used jet trainer in the world. Licence-production took place in Poland (as the Lim-3), Czechoslovakia (as the CS-102) and China (Type 2 or TF-2) and probably at

least 5,000 were constructed, about 30 per cent of the total of all versions of MiG-15. Few fighter versions are left today, but the UTI trainer has shown itself extremely tough and durable, and remains in use in about 30 countries, though in many of them utilization is poor, mainly through poor support and lack of spares.

Mikoyan/ Gurevich MiG-17

MiG-17, -17P, -17F (Lim-5P and -5M, S-104, F-4), -17PF and -17PFU (NATO name "Fresco")

Origin: The design bureau of Mikoyan and Gurevich, Soviet Union; licence-production as described in the text.

Type: Single-seat fighter; (PF, PFU) limited all-weather interceptor.

Engine: (-17, -17P) one 5,952lb (2700kg) thrust Klimov VK-1 single-shaft centrifugal turbojet; (later versions) one 4,732/7,452lb (3380kg) VK-1F with afterburner.

Dimensions: Span 31ft (9·45m); length (all) 36ft 3in (11·05m); height 11ft (3·35m).

Weights: Empty (all) about 9,040lb (4100kg); loaded (F, clean) 11,773lb (5340kg); maximum (all) 14,770lb (6700kg).

Performance: Maximum speed (F, clean at best height of 9,840ft) 711mph (1145km/h); initial climb 12,795ft (3900m)/min; service ceiling 54,460ft (16,600m); range (high, two drop tanks) 913 miles (1470km).

Armament: (-17) as MiG-15, one 37mm and two 23mm NS-23; (all later versions) three 23mm Nudelmann-Rikter NR-23 cannon, one under right side of nose and two under left; four wing hardpoints for tanks, total of 1,102lb (500kg) of bombs, packs of eight 55mm air-to-air rockets or various air-to-ground missiles.

History: First flight (prototype) January 1950; service delivery, 1952; service delivery (F-4) January 1956; final delivery (Soviet Union) probably 1959.

Development: Only gradually did Western observers recognise that the MiG-17 is not a modified MiG-15 but a totally redesigned aircraft. Many thousands were built in the Soviet Union, Poland, Czechoslovakia and China, but the numerous variants have today largely faded from the scene in WP air forces, and survive only as advanced trainers and squadron hacks or research aircraft. The only MiG-17s remaining in WP inven-

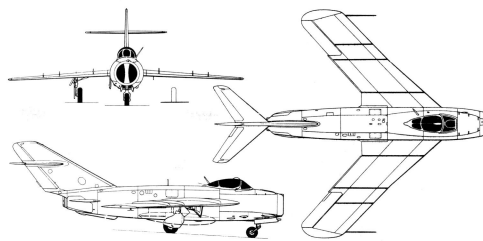

tories in 1980 were believed to be about 30 in the East German LSK, a larger number in the Czech CL (at last giving way to MiG-23 and 27 versions), eight complete squadrons in Bulgaria, one regiment of about 60 licence-built Lim-6 in Poland, a small number in Hungary and about 50 ageing examples in Romania.

Above: Three-view of MiG-17F (Fresco-C).

Below: Early Mig-17 fighters in service with the AV-MF Black Sea Fleet. Some are still in use.

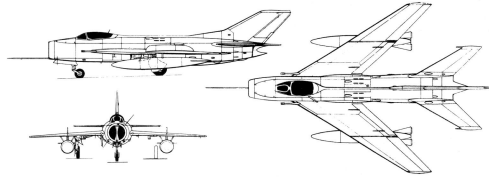

Mikoyan/ Gurevich MiG-19

MiG-19, -19S, -19SF (Lim-7, S-105, F-6), -19PF and -19PM; NATO name "Farmer"

Origin: The design bureau named for Mikoyan and Gurevich, Soviet Union; licence-production as described in the text.

Type: Single-seat fighter (PF, PM, all-weather interceptor).

Engines: (-19, -19S) two 6,700lb (3,040kg) thrust (afterburner rating) Mikulin AM-5 single-shaft afterburning turbojets; (-19SF, PF, PM) two 7,165lb (3250kg) thrust (afterburner) Klimov RD-9B afterburning turbojets.

Dimensions: Span 29ft 6½in (9m); length (S, SF, excluding pitot boom) 42ft 11¼in (13·08m); (-19PF, PM) 44ft 7in; height 13ft 2¼in (4·02m).

Weights: Empty (SF) 12,698lb (5760kg); loaded (SF, clean) 16,755lb (7600kg); (maximum, SF) 19,180lb (8700kg); (PM) 20,944lb (9500kg).

Performance: Maximum speed (typical) 920mph at 20,000ft (1480km/h, Mach 1·3); initial climb (SF) 22,640ft (6900m)/min; service ceiling (SF) 58,725ft (17,900m); maximum range (high, with two drop tanks) 1,367 miles (2200km).

Armament: See text.

History: First flight, September 1953; service delivery early 1955; first flight (F-6) December 1961.

Development: With its I-350 prototype of September

Above: Three-view of standard MiG-19SF.

1953 the MiG bureau established itself in the very front rank of world fighter design. Powered by twin axila engines and with a wing swept at the 25 per cent chord line at the bold angle of 55° it was supersonic on the level, and gave rise to a profusion of MiG-19 production versions. By 1960 this basic type was beginning to be undervalued by the West, and even regarded as obsolescent, and it was a matter for comment when China abandoned the later MiG-21 and returned to mass-production of the F-6 (MiG-19SF and PF). Today it is recognised that this is a remarkable air-combat aircraft with excellent turn radius and ex-

tremely powerful 30mm guns, but though many thousands were built in WP countries none are in the combat inventory of the Soviet Union. A few hundred, mainly of the SF fighter/bomber type, remain in WP service, including some 36 in Bulgaria, and no fewer than 15 squadrons in Romania.

Below: A Russian (probably Frontal Aviation) MiG-19F, with "Scan Odd" gun-ranging radar, in landing configuration. Large numbers of these and other MiG-19 versions are still flying with various Communist countries.

Mikoyan/ Gurevich MiG-21

MiG-21, 21F (S-107), 21FA, 20PF, 21FL, 21PFS, 21PFM, 21PFMA, 21M, 21R, 21MF, 21SMT, 21bis, 21U, 21US and 21UM plus countless special versions. Several versions made in China as F-7.

Origin: The design bureau named for Mikoyan and Gurevich; Soviet Union licence-production as described in the text.

Type: Single-seat fighter; (PFMA and MF) limited all-weather multi-role; (R) reconnaissance; (U) two-seat trainer.

Engine: In all versions, one Tumansky single-shaft turbojet with afterburner (-21) R-11 rated at 11,240lb (5100kg) with afterburner; (-21F) R-11-F2-300 rated at 13,120lb (5950kg); (-21FL, PFS, PFM and PFMA) R-11-G2S-300 rated at 13,668lb (6200kg); (-21MF and derivatives) R-13-300 rated at 14,500lb (6600kg). (Fishbed-N) Tumansky R-25 rated at 16,535lb (7500kg).

Dimensions: Span 23ft 5½in (7·15m); length (excluding probe) (-21) 46ft 11in; (-21MF) 48ft 0½in (14·6m); height (little variation, but figure for MF) 14ft 9in (4·5m).

Weights: Empty (-21) 11,464lb (5200kg); (-21MF) 12,346lb (5600kg); maximum loaded (-21) 18,740lb (8500kg); (-21MF) 21,605lb (9800kg) (weight with three tanks and two K-13A, 20,725lb).

Performance: Maximum speed (MF, but typical of all) 1,285mph (2070km/h, Mach 2·1); initial climb (MF, clean) 36,090ft (11,000m)/min; service ceiling 59,050ft (18,000m); range (high, internal fuel) 683 miles (1100km); maximum range (MF, high, three tanks) 1,118 miles (1800km).

Armament: See text.

History: First flight (E-5 prototype) late 1955; (production -21F) late 1957; service delivery early 1958.

Development: Undoubtedly the most widely used combat aircraft in the world in the 1970s, this trim little delta has established a reputation for cost effectiveness and in its later versions it also packs a more adequate multi-role punch. It was designed in the 18 months following the Korean War. While Sukhoi developed large supersonic fighters to rival the American F-100, the Mikoyan-Gurevich bureau, by now led only by Col-Gen Mikoyan (who died in 1970), concentrated on a small day interceptor of the highest possible performance. Prototypes were built with both swept and delta wings, both having powered slab tailplanes, and the delta was chosen for production. At least 30 pre-production aircraft had flown by the time service delivery started and the development effort was obviously considerable. The initial MiG-21 abounded in interesting features including Fowler flaps, fully powered controls, upward ejection seat fixed to the rear of the front-hinged canopy (which incorporated the whole front of the cockpit enclosure except the bullet-proof windshield) to act as a pilot blast-shield, and internal fuel capacity of only 410 gal. Armament was two 30mm NR-30 in long fairings under the fuselage, the left gun usually being replaced by avionics. Part of these avionics serve the two K-13 ("Atoll") missiles carried on wing pylons on the slightly more powerful 21F. This had radar ranging, 515 gal fuel broader fin, upward-hinged pitot boom attached under the nose (to prevent people walking into it) and two dorsal blade aerials. Czech-built aircraft (still called 21F) did not have the rear-view windows in the front of the dorsal spine. The F was called "Fishbed C" by NATO and Type 74 by the Indian Air Force; it was also the type supplied to China in 1959 and used as the pattern for the Chinese-built F-7. As the oldest active variant it was also the first exported or seen in the West, the Finnish AF receiving the 21F-12 in April 1963.

At Tushino in 1961 the prototype was displayed of what became the 21PF, with inlet diameter increased from 27in to 36in, completely changing the nose shape and providing room for a large movable centre-body housing the scanner of the R1L (NATO "Spin Scan") AI radar. Other changes include deletion of guns (allowing simpler forward airbrakes), bigger mainwheels (causing large fuselage bulges above the wing), pitot boom moved above the inlet, fatter dorsal spine (partly responsible for fuel capacity of 627gal) and many electronic changes. All PF had an uprated engine, late models had take-off rocket latches and final batches had completely new blown flaps (SPS) which cut landing speed by 25mph and reduced nose-up attitude for better pilot view. The FL was the export PF (L = *lokator*, denoting R2L radar) with even more powerful engine. Like the F models rebuilt in 1963–64, this can carry the GP-9 gunpack housing the excellent GSh-23 23mm twin-barrel gun, has a still further

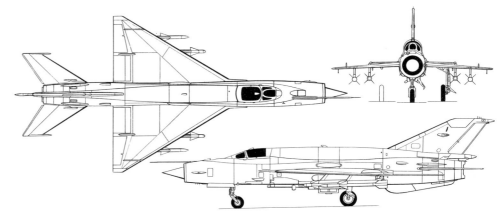

Above: Three-view of MiG-21 SMT (Fishbed-K).

broadened vertical tail and drag-chute repositioned above the jetpipe. The PFS was the PF with SPS blown flaps while the PFM was a definitive improved version with another 19in added to the fin (final fillet eliminated), a conventional seat and side-hinged canopy, and large flush aerials in the fin. One-off versions were built to prove STOL with lift jets and to fly a scaled "analogue" of the wing of the Tu-144 SST. The very important PFMA, made in huge numbers, was the first multi-role version, with straight top line from much deeper spine (housing equipment and not fuel and holding tankage to 572gal), and four pylons for two 1,100lb and two 551lb bombs, four S-24 missiles and/ or tanks or K-13A missiles. The 21M has an internal GSh-23 and since 1973 has been built in India as Type 88. The 21R has multi-sensor reconnaissance internally and in pods and wing-tip ECM fairings, as do late models of the 21MF, the first to have the new R-13 engine. The RF is the R-13-powered reconnaissance version. One of the few variants still in production is

the SMT, with fuel restored to the spine and more comprehensive avionics including tail-warning radar.

Code-named "Mongol" and called Type 66 in India, the U is the tandem trainer the US has SPS flaps and UM the R-13 engine and four pylons. Many other versions have been used to set world records. About 10,000 of all sub-types have been built, and in 1977 output was continuing at perhaps three per week in the Soviet Union, with a much lower rate in India; in early 1976 N Korea was said to be also in production. Many of the early models of this neat fighter were sweet to handle and quite effective day dogfighters, but the majority of the subtypes in use have many adverse characteristics and severe limitations.

In late 1976 a new version appeared, the MiG-21bis (Fishbed L); this is a cleaned-up and refined MiG-21MF with Tacan-type navigation and other improvements. Production was continuing in 1980 with a further version, the Fishbed-N, with a new engine and improved avionics.

Left: One of the several versions known as MiG-21 bis (in this case the type called Fishbed-L by NATO), with Tacan but still powered by the R-13-300 turbojet instead of the R-25.

Below: Another of the so-called Fishbed-L version, which has the new airframe of the MiG-21 bis family (with enlarged dorsal fairing and other changes) but retains the existing engine. Probably more than 8,000 MiG-21s have been built, virtually all of them in the Soviet Union.

Mikoyan/ Gurevich MiG-23

MiG-23, -23S and -23U ("Flogger")

Origin: The design bureau named for Mikoyan and Gurevich, Soviet Union; no production outside the Soviet Union yet reported.

Type: (-23S, Flogger B) single-seat all-weather interceptor with Flogger E export variant of unknown designation; (-23U, Flogger C) dual-control trainer and ECM platform.

Engine: One Tumansky afterburning turbofan, believed to be an R-29B rated at 17,640lb (8000kg) dry and 25,350lb (11,500kg) with afterburner.

Dimensions: (Estimated) Span (72° sweep) 28ft 7in (8·7m), (16°) 47ft 3in (14·4m); length (export) 53ft (16·15m), (S, U) 55ft 1½in (16·80m); height 13ft (3·96m).

Weights: (Estimated) empty 17,500lb (7940kg); loaded (clean or fighter mission) 30,000lb (13,600kg); maximum permissible 33,000lb (15,000kg).

Performance: Maximum speed, clean, 840mph (1350km/h, Mach 1·1) at sea level; maximum speed, clean, at altitude, 1,520mph (2445km/h, Mach 2·2); maximum Mach number with missiles (MiG-23S) about 2; service ceiling about 55,000ft (16,765m); combat radius (hi-lo-hi) about 400 miles (640km).

Armament: (-23S) one 23mm GSh-23 twin-barrel gun on ventral centreline, plus various mixes of air/air missiles which usually include one or two infra-red or radar-homing AA-7 "Apex" and/or infra-red or radar-homing AA-8 "Aphid", the latter for close combat; (-23U) none reported.

History: First flight, probably 1965; (first production aircraft) believed 1970; service delivery, believed 1971.

Development: Revealed at the 1967 Moscow Aviation Day, the prototype swing-wing MiG-23 was at first thought to be a Yakovlev design, though it appeared in company with a jet-lift STOL fighter having an identical rear fuselage and tail and strong MiG-21-like features (though much bigger than a MiG-21). Over the next four years the Mikoyan bureau greatly developed this aircraft, which originally owed something to the F-111 and Mirage G. By 1971 the radically different production versions, the -23S fighter and -23U trainer, were entering service in quantity, and by 1975 several hundred had been delivered to Warsaw Pact air forces and also to Egypt. Today Egypt is believed no longer to operate the type, but large deliveries have been made to other countries. The MiG-27 attack version is described separately.

There are three main versions. The first to enter service was the MiG-23S all-weather interceptor, with

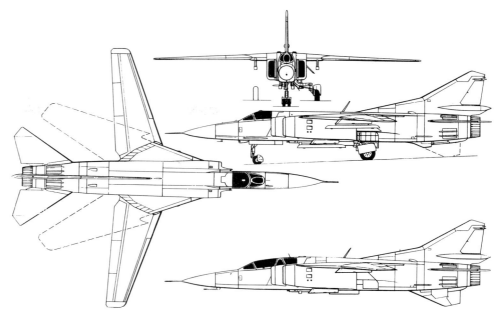

powerful highly-afterburning engine, "High Lark" nose radar (said in 1973 by the then Secretary of the USAF to be "comparable with that of the latest Phantom") and, almost certainly, a laser ranger and doppler navigator. ECM and other EW equipment is markedly superior to anything fitted in previous Soviet aircraft and apparently as good as comparable installations in Western fighters (other than the F-15).

Several hundred S models are in service with the IA-PVO and Warsaw Pact air forces, and they are replacing the Su-9 and -11 and Yak-28P. Missiles are carried on a centreline pylon (which often carries a drop-tank instead), on pylons under the inlet ducts and under the fixed wing gloves (centre section). For overseas customers a simplified sub-type is in production, with the same high-Mach airframe and systems as the -23S fighter but lacking the latter's radar (NATO calls this model "Flogger E" but the Soviet designation was unknown as this book went to press). The third MiG-23 so far seen is the tandem two-seat -23U, used for conversion training and as an ECM and reconnaissance platform. This again has the fighter's high-speed airframe and systems, but has not been seen with any weapons or delivery systems.

Above: Three-view of MiG-23S (Flogger-B) with (immediately above) a -23C (Flogger-C).

Below: Side elevation of a MiG-23S (Flogger-B) all-weather interceptor of the PVO. This example was fitted with a radome smaller than that normally fitted.

Foot of page: The six MiG-23 fighters from Kubinka airbase which visited Finland and France in the summer of 1978. Called Flogger-G by NATO, this version is not only simplified (possibly prior to flying to the West) but also has a smaller dorsal fin than all other versions known to be in service.

Mikoyan/ Gurevich MiG-25

MiG-25 ("Foxbat A"), -25R and -25U

Origin: The design bureau named for Mikoyan and Gurevich, Soviet Union.

Type: "Foxbat A" (believed to be MiG-25S), all-weather long-range interceptor; MiG-25R, reconnaissance; MiG-25U, tandem-seat dual trainer with stepped cockpits.

Engines: Two Tumansky R-266 afterburning turbojets each rated at 27,000lb (12,250kg) with full augmentation.

Dimensions: Span 46ft (14·0m); length ("A") 73ft 2in (22·3m), (R) 74ft 6in (22·7m), (U) about 76ft (23·16m); height 18ft 6in (5·63m).

Weights: (Fighter) empty 44,000lb (19,960kg); normal loaded 68,350lb (31,000kg); maximum loaded with external missiles or tanks 77,000lb (34,930kg).

Performance: (Estimated) maximum speed at altitude 2,100mph (3380km/h, Mach 3·2); initial climb, about 50,000ft (15,240m)/min; service ceiling 73,000ft (22,250m); high-altitude combat radius without external fuel, 700 miles (1130km).

Armament: ("-A") four underwing pylons each carrying one AA-6 air-to-air missile (two radar, two infra-red) or other store; no guns; ("B", "D", none; ("E") six new AAM called "AA-X-9").

History: First flight (E-266 prototype) probably 1964; (production reconnaissance version) before 1969; (production interceptor) probably 1969; service delivery (both) 1970 or earlier.

Development: This large and powerful aircraft set a totally new level in combat-aircraft performance. The prototypes blazed a trail of world records in 1965–67 including closed-circuit speeds, payload-to-height and rate of climb records. The impact of what NATO quickly christened "Foxbat" was unprecedented. Especially in the Pentagon, Western policymakers recognised that here was a combat aircraft that outclassed everything else, and urgent studies were put in hand for a new US Air Force fighter (F-15 Eagle) to counter it. By 1971 at

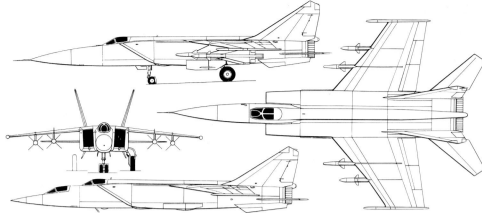

Above: MiG-25 and side-view of MiG-25U.

least two pairs of reconnaissance aircraft were flying with impunity over Israel, too high and fast for Phantoms to catch, while others have made overflights deep into Iran. This version is different in many respects, the nose having cameras instead of a "Fox Fire" radar, and other sensors being carried under the large body. Both versions have twin outward-sloping vertical tails, single mainwheels and a flush canopy shaped for speed rather than pilot view. From the start the main development effort has been applied to the basic MiG-25 (so-called "Foxbat A") interceptor, which has been developed in structure, systems and armament since first entering service with the PVO. In 1975 the original AA-5 missiles were supplemented, and later replaced, by the monster AA-6 "Acrid", which is easily the biggest air/air missile in service in the world. The radar-homing version has a length of about 20ft 2in (6·15m) and effective range of 28 miles (45km); the infra-red missiles have a length of just over 19ft (5·8m) and range of some 12·5 miles (20km). Another major im-

provement since entering service is flight-refuelling capability, not yet fitted to all MiG-25 versions. The detailed inspection of an interceptor version landed at Hakodate AB, Japan, on 6 September 1976, showed that in service pilots are forbidden to use the limits of the available flight performance, presumably to avoid thermal fatigue of the airframe; it also showed this particular machine to have early "Fox Fire" radar comparable in basic technology with the AWG-10 Phantom radar (as would be expected). Radars in current production are unquestionably solid-state pulse-doppler types able to look down and track low-flying aircraft against ground clutter. Several MiG-25s, most of them MiG-25R models on ELINT missions, have been plotted by Western radars at Mach 2·8. It should be emphasized that at this speed the MiG-25 — and any other aircraft — flies in a straight line. The MiG-25 was not designed for air combat, and if it became involved in a dogfight its speed would — like any other aircraft — soon be subsonic. The MiG-25U trainer carries neither weapons nor sensors, but is needed to convert pilots to what is still, 15 years after design, a very advanced and demanding aircraft.

Left: There are at least two reconnaissance versions of the MiG-25. This example is of the species called Foxbat-B by NATO, with comprehensive camera installation, as well as various IR or radar sensors around the nose. Another version, dubbed Foxbat-D, has no cameras but carries a large SLAR (side-looking airborne radar).

Below: One of the best illustrations of the basic MiG-25 interceptor, called Foxbat-A by NATO. Its main armament usually comprises four of the giant "AA-6 Acrid" missiles, two semi-active radar homing and two homing on the target's IR (heat) emission. It is thought that over 400 had been built by 1976.

Mikoyan/ Gurevich MiG-27

MiG-27 "Flogger D" and "Flogger F"

Origin: The design bureau named for Mikoyan and Gurevich, Soviet Union; no production outside the Soviet Union yet reported.

Type: Single-seat tactical attack, probably with reconnaissance capability.

Engine: One Tumansky R-29B afterburning turbofan rated at 17,640lb (8000kg) dry and 25,350lb (11,500kg) with full afterburner.

Dimensions: Similar to MiG-23 except fuselage nose is longer but pitot head shorter giving fractionally shorter overall length; height about 15ft (4·6m).

Weights: (estimated): Empty 17,300lb (7850kg); maximum loaded 39,130lb (17,750kg).

Performance: Maximum speed at low level (clean) about Mach 1·2, (maximum weight) subsonic; maximum speed at high altitude (clean) about 1,055mph (1700km/h, Mach 1·6); take-off to 50ft (15m) at 34,600lb (15,700kg) 2,625ft (800m); service ceiling (clean) about 50/000ft (15,250m); combat radius with bombs and one tank (hi-lo-hi) 600 miles (960km); ferry range (wings spread with three tanks) over 2,000 miles (3200km).

Armament: One 23mm six-barrel Gatling-type gun in belly fairing; seven external pylons (centreline, fuselage flanks under inlet ducts, swing wing gloves and swing-wings) for wide range of ordnance including guided missiles (AS-7 "Kerry") and tactical nuclear weapons to total weight of 4,200lb (1900kg). All ECM are internal and all pylons are thus usable by weapons or tanks. Those on the outer wings are not always fitted; they are piped for drop tanks, but do not pivot and thus may be loaded only when the wings remain unswept.

History: First flight, possibly about 1970; service delivery, before 1974.

Development: Derived from the same variable-geometry prototype flown by the MiG bureau at the 1967 Aviation Day, this aircraft was at first called "MiG-23B" in the West but is now known to have a different Soviet service designation that is almost certainly MiG-27. Bureau numbers are generally unknown for the MiG series; Mikoyan himself died in December 1970 and Gurevich in November 1976, and recent designs are known only by their service numbers. Compared with the MiG-23 this attack

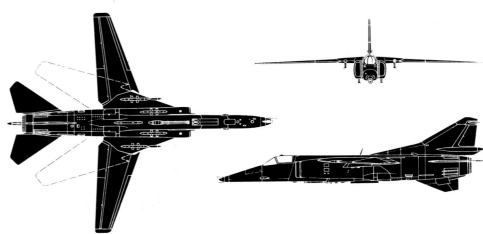

Above: Three-view of MiG-27 Flogger-D showing range of sweep and with underfin down.

version carries heavier loads and is simpler and optimised for low-level operation. The air-frame-differs in having a shallower nose with a flat pointed profile housing mapping/terrain-following radar, laser ranger, doppler radar and radio altimeter, with good pilot view ahead and downward. The cockpit is heavily armoured. The engine is more powerful than that of the MiG-23 but is fed by fixed inlets and has a shorter and simpler nozzle. Main wheels are fitted with large low-pressure

tyres, and special provision is made for rough-field operation. Internal ECM equipment is extensive, and pods on the wing-glove leading edges appear to contain an opto-electronic seeker (left) and passive radar receiver (right). Internal fuel capacity is estimated at 1,183 Imp gallons (5380lit) including fuel in the fin; no provision for flight refuelling has been noted. The "Flogger F" has the engine installation and gun of the MiG-23, with variable inlets, and lacks the comprehensive MiG-27 avionics. These are thought to be development aircraft or an export version. Possible problems with the basic ajrcraft are suggested by reports that in a few months the Syrian AF has written off 13 out of 50 supplied.

Left: Frontal Aviation pilots about to fly a training mission in their MiG-27 Flogger-Ds. Note the wings parked at full sweep and canopy curtain.

Below: A puzzling MiG-27 (Flogger-D type) with variable-geometry air inlets resembling those of the MiG-23 family.

Mil Mi-6 and Mi-10

Mi-6 ("Hook"), Mi-10 and -10K ("Harke")
Origin: The design bureau named for Mikhail Mil, Soviet Union.
Type: -6, heavy transport helicopter; -10, crane helicopter for bulky loads; -10K, crane helicopter.
Engines: (-6, -10) two 5,500shp Soloviev D-25V single-shaft free-turbine engines driving common R-7 gearbox; (-10K) two 6,500shp D-25VF.
Dimensions: Main rotor diameter 114ft 10in (35m); overall length (rotors turning) (-6) 136ft 11½in (41·74m); (-10, -10K) 137ft 5½in (41·89m); fuselage length (-6) 108ft 10½in (33·18m); (10, -10K) 107ft 9¾in (32·86m); height (-6) 32ft 4in (9·86m); (-10) 32ft 2in (9·8m); (-10K) 25ft 7in (7·8m).
Weights: Empty (-6, typical) 60,055lb (27,240kg); (-10) 60,185lb (27,300kg); (-10K) 54,410lb (24,680kg); maximum loaded (-6) 93,700lb (42,500kg); (-10) 96,340lb (43,700kg); (-10K) 83,776lb (38,000kg) with 5,500shp engines (90,390lb, 41,000kg expected with D-25VF engines).
Performance: Maximum speed (-6) 186mph (300 km/h) (set 100km circuit record at 211·36mph, beyond flight manual limit); (-10) 124mph (200km/h); service ceiling (-6) 14,750ft (4500m); (-10, -10K, limited) 9,842ft (3000m); range (-6 with half payload) 404 miles (650km); (-10 with 12,000kg platform load) 155 miles (250km); (-10K with 11,000kg payload, 6,500shp engines) over 280 miles (450km).
Armament: Normally none, but Mi-6 often seen with manually aimed nose gun of about 12·7mm calibre.
History: First flight (-6) probably early 1957; (-10) 1960; (-10K) prior to 1965.
Development: Development by Mikhail L. Mil's design bureau at Zaporozhye of the dynamic system (rotors and shafting) of the Mi-6 was a task matched only by Soloviev's development of the huge R-7 gearbox, which weighs 7,054lb (much more than the pair of engines). By far the biggest rotor system yet flown, this served to lift by far the biggest helicopter, the Mi-6 (NATO code name "Hook"), which quickly set world records for speed and payload, though the normal load is limited to 26,450lb (12,000kg) internally, loaded via huge clamshell rear doors, or 19,840lb (9000kg) externally slung. About 500 have been built, possibly half being in military use. Most have the rotor unloaded in cruising flight (typically 150mph) by a fixed wing of 50ft 2½in span. These huge helicopters have played an active role in field exercises carrying troops (typically 68) and tactical missiles or vehicles in the class of the BRDM. The Mi-10 (code name "Harke") has lofty landing gears which enable it to straddle a load, such as a bus or prefabricated building, 3·75m (12ft 3½in) high; heavy loads weighing 33,070lb (15,000kg) and up to over 65ft in length have been flown. It uses a TV viewing system for load control, but the short-legged Mi-10K has an under-nose gondola.

Right: An Mi-6 with external long-range tanks, 164 lmp gal (745 litres) on the left and 150 gal (682 litres) on right.

Below: This Mi-10 (Harke) is one of the original long-legged type designed to straddle its load.

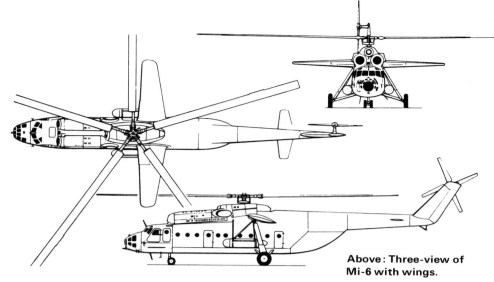

Above: Three-view of Mi-6 with wings.

Mil Mi-8

Mi-8, Mi-8T (NATO names "Hip", "Haze"), Mi-14

Origin: The design bureau named for Mikhail Mil, Soviet Union.

Type: General utility helicopter for internal loads and externally mounted weapons; "Haze", ASW.

Engines: Two 1,500shp Isotov TV2-117A single-shaft free-turbine engines driving common VR-8A gearbox.

Dimensions: Main rotor diameter 69ft 10$\frac{1}{2}$in (21·29m); overall length, rotors turning, 82ft 9$\frac{3}{4}$in (25·24m); fuselage length 60ft 0$\frac{3}{4}$in (18·31m); height 18ft 6$\frac{1}{2}$in) (5·65m).

Weights: Empty (-8T) 15,026lb (6816kg); maximum loaded (all) 26,455lb (12,000kg) (heavier weights for non-VTO operation).

Performance: Maximum speed 161mph (260km/h); service ceiling 14,760ft (4500m); range (-8T, full payload, 5 per cent reserve at 3,280ft) 298 miles (480km).

Armament: Optional fitting for external pylons for up to eight stores carried outboard of fuel tanks (always fitted); typical loads eight pods of 57mm rockets, or mix of gun pods and anti-tank missiles (Mi-8 not normally used in anti-tank role).

History: First flight 1960 or earlier; service delivery of military versions, before 1967.

Development: Originally powered by a single 2,700 shp Soloviev engine, the Mi-8 soon appeared with its present engines and in 1964 added a fifth blade to its main rotor. It has since been the chief general utility helicopter of the Warsaw Pact powers and many other nations. By mid-1974 it was announced that more than 1,000 had been built, the majority for military purposes and with about 300 having been exported. Since then the Mi-8 has continued in production. The basic version is a passenger and troop carrier normally furnished with quickly removable seats for 28 in the main cabin. The -8T is the utility version without furnishing and with circular windows, weapon pylons, cargo rings, a winch/pulley block system for loading and optional electric hoist by the front doorway. All versions have large rear clamshell doors (the passenger version having airstairs incorporated) through which a BRDM and other small vehicles can be loaded. "Haze" has AS radar, MAD bird and weapons.

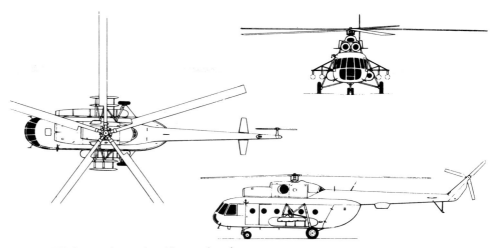

Above: Mi-8 assault version (four pylons).

Above: An Mi-14, called V-14 by the AV-MF Naval Air Force and Haze by NATO.

Below: One of the Jugoslav military (Hip) versions, pictured with a slung load.

Mil Mi-24

Mi-24 versions with NATO names "Hind-A" to "Hind-F"

Origin: The design bureau named for Mikhail Mil, Soviet Union.

Type: Tactical multi-role helicopter.

Engines: Two turboshafts of estimated 1,500shp each, derived from Isotov TV2-117A but shorter.

Dimensions: (Estimated) diameter of five-blade main rotor 55ft 9in (17m); length overall (ignoring rotors) 55ft 9in (17m); height overall 14ft (4·25m).

Weights: (Estimated) empty 14,300lb (6500kg); maximum loaded 25,400lb (11,500kg).

Performance: Maximum speed 170mph (275km/h); general performance, higher than Mi-8.

Armament: (Hind-A) usually one 12·7mm gun aimed from nose; two stub wings providing rails for four wire-guided anti-tank missiles and four other stores (bombs, missiles, rocket or gun pods). (Hind-B) two stub wings of different type with four weapon pylons.

History: First flight, before 1972; service delivery, before 1974.

Development: Appearance in East Germany of this totally new helicopter in 1974 heralded a fantastic strengthening of the only area in which Soviet forces had previously been outclassed by those of the United States. The Mi-24 is a substantial machine in the same size and power class as the later Sikorsky UH-60 Black Hawk, and since 1974 a number considerably exceeding 1,000 have gone into service mainly with Air Armies in occupied countries of Eastern Europe. "Hind-A" is an assault transport, with crew of four, seats for eight armed troops in the main cabin, various sensors and large weapon "wings" carrying four "Swatter" anti-tank missiles (by 1980 being replaced by the even more lethal tube-launched "Spiral") as well as other stores which can include 128 rockets of 57mm calibre. "Hind-B" carries fewer weapons and may have been a pre-production model. "Hind-C" is a cleaned-up variant without the usual nose gun and sensors, and may be the so-called A-10 (possibly a true designation) used to set various speed records in the hands of women pilots at up to 368·4km/h (229mph) and in one case powered by 2,200snp TV3-117 engines. "Hind-D" is a gunship with redesigned front fuselage (see drawing) and tail rotor on the left; it is extremely well equipped with night and all-weather sensors. "Hind-E" has not been reported, but "Hind-F" is a variant in East Germany in 1979 with six anti-tank missiles.

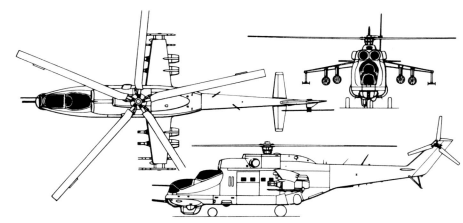

Above: Three-view of Mi-24 gunship Hind-D.

Above: One of the first examples of the so-called Hind-A version to be seen with the Group of Soviet Forces in Germany.

Below: Dusk picture of Hind-D gunships on exercise. By 1980 there were at least eight major versions of Mi-24s in service.

Myasishchev M-4

M-4 (three versions, known to West as "Bison A, B and C")
Origin: The design bureau of Vladimir M. Myasishchev, Soviet Union.
Type: "Bison-A", originally heavy bomber, now tanker; B, maritime reconnaissance; C, multi-role reconnaissance and electronic warfare.
Engines: (A) four 19,180lb (8700kg) Mikulin AM-3D single-shaft turbo-jets; (B and C) four 28,660lb (13,000kg) Soloviev D-15 two-shaft turbojets.
Dimensions: (A) estimated, span 165ft 7½in (50·48m); length 154ft 10in (47·2m); height 46ft (14·1m).
Weights: Estimated, empty (A) 154,000lb (70,000kg); (B, C) 176,400lb (80,000kg); maximum loaded (A) 352,740lb (160,000kg); (B, C) 375,000lb (170,000kg).
Performance: (Estimated) maximum speed (all) 560mph (900km/h); service ceiling (A) 42,650ft (13,000m); (B, C) 49,200ft (15,000m); range (all) 6,835 miles (11,000km) with 9,920lb (4500kg) of bombs or electronic equipment.
Armament: (A) ten 23mm NR-23 cannon in manned turret in tail and four remotely controlled turrets above and below front and rear fuselage (two guns in each turret); internal bomb bays in tandem for at least 22,050lb (10,000kg) stores; (B, C) six 23mm cannon in two forward turrets and tail turret; internal bay for at least 10,000lb (4500kg) stores. In many versions a single 23mm gun is fixed on the right side of the nose, firing ahead.
History: First flight, probably 1953; service delivery, probably 1955; final delivery, probably about 1958.
Development: A single example of this large aircraft took part in the 1954 May Day parade fly past over Moscow, its size being gauged from the escorting

Right: This so-called Bison-B was seen and photographed by an RAF Lightning near Scotland. Most of this version retained the manned rear turret.

Below: Tanker's view of a Bison-C acting as receiver in refuelling by the British probe/drogue method (for which no licence fee was ever paid). About 31 Bison tankers are now in use. They are not included in the SALT agreement tally of bombers.

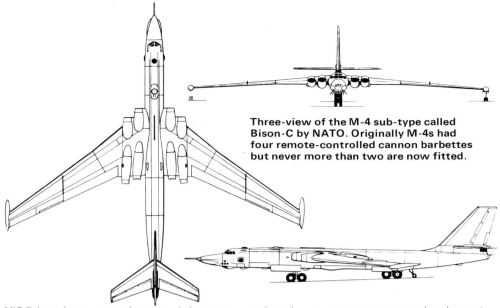

Three-view of the M-4 sub-type called Bison-C by NATO. Originally M-4s had four remote-controlled cannon barbettes but never more than two are now fitted.

MiG fighters. It was expected to appear in large numbers, but little was heard of it for years. In fact a useful run of about 150 had been delivered, at first being used as bombers ("Bison A"). In 1959 a re-engined aircraft, called Type 201-M, set up world records by lifting a payload of 10,000kg (22,046lb) to 50,253ft (15,317m) and the formidable weight of 55,220kg (121,480lb) to 2000m (6,561ft). By this time the M-4 bombers were being likewise fitted with more powerful engines, and their role changed from bomber to long-range oversea reconnaissance, ECM and, in some cases, flight-refuelling tanker. All aircraft were given large fixed FR probes, the rear turrets were removed and a vast amount of special reconnaissance equipment fitted, with from five to 17 aerials visible all over the aircraft. In the "Bison C" sub-type a large search radar fills the engine nose, lengthening the nose by about 6ft and changing its shape. Since 1967 these now obsolescent aircraft have been frequently encountered on probing missions far over the Arctic, Atlantic, Pacific and else-elsewhere, at both high and low levels, the C-model having been seen most frequently. In the SALT II agreement the number of M-4 tankers of "Bison-A" type was given as 31.

Sukhoi Su-7

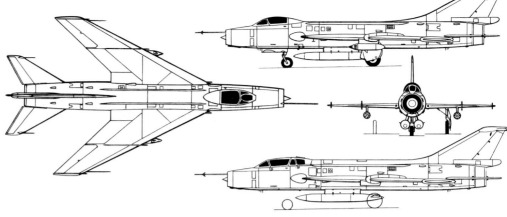

Su-7B, -7BM, -7BMK and -7U; NATO name "Fitter"
Origin: The design bureau of Pavel A. Sukhoi, Soviet Union.
Type: Single-seat close-support and interdiction; (-7U) dual-control trainer.
Engine: One Lyulka AL-7F turbojet rated at 15,430lb (7000kg) dry or 22,046lb (10,000kg) with maximum afterburner.
Dimensions: Span 29ft 3½in (8·93m), length (all, incl probe) 57ft (17·37m); height (all) 15ft 5in (4·70m).
Weights: Empty (typical -7) 19,000lb (8620kg), maximum loaded (typical -7) 30,000lb (13,610kg).
Performance: Maximum speed, clean, at altitude, (all) 1,055mph (1700km/h, Mach 1·6), initial climb (-7BM) 29,000ft (9120m)/min; service ceiling (-7BM) 49,700ft (15,150m); range with twin drop tanks (all) 900 miles (1450km).
Armament: (-7) two 30mm NR-30 cannon, each with 70 rounds; four wing pylons, inners rated at 1,653lb (750kg) and outers at 1,102lb (500kg), but when two tanks are carried on fuselage pylons total external weapon load is reduced to 2,205lb (1000kg).
History: First flight (-7 prototype) not later than 1955; service delivery (-7B) 1959.
Development: Two of the wealth of previously unknown Soviet aircraft revealed at the 1956 Aviation Day at Tushino were large Sukhoi fighters, one with a swept wing (called "Fitter" by NATO) and the other a tailed delta (called "Fishpot"). Both were refined into operational types, losing some of their commonality in the process. The delta entered service as the Su-9 and -11, described separately. The highly-swept Su-7 was likewise built in very large numbers, optimised not for air superiority but for ground attack. As such it has found a worldwide market, and despite severe shortcomings has been exported in numbers which exceed 700. All Sukhoi combat aircraft have been made within the Soviet Union. The good points of the Su-7 family are robust structure, reasonable reliability and low cost; drawbacks are vulnerability to small-calibre fire and the impossibility of getting adequate field length, weapon load and radius of action

all together. There are many variants. The original -7B was quickly superseded by the more powerful -7BM, with twin ribbon tail chutes. The most common export model is the -7BMK with low-pressure tyres and other changes to improve behaviour from short unpaved strips. The -7U is the tandem dual trainer. Since 1964 many BMK have been seen with take-off rockets and four wing pylons.

Above: Three-view of Su-7BMK (still known as Fitter-A) with side-view of -7U Moujik.

Below: Very large numbers of Su-7B ground-attack fighters were built, but those remaining in FA service are trainers.

Sukhoi Su-9 and Su-11

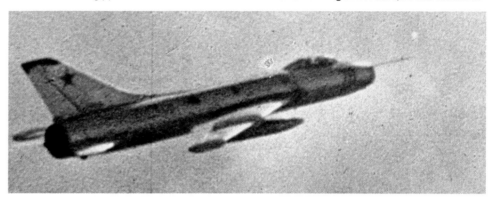

Su-9 "Fishpot B", Su-9U "Maiden" and Su-11 "Fishpot C"
Origin: The design bureau named for Pavel O. Sukhoi, Soviet Union.
Type: Single-seat all-weather interceptor (Su-9U, two-seat trainer).
Engine: One Lyulka single-shaft turbojet with afterburner; (Su-9 and -9U) AL-7F rated at 19,840lb (9000kg) thrust with maximum afterburner; (Su-11) AL-7F-1 rated at 22,046lb (10,000kg).
Dimensions: Span 27ft 8in (8·43m); length (-9, -9U) about 54ft (16·5m), (-11) 57ft (17·4m); height 16ft (4·9m).
Weights: (All, estimated) empty 20,000lb (9070kg); loaded (typical mission) 27,000lb (12,250kg), maximum) 30,000lb (13,610kg).
Performance: (-11, estimated) maximum speed (clean, sea level) 720mph (1160km/h, Mach 0·95), (clean, optimum height) 1,190mph (1910km/h, Mach 1·8), (two missiles and two tanks at optimum height) 790mph (1270km/h, Mach 1·2); initial climb 27,000ft (8230m)/min; service ceiling (clean) 55,700ft (17,000m); range (two missiles, two tanks) about 700 miles (1125km).
Armament: (-9) four AA-1 "Alkali" air-to-air missiles; (-9U) same as -9, or not fitted; (-11) two AS-3 "Anab" air-to-air missiles, one radar and the other IR.
History: First flight (-9) before 1956; (-11) probably 1966; service delivery (-9) probably 1959, (-11) 1967.
Development: When first seen, at the 1956 Tushino display, one prototype delta-winged Sukhoi fighter had a small conical radome above the plain nose inlet, while a second had a conical centrebody. The latter arrangement was chosen for production as the Su-9, though development was rather protracted. At first sharing the same engine installation, rear fuselage and tail as the Su-7, the Su-9 eventually came to have no parts exactly common. No gun was ever seen on an Su-9 by Western intelligence, the primitive missiles being the only armament. At least 2,000 were built, an additional number, probably supplemented by conversions, being tandem-seat trainers with a cockpit slightly different from that of the Su-7U. The Su-11 is

Above: Three-view of Su-11 with Anab AAMs.

Right: This PVO all-weather interceptor is an Su-11, most of which have been replaced by the Su-15 in first-line units. It is an appreciably larger aircraft than the superficially similar MiG-21.

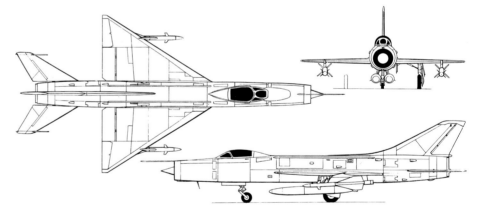

cleaned up in every part of the airframe, has a longer and less-tapered nose with larger radar centrebody, completely different armament (still without guns) and a fuselage similar to the Su-7B with external duct fairings along the top on each side. Though much larger and more powerful than the MiG-21, these interceptors have an almost identical tailed-delta configuration. Unlike the MiG-21 they have all-weather capability (interpreted as "night and rain" rather than true all-weather), but are still limited in radius, endurance and armament. In the early 1970s as many as 800 of both types were in service with the IA-PVO, but by 1980 nearly all had been replaced by Su-15s and other types. Many may have been converted into dual-control "Maiden" trainers, including some that are basically Su-11s.

Sukhoi Su-15

Versions known to the West are code-named "Flagon-A to -E"
Origin: The design bureau of Pavel O. Sukhoi, Soviet Union.
Type: Most versions, all-weather interceptor.
Engines: Two afterburning engines, believed to be Tumansky R-25 turbofans each rated at 9,000lb (4000kg) dry and 16,530lb (7500kg) with afterburner.
Dimensions: Span (A) 31ft 3in (9·50m), (D) about 36ft (11·0m); length (all) 70ft 6in (21·50m); height 16ft 6in (5·0m).
Weights: (Estimated) empty (A) 24,000lb (10,900kg), (D) 26,000lb (11,800kg); normal loaded (A) 35,275lb (16,000kg); maximum loaded (D) 46,000lb (21,000kg).
Performance: (Estimated) maximum speed at altitude, with two missiles, 1,520mph (2445km/h, Mach 2·3); initial climb 35,000ft (10,670m)/min; service ceiling 65,000ft (19,800m); combat radius 450 miles (725km); ferry range about 1,400 miles (2250km).
Armament: Two underwing pylons normally carry one radar "Anab" and one infra-red "Anab"; two fuselage pylons normally carry drop tanks, often with a 23mm GSh-23 two-barrel cannon between them; other missiles such as AA-6 or AA-7 are probably now being carried (but not yet seen by the West).
History: First flight (Su-15 prototype) probably 1964; (production Su-15) probably 1967.
Development: Following naturally on from the Su-11, and strongly resembling earlier aircraft in wings and tail, the Su-15 has two engines which not only confer increased performance but also leave the nose free for a large AI radar. The initial "Flagon-A" version entered IA-PVO Strany service in 1969. "Flagon-B" is a STOL rough-field version with three lift jets in the fuselage and a revised "double delta" wing. "Flagon-C" is the Su-15U dual trainer, "-D" is basically a "-B" without lift jets, and "-E" has completely updated electronics and the same extended wing but with further leading-edge improvements; the latest and probably final version is "Flagon-F" with an ogival radome suggesting use of a larger aerial and possibly a completely new radar. It has been speculated that some late examples have an internal gun. In 1971 a US official estimated that 400 Su-15 were in service, with production at

about 15 monthly. In early 1976 an estimate of PVO establishment gave the number of all Su-15 versions in combat service as 600. Since then production has continued and today these extremely high-performance aircraft are judged to provide more than half the total PVO force of 2,600 all-weather interceptors, roughly 2,450 more than in any other air force!

Above: Three-view of Su-15 Flagon-F.

Below: IA-PVO officers in a very posed propaganda picture (ladders both sides of the cockpit) with an Su-15 Flagon-D.

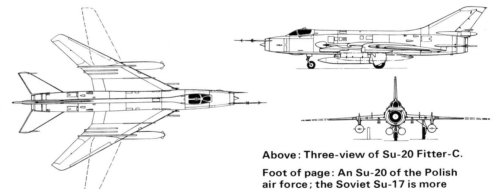

Sukhoi Su-17 and Su-20

Su-17 "Fitter C", Su-20 and Su-22
Origin: The design bureau named for Pavel O. Sukhoi, Soviet Union.
Type: Single-seat attack and close-support aircraft.
Engine: (-17) one Lyulka AL-21F-3 single-shaft turbojet with afterburner rated at 17,200lb (7800kg) dry and 25,000lb (11,340kg) with maximum afterburner, (-20, -22) believed to be AL-7F-1 rated at 22,046lb (10,000kg).
Dimensions: (all): Span (28°) 45ft 11¼in (14·00m), (62°) 34ft 9½in (10·60m); length (incl probe) 61ft 6¼in (18·75m); height 15ft 7in (4·75m).
Weights: (-17 estimated, -20 and -22 slightly less) empty 22,046lb (10,000kg); loaded (clean) 30,865lb (14,000kg), (maximum) 41,887lb (19,000kg).
Performance: (-17, clean) maximum speed at sea level 798mph (1284km/h, Mach 1·05), maximum speed at optimum height 1,432mph (2305km/h, Mach 2·17); initial climb 45,275ft (13,800m)/min; service ceiling 59,050ft (18,000m); combat radius with 4,410lb (2000kg) external stores (hi-lo-hi) 391 miles (630km).
Armament: Two 30mm NR-30 cannon, each with 70 rounds, in wing roots; eight pylons under fuselage, fixed gloves and swing-wings for maximum external load of 11,023lb (5000kg) including the AS-7 "Kerry" air-to-surface missile (-20, -22, six pylons).

Above: Three-view of Su-20 Fitter-C.

Foot of page: An Su-20 of the Polish air force; the Soviet Su-17 is more powerful.

History: Service delivery 1970 (-17); 1972–3 (-20).
Development: A logical direct modification of the somewhat limited Su-7B, the Su-17 has variable-geometry "swing-wings" pivoted far outboard, hinged to a slightly modified -7B centre section with strengthened landing gear. At maximum sweep the trailing edge of the centre section aligns with the outer section, and it carries two shallow fences on each side. At the pivots are large square-fronted fences combined with pylons which are stressed to carry 2,200lb (1000kg) stores which in the Polish Su-20 are invariably drop tanks with nose fins. The swing-wings carry full-span slats,

slotted ailerons and flaps which retract inside the centre section. Compared with the Su-7B the result is the ability to lift twice the external load from airstrips little more than half as long, and climb and level speed at all heights are much increased, even in the lower-powered Su-20 and export Su-22. Equipment in the -17 includes SRD-5M "High Fix" radar, an ASP-5ND fire-control system and comprehensive communications and IFF. Landing performance is so much better than the -7B that a braking chute is not fitted; in its place is the aft-facing aerial for a Sirena 3 radar homing and warning system at the rear of the prominent dorsal spine.

Sukhoi Su-24

Su-24 versions known to NATO as "Fencer"

Origin: The design bureau of Pavel O. Sukhoi, Soviet Union.

Type: Two-seat multi-role combat aircraft.

Engines: Two afterburning turbofan or turbojet engines, probably two 24,500lb (11,113kg) Lyulka AL-21F3.

Dimensions: (Estimated) span (spread, about 22°) 56ft 3in (17·5m), swept (about 72°) 31ft 3in (9·53m); length 69ft 10in (21·29m); height 21ft (6·4m).

Weights: (Estimated) empty 35,000lb (15,875kg); maximum loaded 70,000lb (31,750kg).

Performance: (Estimated) maximum speed, clean, 950mph (1530km/h, Mach 1·25) at sea level, about 1,650mph (2655km/h, Mach 2·5) at altitude; initial climb, over 40,000ft (12,200m)/min; service ceiling, about 60,000ft (18,290m), combat radius with maximum weapons, about 500 miles (805km); ferry range, over 2,500 miles (4025km).

Armament: One 23mm GSh-23 twin-barrel cannon in lower centreline; at least six pylons on fuselage, fixed and swinging wings, for wide range of stores including

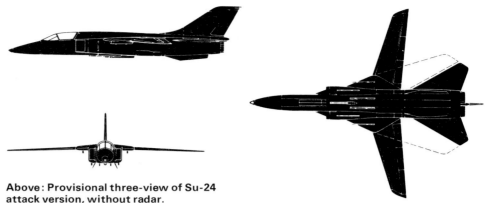

Above: Provisional three-view of Su-24 attack version, without radar.

guided and unguided air-to-ground or air-to-air missiles.

History: First flight, probably about 1970; service delivery, 1974 or earlier.

Development: First identified publicly in the West by the Chairman of the US Joint Chiefs of Staff, who

described it as "the first modern Soviet fighter to be developed specifically as a fighter-bomber for the ground-attack mission", this aircraft will probably be the chief tactical attack aircraft of the Soviet V-VS throughout the early 1980s. Until 1980 it was thought

Tupolev Tu-16

Tupolev bureau designation, Tu-88; NATO names "Badger-A" to "Badger-K". Chinese designation B-6.

Origin: The design bureau of Andrei N. Tupolev, Soviet Union; built (probably without licence) at Shenyang, China.

Type: Designed as strategic bomber; see text.

Engines: Believed in all versions, two Mikulin AM-3M single-shaft turbo-jets each rated at about 20,950lb (9500kg).

Dimensions: Span (basic) 110ft (33·5m) (varies with FR system, ECM and other features); length (basic) 120ft (36·5m) (varies with radar or glazed nose); height 35ft 6in (10·8m).

Weights: Empty, typically about 72,750lb (33,000kg) in early versions, about 82,680lb (37,500kg) in maritime/ECM roles; maximum loaded, about 150,000lb (68,000kg).

Performance: Maximum speed, clean at height, 587mph (945km/h); initial climb, clean, about 4,100ft (1250m)/min; service ceiling 42,650ft (13,000m); range with maximum weapon load, no missiles, 3,000 miles (4,800km); extreme reconnaissance range, about 4,500 miles (7250km).

Armament: In most variants, six 23mm NR-23 cannon in radar-directed manned tail turret and remote-aimed upper dorsal and rear ventral barbettes; versions without nose radar usually have seventh NR-23 fixed firing ahead on right side of nose. Internal weapon bay for load of 19,800lb (9000kg), with certain versions equipped to launch missiles (see text).

History: First flight (Tu-88), believed 1952; service delivery 1954; final delivery (USSR) about 1959, (China) after 1975.

Development: Representing a simple and low-risk approach to the strategic jet-bomber requirement, the

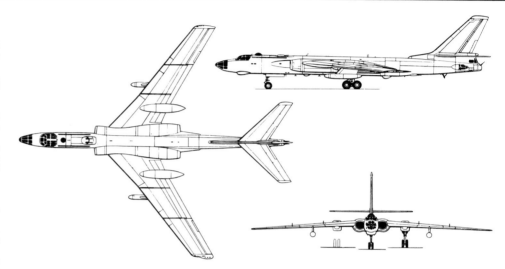

Above: Three-view of Tu-16 Badger-F.

Tu-88 prototype was generally in the class of the Valiant but incorporated heavy defensive armament. Technology throughout was derived directly from the Boeing B-29, which Tupolev's bureau had in 1945–53 built in large numbers as the Tu-4. The first ("Badger A") version had blind-bombing radar and glazed nose, and a few were supplied to Egypt and Iraq. The B carried two "Kennel" cruise missiles on underwing pylons and served the AV-MF (Navy) and Indonesian AF. C carried the large "Kipper" stand-off missile on the centre-line, with panoramic nose radar for ship search

and missile guidance. D is a maritime reconnaissance type, with comprehensive radars and ECM. E is a photo and multi-sensor reconnaissance type, F is an E with major new ECM and ESM installations, and G is an updated B which launched many missiles against Israel in 1973. H is a stand-off or escort electronic-warfare platform with many new equipments including powerful chaff dispensers. J is a specialized ECM jammer with further new electronics including a "canoe radome" projecting from the former bomb bay. K is another electronic reconnaissance model, with various new aerials including deep blisters at the front and rear of the former bomb bay.

Tupolev Tu-26

Two main versions with NATO code names "Backfire-A" and "-B"

Origin: The design bureau named for Andrei N. Tupolev, Soviet Union.

Type: Reconnaissance bomber and missile platform with probable crew of four.

Engines: Two afterburning turbofans, probably Kuznetsov NK-144 two-shaft engines each with maximum rating of 48,500lb (22,000kg).

Dimensions: Span (15°) 113ft (34·44m), (56°) 86ft (26·2m); length (excluding probe) 132ft (40·23m); heights 33ft (10·1m).

Weights: (Estimated) 99,250lb (45,000kg) maximum loaded 270,000lb (122,500kg).

Performance: (Estimated, "Backfire B") maximum speed at altitude 1,320mph (2125km/h, Mach 2·0); speed at sea level, Mach 0·9; service ceiling over 60,000ft (18,290m); maximum combat radius on internal fuel 2,110 miles (3400km); ferry range, about 5,900 miles (9500km).

Armament: Internal weapon bay(s) for free-fall bombs up to largest thermonuclear sizes, with provision for carrying two AS-6 stand-off missiles (often only one) on external wing racks; nominal weapon load 17,500lb (7935kg).

History: First flight (-A prototype) not later than 1969; (-B) probably 1973; entry to service, probably 1974.

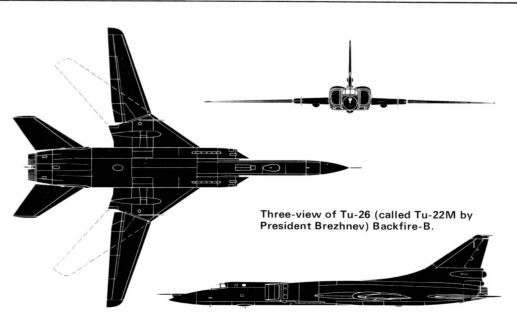

Three-view of Tu-26 (called Tu-22M by President Brezhnev) Backfire-B.

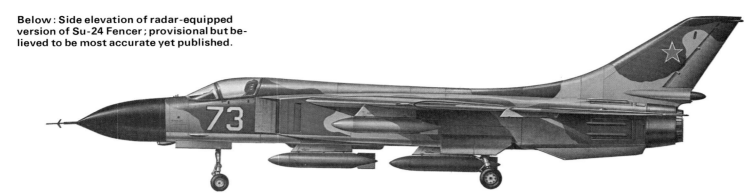

to be the Su-19 but it is now known to be the Su-24 (an even-numbered "bomber" designation). Like the rival but much smaller MiG-27, the Su-24 is an extremely clean machine strongly reminiscent of the F-111 and Mirage G, having side-by-side seats and wing and tailplane at the same level, as in the US machine, yet following the French aircraft in general layout. In general capability the nearest Western equivalent is the F-14 Tomcat, which shows just how formidable this aircraft is. Whereas "Foxbat" was on many Western lips in the 1960s, so was "Fencer" a big scare-word in the 1970s. Features of the first service version include a typical Sukhoi tail, but with ventral fins; double-shock side inlets; full-span slats and double-slotted flaps; and very extensive avionics (thought to include a multi-mode attack radar, doppler, laser ranger and very comprehensive EW/ECM installations).

Tupolev Tu-20

Tupolev bureau designation, Tu-95 for versions with NATO names "Bear-A" to "Bear-E" and Tu-142 for version called "Bear-F".
Origin: The design bureau of Andrei N. Tupolev, Soviet Union.
Type: Designed as strategic bomber, see text.
Engines: Four 14,795ehp Kuznetsov NK-12M single-shaft turboprops.
Dimensions: Span 159ft (48·5m); length 155ft 10in (47·50m) (certain versions differ by up to 6ft); height 38ft 8in (11·78m).
Weights: Empty, probably about 160,000lb (72,600kg); maximum loaded (estimate) about 340,000lb (154,000kg).
Performance: Maximum speed (typical Bear, clean) 540mph (870km/h); service ceiling, about 44,000ft (13,400m); range with 25,000lb (11,340kg) bomb load, 7,800 miles (12,550km).
Armament: Normally six 23mm NS-23 in radar-directed manned tail turret and remote-aimed dorsal and ventral barbettes (defensive guns often absent from late conversions); internal weapon bay for load of about 25,000lb (11,340kg).
History: First flight (prototype) mid-1954; service delivery, 1956; final delivery, probably about 1962.
Development: Making use of identical systems, techniques and even similar airframe structures as the Tu-16, the Tu-95 (service designation, Tu-20) is much larger and has roughly double the range of its turbojet predecessor. The huge swept wing, forming integral tanks, was a major accomplishment in 1952–54, as were the monster turboprop engines and their eight-blade 18ft 4½in (5·6m) contraprops. The basic bomber called "Bear A" had a glazed nose, chin radar and gun-sight blisters on the rear fuselage. First seen in 1961, "Bear B" featured a solid nose with enormous radome,

Above: Three-view of Tu-20 of Bear-D.

refuelling probe and centreline attachment for a large cruise missile ("Kangaroo"). C appeared in 1964 with a large new blister on each side of the fuselage (on one side only on B), while D was obviously a major ECM/ESM reconnaissance type with chin radar, very large belly radar, and from 12 to 21 avionic features visible from stem to stern. E is a multi-sensor reconnaissance conversion of A, while F is a recent further conversion for anti-submarine warfare with an extended forward fuselage, longer inboard nacelles (said to be for aerodynamic reasons), completely changed avionic and sensor installations, and rear-fuselage stores bays, one replacing the lower rear gun barbette. Under the SALT II agreement it is agreed that this version, about 25 of which are in use, need not be counted as a strategic bomber.

Development: Owing to the obvious inability of the Tu-22 to fly strategic missions the Tupolev bureau designed this far more formidable aircraft, larger in size and fitted with a swing-wing. "Backfire-A" was apparently not a very successful design, with multi-wheel main gears folding into large fairings projecting in typical Tupolev fashion behind the only moderately swept wing. About half the gross wing area was fixed, just the outer portions swinging through a modest arc. Today's "Backfire-B", which is believed to have the service designation of Tu-26, has no landing-gear boxes and is improved in other ways, though the details are still largely a matter for conjecture. The large engines are fed through wide inlet ducts which probably pass above the wing; a flight refuelling probe is fitted above the nose, but even without this "Backfire-B" has an endurance of some ten hours. The Chairman of the US Joint Chiefs of Staff said in 1974: "It is expected to replace some of both the current medium and heavy bombers and, when deployed with a compatible tanker force, constitutes a potential threat to the continental United States." The speed of development is also disquieting to the West, because these aircraft were being encountered on long oversea missions in early 1975. Even in 1977 details of the aircraft were sparse, not even its correct Soviet bureau or service designations having surfaced publicly. It is believed to have a crew of three, a very large radar and extremely sophisticated ECM/EW fits. The internal bomb load has been estimated at the low level of 17,500lb (B-1 carries 6·5 times as much), and the Russian insistence on having a radar-directed tail cannon is believed to have prevailed over those who think such installations a waste of cost and payload. Unusual features include the double-taper outer wings pivoted no less than 19ft from the centreline; another puzzle is where the landing gears are in the main production (B) version. Production rate is estimated at 30 per year, the figure President Brezhnev assured President Carter would not be exceeded, and number in service in 1980 is put at about 200. The Soviet president's statement designated this aircraft "Tu-22M"; M in Russian normally stands for *modi-* *fikatsirovanni*, or modified, but comparison with the Tu-22 will show that the two have little in common apart from a family likeness on a vastly different scale of size, weight and power. President Brezhnev insisted the aircraft was not of intercontinental range and that such range would not be imparted "in any other manner, including by in-flight refuelling" — again a strange statement since the only clear pictures available have shown a flight refuelling probe already fitted!

Below: Side elevation of Tu-26 (Tu-22M) Backfire-B in AV-MF colour for Arctic use, with "SA-6 Kingfish" missile.

Tupolev Tu-22

Tu-22 in versions known to West as "Blinder A" to "Blinder D"; Tupolev bureau, Tu-105
Origin: The design bureau of Andrei N. Tupolev, Soviet Union.
Type: Originally bomber; see text.
Engines: Two afterburning turbojets, of unknown type, each with maximum rating estimated at 27,000lb (12,250kg).
Dimensions: Span 90ft 10½in (27·70m); length (most versions) 132ft 11½in (40·53m); height 35ft 0in (10·67m).
Weights: Empty, about 85,000lb (38,600kg); maximum loaded, about 185,200lb (84,000kg).
Performance: Maximum speed (clean, at height) 920mph (1480km/h, Mach 1·4); initial climb, about 11,500ft (3500m)/min; service ceiling 59,000ft (18,000m); range (high, internal fuel only) 1,400 miles (2250km).
Armament: One 23mm NS-23 in radar-directed barbette in tail; internal weapon bay for at least 20,000lb (9070kg) of free-fall bombs or other stores or

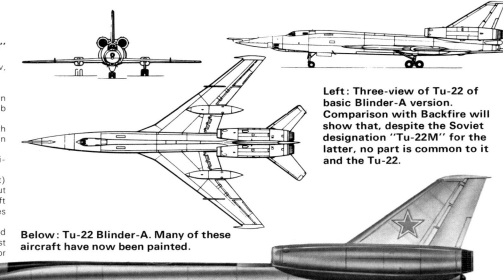

Left: Three-view of Tu-22 of basic Blinder-A version. Comparison with Backfire will show that, despite the Soviet designation "Tu-22M" for the latter, no part is common to it and the Tu-22.

Below: Tu-22 Blinder-A. Many of these aircraft have now been painted.

(Blinder B) one "Kitchen" stand-off cruise missile semi-recessed under centreline.
History: First flight, well before public display in 1961; service delivery, probably 1963.
Development: Having an efficient wing closely related to that of the Tu-28P, this supersonic bomber is a large aircraft with a bigger body and higher gross weight than the USAF B-58 Hustler. Typical crew appears to be a pilot, upward-ejecting, and two more members in tandem at a lower level who eject downwards. "Blinder A" was a reconnaissance aircraft, seen in small numbers. B carried the stand-off missile, had a larger nose radar and semi-flush FR probe. C is the main variant, used by Naval Aviation for oversea ECM/ESM surveillance, multi-sensor reconnaissance and with limited weapon capability. D is a dual trainer with stepped cockpits. Recent versions appear to have later engines (probably turbofans) with greater airflow. There have been persistent reports of an interceptor version, but this seems unlikely. The abiding short-coming of the Tu-22 has been limited range, only partially alleviated by flight refuelling.

Right: Gears retract following takeoff of a Tu-22 of the type called Blinder-D by NATO. The chief feature distinguishing this version is the additional instructor cockpit behind and higher than the first.

Tupolev Tu-126

Design bureau Tu-126; service designation, possibly Tu-24 (NATO name "Moss")
Origin: The design bureau named for Andrei N. Tupolev, Soviet Union.
Type: Airborne warning and control system.
Engines: Four 14,795ehp Kuznetsov NK-12MV single-shaft turboprops.
Dimensions: Span 167ft 8in (51·10m); length 182ft 6in (55·48m), (with FR probe) 188ft 0in (57·30m); height overall 52ft 8in (16·05m).
Weights: Empty (estimate) 198,400lb (90,000kg); maximum loaded 375,000lb (170,000kg).
Performance: Probable maximum speed 500mph (805km/h); on-station height 40,000ft (12,200m); normal operational endurance 18hr; ferry range at least 6,000 miles (9,650km).
History: First flight probably 1962–64; service delivery not later than 1967.
Development: Tupolev's family of swept-wing turboprops, bigger and faster than any others ever put into service, began with the long-range bomber Tu-95 (service designation Tu-20). From this evolved the considerably bigger Tu-114 civil airliner and the same-size Tu-114D special transport. The Tu-114 was never used as the basis for a large military freighter, but it was tailor-made for the Tu-126 AWACS (airborne warning and control system). Even examination of photographs indicates that this is a sophisticated and highly developed aircraft. Though details are sparse in the West, it is unlikely that its surveillance radar can quite equal that of the Boeing E-3A. On the other hand there is an element of wishful thinking in the supposed US belief that it is "of limited effectiveness over water and ineffective over land." At least one Tu-126 was detached with its crew to serve with the Indian Air Force during the 1971 fighting with Pakistan. The number in Soviet service in 1976 was put at "at least ten" but ten times that number would be needed to patrol even the main sections of the Soviet frontier.

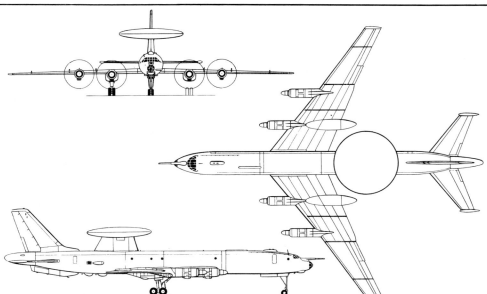

Above: Three-view of Tu-126, called Moss.

Right: Though at least 28 Tu-114 airframes were available it is believed that half that number of Tu-126 were completed.

Tupolev Tu-28P

Tu-28 versions of unknown designation; Tupolev bureau, Tu-102

Origin: The design bureau of Andrei N. Tupolev, Soviet Union.

Type: Long-range all-weather interceptor.

Engines: Originally, two large axial turbojets of unknown type, each with afterburning rating of about 27,000lb (12,250kg), probably similar to those of Tu-22; later versions, afterburning turbofans of about 30,000lb (13,610kg) each, as in later Tu-22.

Dimensions: (Estimated) span 65ft (20m); length 85ft (26m); height 23ft (7m).

Weights: (Estimated) empty 55,000lb (25,000kg); maximum loaded 100,000lb (45,000kg).

Performance: (Estimated) maximum speed (with missiles, at height) 1,150mph (1850km/h, Mach 1·75); initial climb, 25,000ft (7500m)/min; service ceiling (not gross weight) about 60,000ft (18,000m); range on internal fuel (high Patrol) about 1,800 miles (2900km).

Armament: No guns seen in any version; mix of infrared homing and radar-homing "Ash" air-to-air guided missiles, originally one of each and since 1965 two of each.

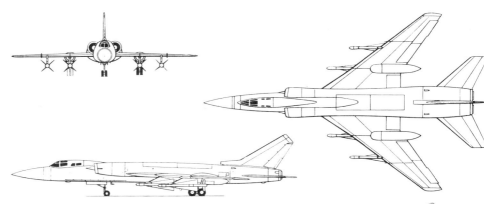

Above: Three-view of Tu-28P with Ash AAMs.

Below: Side elevation of a Tu-28P long-range interceptor of the IA-PVO. By 1980 these aircraft were beginning to be withdrawn.

History: First flight, believed 1957; service delivery, probably 1961.

Development: Largest fighter known to be in service in the world, this formidable machine is essentially conventional yet has the greatest internal fuel capacity of any fighter and the biggest interception radar known to exist. It was one of a number of supersonic types produced by the Tupolev bureau with technology explored with the family of aircraft of the late 1950s known to NATO as "Backfin" (another is the Tu-22). Like the others the Tu-28P has a distinctive wing with sharply kinked trailing edge, the outer 45° panels being outboard of large fairings extending behind the trailing edge accommodating the four-wheel bogie landing gears. Two crew sit in tandem under upward-hinged canopies, and all armament is carried on wing pylons. Early versions had twin ventral fins and usually large belly fairings, but these features are absent from aircraft in current service. The Tu-28P would be an ideal strategic patrol fighter to operate in conjunction with the "Moss" AWACS.

Right: For many years the Tu-28P has been the world's largest type of fighter — strictly an all-weather interceptor, which does not engage in dogfights.

Yakovlev Yak-28P

Yak-28 attack versions, -28P, -28R and -28U
Origin: The design bureau of Alexander S. Yakolev, Soviet Union.
Type: 28 (unknown designations) two-seat attack; (P) all weather interceptor; (R) multi-sensor reconnaissance; (U) dual-control trainer.
Engines: Two Tumansky RD-11 single-shaft afterburning turbojets each with maximum rating of 13,120lb (595kg); certain sub-types have RD-11-300 rated at 13,670lb (6200kg).
Dimensions: (Estimated) span 42ft 6in (12·95m) (some versions have span slightly less than standard); length (except late P) 71ft 0½in (21·65m); (late 28P) 74ft (22·56m); height 12ft 11¾in (3·95m).
Weights: Empty (estimated, typical) 24,250lb (11,000kg); maximum loaded (U) 30,000lb (13,600kg); (others) 35,300—41,000lb (16,000—18,600kg).
Performance: (Estimated) maximum speed at altitude 735mph (1180km/h, Mach 1·13); initial climb 27,900ft (8500m)/min; service ceiling 55,500ft (16,750m); range (clean, at altitude) 1,200—1,600 miles (1930—2575km).
Armament: (Attack versions) one 30mm NR-30 cannon on both sides of fuselage or on right side only; fuselage weapon bay for internal load of freefall bombs (estimated maximum, 4,400lb, 2000kg); hard-points or pylons between drop-tank attachments and outrigger gears for light loads (usually pod of 55mm rockets); (28P) two "Anab" air-to-air guided missiles, one radar and the other infra-red in some aircraft, two additional pylons for two K-13A ("Atoll") missiles, both "Anab" then being radar homers; (R) believed none; (U) retains weapon bay and single gun.
History: First flight, before 1961; (production attack and interceptor versions) before 1961; service delivery

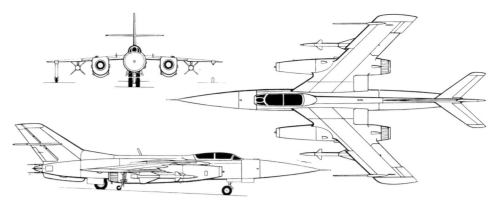

Above: Three-view of Yak-28P with definitive pointed radome and Anab missiles similar to those carried by the Su-11.

Below: Side elevation of a Yak-28P as in service throughout the 1970s with the IA-PVO. Though still a major type in the Soviet inventory, by 1980 these interceptors were being withdrawn from first-line units and assigned to other duties.

not later than mid-1962; final delivery, before 1970.
Development: Obviously derived from the Yak-25/26/27, the Yak-28 is a completely new aircraft, with high wing of different form, new engines, steerable twin-wheel nose gear and considerably greater weight. Early attack versions had slightly shorter fuselage and shorter nacelles ahead of the wing; many hundreds (possibly thousands) of glazed-nose attack 28s (code name "Brewer") were built, most having been rebuilt as ECM and other specialist tactical machines. The Yak-28P (code name "Firebar") remains a leading interceptor, its "Skip Spin" radar being enclosed in a much longer and more pointed nose from 1967. The 28U trainer (code name "Maestro") has a separate front (pupil) cockpit with canopy hinged to the right. Many 28R versions ("Brewer D"), with cameras and various non-optical sensors, may be converted attack aircraft. Flight refuelling is not fitted.

Right: A Yak-28P landing with full flap and tailplane at full negative incidence. This aircraft has the original short radome and is probably an advanced trainer with operational capability.

Below: A flight of three of the original version of Brewer-A attack aircraft, with airframe basically similar to Firebar (Yak-28P). Large numbers of Yak-25, 26, 27 and 28 were built from 1960 onwards and, though differing in important respects, most of the survivors are being converted for EW/ECM and training.

Yakovlev Yak-36

Yak-36 "Forger A" and -36U (?) "Forger B"
Origin: The design bureau of Aleksander S. Yakovlev, Soviet Union.
Type: Single-seat VTOL naval attack (and possibly reconnaissance) aircraft ("Forger B") two-seat dual trainer.
Engines: One lift/cruise turbojet or turbofan of unknown type with estimated maximum thrust of 17,000lb (7710kg); two lift jets of unknown type with estimated thrust of 5,600lb (2540kg) each.
Dimensions (estimated): Span 25ft (7·6m); length (A) 49ft 3in (15·0m), (B) 58ft (17·7m); height 13ft 3in (4·0m); width with wings folded 14ft 10in (4·51m).
Weights (estimated): Empty 12,000lb (5450kg) (B slightly heavier); maximum loaded 22,050lb (10,000kg).
Performance (estimated): Maximum speed at sea level 722mph (1160km/h, Mach 0·95); maximum level speed at optimum height 860mph (1380km/h, Mach 1·3); service ceiling about 50,000ft (15,250m); radius on hi-lo-hi attack mission without external fuel, not greater than 200 miles (320km).
Armament: Contrary to early reports there appears to be no internal gun; four pylons under the non-folding wing centre section carry gun pods, reconnaissance pods, ECM payloads, bombs, missiles (said to include AA-2 "Atoll" AAM and AS-7 "Kerry" ASM) and tanks. Maximum external load, about 4,000lb (1814kg). (B two-seater) none seen.
History: First flight probably about 1971; service delivery possibly 1975.
Development: At the 1967 show at Domodedovo a single V/STOL jet-lift research aircraft gave a convincing display of hovering and transitions. Called "Freehand" by NATO, it was at first thought to be the Yak-36, but this is now believed to be the service designation of the combat aircraft carried above *Kiev*,

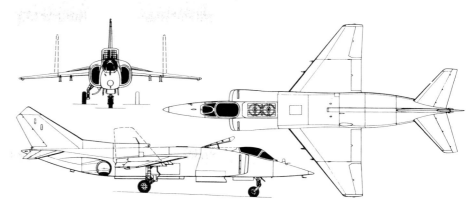

Above: Three-view of Yak-36 Forger-A.

the first of the large Soviet carriers (officially classed as anti-submarine cruisers) which also carry ASW helicopters and an unprecedented array of shipboard weapons. The "Freehand", of which fewer than ten are thought to have been built, conducted trials from a specially built platform on the carrier *Moskva*. It provided information to assist the design of the Yak-36, which probably has the same large lift turbofan engine plus aft-angled lift jets behind the cockpit. To take off, the three engines must be used together and a vertical ascent made, the main nozzles being rotated to about 100° to balance the rearward thrust of the lift jets. STOL takeoffs are not thought to be possible, neither is Viffing (vectoring in forward flight) to increase combat manoeuvrability. The design is simple, though one wonders why the wing was mounted in the mid-position instead of the much lighter solution of putting it above the main engine. The latter has plain inlets with a row of auxiliary doors as on the Harrier, but super-

sonic speed at height is judged possible in the clean condition. Other features include Fowler flaps, large ailerons on the folding outer wings, wingtip and tail control nozzles, a ram inlet duct in the dorsal spine, rear airbrakes, a large vertical tail with dielectric tip, and a dielectric nosecap probably covering a small ranging radar. The "Forger" B has a completely different tandem-seat nose angled downwards and a lengthened rear fuselage to preserve directional stability. The development squadron aboard *Kiev* on her shakedown cruise from the Nikolayev yard to Murmansk flew intensively, and observers especially noted the repeated precision of take-offs and landings, indicating ship guidance. Even this aircraft is almost certainly an interim type.

Below: An excellent US Navy photograph of a Forger-A, without auxiliary inlet doors, approaching the flight deck of *Kiev*.

New military aircraft

During the few months prior to publication information became available on several reported new types of Russian military aircraft, for which positive identities, data and illustrations are lacking (though unconfirmed guesses have appeared in the American Press).

New heavy bomber
In Annual Report for 1979 the US Secretary for Defense stated "We now expect to see the first prototype of a new modern heavy bomber in the near future. If deployed, this aircraft would presumably replace the "Bisons" and "Bears" as the backbone of the Soviet intercontinental bomber force". Surprisingly, no mention of this aircraft was made in the SALT II agreement in June 1979, but there have since been many reports and rumours concerning this programme. What appears to be beyond dispute is that such a programme exists, and that the first aircraft entered flight test before early 1980. It is generally ascribed to the Tupolev bureau, probably because of its appearance outside the Tupolev bureau's development centre at Kazan where the Tu-144 and "Backfire" were developed. Several observers have positively stated that the new bomber has variable geometry (ie, so-called swing-wings). It has been suggested that its engines may be the advanced variable-bypass Koliesov turbofans fitted to the Tu-144D and described by the Soviet Deputy Minister for Civil Aviation as "50 per cent more

economical in operation". American reports identify two aircraft, one a large (390,000lb, 176,900kg) subsonic missile platform known as Bomber H, and the other a 250,000lb (113,400kg) Mach 2·3 variable-geometry penetrator called Bomber X.

New fighter
As early as 1977 there were persistent reports of a new fighter from the MiG bureau — possibly based on no better evidence than the ten years that had then elapsed since the emergence of the first MiG-23 prototypes, the latest known basic MiG design. By 1979 the US Press was publishing artist's impressions of an aircraft looking like a copy of the American F-18 — a highly suspect conclusion — and said to be known to the US Department of Defense as 'Ram L' from its initial sighting in a satellite picture of the flight-test centre at Ramenskoye. Subsequent reports have suggested weights, engine thrust and armament, but, though all are plausible, these reports appear to be based on little evidence. By 1980 this aircraft, armed with the same radar and AA-X-9 missiles as the Advanced Foxbat MiG-25M, was credited to the Sukhoi bureau. Ram K was said to be a much larger swing-wing all-weather interceptor which, unlike Ram L and despite weighing an estimated 60,000lb (27,200kg) is single-engined!

New close-support aircraft
Entry to service of the USAF A-10 close-support aircraft may be in part responsible for a rash of reports of a Russian aircraft in the same general category. Ram J

is the US code for a Mach 0·9 machine with two R-13 or R-25 engines in the fuselage above the wing, the latter having ten pylons. The Su-25 is said to be a new close-support machine in almost the same class, with Mach 0·8 speed, similar dimensions (span of unswept wing 47ft (14·33m) and two 30mm guns.

New heavy-lift helicopter
The US Army FY80 budget statement to Congress stated that the Soviet Union "may be on the verge of developing an operational heavy-lift helicopter — a system we do not possess. . . . They . . . have developed prototypes of a new heavy-lift helicopter called 'Halo' Halo, of course, is the Western code-name, not a Russian one, and it would be premature even to suggest that the HLH is a design by the Mil bureau, though at the 1979 Paris Show Mil engineers said that they were working on helicopters with an installed power up to 18,648kW (25,000shp). Unofficial Western reports state that Halo resembles the 23-year-old Mi-6 in layout, though the fuselage is almost certainly much larger in cross-section.

New naval helicopter
The FY79 *US Military Posture* statement to Congress announced, after describing earlier Soviet helicopters, "Another new naval helicopter is projected in the mid-1980s for ASW and reconnaissance roles". This again has sparked off amplifying comments in the US Press, but it is difficult to determine to what extent these have any basis in fact.

The Modern Soviet Navy

Of all the areas in which the Soviet Union has expanded its capability none has created such a general impression in the West as that of the Soviet Navy. This probably arises from the fact that Soviet naval ships can be seen around the coasts of Western countries and thus seem some-how to be a more direct threat than the air or ground forces. Whatever the reason, the fact is that the Soviet Navy is now the second most powerful in the world. Soviet ships are very heavily armed, but do have limitations and might not fare as well in war as some experts predict.

Captain J. E. Moore, RN

Although the main focus of interest today is upon the astonishing rise of the Soviet Navy's capabilities and power in the last 20 years, this must be viewed as part of a lengthy and, at times, painful evolution. Unlike the German navy of Kaiser Wilhelm II and Tirpitz, which was created from virtually nothing, the history and tradition of the Russian fleet stretches back over 250 years, a period during which operations against Sweden, Turkey, France and Great Britain brought such names as Apraksin, Ushakov, Senyavin and Makarov to the fore. In common with other navies the Russian fleet suffered from contraction and neglect in times of peace. Imaginative ideas were stultified by bureaucracy. By the time of the outbreak of the Russo–Japanese War in 1904

The Soviet aircraft carrier *Minsk* at sea in the Mediterranean. Parked on the flight-deck are four Kamov Ka-25 (Hormone) helicopters and seven Yakovlev Yak-36 (Forger) vertical take-off and landing attack aircraft.

the Russian fleet was fourth in the world in numbers, but ill-led and poorly trained, with its morale sapped by the wide gulf between officers and men. The geographical position of Russia also caused wide dispersion of the available forces and these were soundly defeated by the Japanese.

New building programmes were slow in realisation and thus, by the outbreak of World War I in 1914, the navy was sadly lacking in modern ships. Its performance during the war with Germany was inadequate and the Revolution of October 1917 (November 1917 in the revised calendar) found it of poor quality, with its ratings only too ready to join with the revolutionaries.

The foundation of the Workers' and Peasants' Red Navy dates from Lenin's decree of 11 February 1918, but little was done to provide modern ships. Small groups operated against the Allied and White Russian forces, but the manpower was much diluted by the purge which followed the sailors' demands for free elections in February 1921. War damage to Russian shipyards delayed the building and refitting of ships, and by 1924 this meagre fleet consisted of two battleships, a cruiser, 18 destroyers and nine submarines. Two years later the Defence Council authorised the construction of 12 submarines, 18 escorts and a number of light forces, a decision which was built into the first 5-year plan in 1928. Although there is no evidence that the escort vessels were built, the submarine programme continued at an increased rate until, by the time of the German invasion of Russia in June 1941, 213 submarines were complete, with another 91 on the slips and running trials. Meanwhile Stalin, impelled in later years by the lessons of the Spanish Civil War, had set his sights on an impressive surface fleet. In addition to the three old battleships, 10 cruisers and 60 destroyers, a further three battleships, 12 cruisers and 45 destroyers were on the building slips in 1941. Few of them were, however, to be completed.

Although the ships available to the USSR were considerably more numerous than those of the German navy when hostilities began in 1941, the performance of the Soviet Navy was inefficient and ineffective. This was due in large measure to the fact that a great number of the experienced officers in the fleet had been removed and executed in the purges started by Stalin in 1934. The standard of material efficiency in the fleet was low, training had suffered and only when Allied ships were transferred on loan did the Soviet Navy learn of new sensors such as sonar and radar.

In July 1945 Stalin ordered that a fleet 'still stronger and more powerful' should be provided but, as after the previous war, the destruction of the main surface-ship building yards hampered the fulfilment of this instruction. As the yards were repaired so did construction begin, but the designs remained basically those of the prewar years. At the same time, though, new classes were being laid out on the drawing-board. These benefited from the lessons learned from the recent war and were indications of new and advanced attitudes among Soviet naval constructors. The last stage of the Stalinist period (1945–1953) saw radical changes under way. The very numerous 'Whiskey'

class submarines and their larger companions of the 'Zulu' class were, at the time, equalled by very few Western boats; the naval air force reached a strength of 4,000 aircraft; and research into missiles for maritime purposes was well advanced.

The interregnum which came between Stalin's death and the accession to power of Khrushchev saw a dramatic change in the Soviet naval programmes. In January 1956 Admiral Sergei Gorshkov was appointed as Commander-in-Chief of the Navy at the age of 45. This post, which has no equivalent in Western navies, combines the duties once vested in the British First Lord of the Admiralty and the First Sea Lord, and 24 years later, Admiral Gorshkov still holds the reins. These 24 years have seen the totally dramatic renaissance of the Soviet fleet. Fourth in strength the Russian navy may have been in 1904 – today it challenges the power of the United States Navy, is a fleet which leads the world in certain aspects and has learned lessons of tactics, seamanship and worldwide operations in a period which would have been thought absurdly short a quarter of a century ago.

Admiral Gorshkov inherited a number of advantages when he assumed command. The first submarine-oriented ballistic missile had been test-launched in the previous year, two years before the USA laid down a ballistic-missile submarine. Within months of his appointment the first 'Zulu V' class was at sea, mounting two SSN-4 'Sark' missiles with a range of 350 miles. At the same time plans were in hand for the building of the new 'Krupny' class, the world's first destroyers armed with surface-to-surface missiles (SSMs), aimed at defence against Western aircraft-carriers. Also in hand were the 'Kildin' class destroyers with a missile armament similar to the 'Krupnys' and the 'Whiskey Twin Cylinder' submarines armed with twin SSN-3 launchers – all aimed at the prevention of seaborne attacks on the USSR.

Programmes in the immediate future were similarly reactive to the possibility of external assault – missile-firing fast attack craft of the 'Osa' and 'Komar' classes, cruisers of the 'Kynda' class with SSMs and then ships with surface-to-air missiles as the naval air force lost its own fighter squadrons and the fleet was planned to operate further from Russia's coasts.

The final phase began in 1967 with the 'Moskva' helicopter cruisers, followed by

Below: Twenty of the 29 Echo II nuclear boats are armed with SSN-12 cruise missiles, presenting a still-useful, if noisy, example of 'forward defence' of the USSR.

Soviet Naval Strengths

Ship type	Class	In Service	In Reserve	Under Construction (estimated)
Submarines				
SSBN	Typhoon	–	–	1
SSBN	Delta III	7	–	3
SSBN	Delta II	5	–	–
SSBN	Delta I	19	–	9
SSBN	Yankee	34	–	4
SSBN	Hotel II/III	8	–	–
SSB	Golf I/II	20	–	–
SSGN	Papa	1	–	–
SSGN	Charlie I/II	15	–	2
SSGN	Echo II	29	–	–
SSG	Juliett	16	–	–
SSG	Whiskey	8	–	–
SSN	Alfa	2	–	2
SSN	Victor I/II	22	–	?
SSN	November	13	–	–
SSN	Echo	5	–	–
SS	Tango	10	–	2 p.a.
SS	Bravo	4	–	–
SS	Foxtrot	60	–	–
SS	Zulu IV	10	9	–
SS	Romeo	12	–	–
SS	Whiskey	50	80	–
SSR	Whiskey Canvas Bag	3	–	–
SS	Quebec	4	15	–
Aircraft Carriers				
CVN	?	–	–	1
CVG	Kiev	3	–	1
Helicopter Cruisers				
CHG	Moskva	2	–	–
Cruisers				
CGN	Sovietski Soyuz	1	–	1 +
CG	Kirov	–	–	3 +
CG	Kara	7	–	3
CG	Kresta II	10	–	–
CG	Kresta I	4	–	–
CG	Kynda	4	–	–
CG	Sverdlov	1	–	–
CA	Sverdlov	7	2	–
CC	Sverdlov	2	–	–
Destroyers				
DDG	Kashin	19	–	–
DDG	Kildin	4	–	–
DDG	Kanin	8	–	–
DDG	SAM Kotlin	8	–	–
DD	Kotlin	14	4	–
DD	Skory	20	15	–
Frigates				
FFG	Krivak	24	–	3 p.a.
FF	Koni	2	–	4 p.a.
FF	Mirka	20	–	–
FF	Petya	48	–	–
FF	Riga	40	8 +	–
FF	Kola	3	–	–
Corvettes				
	Tarantul	2	–	1 p.a.
	Grisha	35	–	3 p.a.
	Nanuchka	19	–	4 p.a.
	Poti	64	–	–
Ocean Minesweepers				
MSO	Alesha	3	–	–
MSO	Natya	34	–	3 p.a.
MSO	Yurka	49	–	–
MSO	T 58	17	–	–
MSO	T 43	73	80	–
Minehunters				
MCM	Sonya	30	–	4 p.a.
Coastal Minesweepers				
MSI	Zhenya	4	–	–
MSI	Vanya	72	–	–
MSI	Sasha	10	–	–
Light Forces				
FACH(M)	Sarancha	3	–	?
FAC(M)	Osa I/II	120	–	?
PG	SO 1	55	–	–
PC	Slepen	1	–	–
PC	Stenka	87	–	2 p.a.
PC	Shershen	50	–	–
PT	P 6	8	–	–
PH	Babochka	1	–	–
PH	Pchela	20	–	–
PHM	Matka	6	–	–
PHT	Turya	34	–	–
Amphibious Ships (large)				
LPD	Ivan Rogov	2	–	?
LST	Ropucha	13	–	–
LST	Alligator	14	–	–
LCT	Polnochniy	60	–	–
Depot and Support (large)				
AS	Ugra	7	–	–
AS	Don	6	–	–
AS	Dnepr	5	–	–
AM	Lama	6	–	–
AM	Amga	4	–	–
AR	Amur	18	–	?
AR	Oskol	12	–	–
AS	Tomba	4	–	–
Intelligence Collectors				
AGI	(Various)	55	–	?

Ship type	Class	In Service	In Reserve	Under Construction (estimated)
Radar Pickets				
AGR	T 43/AGR	12	–	–
Survey Ships				
AGS	(Various)	84	–	–
Training Ships				
	Ugra	2	–	–
	Smolny	3	–	–
	Chapaev	1	–	–
Replenishment Ships				
AOE	Berezhina	1	–	?
AOE	Boris Chilikin	6	–	1 p.a.
AOE	Manych	2	–	–
AOR	Dubna	3	–	–
AOR	Sofia	1	–	–
AOR	Kazbek	3	–	–
AO	(Various)	33	–	–

Note: The USN system of ship categories is used. In this the first one or two letters denote the type of ship, with the final letter denoting the armament, or, in the case of the letter 'N', that the ship is nuclear powered. Thus;

A	= Auxiliary vessel.		DD	= Destroyer; gun-armed.
AM	= Missile supply ship.		DDG	= Destroyer; guided-missile armed.
AO	= Oiler.			
AOE	= Fast combat support ship.		FF	= Frigate; gun-armed.
AOR	= Replenishment oiler.		FFG	= Frigate; guided-missile armed.
AGI	= Miscellaneous; intelligence gatherer.		LCT	= Landing craft; tanks.
			LPD	= Landing platform; dock.
AGR	= Miscellaneous; radar picket.		LST	= Landing ship; tanks.
AR	= Repair ship.		MCM	= Mine counter-measure ship.
AS	= Submarine tender.		MSI	= Minesweeper, inshore.
C	= Cruiser.		MSO	= Minesweeper, offshore.
CA	= Cruiser; gun-armed.		SS	= Submarine; conventional.
CC	= Cruiser; command ship.		SSB	= Submarine; conventional
CG	= Cruiser; guided-missile armed.			power; ballistic missile armed.
CGN	= Cruiser; guided-missile armed; nuclear powered.		SSG	= Submarine; conventional power; guided missile armed.
CHG	= Cruiser; helicopter carrier; guided-missile armed.		SSN	= Submarine; attack; nuclear powered.
CVN	= Aircraft carrier; nuclear-powered.		SSR	= Submarine; conventional power; radar picket.
CVG	= Aircraft carrier; guided-missile armed.			

Fleet Strengths*

Ship type	Northern	Baltic Fleet	Black Sea and Caspian Sea	Pacific	Total
Submarines					
SSBN	49	–	–	24	73
SSB	8	6	–	6	20
SSGN	28	–	–	17	45
SSG	12	2	4	6	24
SSN	32	1	–	13	46
SS	20	5	38	44	153
Aircraft Carriers					
CVG	1	–	–	1	2
CHG	–	–	2	–	2
Cruisers					
CGN	–	1	–	–	1
CG	9	1	11	7	28
CA	1	3	2	3	9
Destroyers					
DDG	8	5	16	10	39
DD	11	13	12	17	53
Frigates					
FFG	5	10	4	7	26
FF, corvettes	47	43	44	49	183
Fast attack craft (missile armed)	39	36	39	55	169
Light forces	32	140	158	111	441
Minesweepers	65	156	80	103	404
Amphibious Ships					
LPD	1	–	–	1	2
LST	2	10	4	9	25
LCT, LCU	11	26	56	46	139
Support Shipping (large)					
Depot ships	25	2	17	21	65
Service ships	21	3	14	16	54

Notes:
* The fleet strengths are approximate and vary with out-of-area deployments. For example, the Mediterranean squadron is found from the Black Sea fleet, while the Indian Ocean squadron is detached from the Pacific Fleet. Numbers can also fluctuate due to ships being in transit, or in refit.
** Source: Information derived from Jane's Fighting Ships 1979–80.

Above: A Soviet nuclear-powered submarine of the Delta-I class. It carries 12 ballistic missiles. A lengthened boat carrying 16 missiles is entering service.

Right: Admiral of the Fleet of the Soviet Union Sergei Georgiyevich Gorshkov. Few men have placed such a personal seal on a service and Admiral Gorshkov will go down in history as one of the greatest naval administrators.

Far right: A Yankee class submarine. Thirty-four of these boats have been built, and they maintain constant patrols off the Atlantic and Pacific seaboards of the United States.

the all-purpose cruisers of the 'Kresta I', 'Kresta II' and 'Kara' classes, and the multiple-armed destroyers of the 'Krivak' class. With the completion of the first aircraft-carrier of the 'Kuril' class Admiral Gorshkov has achieved his aim of the creation of a balanced fleet, 'a powerful ocean-going navy' in his own words.

Submarine development

Since the first major building programme of 1926 the Soviet Navy has laid great emphasis on submarine construction. This was originally due to the defensive role planned for the fleet and, later, because the widely dispersed submarine yards were the only ones to survive the German attacks between 1941 and 1945. The first boats were little more than improved editions of World War I designs and this tendency continued until 1950. In this period of 24 years huge numbers of submarines were completed, a programme equalled only by that of Germany in the war years. Thus, in the immediate postwar period, the boats included in the Soviet order-of-battle were well behind modern developments. But in 1951 the first of a class which was eventually to number 240 in the next six years joined the fleet. This was the 'Whiskey' class, a design which had clearly profited greatly from German experience. Of some 1,350 tons dived displacement, with six torpedo-tubes and a submerged speed of 15 knots, they looked not unlike the German Type XXI boats,

and were to be the basic hulls for no less than eight variants. These ranged from the original type with twin guns, to the 'Canvas Bag' radar pickets and the 'Long Bin' fitted with four SSN-3 cruise-missile launchers. At the same time a larger version, the 'Zulu' class, began to appear and this submarine was chosen as the first conversion for ballistic missile operations. The first of six was completed in 1956 and carried two 350-mile SSN-4 missiles.

By then the forerunners of the present nuclear submarine fleet were under construction, in the form of the 'November' class. Displacing over 4,000 tons, they were fast but noisy, characteristics shared by the 'Echo I' and 'II' classes of nuclear boats which followed them and which were armed with six and eight SSN-3 cruise-missiles respectively. These were clearly aimed at the forward defence of the USSR, as also were the 16 'Juliet' class of diesel submarines with four SSN-3 tubes. Not only cruise-missile boats joined the fleet – the diesel-propelled 'Golf' class and the nuclear 'Hotel' class followed rapidly in the early 1960s, both originally carrying SSN-4 missiles which were later replaced in many cases by the 700-mile SSN-5 'Serb' missiles.

There was now a pause before the next three major classes were reported – the 'Victor' fleet submarine, the 'Charlie' cruise-missile submarine and the 'Yankee' ballistic-missile submarine. All included improved hull and reactor designs, and were faster and

better armed. 'Victor' had eight torpedo-tubes, 'Charlie' eight tubes for the 30-mile SSN-7 missile which could, for the first time, be launched under water, and 'Yankee' carried 16 tubes for the new 1,300-mile SSN-6 'Sawfly' ballistic missiles. Improvements to all three have been launched, the 'Victor II', 'Papa' and 'Delta' classes, but it is the last which has caused the greatest change in today's balance of naval power. Armed with 12 4,200-mile SSN-8 missiles, this class can cover targets throughout Canada, the USA and the whole of Asia without leaving the Barents or Greenland Seas. The next monster, the 'Delta II', carries 16 of these missiles in a hull of 11,750 tons, the largest class of submarine ever built. They are an impressive addition to today's fleet of some 350 submarines, which now includes an increasing number of 'Delta III' class. Of similar dimensions to the 'Delta II' this carries 16 SS-N-18 missiles with a range of 5,200 miles.

The most advanced nuclear submarine in the world was completed in Leningrad in 1970. This was the first of the 'Alfa' class which had many early teething problems. Now in slow series production, this submarine, which is 60 feet shorter and, at 3,300 tons, 2,400 tons less than the 'Victor II', has a titanium hull giving a diving depth of 3,000 feet. A new type of reactor provides power for 40 knots and the whole presents a major problem to all those concerned with Western A/S defence.

Aircraft-carrier development

Although the Russian and Soviet navies have, since 1910, recognised the place of aircraft in maritime warfare, it was not until 1937 that plans were laid for the building of true aircraft-carriers. This intention was overtaken by the war with Germany and, in the postwar years, there was much difference of opinion in Soviet naval circles about the value of this type of ship. However, in 1967 the *Moskva* was produced, first of a pair of 17,000-ton helicopter-carriers. With a flight-deck occupying the after half of the ship and with a complement of 18 Kamov Ka-25 'Hormone' helicopters, these were clearly intended for anti-submarine operations.

Five years after *Moskva*'s appearance came reports of the first of the 38,000-ton 'Kiev' class aircraft-carriers. With an angled flight-deck these new ships, of which four will be in commission by 1984, are designed to operate VTOL aircraft and helicopters. As such they were a logical advance towards the achievement of a balanced fleet capable of worldwide operations.

But in 1976 Admiral Gorshkov, in his book 'The Sea Power of the State', was discussing 'sea control' and clearly considered that the USSR had not yet achieved the aim of the 'balanced fleet'. Now (1980) with a nuclear-powered aircraft-carrier, probably with a conventional fixed-wing aircraft capability, under construction at Severodvinsk and with four new classes of cruiser building in other yards, the Soviet Navy can look forward to a period when, if manpower is adequate, it will have not only ASW capability but the means to exercise sea control in specific areas. Gorshkov will have his 'balanced fleet' by the mid-1980s.

Cruiser development

The cruiser strength of the Soviet Navy during the early post-Revolutionary days was confined to two ships completed and three building. In 1935 the first pair of the 9,000-ton 'Kirov' class, a new design to meet the needs of the second 5-year plan, joined the fleet. Six of these were eventually built, to be followed by the larger 'Frunze' or 'Chapaev' class. Five of these were finished and gave place in the yards to the 18,000-ton 'Sverdlov' class with 6-inch guns. Twenty-four of these were planned but, as their construction coincided with the end of the Stalin era and the subsequent eruption of new thoughts on naval programmes, only 14 were completed. The last commissioned in 1956, six years before the first of the 'Kynda' class appeared.

The ships of the 'Kynda' class were apparently the first guided-missile vessels designed from scratch – the preceding missile destroyers were conversions of earlier hull designs. Armed with two quadruple SSN-3 cruise-missile mountings and a twin SAN-1 mount on a 6,000-ton hull, they had no helicopter and a light gun armament. In 1967 the 'Kresta I' class appeared – larger at 8,000 tons, with an embarked helicopter but carrying only half the number of missiles and with smaller guns. However, she did carry two twin SAN-1 mountings for aircraft defence, and these were replaced by twin SAN-3s in the next class, 'Kresta II'. The main change in this class was in the replacement of the long

range SSN-3s by two quadruple launchers for SS-N-14 missiles, primarily anti-submarine but with a probable anti-ship capability. The first of the 'Kara' class appeared in March 1973 with a missile armament similar to that of 'Kresta II' and with the addition of two twin SAN-4 launchers, the new 'Gatling' anti-aircraft mounting, larger guns and an increased anti-submarine armament. This class continued in series production until 1977.

In December 1977 a ship was launched at Leningrad which was the logical complement of the nuclear-propelled aircraft-carrier at Severodvinsk. This was *Kirov*, a 32,000-ton battle-cruiser with nuclear propulsion, a stack of missiles and air-capable. Operational in 1980 she is the first of an increasing class which, with the three other new classes of cruiser now (1980) under construction, will provide long-range sea control task forces long into the future.

Destroyer development

The considerable force of destroyers in the Tsarist navy was reduced to 15 by 1924 and by June 1941 had reached a total of only 60. Four years later the total, including lend/lease ships, a few captured from the Germans and the small number completed during the war, was down to 48. These were, on the whole, inefficient ships by

Above left: Having carefully built up an effective and modern surface fleet, Admiral Gorshkov has turned to a seaborne air arm, which has reached maturity with the Kiev-class carriers of 38,000 tons and the VTOL Yak-36 fighters.

Left: The first of the Soviet aircraft carrier designs was the Moskva class of two ships, which carry 18 Ka-25 Hormone ASW helicopters.

Below left: The Soviet Navy tends to mount a heavy armament on its carriers. Seen here on the *Moskva* is one of the two twin SA-N-3 mounts, while above it are the two 'Headlight' radars used to control the surface-to-air missiles.

Above: The Krivak-I class frigate *Bodry*, seen here in the English Channel. Some 24 of these well-designed ships are in service and building continues at about 3 a year.

Below right: Another striking design is the Kresta-II anti-submarine cruiser. Seen on this ship – *Admiral Makarov* – is the heavy armament and 'copter pad and hangar aft.

Western standards. Their numbers were augmented by new construction, but these were also ships of prewar design.

It was not until 1949 that there appeared the first postwar destroyers, the 3,100-ton 'Skory' class, of which 70 were eventually completed. These were conventional all-gun ships, as were their successors of the 'Tallin' and 'Kotlin' classes of 1954–1955. At this point the Soviet Navy produced its first missile-armed destroyers: four 'Kotlin' hulls were converted to 'Kildins' with a single SSN-1 (130-mile) surface-to-surface missile-launcher and eight more into 'SAM Kotlins' with a twin SAN-1 surface-to-air launcher. These conversions of 1957–1962 were among the first ships so fitted, and were followed by the 4,650-ton 'Krupny' class of eight ships, the lead ship appearing in 1960. They had originally been designed

as large all-gun destroyers and some underwent a further conversion in 1967–1971 when their two SSN-1 launchers were replaced by a twin SAN-1 mounting and more anti-submarine (A/S) weapons. Since then all of the remainder have been similarly changed, the whole group being known as the 'Kanin' class. The emphasis on surface-to-air missiles in destroyers was continued in the 'Kashin' class of 4,500 tons with two twin SAN-1 mountings, first seen in 1962. These were the world's first all-gas-turbine major warships and have become a numerous and effective group. So successful have they been, in fact, that their successors, the 1971 'Krivak' class, continued this method of propulsion. The latter's armament was, however, totally different: a quadruple launcher for the new SSN-14 25-mile anti-submarine missile and two 'pop-up' SAN-4 launchers were backed by four 76mm guns, eight torpedo-tubes and the advantage of a variable depth sonar. The lack of a helicopter, a deficiency partially rectified by the provision of a helicopter pad,

in the new conversion of the 'Kashins', may need attention in the future. All-in-all though, the Soviet destroyer force consists of powerful ships with good sea-keeping qualities and all capable of speeds of 32–35 knots.

Frigate and corvette development

In 1945 there was a motley group of escort ships available, but it was not until 1950 that the early ships of the 1,900-ton 'Kola' class appeared. This was a postwar design and was closely followed by the 'Rigas' of 1,600 tons and capable of 28 knots. Both these classes were conventional ships capable of escort duties, and the production of 'Rigas' continued until 1959. After a pause of two years came the 'Petya' class of 1,150 tons fitted with gas-turbines and diesels, an ideal combination for A/S ships. This task was further assisted by the provision of a heavier A/S armament of torpedoes and rocket-launchers, a layout continued in the succeeding 'Mirka' class. Sixty-five of these two classes were completed by 1969, a

Above: The 'SAM Kotlin' class destroyer *Bravy* lies at anchor while serving with the Soviet Navy's Meditteranean Squadron. This was the first Kotlin to be converted.

Above right: A Kara-class anti-submarine cruiser at anchor. There are nine of these powerful ships in service, with one more joining the fleet each year. The large quadruple launcher abreast the bridge is for SS-N-14 anti-submarine missiles.

Left: Although the Nanuchka-class guided missile corvette entered service ten years ago, this remains a unique concept, with a heavy missile armament (and a twin 57mm turret) on a 950 tonne hull.

Below: A destroyer of the 'Modified Kashin' class; these were the first major warships in the world to depend entirely upon gas-turbine power.

powerful group which has not been further augmented.

The corvette type was first represented by the 380-ton 'Kronstadt' class, 230 of which were built between 1948 and 1956. Smaller at 250 tons were the 'SO Is', about 100 being built between 1957 and 1961 before the gas-turbine/diesel propulsion form appeared in the 600-ton 'Poti' class. Seventy of these were followed by the impressive 'Nanuchka' class in 1969. Of 850 tons, their design provided a really sea-worthy hull for the very powerful armament of six 150-mile SSN-9 surface-to-surface missiles, a twin SAN-4 cylinder as well as A/S rocket launchers and a twin 57-mm gun mounting. This class is designed as part of a strike-force, while the contemporary 'Grisha' class is clearly an A/S design. Slightly smaller than 'Nanuchka', these have

an A/S armament, an SSN-4 mounting (replaced by an additional twin 57-mm gun mounting in later ships) and a gas-turbine/diesel layout. Once again this group shows variety and innovation, and provides a valuable force for any commander.

Amphibious forces development

The 12,000-strong Soviet Naval Infantry was re-established in 1961–1962 and was, at that time, provided with a number of Landing Craft (Utility), only one class being of any notable size. But in 1963–1964 a pattern of new construction appeared – the 800-ton 'Polnocny' class Landing Craft (Tank) (LCT) and the 5,800-ton 'Alligator' class Landing Ship (Tank) (LST). Both have proved to be successful designs, 60 of the former and 14 of the latter now being in service. The first ships of the replacement class of LCTs, the 'Ropucha' class, were completed in Poland. The completion in 1975, also in Poland, of the first of the 13,100-ton 'Ivan Rogov' class was an indication of an intention to provide a long-range amphibious force. With a helicopter hangar and two landing decks she also carries small hovercraft and a battalion of Naval Infantry. In considering amphibious affairs the backing available from the very large Soviet merchant navy must always be remembered, as must the increasing Soviet emphasis on hovercraft.

Mine warfare development

Russia has always been interested in the use of the moored or bottom mine. All the earlier surface ships had a minelaying capability, as do all modern submarines and many aircraft. Very few specialised minelayers exist in the Soviet Navy today, but a considerable force of some 200 ocean minesweepers and 200 coastal and inshore minesweepers are kept in commission. All forms of minesweeping are available. The forces are kept well up-to-date, the latest coastal

sweepers of the 'Zhenya' and 'Sonya' classes being reported as having GRP (glass-reinforced plastic) hulls.

Light forces development

Soviet interest in fast attack craft dates from 1927, when two coastal motor boats (CMBs) were bought. These were followed by several Italian designs, and by 1941 about 140 such craft were in commission. In the postwar years indigenous designs were used for the small 'P2' and 'P4' classes, which were followed by the 600 craft of the 'P6', '8' and '10' classes. These were 66-ton boats, with 21-inch torpedoes, some having hydrofoils, some gas-turbines. The main variant of this hull-design was the 'Komar', carrying two 'Styx' missiles. At the same time in 1960 there appeared the first of the 'Osa' class, with four 'Styx' launchers on a 200-ton hull. These craft have remained the main strike force since then, while considerable numbers of both torpedo and patrol craft, including hydrofoils, have been added to the inventory. In addition some 100 craft are employed on patrol duties on the Danube, Amur and Ussuri rivers as well as the Caspian Sea.

Support forces

In the earlier stages of the build-up of the Soviet fleet, the main emphasis in this sphere was on depot and repair ships. Twelve classes, varying from the 7,000-ton 'Ugra' and 'Don' submarine depot ships to the 3,000-ton 'Oskol' repair ships, provide a total of 61 vessels designed for duties as diverse as submarine maintenance and the provision of missiles. The provision of afloat replenishment of both fuel and stores 20 years ago was entirely confined to tankers and store-ships taken from trade. In 1971 the first custom-built fleet replenishment ship, *Boris Chilikin*, appeared and was soon followed by five more 23,000-ton ships and two of a smaller edition. In 1977 the 36,000-

ton *Berezina* was completed, designed to provide support for aircraft-carriers.

Survey, research and intelligence ships

The past 20 years have seen the growth of an enormous fleet of these various types of ships. Today 120 survey ships, 25 so-called 'Space Associated' ships, 30 major and many minor ships on research duties and 193 fishery research ships provide a vast flow of data on the world's oceans. While much of this is basic scientific information, there is little that is not to some extent of military value. The intelligence-gatherers (AGIs) have increased their numbers from four in 1963 to 54 today. Their duty is to monitor Western naval movements and exercises, an activity from which a great fund of both communications and tactical knowledge has been built up, materially assisting in the training of the Soviet Navy.

Naval aviation

Despite a reduction from 4,000 aircraft in 1956 to 1,200 today, the Soviet naval air force is a very important part of the fleet. A considerable part of the cut resulted from the transfer of air-defence duties to the Air Force but the Soviet naval air force has retained maritime reconnaissance and strike tasks and ASW duties. These are carried out by a wide range of aircraft from the huge Tu-95 'Bear' to the 'Hormone' helicopter and include the variable-geometry 'Backfire' bomber. The operation of these aircraft worldwide has been greatly assisted by the increasing availability of foreign air-fields in such places as Cuba, Guinea, Ethiopia and Aden. (A fuller discussion of Soviet naval aviation will be found in the chapter on the Soviet Air Forces.)

Command and control

In considering this aspect of Soviet naval affairs it must be remembered that these are far more interwoven with the political organisation than in any Western navy. This is true at all levels from the Central Committee and the Defence Ministry down to the political officer in an individual ship. Partly as a result of this there is far more centralised control of fleets and ships than in the West. The C-in-C of the Navy

Above right: A decontamination monitoring operator assessing the radiological level on a 30mm gun turret on a fast attack craft. This is a frequent drill in a force which regards nuclear weapons as normal.

Right: SS-N-3 (Shaddock) missiles in a twin launcher on a Kresta-I class cruiser. Range is estimated to be 100 nautical miles and the missile has a nuclear warhead.

Below: Another notable development has been the expansion of the Soviet Naval Infantry into a sizeable corps, well-equipped and well-trained. Here a platoon is coming ashore in its BTR-60P APCs.

Top: These two Turya-class patrol hydrofoils are en route to Cuba in February 1979. These craft are armed with four 21 in torpedo tubes, a twin 25mm mount (forward) and a twin 57mm mount (aft).

Above: A fully-enclosed floating dock, of the type used to service submarines in the very cold conditions experienced in the Northern Fleet area. The Soviet Navy has bought a number from the West lately.

exercises this control on the instructions of the Central Committee, with the assistance of six deputies and a large naval staff, the whole being under the eye of the General Staff. His is an organisation which is reflected in the various fleet commands. These, the Northern, Baltic, Black Sea and Pacific Fleets, are each controlled by staffs of a similar pattern to that found in Moscow. Autonomy is not a word welcome in the Soviet Union except at the most senior levels, and this is the second fact to be remembered in considering the operations of the Soviet Navy.

Entry and training

With a little under 500,000 people involved, the Soviet Navy has an enormous training task. In a fleet manned entirely by conscripted junior ratings, a great weight of responsibility rests on the officers and senior rates. Both are drawn from volunteers and the first receive a highly technical training in one of 11 establishments. During this period they are given an efficient indoctrination, both professional and political, into their future life. Some of this time is now spent at sea and when they receive their first appointments they may expect a long period in the same ship, sometimes moving from a junior position to command. This, in a number of cases, is achieved at an early age, although the more sensitive ships and submarines are reserved for the very senior.

The reason that so much depends on the

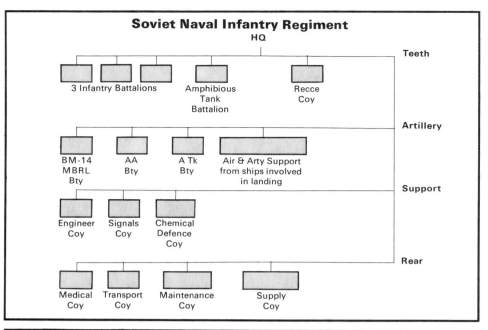

Soviet Naval Infantry Regiment

HQ

Teeth

3 Infantry Battalions | Amphibious Tank Battalion | Recce Coy

Artillery

BM-14 MBRL Bty | AA Bty | A Tk Bty | Air & Arty Support from ships involved in landing

Support

Engineer Coy | Signals Coy | Chemical Defence Coy

Rear

Medical Coy | Transport Coy | Maintenance Coy | Supply Coy

Warsaw Pact Naval Assault Ships

Ships	North	Baltic	Black	Pacific	Total
Soviet					
Ivan Rogov		1			1
Alligator/Ropucha LST	5	5	5	10	25
MP4—Polnocny LSM	variable				75
Hovercraft					61
Polish					
Polnocny		23			23
LCM		20			20
E. German					
Frosch LST		9			9
Robbe LSM		9			9
Labo LCT		2			2

beyond these wide boundaries they are described as 'out-of-area'. However, within the local commands a number of minor bases provide support and repair services for the ships of their fleet. There are also numerous commercial ports which have naval facilities.

In some cases these bases coincide with the areas where naval ship-building takes place. In the west these ports suffered great damage in both world wars but all were rapidly brought back to full production. The north, virtually unharried in the past, has a major building yard at Severodvinsk, there are five yards in the Leningrad area and four smaller yards on the Baltic. While major submarine building takes place at Gorkiy on the Volga, the main big-ship building base is at Nikolayev close to the Black Sea. In the east the yards at Komsomolsk and Khabarovsk on the Amur river produce destroyers and submarines, and there are other fitting-out yards in the area. With nearly 20 yards available for naval construction the Soviets thus have a very major capability in this field.

Deployment

Admiral Gorshkov has shown very clearly that he understands the mission of the Soviet Navy abroad. While claiming in 1967 that his fleet was fully capable of offensive operations, he has recently stated that 'The Soviet Navy is a powerful factor in the creation of favourable conditions for the building of Socialism and Communism, for the active defence of peace and for strengthening international security.' With the worldwide deployments that have become the standard method of operation of the

Below: A Kynda-class missile cruiser refuels at sea from a Boris Chilikin-class fleet replenishment ship, the *Vladimir Kolechtisky*. The Chilikin-class, completed in 1971, were the first purpose-built underway support ships in the Soviet Navy. Six are in service, supplying both liquids and solids. They indicate the Soviets' awareness of the need for, and considerably increasing capability of, resupplying a widely dispersed fleet.

officers is that the ratings are conscripted at 18 and after six months training serve for 2½ years with the fleet. At 21 they may have become petty officers and, at this age and if they volunteer, will be signed on as chief petty officers. As they lack experience it is not surprising that they rely largely on their seniors for direction. The biannual intake of junior ratings, earning some £50 per year, is 60,000 and this means a continual state of

flux in all ships, a situation which is not conducive to efficiency.

Bases and shipbuilding

Each of the four fleets has a main shore-base – the Northern Fleet at Severomorsk, the Baltic at Baltiysk, the Black Sea at Sevastopol and the Pacific at Vladivostok. All four fleets have large local exercise areas and when their ships are deployed

Soviet Navy, this statement can only be construed as an intention to use that fleet for political purposes.

With this in mind it is interesting to observe the areas to which these ships have been dispatched since 15 years ago. At this time the first signs of a permanent Soviet presence in the Mediterranean were seen, a presence which was rapidly reinforced to a total of some 100 ships during the Arab–Israeli war of 1973, when these could have inhibited US 6th Fleet action there.

This is possibly the best-known area of Soviet naval expansion but is by no means the only one needing consideration. In the Caribbean, the scene of Soviet humiliation off Cuba in 1962, their survey ships continue to operate and a large fishery base has been built at Havana. By 1969 confidence had been restored sufficiently for a Soviet naval squadron to visit the area. Since then frequent similar visits have taken place and 'Bear' reconnaissance aircraft are now welcome in that island.

Similar facilities exist in Conakry, the capital of Guinea in West Africa, where Soviet ships responded rapidly to President Sekou Touré's call for help after an abortive invasion. Further south, Angolin ports are available and Mozambique has valuable safe havens. These, with facilities at Aden and Hodeida, provide the Soviet squadron, which has been in the Indian Ocean since 1968, with valuable base support as well as forward airfields for both reconnaissance and strike aircraft of the Soviet naval air force.

As Soviet interest in Mauritius and Vietnam continues, their ships are ever-present in a worldwide deployment impossible only 15 years ago.

Right: These Aist-class hovercraft are the latest machines developed specifically for the use of the Soviet Naval Infantry. It is similar to the British SR.N-4, but this is a unique and effective Soviet design.

Below: The essential raw material of Admiral Gorshkov's navy: conscripted ratings are not considered entirely efficient, and are very dependent on their officers. These are on an exchange visit to the US.

The future

Once its new aircraft-carriers are in commission, the Soviet Navy will have a well-balanced fleet. However, the numbers of ships in the fleet are clearly limited by the manpower available and, although this is a variable governed by the Central Committee, it has possibly now reached a level unlikely to be exceeded in the near future. While the ships themselves possess increasingly efficient weapons and are capable of worldwide operations, there are many other factors which must be considered in assessing a country's capability at sea. Chief of these is training and the capability of those who man the ship. Present indications are that the officer corps of the Soviet Navy is both self-reliant and efficient despite centralised control. The same is not true of the junior conscripted ratings, and these must remain the weakest link, as will always be true under such a system. But it is wrong either to over- or under-estimate this navy. It is perfectly capable of remaining an efficient political weapon for many years to come, although its capabilities in drawn-out hostilities might be questionable.

Soviet Warships

Bill Gunston

This section is not intended to be an exhaustive catalogue of all Soviet warships, but rather to display the growing variety of classes. Soviet ships are very heavily armed in comparison with Western ships of equivalent size, but this is not the whole story, however, for few missile reloads are carried, range is relatively poor, and crew conditions cramped. Further, for all its peacetime exercises, the Soviet Navy has never conducted a campaign in distant waters. But it cannot be denied that the naval architects are skilled and imaginative, world leaders in some fields.

Kiev class V/STOL cruisers

Displacement: About 32,000 tons (38,000 full load).
Dimensions: Estimated length overall 899ft (274m); deck width overall about 158ft (48m); beam 92ft (28m).
Aircraft: Estimated 43; mix of jet V/STOLs and helicopters (27 'Hormone-A', 3 'Hormone-B', 12 'Forger-A', 1 'Forger-B').
Armament: Four twin SS-N-12 bombardment missiles on foredeck (believed to be associated with retractable radar above bows); two twin SA-N-3 SAM; two twin SA-N-4 SAM; one twin SUW-N-1 ASW; two twin 76mm guns; eight 30mm 'Gatling'.
Propulsion: Four sets steam turbines, 40,000shp on each of four shafts, 32kt.

Easily the biggest warship ever built in the Soviet Union, *Kiev* was built in 1968–73, spent 1973–75 fitting out at the Nikolayev yard and in late 1975 was working up in the Black Sea. Before this volume appears she may be in the Mediterranean. Like all modern Soviet warships she is extremely bold, modern, ingenious and formidable. Her fore part is a missile cruiser packed with SSMs, SAMs and AS (anti-submarine) weapons; her stern is a simple V/STOL carrier with an extremely long 6° angled deck. This provides seven spots for V/STOL aircraft and helicopters (see Aircraft section for roles of two types of 'Forger' and two types of 'Hormone'). By 1980 there were three ships of this class in commission, named

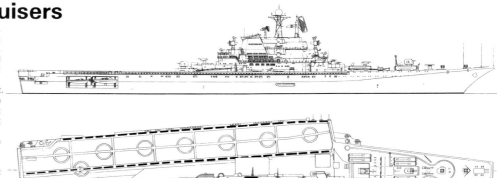

Kiev, *Minsk* and *Kharkov*, with a fourth, believed to be *Novorossisk*, on the slipway at the so-called Nikolayev South yard which has built all the Soviet Navy's new large surface ships. Predictably, these impressive

Above: The excellent lines and heavy armament of the Kiev class show the skill and ingenuity of Soviet naval designers. The plan view shows how the deck area has been divided into clearly defined parts: flight-deck, superstructure, and weapons area. The multiplicity of weapons and electronic systems is also apparent.

vessels, called anti-submarine cruisers by the Russians, are very fully equipped, there being at least 13 radars, comprehensive ECM and two installations of VDS (variable-depth sonar).

Left: *Kiev*, at sea with Kamov Ka-25 helicopters and a Yakovlev Yak-36 (Forger) VTOL aircraft on the flight-deck. The door on the stern is probably for a Variable Depth Sonar (VDS); the large number of close defence weapons can also be seen.

Below: The remarkable accumulation of weapons on *Kiev's* foredeck includes two 12-barrel MBU 2500 AS rocket launchers, two twin SAN-3 SAM launchers, a twin 76mm gun turret and eight SSN-12 ASM launchers. No Western carrier mounts so many weapons systems.

Moskva, Leningrad helicopter cruisers

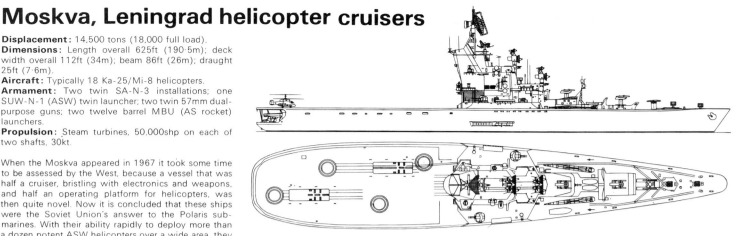

Displacement: 14,500 tons (18,000 full load).
Dimensions: Length overall 625ft (190·5m); deck width overall 112ft (34m); beam 86ft (26m); draught 25ft (7·6m).
Aircraft: Typically 18 Ka-25/Mi-8 helicopters.
Armament: Two twin SA-N-3 installations; one SUW-N-1 (ASW) twin launcher; two twin 57mm dual-purpose guns; two twelve barrel MBU (AS rocket) launchers.
Propulsion: Steam turbines, 50,000shp on each of two shafts, 30kt.

When the Moskva appeared in 1967 it took some time to be assessed by the West, because a vessel that was half a cruiser, bristling with electronics and weapons, and half an operating platform for helicopters, was then quite novel. Now it is concluded that these ships were the Soviet Union's answer to the Polaris submarines. With their ability rapidly to deploy more than a dozen potent ASW helicopters over a wide area, they would have been formidable to the submarines armed with Polaris A-1, but less effective against Polaris A-3 and Poseidon carriers. The second of these 'helicopter cruisers' was finished in 1969, and no more were built their place in the vast Nikolayev yards being taken by the much bigger Kiev class. They operate in the Atlantic, Mediterranean, Red Sea and Barents Sea. In 1974 Leningrad used Mi-8 helicopters to help sweep the Suez canal free from mines, but their main complement is of the Ka-25 type. Originally they were fitted with ten torpedo tubes.

Above: Moskva class anti-submarine cruiser. Only two have been built.

Below: A US Navy Neptune aircraft shadows a Moskva class cruiser. Although they bear a superficial resemblance to the earlier French *Jeanne d'Arc*, these ships are in fact a purely Soviet concept and provide a good balance between functions. They are excellent seaboats.

Above: A Nimrod submarine hunter of the RAF flies over *Moskva*. Note the open dooar at the foot of the huge 'mack' and the aircraft lift.

Below: *Moskva*, showing the missile launchers, radar antennas on the superstructure and two Kamov Ka-25 helicopters on the flightdeck.

Echo II class missile submarines

Displacement: 5,800 tons (Echo I, about 5,000 tons) submerged; 4,800 surface (Echo I, 4,600).
Dimensions: Length overall 386ft (117m) (Echo I, 381ft, 116m); beam 30ft 2in (9·2m); draught 26ft (7·9m).
Armament: Eight launch tubes for SS-N-3 cruise missiles (Echo I had only six); six 21in (533mm) torpedo tubes in bow; four 16in (406mm) AS tubes in stern.
Propulsion: Nuclear (pressurized water reactor); twin turbines, two shafts each with 15,000shp steam turbine, submerged speed 25kt.

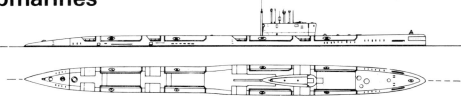

Echo-II class SSGN; 5,800 tons: 29 built.

These large and probably formidable vessels have for many years formed an important part of the Soviet Navy's offensive firepower at sea. Forming a natural follow-on to the Juliett class, they have bigger hulls generally similar to those of the November class, and doubtless powered by the same nuclear installation (the first to be developed in the Soviet Union). The first five were equipped with three pairs of N-3 launch tubes, but they were later removed and these boats are patrol SSNs. Then the decision was taken to lengthen the hull and incorporate a fourth pair, resulting in the impressive E-II class. The first of these appeared in 1962 or 1963, and the considerable total of 29 was built by 1967. The Echo II class have since been seen in many parts of the world, operating with both the Northern and Pacific fleets. They still constitute a great threat to allied surface ships of all kinds.

Right: A damaged Echo-II class submarine limps homewards; this very clear picture was taken by a Nimrod aircraft of the Royal Air Force. These large submarines mount eight tubes for the SS-N-3 anti-shipping cruise missile and are presumed to be designed to counter Western strike carriers and their associated task forces. The large wells in the casing result in an exceptionally noisy hull, which makes detection relatively simple.

Juliett class missile submarines

Displacement: 3,550 tons; 2,800 surface.
Dimensions: Length overall 285ft (86·7m); beam 33ft (10·1m); draught 23ft (7m).
Armament: Four launch tubes for SS-N-3 cruise missiles; six 21in (533mm) torpedo tubes in bow: two or four 16in (406mm) AS tubes in stern.
Propulsion: Diesel-electric; three shafts, each with 2,000shp, speed about 16kt surface or submerged.

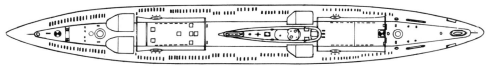

Though representing a tremendous advance over the crude missile conversions of the Whiskey class, the excellent Julietts were in turn overtaken by the bigger and heavier-armed Echo series. Nevertheless they are nimble and much cheaper than an Echo, and 16 were commissioned in 1962–66. They are well equipped with sonar and communications, and have proved very successful. They are essentially Foxtrots with enlarged hulls equipped with the hydraulically elevated missile tubes. The latter were derived from the crude system proved on Whiskey class vessels. Normally stowed horizontally, flush with the tall deck casing, they are elevated to a firing angle of just under 20°. Many submarines of this class, nearly all having small individual differences in equipment, have been seen in the Mediterranean and Atlantic.

Juliett class SSG; 3550 tons; 16 built.

Below: A Juliett class submarine underway off Spain. These boats are armed with four SS-N-3 launchers and ten torpedo tubes.

Victor class submarines

Displacement: 5,100 tons submerged; 4,300 surface.
Dimensions: Length overall 307ft 9in (94m); beam 32ft 10in (10m); draught 23ft 11in (7·3m).
Armament: Eight 21in (533mm) torpedo tubes.
Propulsion: Nuclear (pressurized water reactor); single shaft with 30,000shp, submerged speed about 33kt.

This class is unusual in the Soviet Navy in carrying only the submarine's traditional armament of anti-ship torpedoes. Thus, the Victors are attack submarines, and they are extremely fast and dangerous craft, able to sink virtually any kind of surface vessel. They carry the latest and most lethal Soviet torpedoes, which are continually being updated and improved and appear to have overtaken even the latest Freedom, Tigerfish and Alcatel torpedoes used in the West. Victors have fat, streamlined hulls, but retain a traditional upper deck casing with free flood holes (which make them noisier to underwater sonics sensors than corresponding Western boats). At least 16 were in use by early 1976, on patrol in all parts of the world. By 1972 the Leningrad yard had switched to the larger (5,700-ton) Victor II, six of which were commissioned by 1979.

Victor class SSN; 5100 tons; 22 built.

Below: A Victor-II class submarine transits the Malacca Straits (between Indonesia and West Malaysia) at speed. These boats are fast and relatively silent, which makes them very dangerous to Western navies.

Zulu class submarines

Displacement: 2,300 tons submerged; 1,900 surface.
Dimensions: Length overall 295ft 4in (90m); beam 23ft 10in (7.3m); draught 19ft (5.8m).
Armament: Originally built with ten 21in (533mm) torpedo tubes (six bow, four stern); some converted to other weapons.
Propulsion: Three diesels, with total output 10,000shp; three electric motors with total output 3,500hp; speed 18kt on surface, 15kt submerged.

Considerably larger than the Whisky class, these long-range patrol submarines were likewise designed (possibly with the help of German engineers) immediately after World War II to incorporate all the lessons that could be learned from the German Type XXI. They were larger than the famed German boat, enabling radius of action to be extended to about 25,000 miles, despite having the large complement of six officers and 64 ratings and room for 24 torpedoes or ten torpedoes and 40 mines. About 35 were built in 1951—55. At least seven were converted in 1955—57 to carry and fire three SS-N-4 ballistic missiles (Zulu V class). The rest have been modified in various ways, and those remaining are mostly described as Zulu IV boats, with extended conning towers.

Zulu class SS; 2300 tons; 28 built.

Below: The Zulu class was built in the early 1950s to incorporate the best design features of the German Type XXI boats. 28 were built, of four distinct types. Finally, six were converted (Zulu-V) to become the first Soviet ballistic missile submarines.

Delta class missile submarines

Displacement: About 9,300 tons submerged; 8,400 surface. (Delta II about 11,750 tons).
Dimensions: Length overall 446ft (136m); beam 38ft (11·6m); draught 33ft (10·2m).
Armament: Twelve missile launch systems for SS-N-8, with vertical expulsion tubes each about 48ft long and faired into hull by large casing aft of conning-tower sail; believed to be six 21in torpedo tubes in bow. Delta II, sixteen missiles.
Propulsion: Nuclear (pressurized water reactor), about 60,000shp, submerged speed about 30kt.

Largest submarines in service in the world, the formidable Delta class (the name is simply a NATO code, in the absence of a known Soviet designation) have been in quantity production since 1971. Though only one delivery system for Soviet strategic thermonuclear warheads, they already outstrip in number the

Delta class SSBN; 9300 tons; 344 built.

strategic missile forces of the Western nations, and continue in production at the rate of about four per year. All these monster ships are being built at the vast complex at Severodvinsk, which has a greater construction potential than all the submarine yards in the USA combined. The Deltas are in most respects the most potent warships ever operated, with missiles having a range of 4,200 nautical miles (4,830 miles). Delta-II replaced the earlier type in production in 1977 (on the slip in late 1973), with five built. Production then switched to the even more formidable Delta-III,

of which seven or eight had been completed by late 1979, with three more building. As this book went to press the Soviet Union had about 1,090 ballistic missiles at sea.

Below: A Delta-I class submarine at sea. The long casing covering the missiles abaft the fin stands well proud of the hull, its size a result of the length of the SS-N-8 missiles (46.3ft)

Yankee class missile submarines

Displacement: About 9,300 tons submerged; 7,800 tons surface.
Dimensions: Length overall 427ft (130m); beam 38ft (11·6m); draught 26ft (8m).
Armament: Sixteen missile launch systems for SS-N-6, with vertical expulsion tubes extending just above the circular hull and faired inside a flat-topped upper deck. In the bows, six 21in (533mm) torpedo tubes.
Propulsion: Nuclear (pressurized water reactor), about 30,000shp, submerged speed about 30kt.

With a general arrangement identical to that of the US Polaris submarines, the Yankee class were designed in the early 1960s, put into high-rate production and first reported by the Western nations in 1968. Four boats were delivered in that year, and output then climbed to eight in 1971, the final total being 34, reached in 1976. Far more formidable than the earlier Golf and Hotel classes, the Yankee was deficient only in its missiles, which were still somewhat large in bulk and short in range compared with the US counterparts. Thus, on their first deployment the Yankees had to stand close in to the US coast to get coverage over most of the United States, and there was still a band between the Rockies and Mississippi that could not be reached. Later the N-6 missiles were updated, and by 1980 it was believed that 20 of this class were Yankee-I with N-6 Mod 1, 13 were Y-II with N-6 Mod 3, and one (Y-III?) had 12 tubes with the new N-17 missile.

Right: The Yankee class is armed with 16 SS-N-6 Mod 3, which delivers three MRVs.

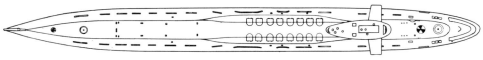

Yankee class SSBN; 9,300 tons; 34 built.

Hotel class missile submarines

Displacement: 5,600 tons submerged; 4,750 surfaced.

Dimensions: Length overall 377ft (115m); beam 29ft 10in (9·1m); draught 25ft (7·6m).

Armament: Three missile launch systems for SS-N-5, with the vertical expulsion tubes extending from the keel to near the top of the conning tower. In the bow, six 21in (533mm) torpedo tubes; in the stern, four 16in (406mm) anti-submarine torpedo tubes.

Propulsion: Nuclear (pressurized water reactor); two shafts each with 15,000shp steam turbines, submerged speed about 26kt.

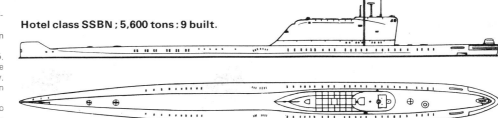

Hotel class SSBN; 5,600 tons; 9 built.

The Soviet wish to pour out armaments, regardless of cost, is well illustrated by this class, built in 1958–62. By the time the first was on the slipway it was known to be obsolete, yet eight were subsequently commissioned. Hull and reactor are similar to Echo-II. Originally fitted with the N-4 missile, they were only marginally useful vessels, though retaining full torpedo armament and capable of secondary employment in the attack role. From 1963 all nine Hotel submarines were converted to launch the N-5 missile, being restyled Hotel-II, and subsequently spent almost their whole operational career off the coasts of North America (including northern Canada). One, called Hotel-III, was rebuilt to carry six SS-N-6 missiles.

Right: A Hotel class submarine photographed some 600 miles Northeast of Newfoundland on February 29, 1972, apparently in trouble. This type is armed with three ballistic missiles, which are mounted vertically in the fin. Hotel-I had to surface to fire, but Hotel-II has SS-N-5 which can be launched submerged. Hotel-III was a single-ship conversion used to test fire the SS-N-8 which now equips the Delta class.

November class submarines

Displacement: About 5,000 tons submerged; 4,200 surface.

Dimensions: Length overall 361ft (110m); beam 29ft 8in (9·1m); draught 21ft 9in (6·7m).

Armament: Bow, eight 21in (533mm) torpedo tubes; stern, four 16in (406mm) anti-submarine torpedo tubes.

Propulsion: Nuclear (pressurized water reactor); twin steam turbines, 15,000shp on each of two shafts, submerged speed about 28kt.

These large and generally conservatively designed boats were the first Soviet submarines to have nuclear propulsion. To a considerable degree the technology was based upon intelligence information from the United States in 1955, though at that time the Soviet Union had not appreciated the advantages of the streamlined 'spindle' hull first seen in the US Navy Albacore. Accordingly the Novembers were given long conventional hulls with two screws. By 1963 a total of 13 had been commissioned, despite the fact that they had long since been overtaken by later technology, showing yet again how indifferent the Soviet Union is to heavy arms expenditure. In any case, anti-ship Attack and Fleet submarines never had the same priority as the purely offensive missile submarines, once the latter had been brought to the operational stage in the late 1950s.

November class SSN; 5000 tons; 13 built.

Below: Another Soviet submarine in distress in the Atlantic, this time a November class nuclear-powered boat. One of this class sank off the southwest of the United Kingdom in April 1970. The hull shape is by no means ideal for fast, quiet underwater performance and the many free-flood holes in the casing must create a lot of noise.

Foxtrot class submarines

Displacement: 2,400 tons submerged; 1,950 surface.
Dimensions: Length overall 297ft (90·5m); beam 24ft 1in; draught 19ft (5·8m).
Armament: Bow, six 21in (533mm) torpedo tubes; stern, four 16in (406mm) tubes.
Propulsion: Diesel-electric, three shafts, each with 2,000shp set, speed about 18kt surface or submerged.

Though they are only patrol submarines, with traditional diesel-electric propulsion and torpedo armament, the Foxtrots have been built in greater numbers than any other single class of submarine in the world since the preceding Soviet patrol class known to the West as Whisky vessels. The first Foxtrots appeared about 1958, and they stayed in production at the rate of seven a year to a total of 60, all delivered from

the long-established yards of Sudomekh and at Leningrad. Though bigger than the Zulu class, and with less-powerful diesels, they actually have marginally better performance. By all accounts the Foxtrots have been extremely successful, and they have been frequently encountered by Western patrol aircraft all over the world. Since 1968 many units of this class have been sold or given to other countries and production for export is continuing.

Foxtrot class SS; 2400 tons; 60 built.

Below: A Soviet Foxtrot class conventional patrol submarine in Arctic waters. Sixty of these boats were built making it the second largest class of post-War submarine, although it was initially planned to build no less than 160.

Romeo class submarines

Displacement: 1,800 tons submerged; 1,400 tons surface.
Dimensions: Length overall 252ft (77m); beam 24ft (7·3m); draught 18ft (5·5m).
Armament: Bow, six 21in (533mm) torpedo tubes; two more in stern.
Propulsion: Diesel-electric; two shafts, each with 2,000hp set; speed about 17kt on surface, 16kt submerged.

These patrol submarines were a direct development of the mass-produced Whisky class, rather more than 20 being built between 1958 and 1960, eight of which were exported. It is especially significant that they were built as new submarines, at a time when over 200 Whiskeys were available for modernization. They have hulls slightly longer and with fractionally greater beam than the Whiskey class, improved electric propulsion, new conning towers, and — most important of all — a much later and more comprehensive suite of sonar sensor and communications equipment. They are medium-range vessels, which tend to stay relatively close to Soviet shores (though similar submarines are in production in China, and six were sold or given to the Egyptian Navy in 1966). It is expected that the Romeo class will be withdrawn from front-line duty by 1980, thereafter being used mainly for training and research.

Right: The elegant lines of a Romeo class submarine on patrol in the Atlantic. At one time it was planned to build 560 Romeos.

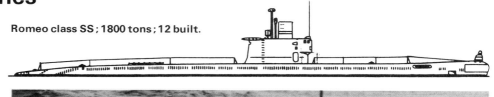

Romeo class SS; 1800 tons; 12 built.

Quebec class submarines

Displacement: 740 tons submerged; 650 surface.
Dimensions: Length overall 185ft (56·4m); beam 18ft (5·5m); draught 13ft 3in (4·0m).
Armament: Four 21in (533mm) torpedo tubes, in bow.
Propulsion: One 3,000shp diesel; three shafts each with 800/900hp electric motor, speed about 18kt on surface, 16kt submerged.

These are the only small submarines built in the Soviet Union since World War II (denoting a sharp contrast with the pre-war policy, when coastal short-range types strongly predominated). About 25 were built

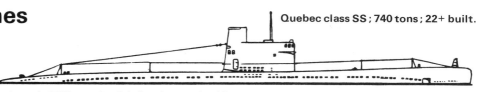

Quebec class SS; 740 tons; 22+ built.

in the early 1950s, one batch believed to number 13 having been delivered in 1955 from the Sudomekh yard at Leningrad. They are believed to have been efficient and successful craft, and some are still in operational service. Probably the chief reason for their relatively small number is their limited cruising range of about 7,000 miles, which severely hampers their

deployment in the context of the vast size of the Soviet Union and its growing interest in dominating all parts of the world. One of their attractive features was that they could be built at dispersed plants and transported in prefabricated sections to a final assembly yard, which is no longer possible with the much larger submarines of today.

Charlie class cruise-missile submarines

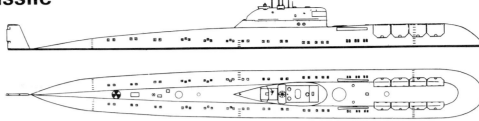

Displacement: 3,900 tons (surface), 4,700 tons (submerged).
Dimensions: Length overall 308ft (93·9m); beam 32ft 10in (10m); draught 24ft 7in (7·5m).
Armament: Eight tubes for launching SS-N-7 missiles (see comments below); six 21in (533mm) torpedo tubes.
Propulsion: Nuclear reactor, steam turbine of about 30,000shp, single screw at tip of hull; submerged speed 27kt.

First seen in 1968, this class of submarine is still something of an enigma. The basic vessel is fast and streamlined, having a fat spindle-type hull with the most powerful (second-generation) Soviet naval reactor installation. The conning tower is squat and well profiled, and altogether these vessels probably have the highest performance of any Soviet submarines (though their free-flood holes under the separate deck casing make them noisier than Western boats). They have become common in the Mediterranean and in many

other areas, though their modest production rate of about three per year means that the total number is still only about 12, plus three or four larger Charlie II with eight torpedo tubes. believed able to fire SS-N-15, said to be long-range AS missile. They appear to have a deck installation for a new type of cruise missile, appreciably smaller than the N-3 but similar in concept. Called N-7 by NATO, these missiles are thought to have a range of 56km (30 miles) and to be capable of being fired from below the surface. Little is known of N-7/'Charlie' fire control and guidance.

Charlie class SSGN; 4700 tons; 15+ built.

Below: A Charlie class submarine. This class is fitted with eight tubes for the SS-N-7 cruise-missile, which can be launched while the submarine is submerged. Twelve Charlie-I boats were built before production switched to the somewhat larger Charlie-II. This latter type has a submerged speed of 33 knots, a very creditable performance for a missile-armed boat.

Sverdlov class cruisers

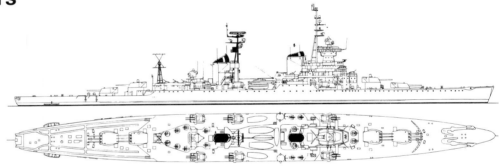

Displacement: About 17,500 tons (full load); as converted, usually fractionally less.
Dimensions: Length overall 656ft (200m); beam 72ft 3in (22m); draught 24ft 6in (7·5m).
Armament: See text.
Propulsion: Geared steam turbines with 110,000shp on two shafts, maximum speed 30kt.

During World War II these fine cruisers were designed to have four triple 6in gun turrets and dozens of smaller dual-purpose guns, plus two quintuple 21in (533mm) torpedo tubes. A class of 24 was planned, 20 keels were laid, 17 hulls launched and, by 1956, 14 cruisers commissioned. Two have now been passed to other navies or placed in reserve, and the remainder have been rebuilt in contrasting ways. The first four versions, in 1969–71, were of *Dzerzhinski, Admiral Senyavin, Mikhail Kutuzov* and *Ahdanov*. In general, the rebuilt programmes have involved reduction in the number of 6in turrets, addition of a vast amount of radar and electronics, surface-to-air and other missile systems, helicopters (with pads and hangars) and other equipment of which some is still not identified.

Torpedo tubes have been removed, but minelaying installations usually remain. Two of these large cruisers are serving as strategic command ships (*Zhdanov* and *Senyavin*), with two twin SA-N-4, 16 30mm 'Gatlings' and communications, radars, displays, computers and other installations to direct the whole operations in a theatre.

Sverdlov class cruiser; 17500 tons; 14 built.

Below: The Soviet cruiser *Sverdlov,* nameship of the class, photographed from HMS *Andromeda's* Wasp helicopter. The Soviet Navy shows a remarkable affection for these ships after 30 years' service.

Kara class cruisers

Kara class CG; 9600 tons; 10+ built.

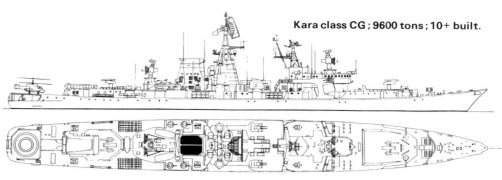

Displacement: 8,200 tons (9,600 full load).
Dimensions: Length overall, about 570ft (174m); beam 60ft (18m); draught 20ft (6·2m).
Armament: Bombardment missiles, two quadruple launcher boxes for SS-N-14 (each side of bridge); surface-to-air missiles, two twin launch installations for SA-N-3 (fore and aft) and two retractable twin installations of SA-N-4 (each side of mainmast); AS weapons, two 16-barrel MBU launchers (foredeck) and two 6-barrel MBU launchers (aft); guns, two twin 3in (76mm) each side between bridge and mast, four 23mm 'Gatling' abaft funnel; torpedoes, two sets quintuple 533mm tubes each side between funnel and hangar.
Propulsion: Four gas turbines, 120,000hp, two shafts, maximum speed 32kt.

When the lead-ship of this class, Nikolayev, steamed into the Mediterranean on 2 March 1973 she cast yet a further mantle of gloom over naval defence observers in the West. She was like previous Soviet cruisers only more so'. In other words she fairly bristled with an array of weapons and electronics that no ship in any Western navy can even remotely begin to match. On top of this, she has proved to be a good sea-boat, with excellent reliability and fine all-round performance.

Compared with immediate predecessors, such as the Kresta II ships, the Kara class escape from squeezing too many quarts into a pint pot. Their hulls are larger, the propulsion system more compact and their interior design apparently outstanding. On the small fantail at the stern is a platform for a Ka-25 'Hormone A' helicopter for AS use. Below the platform is a variable-depth sonar (VDS), and all-round AS capability of these big cruisers is formidable, especially as it is now realized that SS-N-14 has major AS effectiveness.

Petropavlovsk and *Tashkent* of this class have new missiles ahead of the bridge, said to be SA-N-10 with anti-missile capability. The missile/gun AA firepower of this class is also impressive and deficiencies are conspicuously absent. Deliveries by 1980 totalled nine, with at least one more fitting out.

Below: The antenna complexes on the Kara class cruiser *Ochakov* are clearly seen, dominated by the huge 'Top Sail' 3-D radar.

Kresta I class cruisers

Kresta-I class; 7500 tons; 4 built.

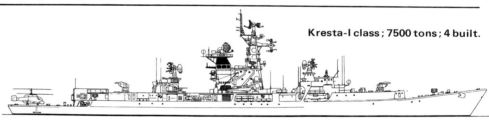

Displacement: 6,000 tons (7,500 full load).
Dimensions: Length overall 510ft (155·5m); beam 55ft (16·8m); draught 19ft 8in (6m).
Armament: Bombardment missiles, two twin launchers for SS-N-3 abeam of bridge; surface-to-air missiles, two twin installations for SA-N-1 ahead of bridge and ahead of hangar (B and X positions); AS weapons, two 12-barrel MBU launchers (foredeck) and two 6-barrel MBU launchers (each side of hangar); guns, two pairs 57mm (abeam rear radar tower); torpedoes, two sets quintuple 21in (533mm) aft of funnel.
Propulsion: Two sets steam turbines, 100,000shp, maximum speed 34kt.

Though overtaken by swiftly galloping technology, these four ships marked the turning point in Soviet naval construction, together with the contemporary Kashin class. Prior to 1960 Soviet surface vessels were not exceptional; afterwards, largely through the force-ful direction of Admiral Gorshkov, they became the fear and envy of other navies. The Kresta class set designers and constructors firmly on the road towards packing incredible arrays of weapons and electronics into modest hulls. Four were built, in 1967–70, and the first to be modernized, *Vice-Admiral Drozd* has new radars and four 23mm 'Gatlings'. They are unusual in carrying the Ka-25 helicopter in its 'Hormone B' form for over-the-horizon targeting of the N-3 long-range missiles. These were the last surface ships to carry the N-3 missile, which was superseded by the smaller, multiple-reload N-14. It was the need to provide for over-the-horizon target guidance for N-3 that led to the K-I class carrying a helicopter, for the first time in a Soviet warship.

Right: A Kresta-I class cruiser operating as part of a task group in the Atlantic in October 1971. These were the first design to be directly influenced by Admiral Gorshkov.

Kresta II class cruisers

Kresta-II class; 7600 tons; 10 built.

Displacement: About 6,140 tons (7,600 full load).
Dimensions: Length overall 520ft (158m); beam 55ft (16·8m); draught 19ft 8in (6m).
Armament: Bombardment missiles, two quadruple launchers for SS-N-14 abeam of bridge; surface-to-air missiles, twin installation for SA-N-3 ahead of bridge and ahead of hangar (the traditional B and X positions); AS weapons, two 12-barrel MBU launchers (foredeck) and two 6-barrel MBU launchers (aft); guns, two pairs 57mm (each side of 'mainmast', rear radar tower). four pairs 30mm (abeam 'foremast', main radar tower); torpedoes, two sets quintuple 21in (533mm) tubes aft of funnel.
Propulsion: Two sets steam turbines, 100,000shp, maximum speed about 34 knots.

Left: A Kresta-II class guided-missile cruiser photographed while shadowing a NATO exercise in 1975. Shown to advantage are the tiny helicopter landing platform and the folding-roofed hangar for the Ka-25 (Hormone-A) helicopter.

Below: Soviet naval designers seem to be able to pack more weapons and electronic equipment onto a given size of hull than those in the West, as is shown clearly in this picture of a Kresta-II class cruiser. The ten ships of this class are designated 'large anti-submarine vessels'.

With these ships the Soviet naval designers went considerably further than in the Kresta I class and demonstrated their amazing ability to fit the weapons and electronics of the largest modern 'capital ship' into a hull not much bigger than a destroyer. Put another way, there are many Western naval vessels of similar size, but all have a much smaller range of weapons and electronics. Especial emphasis must be laid on the electronics, because radar, ECM and communications are the most vital installations in any combat platform and the Soviet Union has leapt in a decade from inferiority to superiority in such matters. The K-II ships positively bristle with a wealth of installations indicative of the most lavish funding, and they are extremely formidable in a wide range of roles, concentrating on AS (anti-submarine), the primary purpose of the N-14 missile. Ten were built.

Kynda class cruisers

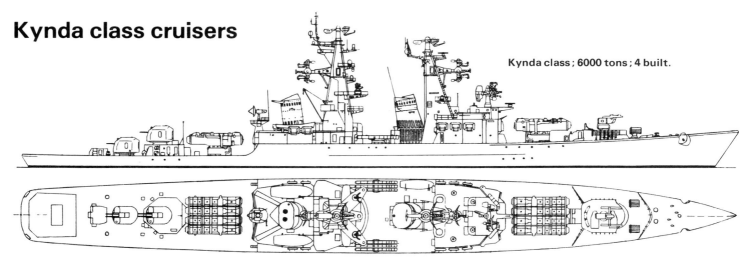

Kynda class; 6000 tons; 4 built.

Displacement: About 4,500 tons (6,000 full load).
Dimensions: Length overall 465ft 9in (142m); beam 51ft 10in (15·8m); draught 17ft 5in (5·3m).
Armament: Bombardment missiles, two sets quadruple launch tubes for SS-N-3 (ahead of bridge and ahead of gun turrets); surface-to-air missiles, twin installation for SA-N-1 on foredeck; AS weapons, two 12-barrel MBU launchers on foredeck ahead of SA-N-1 launcher; guns, two twin 76mm turrets (at rear, in X, Y positions); torpedoes, two triple 21in (533mm) tubes abaft forefunnel.
Propulsion: Two sets steam turbines, 100,000shp, maximum speed 35kt.

These were the last 'traditional' cruisers built in the Soviet Union; even so, they were redesigned while under construction to carry fewer guns and instead have the huge launch tubes for the N-3 missile. Associated with these long-range weapons are the prominent 'Scoop Pair' search/guidance radars, on the foremast and mainmast. These, however, cannot see beyond the radar horizon, and so to use N-3 missiles at extreme range the Kynda cruisers have to operate in partnership with friendly aircraft, such as the missile-guidance versions of the Tu-95 called 'Bear D'. The next cruiser design, the Kresta I, carried a helicopter for this purpose. Total built was only four, and by 1980 they had not been modernized.

Right: A Kynda class cruiser underway in the Mediterranean. These large ships mark a turning-point in Soviet naval design. They were originally to have been gun-armed but a change of mind during construction led to a mixed armament with eight SS-N-3 launchers, a twin SA-N-1 launcher and two twin 76mm gun turrets in X and Y positions. The SS-N-3 cooperates with Bear-D aircraft for long range firing.

Below: This fine view of a Kynda class cruiser shows the heavy armament which takes up virtually all the deck space, from the MBU anti-submarine projectors on the foredeck to the 76mm turret in Y position on the quarterdeck. The concentration of radar antennas on the masts is also clearly shown. The Kyndas have not been modernised and with their dated missile systems could be of limited value in a conflict.

Kashin class destroyers

Displacement: 3,950 tons (4,950 full load).
Dimensions: Length overall 471ft (143m); beam 52ft 6in (15·9m); draught 19ft (5·8m).
Armament: Surface-to-air missiles, two twin installations for SA-N-1 on upper deck at front and rear (B and X positions); AS weapons. two 12-barrel MBU launchers (high in front of bridge), two 6-barrel MBU launchers aft; guns, two twin 76mm (fore and aft, in A and Y positions); torpedoes, single set of quintuple 21in (533mm) torpedo tubes amidships (on centreline). Six (Kashin-Mod) have four single bins for SS-N-2 abeam the rear funnel (see drawing).
Propulsion: Four sets of gas turbines, 96,000shp on two shafts, maximum speed 35kt.

Above: Kashin modified class DDG; 4950 tons; 6 modified (also 13 unmodified).

When the Kashins appeared in 1962 they were dramatically new and impressive; in particular, they were the first large warships in the world to be powered solely by gas turbines. It is eloquent testimony to the awesome pace of Soviet warship development that within ten years these important ships have been rendered obsolescent. Probably the whole class (originally 20 but one foundered after an explosion in 1974) is being updated; at least one ship has SA-N-1 replaced by two new SAM installations not yet seen on other ships.

Below: A 'Modified Kashin' class guided missile destroyer. Modifications included lengthening the hull by 3.2m(10ft) and adding four SS-N-2 missile launchers on the afterdeck. Extra radar also fitted.

Bottom: An unmodified Kashin class destroyer leaving harbour. These were the first major warships in the world to be powered by gas turbines and the funnels are carefully sited and angled to ensure that the hot efflux has minimal effect on antennas.

Kanin class destroyers

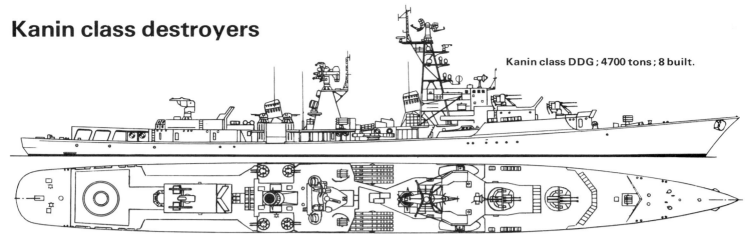

Kanin class DDG; 4700 tons; 8 built.

Displacement: 3,700 tons (4,650 full load).
Dimensions: Length overall 457ft (139·3m); beam 48ft 2in (14·7m); draught 16ft 5in (5m).
Armament: Surface-to-air missiles, one twin installation for SA-N-1 (aft, in X position); AS weapons, three 12-barrel MBU launchers (foredeck and each side abeam 'mainmast'); guns, eight 57mm (two quads, in A and B positions) and eight 30mm (four twins); torpedoes, two sets quintuple 21in (533mm) tubes amidships.
Propulsion: Two sets steam turbines, 84,000shp on two shafts, maximum speed 34kt.

Built as Krupny class destroyers the eight Kanins dispense with the outmoded SS-N-1 installations and instead have completely revised electronics, SAMs, AS weapons, sonar and better helicopter installation. Conversions were all carried out at the Zhdanov Yard at Leningrad where the Krupnys were built in the late 1950s. Though outmoded by today's Soviet ships, in any other Navy the Kanins would be judged large, versatile and extremely effective. They continue to be active in Western waters.

Right: A Kanin class destroyer speeds past the Royal Navy's former carrier *Ark Royal*.

Kildin class destroyers

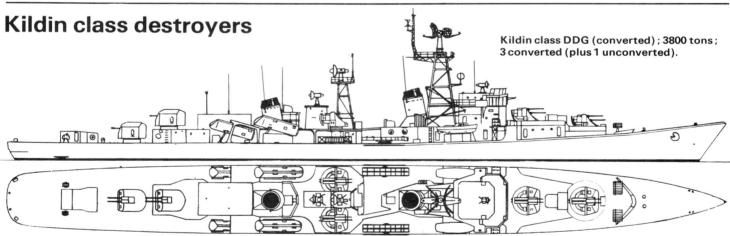

Kildin class DDG (converted); 3800 tons; 3 converted (plus 1 unconverted).

Displacement: 3,000 tons (3,800 full load).
Dimensions: Length overall 415ft (126·5m); beam 42ft 7in (13m); draught 16ft 6in (5·03m).
Armament: Bombardment missiles, four bins for SS-N-2 abeam rear funnel; AS weapons, two 16-barrel MBU on fo'c'sle; guns, two twin 76mm aft, four quad 57mm forward and amidships; two sets twin 21in (533mm) torpedo tubes.
Propulsion: Two sets steam turbines, 72,000shp, maximum speed 36kt.
Originally laid down in 1955 as units of the Kotlin class, these four vessels were completed as the first carriers of the large SS-N-1 cruise missile, carried in a hangar behind the rear funnel and launched from a rather clumsy system riding on a trainable and elevatable rail on the quarterdeck. From 1972 three of the four ships were rebuilt with the four N-2 cruise-missile boxes and augmented gun armament, and are called large rocket ships. The fourth is unlikely to be modernized.

Right: A Soviet Kildin class destroyer in the grey waters of the Atlantic, its probable operational area in a future war.

Kotlin class destroyers

Kotlin class DD ; 3800 tons ; 18 built.

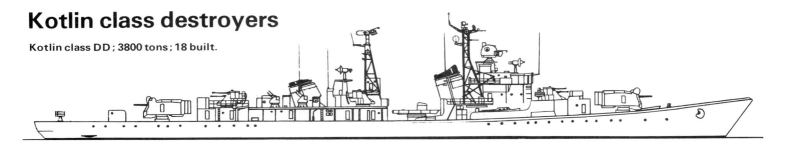

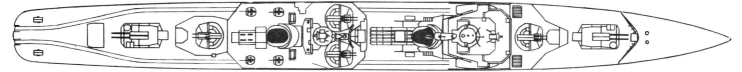

Displacement: Typically about 2,850 tons (3,885 full load).

Dimensions: Length overall 415ft (126·5m); beam 42ft 7in (13m); draught 16ft 1in (4·9m).

Armament: Missiles, none; AS weapons, originally six depth-charge projectors, but replaced progressively by two 16-barrel rocket launchers, guns, originally two twin 5.1in (130mm) at front and rear on flush deck, plus four quad 45mm (front and rear in B and X positions and abeam amidships), but progressively being modified with four or eight 25mm added; torpedoes, originally two sets quintuple 21in (533mm) tubes on centreline amidships and behind rear funnel, but rear set often replaced by deckhouse; mimes, 80 as originally built.

Propulsion: Two sets steam turbines, 72,000shp, maximum speed 36kt.

Immediate successors to the prolific Skory class in the early post-war years, the Kotlins were likewise designed for rapid mass-production and were probably intended to number at least 50. Eventually only about 30 were completed, the last four being modified into the Kildin class. They proved to be seaworthy and reliable, but by later standards are completely outdated. About 15–18 remain in commission, nearly all with significant modifications. *Svetly* has a Ka-25 helicopter for AS duty (so-called 'Kotlin Helo' class, with raised platform immediately below 5·1in gun level at the stern). Electronics, especially radar and communications,

have been progressively updated, and AS gear has been improved by removing TT and DC-projectors and adding the MBU rocket installations. At least eight have been converted to the Kotlin SAM class.

Below: A Kotlin class destroyer in the Philippine Sea during Exercise Okean. The unmodified Kotlins are now completely outdated ; many are in reserve.

Bottom: A Nimrod of the RAF flies over-flies over a Kotlin class destroyer. Note the lack of electronic arrays compared to later Soviet ships.

Kotlin-SAM class destroyers

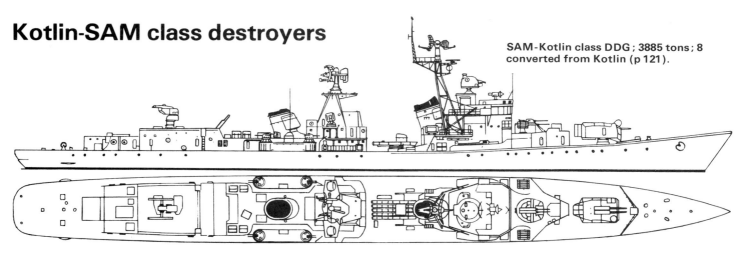

SAM-Kotlin class DDG; 3885 tons; 8 converted from Kotlin (p 121).

Displacement: 2,850 tons (3,885 full load).
Dimensions: Length overall 415ft (126·5m); beam 42ft 7in (13m); draught 16ft 1in (4·9m).
Armament: Surface-to-air missiles, one twin installation for SA-N-1 aft (X position); AS weapons, two 12-barrel MBU launchers (each side ahead of bridge); guns, one twin 100mm (foredeck, A position), one quad 45mm (ahead of bridge, B position) three quads in one ship and, in most, eight 30mm 'Gatlings' (twins abeam rear funnel); torpedoes one set quintuple 21in (533mm) amidships.
Propulsion: Two sets steam turbines, 72,000shp, maximum speed 36kt.

Eight of the useful Kotlin class destroyers were rebuilt in 1960–68 so extensively as to warrant classification as a new class. The four quad 45mm guns were replaced by a single quad 57mm, and an SA-N-1 installation was added together with the Peel Group radar fire control on new electronics towers. The 130mm guns were replaced by a single quick-fire 100mm turret, and the entire interior and deck area was rearranged for greater efficiency with updated equipment. Most of these destroyers have the 30mm guns with associated Drum Tilt radars, further augmenting their capability against aircraft and soft-skinned targets. One was transferred to Poland.

Right: A SAM-Kotlin class destroyer. The conversion consisted of replacing the after twin turret with a SA-N-1 missile launcher and magazine.

Bottom: The destroyer *Bravy*, on Exercise Okean 75, was the prototype in the conversion programme and is the only one to retain the amidships quad 45mm AA mountings and has different funnels.

Krivak class destroyers

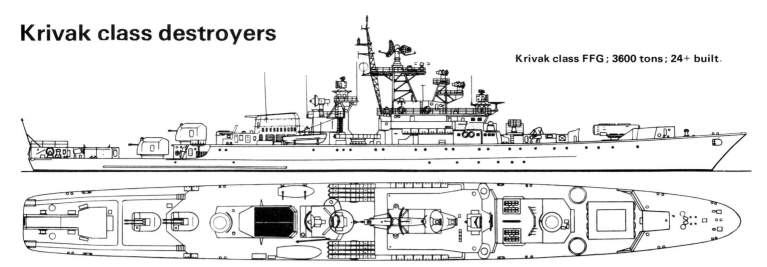

Krivak class FFG; 3600 tons; 24+ built.

Displacement: 3,300 tons (3,600 full load).
Dimensions: Length overall 405ft (123·4m); beam 46ft (14m); draught 16ft 5in (5m).
Armament: Bombardment missiles, quadruple launch tubes for SS-N-14 on foredeck; surface-to-air missiles, two silos for SA-N-4 (one abaft N-14 launch tubes, the other between funnel and guns); AS weapons, two 12-barrel MBU launchers (forward of bridge); guns, two twin 76mm (aft, in X and Y positions) or (Krivak-II) two single 100mm, two twin 30mm (each side abeam bridge); torpedoes, two quadruple sets of 21in (533mm) tubes amidships.
Propulsion: Four sets of gas turbines, total 72,000shp on two shafts, maximum speed 32kt.

These splendid ships perfectly typify the modern Soviet philosophy with surface ships: big on weapons, electronics and power, small on hull. Though classed as destroyers, they pack a bigger punch than almost any Western cruiser, and as well as four multi-reload bombardment missiles have very considerable gun power, SAM capability and outstanding AS effectiveness with VDS (variable-depth sonar) and a large hull-mounted sonar. The Krivaks were among the first ships to appear with the SA-N-4 missile. Not least of their capabilities is reliability and good sea-keeping. By late 1979 there were 17 in commission, with production continuing, plus seven of the big gun Krivak-II class. Soviet designation was originally large-AS ship but was changed to escort. NATO calls this class missile frigates.

Right: A Krivak-II class frigate, photographed from HMS Londonderry's helicopter during Exercise Okean 75.

Below: The Krivaks are handsome, well-designed and efficient escorts.

Riga class frigates

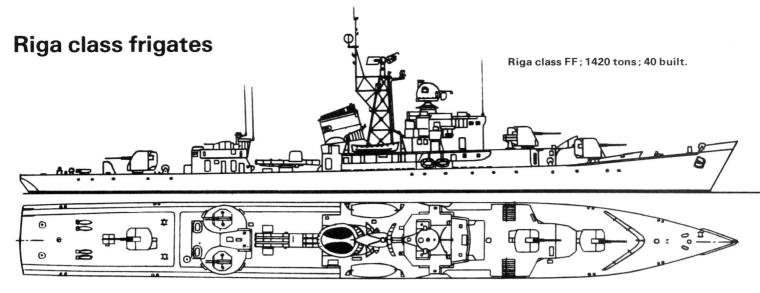

Riga class FF; 1420 tons; 40 built.

Displacement: 1,200 tons (1,600 full load).
Dimensions: Length overall 299ft (91m); beam 33ft 8in (10·2m); draught 11ft (3·4m).
Armament: AS weapons, two 16-barrel AS rocket launchers, four depth-charge projectors; guns, three 3·9in (100mm) (single turrets, in A, B and Y positions) and two twin 37mm; torpedoes, one set triple 21in (533mm) tubes.
Propulsion: Steam turbines, 20,000shp on two shafts, maximum speed 28kt.

About 65 of this trim class were built in the 1950s, to replace the bigger Kola series. Flush-decked, they are relatively conventional, and can carry mines for laying along rails at the stern. Considerable numbers of these vessels have been transferred to other navies, and it is doubtful if the number in Soviet service now exceeds 40. They carry the usual Slim Net search radar, but their overall equipment with electronics is modest in comparison with later vessels in the same category.

Right: The Riga class escorts were built in the 1950s and are now somewhat dated.

Below: The crew of a Riga class escort enjoy the tropical sun off the Philippines. A number of these ships are now in reserve.

Petya class frigates

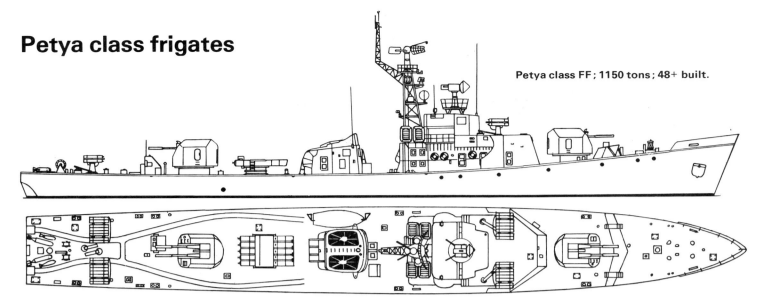

Petya class FF; 1150 tons; 48+ built.

Displacement: 950 tons (1,150 full load).
Dimensions: Length overall 270ft (82·3m); beam 29ft 11in (9·1m); draught 10ft 6in (3·2m).
Armament: AS weapons, two standards, either (Petya I) four 16-barrel AS rocket launchers or (Petya II) two 12-barrel MBU launchers ahead of bridge; guns, usually two twin 76mm (some ships, VDS instead of rear turret); torpedoes, two sets quintuple 16in (406mm) AS tubes (some ships, including most Petya I, only one set).
Propulsion: Combined diesel and gas turbine (CODOG), with one 6,000shp diesel and two

15,000shp gas turbines, giving total of 36,000shp on three shafts, maximum speed 34kt.

The first Petyas were built at Kaliningrad (formerly Königsberg) in 1960, and were among the first production ships with CODOG propulsion in the world. Their extremely squat square funnel was a portent of shapes to come with much bigger ships, but their armament is traditional. Compared with previous frigates their electronic equipment is comprehensive, and Slim Net and Hawk Screech radars are backed up by much other gear. Probably all will

eventually have the MBU launchers and VDS (variable-depth sonar) instead of the aft turret. About 50 were in use by 1980, in several versions.

Below: A Petya-II class frigate. The main identification features of this sub-type are the additional torpedo mount on the stern and the smooth top to the funnel. These small ships were the first in the world to feature CODOG (combined gas turbine and diesel) propulsion.

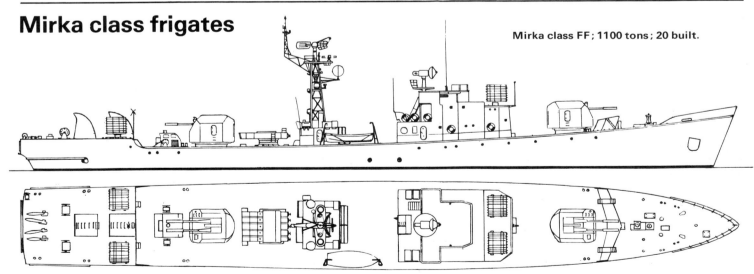

Mirka class frigates

Mirka class FF; 1100 tons; 20 built.

Displacement: 950 tons (1,100 full load).
Dimensions: Length overall 270ft (82·3m); beam 29ft 11in (9·1m); draught 9ft 10in (3m).
Armament: AS weapons, two or four 12-barrel MBU launchers (some, two 16-barrel AS rocket launchers); guns, two twin 76mm; torpedoes, one or two sets of quintuple 16in (406mm) AS tubes.
Propulsion: CODOG, two 6,000shp diesels and two

15,000shp gas turbines, total 42,000shp on two shafts, maximum speed 34kt.

Improved Petyas, these neat frigates were built during the 1960s. Their appearance was at first sight unusual, because (like the prolific Poti corvettes and several other Soviet classes) they have no conventional funnel. In the West they are commonly divided into two

groups, Mirka I having a single set of torpedo tubes aft of the single mast and Mirka II having a second set ahead of it. Nearly all Mirkas seem to use the 12-barrel MBU launcher, but there are variations in equipment and some ships carry VDS (variable-depth sonar) at the stern. The speed of 34kt is almost certainly a conservative estimate. Total in service appears to be 20.

Grisha class corvettes

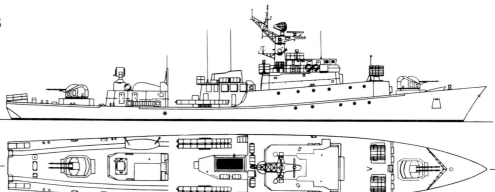

Displacement: 900 tons (1,000 full load).
Dimensions: Length overall 234ft 10in (71·6m); beam 32ft 10in (10m); draught 9ft 2in (2·8m).
Armament: AS weapons, two 12-barrel MBU launchers; surface-to-air missiles, single silo for SA-N-4 in bow; guns, one twin 57mm (stern); torpedoes, two pairs 21in (533mm) tubes at sides amidships.
Propulsion: CODOG, two 9,000shp diesels and one 12,000shp gas turbine, total about 30,000shp on three shafts, maximum speed 30kt.

Newest corvettes in the Soviet Navy, these remarkable vessels show that the brilliance in modern Soviet ship design is not confined to big warships. They have proved to be outstanding sea boats, and to be able to maintain very high speeds even in rough weather. Their versatility is considerable, and they are well equipped with electronic equipment of all kinds. They retain a funnel, a square casing around the combined CODOG uptakes. About three or four of these craft are being delivered each year, the total by 1980 being

about 35. It is difficult to see how these corvettes could be improved, but one may be certain that new designs, with even more advanced weapon systems, are now in production, such as the Tarantul class first seen in 1979.

Grisha class corvette; 1000 tons; 35 built.

Below: A Grisha-III corvette's after-deck showing the 23mm Gatling-type close-in defence system, and the twin 57mm.

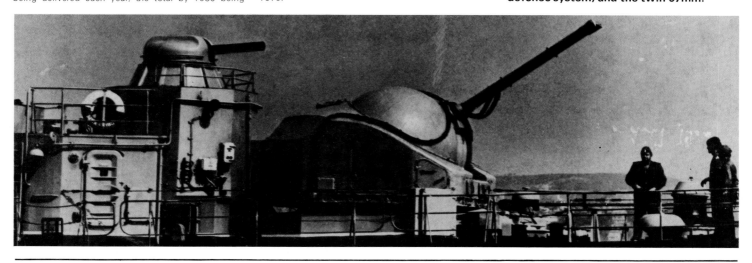

Nanuchka class small missile boats

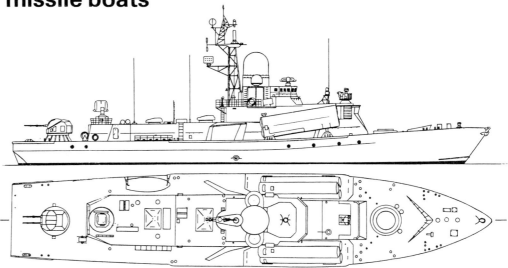

Displacement: 800 tons (about 900 full load).
Dimensions: Length overall 196ft 10in (60m); beam 39ft 7in (12m); draught 9ft 11in (3m).
Armament: Bombardment missiles, two triple boxes for launching SS-N-9 missiles; surface-to-air missiles, twin silo for SA-N-4 in bow; AS weapons, one (sometimes two) 12-barrel MBU launcher; guns, one twin 57mm (aft); some have 76mm gun aft and 30mm 'Gatling'.
Propulsion: Six 4,670shp diesels on three shafts, maximum speed 32kt.

These broad-beamed missile carriers pose a number of enigmas, not least of which is the N-9 missile. The latter is briefly referred to on another page, but appears to be different from the missiles used in all other Soviet naval vessels. They are apparently guided during the initial part of their flight by the large radar housed in a dome on the superstructure, which again was new when it appeared on the first Nanuchka in 1969. Other radars include Slim Net for search, Hawk Screech for the 57mm guns and Skin Head on each side of the large dome. They are markedly larger than previous inshore SSM carriers such as the Osa and Komar classes.

Nanuchka class corvette; 950 tons; 194 built of two types.

Left: The Nanuchka class missile corvettes remain a unique concept and epitomise the willingness of Soviet naval staffs and designers to consider new approaches and to produce revolutionary ships and weapons. The large triple silos for the SS-N-9 anti-ship missiles flank the bridge while the twin 57mm AA mount is on the quarterdeck. The crew of 60 is large for a hull of this size, but is necessitated by the variety of weapons and electronic equipment. Three Nanuchka-IIs were exported to India, specially modified to take SS-N-2 missiles.

Poti class corvettes

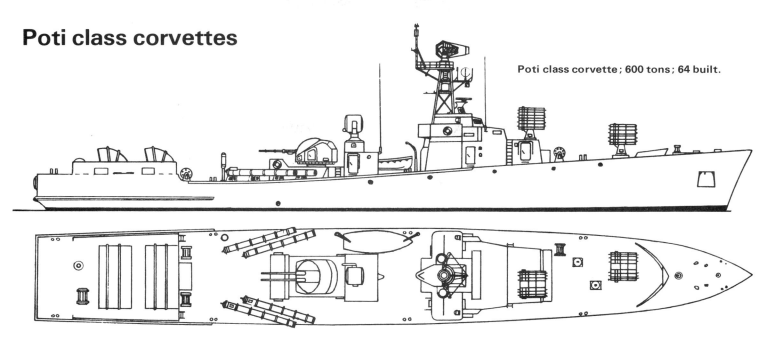

Poti class corvette; 600 tons; 64 built.

Displacement: 550 tons (650 full load).
Dimensions: Length overall 195ft 6in (59·5m); beam 26ft 2in (8m); draught 9ft 2in (2·8m).
Armament: AS weapons, two 12-barrel MBU launchers (foredeck and ahead of bridge, A and B positions); guns, one twin 57mm (high, amidships); torpedoes, two pairs 16in (406mm) AS tubes (at sides, just aft of guns).

Propulsion: CODOG, two 4,000shp diesels on two outer shafts, two 12,000shp gas turbines on two inner shafts, maximum speed about 34kt.

At least 70 of these trim craft have been commissioned since 1961. They were the first CODOG-powered corvettes, and are in consequence markedly faster than their all-diesel predecessors (indeed they virtually began a new class of small high-speed multi-role craft). They have no conventional funnel (stack) and, like the Grisha class which succeeded them, have high freeboard at the bows falling away with a sloping deck. Standard radars include Strut Curve surveillance atop the mast and Muff Cob amidships for gunfire direction.

Osa class small missile boats

Displacement: 165 tons (200 full load).
Dimensions: Length overall 128ft 8in (39·2m); beam 25ft 1in (7·65m); draught 5ft 11in (1·8m).
Armament: Surface-to-surface missiles, two pairs of launchers for SS-N-2A (in tandem on left and right, reloadable only in port); guns, two twin 30mm (front and rear). Osa II class, four tubular launchers for SS-N-11.
Propulsion: Three diesels, 13,000shp on three shafts, maximum speed 32 knots.

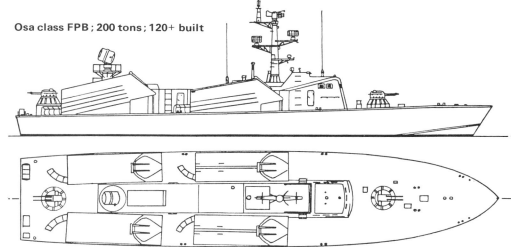

Osa class FPB; 200 tons; 120+ built

Though the prior existence of the remarkable Komar class blunted the impact of these boats on the world naval scene, the sheer number of some 220 of the Osa class have made them a force to be reckoned with. Of these, about 100 have been sold or transferred to other navies, where several have seen action (for example, Indian Osa boats wrought havoc among Pakistani shipping in the war of 1971). Compared with the Komars they are considerably bigger, and better equipped for all-weather operations. Targets are sought on the Square Tie surveillance radar on the masthead, while gunfire is directed by the Drum Tilt on a pylon between the rear missile tubes. In later Osas the missile launchers are tubes, rather than boxes, they are called 'Osa II' class, numbering about 55.

Right: An Osa class missile patrol boat at sea. This class was quite revolutionary when built in the early 1950s, but are being replaced by hydrofoils.

Below: An Osa-II dressed overall for inspection. Osa-I has larger launcher of squarer cross-section for SS-N-2 (Styx), while Osa-II has small, round launchers for SS-N-2 (Mod) missiles. Note beamy, hard-chine hull.

Komar class
small missile boats

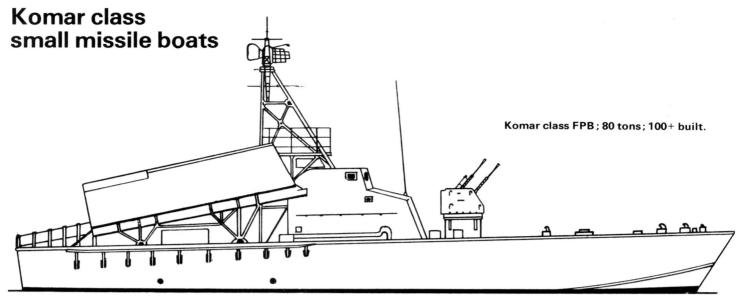

Komar class FPB; 80 tons; 100+ built.

Displacement: 70 tons (80 full load).
Dimensions: Length 83ft 8in (25·5m); beam 19ft 10in (6m); draught 5ft (1·52m).
Armament: Surface-to-surface missiles, two shrouded cylindrical launchers for SS-N-2A (on deck, toed outwards on each side); guns, one twin 25mm (foredeck).
Propulsion: Four 1,200shp diesels, total 4,800shp on four shafts, maximum speed reputedly 40kt.

These small craft did not burst like a bombshell over the world's navies; for several years after their appearance in 1961 they were regarded as odd curiosities. Nobody in any Western navy did anything to counter their menace, nor was any move made to emulate them by developing a similar annihilating bombardment missile that could be carried by small craft in the West. Not until the Egyptians fired N-2As at the Israeli destroyer *Eilat* on 21 October 1967, sinking it with three direct hits, did the rest of the world suddenly recognise that here was a craft as nimble and hard to hit as the traditional MTB or PT-boat which could destroy the largest ships from ranges greater than the biggest gun. About 70 Komars were converted from P6 class patrol boats, most having now been transferred to other navies.

Right: The Komar class were the world's first guided missile armed small patrol boats, mounting two SS-N-2 launchers. They have been replaced by the Osa and later classes, but a few may remain.

Stenka class torpedo boats

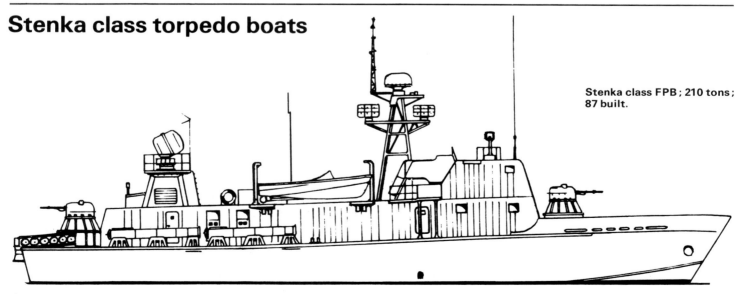

Stenka class FPB; 210 tons; 87 built.

Displacement: 170 tons (210 full load).
Dimensions: Length overall 130ft 8in (39·8m); beam 25ft 1in (7·65m); draught 6ft (1·82m).
Armament: Torpedoes, four 16in (406mm) AS tubes, two in tandem on each side; guns, two twin 30mm (front and rear); AS weapons, depth charge racks at stern.

Propulsion: Three 4,000shp diesels, three shafts, maximum speed 36kt.

The 90-plus boats of this class were based on the Osa, but carry torpedoes instead of missiles. Correctly described as inshore multi-role boats, they are well equipped with electronics and have Square Tie surveillance radar at the masthead. Drum Tilt for gunfire control and a Pot Drum small surveillance scanner atop the lattice tower mast. Extremely fast, the Stenkas have entered service since 1968, and the only unexplained fact about them is how they can be so much faster than the smaller Osas, on less power.

Pchela class patrol hydrofoils

Displacement: (When buoyant) 70 tons (80 full load).
Dimensions: Length overall 82ft (25m); beam 19ft 8in (6m); draught, not relevant when running on foils.
Armament: Two twin 12·7 or 13mm machine guns; depth charge projectors.
Propulsion: Two 2,400shp diesels, on two shafts, maximum speed 45kt.

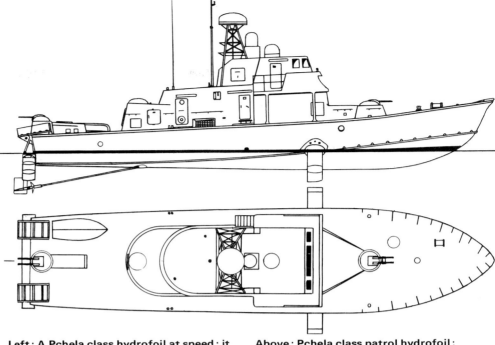

Left: A Pchela class hydrofoil at speed; it is reported that all are KGB-operated.

Above: Pchela class patrol hydrofoil; 80 tons; 20 built.

Most Soviet transport hydrofoil boats use the shallow 'depth effect' foil and are suitable for running over inland waterways. These patrol craft use the surface-piercing system, better adapted to running through a choppy sea. About 40 have been delivered since 1964, most carrying Pot Drum search radar and other electronic installations. None has yet been seen with missiles or torpedo tubes.

Turya class patrol hydrofoils

Turya class hydrofoil; 190 tons; 100+ built.

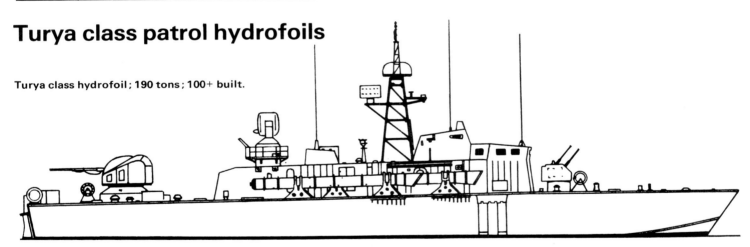

Displacement (or mass): 165 tons (maximum 190 tons).
Dimensions: Length overall 123ft 1in (37.5m), beam 27ft 10½in (8.5m); draught (foilborne) 5ft 11in (1.8m).
Armament: Four 21in (533mm) torpedo tubes, or various missile installations; twin 57mm guns (aft); twin 25mm guns (forward).
Propulsion: Three 5,000shp diesels; foilborne, up to 45kt.

Produced at yards at both ends of the Soviet Union, this refined patrol hydrofoil is in service in considerable numbers (probably 120 by mid-1976) and is appearing with different equipment fits. Most carry 'Pot Drum' and 'Drum Tilt' radars, and appear to be used mainly for ASW roles, cruising as displacement vessels.

Right: A Turya class hydrofoil cruising hull-borne. The Soviet Navy has spent a considerable amount of attention on its coastal forces, producing a variety of types. Development now appears to centre on hydrofoils, using the shallow 'depth effect' foil which are trapezoidal in profile and heavily braced.

Shershen class torpedo boats

Displacement: 150 tons (160 full load).
Dimensions: Length overall 115ft 6in (35·2m); beam 23ft 1in (7m); draught 5ft (1·52m).
Armament: Torpedoes, four 21in (533mm) in tandem on left and right; AS weapons, 12 depth charges; guns, two twin 30mm (front and rear).
Propulsion: Three diesels, total 12,000shp on three shafts, maximum speed 38kt.

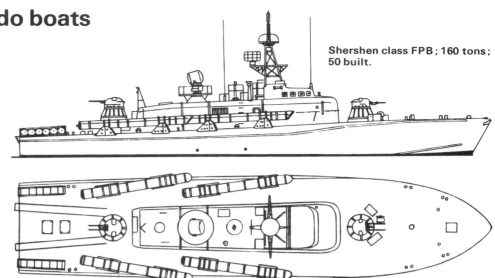

Shershen class FPB; 160 tons; 50 built.

Another class based on the hull of the Osa missile boats, the Shershens are effective torpedo boats with the most modern electronics and the new automatic 30mm gun turrets. About 100 have been built since 1962, of which about half have been sold or transferred to other navies. The torpedoes used in these boats are the large 21in type, not the 406mm species used for AS work. Radars include Drum Tilt for gunfire and Pot Drum for search.

Below: Two shots of Shershen class torpedo boats, showing slight differences, especially in the radar fit. Production of these boats has been completed, with some 50 in Soviet service, and many exported.

P-classes of torpedo boats

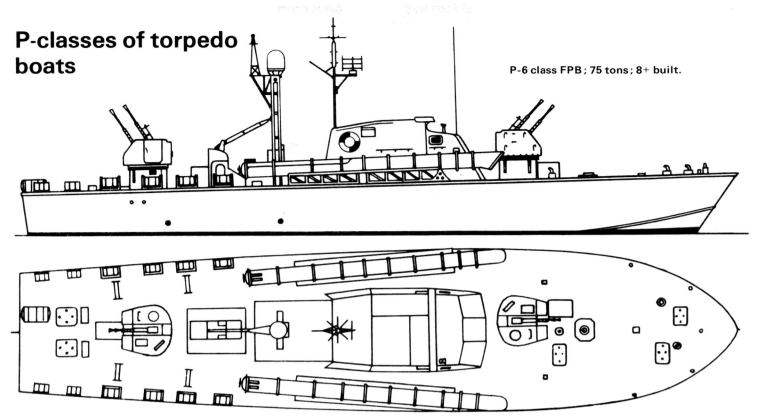

P-6 class FPB; 75 tons; 8+ built.

Displacement: Typically 66 tons (75 full load).
Dimensions: Length overall 84ft 2in (25·7m); beam 20ft (6·1m); draught 6ft (1·83m).
Armament: Torpedoes, usually two 21in (533mm) tubes, left and right; guns, two twin 25mm (front and rear); some boats carry AS weapons or mines instead of torpedo tubes.
Propulsion: P6 class, four 1,200shp diesels, four shafts, maximum speed 43kt; P8 and P10 classes, two

or four gas turbines, total over 6,000shp, maximum speed about 45kt.

Designed in the late 1940s, the P6 class went into production in 1951 and at least 200 were built (some were converted, for example into Komar missile craft). The more powerful P8 and P10 series can be distinguished by the exhaust stack (funnel) behind the changed superstructure. All have Pot Drum search

radar, and many other electronic systems. About 130 of all classes are in Soviet use, and about 200 in other countries (at least 80 were built in China).

Below: P-6 class FPBs at speed. This class shows a distinct resemblance to the American Electric Boat Company boats supplied to the USSR under Lend-Lease in World War II. They are constructed mainly of wood.

Yurka class minesweepers

Displacement: 400 tons (450 full load).
beam 31ft 4in (9·5m); draught 8ft 11in (2·7m).
Armament: Two twin 30mm gun turrets.
Propulsion: Two 2,000shp diesels, two shafts, maximum speed 18kt.

During the 1960s about 49 of these neat MCM (mine counter-measures) ships were commissioned, and they are likely to stay in service for another decade. Hulls are known to be steel.

Right: The 49 ships of the Yurka class were built between 1963 and 1969. Of steel construction, they are powered by two side-by-side diesels and have a range of 1100 miles at 18 knots. They are a very considerable improvement on the T-58 minesweepers which they replaced, and the high freeboard is especially noteworthy.

Natya class minesweepers

Displacement: 650 tons (750 full load).
Dimensions: Length overall 200ft 1in (61m); beam 34ft 1in (10·4m); draught 7ft 2in (2·2m).
Armament: AS weapons, two six-barrel MBU launchers; guns, two twin 30mm, two twin 25mm.
Propulsion: Two 2,400shp diesels, two shafts, maximum speed 18kt.

Currently being produced at the rate of 3–4 per year, the Natyas are standard mine-warfare vessels and about 34 are in commission so far. As might be expected, they are extremely well equipped with MCM (mine countermeasures) gear, and have a large lattice mast bristling from base to tip with electronics. Hull material is not known.

Below: A Natya class minesweeper at sea. Even this is much more heavily armed than its Western equivalents. Some have been deployed to the Mediterranean.

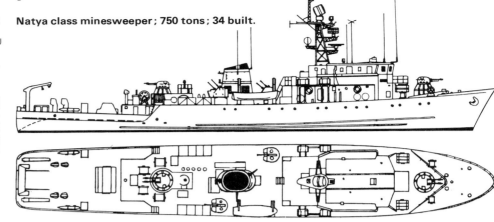

Natya class minesweeper; 750 tons; 34 built.

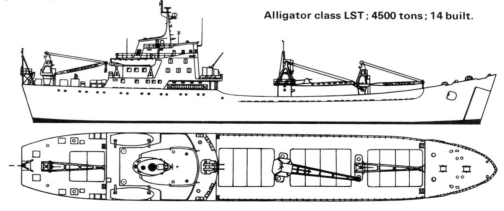

Alligator class landing ships

Displacement: 3,400 tons (4,800 full load).
Dimensions: Length overall 374ft (114m); beam 50ft 11in (15·5m); draught 12ft 1in (3·7m).
Armament: One twin 57mm gun turret.
Propulsion: Diesel, total 9,000shp, maximum speed 18kt.

First commissioned in 1966, at least 14 of these vessels had entered service by 1974, and they were followed by 13 of the newer Ropucha class now being made in Poland at three per year. They are the largest Soviet amphibious assault vessels, with carrying capacity of 1,500 tons and large ramps at both bow and stern. Examples are in use with either one, two or three cranes, the newer one-crane type being predominant.

Below: An Alligator-II LST in the South China Sea, with a class of marines being lectured under the crane jib.

Alligator class LST; 4500 tons; 14 built.

Polnocny class landing ships

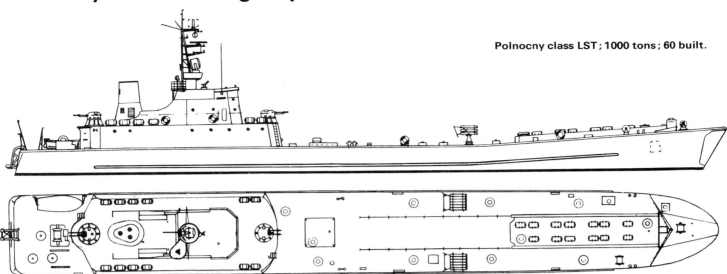

Polnocny class LST; 1000 tons; 60 built.

Displacement: 780 tons (1,000 full load, and see text for Polnocny 'Type IX').

Dimensions: Length overall 246ft (75m), except Type IX 265ft (80·7m); beam 29ft 6in (9m) (Type IX, 27ft 8in, 8·44m); draught 9ft 10in (3m).

Armament: Two 18-barrel rocket launchers (left and right, on foredeck) for bombarding hostile shores; in nearly all, one twin 30mm gun turret.

Propulsion: Two 2,500shp diesels. maximum speed 18kt.

By far the most numerous Soviet amphibious assault ships, the Polnocnys now number about 70, in ten classes. The only significantly different group is the 'Type IX', which has a longer but slightly slimmer hull of greater displacement. Cargo is loaded and unloaded through the full section bow doors, a typical load including six battle tanks. Gun-equipped ships, which are almost standard, have Muff Cob radar atop the superstructure.

Right: This close-up of a Polish Polnocny class LST shows the newly-fitted helicopter platform surrounded by safety nets.

Below: A Polnocny class LST at sea. There are nine versions of this class, all built at the Polish shipyards at Gdansk, releasing Soviet yards for other work.

Ivan Rogov class landing ships

Displacement: 11,000 tons (13,100 full load).
Dimensions: Length overall 522ft (159m); beam 80ft (24·5m); draught 21—28ft (6·5—8·5m).
Armament: Two twin SA-N-4 silos; twin 76mm guns; four 23mm 'Gatling'; two 20-barrel rocket launchers (Army BM-21 type).
Propulsion: Four 5,000shp diesels, maximum speed 20kt.

These impressive vessels began to appear in 1978. ACVs (hovercraft) can be carried in a docking bay and there are spots for helicopters front and rear with flying-control posts and rear hangar. Accommodation is provided for a battalion of troops, 40 battle tanks and support vehicles.

Above and below: Ivan Rogovs can carry a marine battalion, 40 tanks and support vehicles, and can also be fitted out for use as command centres.

Aist class air cushion vehicles

Displacement: 220 tons.
Dimensions: length overall 150ft (45.7m); beam 60ft (18.3m).
Armament: Two twin 30mm cannon.
Propulsion: Two gas turbines driving four propellers and four lift fanx, 70kts.

The Soviet Union, and especially the Navy, has shown itself remarkably eager to seize upon and develop new ideas in marked contrast to the normal conservatism of the Russian character. They have, therefore, been in the forefront of development of the ACV and there are many such craft in civil use, while the navy currently has 52 in commission, 18 with the Baltic Fleet, 18 with the Pacific Fleet and 16 shared between the Black and Caspian Seas.

Eleven 15-ton *Lebed* class have been in service since 1967 and these small craft paved the way for the 27-ton *Gus* class, which is designed to carry 50 Soviet marines on amphibious operations. These ACVs are powered by three 780hp gas turbines; two for propulsion and one for lift, and are a navalised version of the civil *Skate* class. Next to appear was the impressive *Aist* class, which is specifically designed for naval use. Eight are known to be in service, but more will undoubtedly appear, adding significantly to the Soviet capability to carry out rapid, short-range coastal strikes against NATO targets in Scandinavia and on the Baltic.

Above: A Gus class air cushion vehicle (ACV), the navalised version of the 50-seat Skate class, powered by three 780hp gas turbines.

Below: The Soviets have siezed upon the British invention of the ACV; this Aist class has been developed for the Marines.

Ugra class submarine support ships

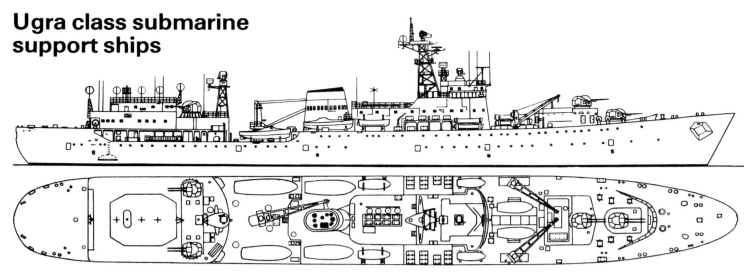

Displacement: 6,750 tons (9,500 full load).
Dimensions: Length overall 463ft 10in (141·5m); beam 57ft 7in (17·6m); draught 22ft 6in (6·9m).
Armament: Usually four twin 57mm, with two Hawk Screech fire-control radars.
Propulsion: Four diesels, 16,000shp, maximum speed 21kt.

These ships are packed with equipment and facilities and are virtually floating dockyards. About ten have been built at Nikolayev since 1961, one being sold to India. They contain elaborate workshops, stores and test facilities for ship systems, weapons and electronics, as well as accommodation for several submarine crews. Among their electronics are Slim Net search radar, Strut Curve and Muff Cob. Still in service are six older Don-class ships. Only two (called Don Helo class) have helicopter provision, which is standard in the Ugras. Type of helicopter varies, but is often a Ka-25 transport version.

Ugra class training ship (developed from submarine tender); 9500 tons; 2 built.

Below: An Ugra class submarine tender. There are seven ships, with a further two converted to training ships as shown above. A further depot ship has been transferred to the Indian Navy. All are well equipped for operations away from base.

Primorye class intelligence ships

Displacement: 5,000 tons.
Dimensions: Length overall 274ft (83·5m); beam 47ft 2in (14·4m); draught 26ft 6in (8m).
Propulsion: Probably two 2,500shp diesels, about 14kt.

Primorye class AGI; 4500 tons; 6 built.

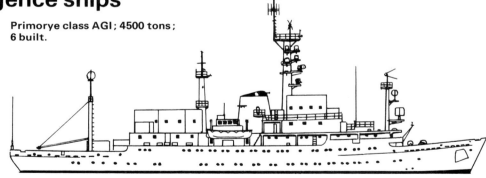

The Soviet Union has more intelligence-gathering ships than the rest of the world combined, a known total of more than 70 vessels. Some are similar to large oceangoing trawlers, many are large and carefully planned, and the six ships of this class are unlike anything else afloat. Their names are Primorye, Kavkaz, Krym, Zabaikalye, Zakarpatye and Zaporozhye. Each is a huge floating intelligence station, linked by the most elaborate communications systems with sensors in smaller ships, in aircraft and probably in the great number of Soviet military satellites which constantly overfly Western territories. The interiors, of course, are unknown, but there seems every likelihood that complete processing (for example, of photographs and electronic signatures) and analysis are performed on board. The results are doubtless transmitted by a secure (satellite) link to Moscow.

Right: A Primorye class intelligence collecting ship. Unlike their predecessors these ships were purpose-built for their role and have complete on-board processing capability. It appears that direct inputs from 'spy' satellites are possible, and that satellites are also used to pass processed information back to the USSR.

Kosmonaut Yuryi Gagarin

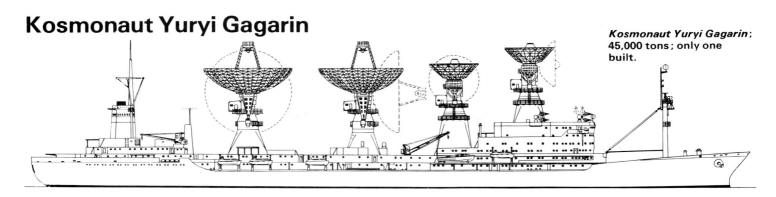

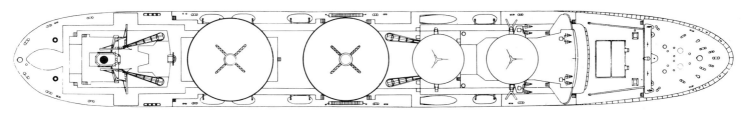

*Kosmonaut Yuryi Gagarin;
45,000 tons; only one
built.*

Displacement: 45,000 tons.
Dimensions: Length overall 773ft 4in (235·7m);
beam 101ft 8in (31m); draught 30ft (9·14m).
Propulsion: Single set geared steam turbines,
19,000shp, maximum speed 17kt.

Largest Soviet research ship, and almost certainly the
largest in the world, this striking vessel was built at
Leningrad in 1970–71, with a hull based on an
established Soviet tanker design. She carries two pairs
of steerable receiver aerial dishes, and their signals are
processed in large laboratories. Her purpose is research
into the control of space vehicles, space communications, upper-atmospheric conditions and other
phenomena. Based at Odessa, she has made several
long voyages. To facilitate accurate positioning (not
necessarily at berthing) she has front and rear lateral
thrusters.

**Right: The extraordinary lines of the 'space
associated' ship *Yuryi Gagarin*. Should all
four antennas be facing forwards their
wind resistance causes a 2 knot speed loss.**

Kosmonaut Vladimir Komarov

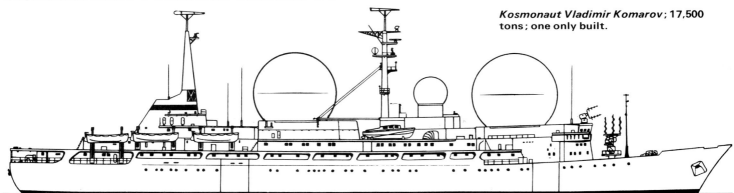

*Kosmonaut Vladimir Komarov; 17,500
tons; one only built.*

Displacement: 17,500 tons.
Dimensions: Length overall 510ft 10in (155·7m);
beam 75ft 6in (23m); draught 29ft 6in (9m).
Propulsion: Two sets of diesels, total 24,000shp,
maximum speed 22kt.

Another of the remarkable Soviet 'space ships'
Komarov was built in 1966 at Leningrad for the
Academy of Sciences ostensibly to study the upper
atmosphere in the Western Atlantic. Her hull is bulged
along each side into huge overhanging sponsons (not
clearly visible in a side view such as the photograph
on this page) and she has appeared in different paint
schemes and with slightly different electronic fits.
The two large and one small radomes are self-evident;
the larger ones could enclose 50ft dishes.

**Right: The space research ship *Kosmonaut
Vladimir Komarov* at sea. Note huge
radomes and 'V-cones' at the mast-heads.**

The Modern Soviet Ground Forces

The most immediate threat to Western Europe is the Soviet Army, with its vast numbers of men and great quantities of equipment. It is not only Europe which is threatened, however, as experience in Afghanistan has shown. One of the basic tenets of Soviet tactical doctrine is that the offensive is the only practicable form of warfare for the Soviet Union, and everything about the army – tactics, organisation, equipment – is designed with this in view. This leads the USSR to produce tanks which are quite unlike the heavy, well-protected machines produced in NATO.

The tank still dominates the Soviet concept of the modern battle, and the USSR has the world's largest tank fleet. Many of the postwar developments in the army have aimed at raising other arms of the ground forces to the level of speed, mobility and protection possessed by the Tank Troops.

Christopher Donnelly

The Soviet Ground Forces constitute a separate arm of service in the Soviet Union, second in importance only to the Strategic Rocket Forces. The 1,825,000 men under the command of General of the Army I. G. Pavlovskii form the very foundation of the Soviet Army; and although in the Khrushchev period their importance was in fact diminished as a result of that politician's belief that any major war would inevitably be waged with strategic nuclear weapons, today the Ground Forces' importance is fully recognised by the leaders of the USSR. As a result the Ground Forces are being constantly strengthened and modernised, to improve their capability to fight either a conventional or a nuclear war.

The various types of troops that make up

Above: The second major arm of the Soviet Army is the artillery, which has always been both efficient and well equipped. These are 130mm M-46 field guns.

Below: The one essential element in any army is the individual man with the rifle. Soviet soldiers are sturdy and patriotic, but some 90 per cent are conscripts.

the formation of the Ground Forces fall into four categories: the teeth arms—motor-rifle (motorised infantry), tank and airborne troops; the artillery – missile troops, air-defence and field artillery; the special troops – engineer, signals and chemical troops; and supporting arms and rear services – transport, medical, traffic control and police etc.

A division is the basic all-arms formation, and the Soviets class their divisions as either Motor-Rifle, Tank or Airborne according to the identity of the major fighting arm in the division. The basic unit of the Soviet Ground Forces is the regiment, which is made up of three or four battalions plus support elements.

Motor-Rifle Battalion organisation

The standard composition of the motor-rifle battalion, the basic motorised infantry sub-unit, is given in a table. The battalion's teeth are its three motor-rifle companies, each of three platoons, each of three sections. A section travels in an armoured personnel carrier (APC) which may be of the BTR-50, BTR-60 or BMP series. In a motor-rifle

division, the infantry in the tank regiment and in one of the three motor-rifle regiments are carried in the BMP; the rest of that division's infantry are carried in the BTR-60P. The BTR-50, which used to carry infantry in tank units and formations, has now been replaced by the BMP in frontline Soviet Armies, but is still common elsewhere. A battalion's artillery support is provided by six 120-mm mortars and, in battalions not equipped with the BMP (which carries an anti-tank missile on each vehicle), an anti-tank platoon of two recoilless anti-tank guns and two anti-tank guided weapons (ATGWs). Battalion logistics support is contained in a 'tail' of only 15–16 vehicles

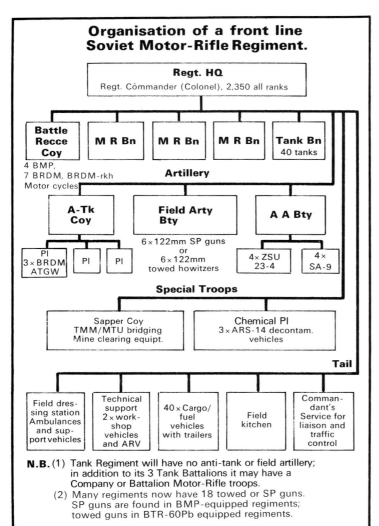

Organisation of a front line Soviet Motor-Rifle Regiment.

Regt. HQ
Regt. Commander (Colonel), 2,350 all ranks

- **Battle Recce Coy** — 4 BMP, 7 BRDM, BRDM-rkh Motor cycles
- **M R Bn**
- **M R Bn**
- **M R Bn**
- **Tank Bn** — 40 tanks

Artillery

- **A-Tk Coy**
  - PI — 3 × BRDM ATGW
  - PI
  - PI
- **Field Arty Bty** — 6 × 122mm SP guns or 6 × 122mm towed howitzers
- **A A Bty**
  - 4 × ZSU 23-4
  - 4 × SA-9

Special Troops

- **Sapper Coy** — TMM/MTU bridging Mine clearing equipt.
- **Chemical PI** — 3 × ARS-14 decontam. vehicles

Tail

- **Field dressing station** Ambulances and support vehicles
- **Technical support** 2 × workshop vehicles and ARV
- 40 × Cargo/fuel vehicles with trailers
- **Field kitchen**
- **Commandant's Service** for liaison and traffic control

N.B. (1) Tank Regiment will have no anti-tank or field artillery; in addition to its 3 Tank Battalions it may have a Company or Battalion Motor-Rifle troops.
(2) Many regiments now have 18 towed or SP guns. SP guns are found in BMP-equipped regiments; towed guns in BTR-60Pb equipped regiments.

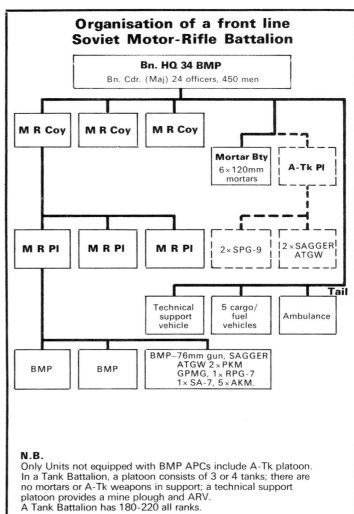

Organisation of a front line Soviet Motor-Rifle Battalion

Bn. HQ 34 BMP
Bn. Cdr. (Maj) 24 officers, 450 men

- **M R Coy**
- **M R Coy**
- **M R Coy**
- **Mortar Bty** — 6 × 120mm mortars
- **A-Tk PI**

- **M R PI**
- **M R PI**
- **M R PI**
- 2 × SPG-9
- 2 × SAGGER ATGW

Tail

- **Technical support vehicle**
- 5 cargo/fuel vehicles
- **Ambulance**

- **BMP**
- **BMP**
- BMP—76mm gun, SAGGER ATGW 2 × PKM GPMG, 1 × RPG-7 1 × SA-7, 5 × AKM.

N.B.
Only Units not equipped with BMP APCs include A-Tk platoon. In a Tank Battalion, a platoon consists of 3 or 4 tanks; there are no mortars or A-Tk weapons in support; a technical support platoon provides a mine plough and ARV.
A Tank Battalion has 180-220 all ranks.

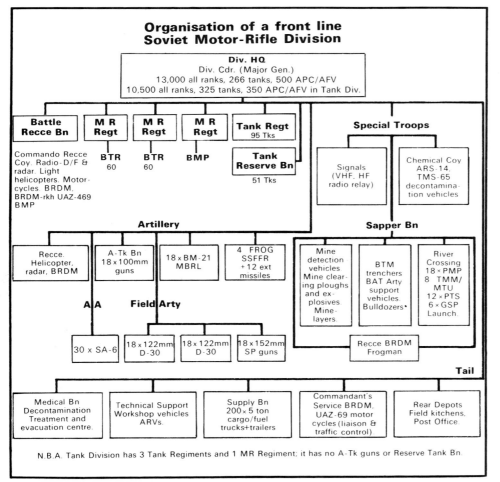

Organisation of a front line Soviet Motor-Rifle Division

Div. HQ
Div. Cdr. (Major Gen.)
13,000 all ranks, 266 tanks, 500 APC/AFV
10,500 all ranks, 325 tanks, 350 APC/AFV in Tank Div.

- **Battle Recce Bn** — Commando Recce Coy. Radio-D/F & radar. Light helicopters. Motorcycles. BRDM, BRDM-rkh UAZ-469 BMP
- **M R Regt** — BTR 60
- **M R Regt** — BTR 60
- **M R Regt** — BMP
- **Tank Regt** — 95 Tks
  - **Tank Reserve Bn** — 51 Tks
- **Special Troops**
  - **Signals** (VHF, HF radio relay)
  - **Chemical Coy** ARS-14, TMS-65 decontamination vehicles

Artillery

- **Recce.** Helicopter, radar, BRDM
- **A-Tk Bn** 18 × 100mm guns
- 18 × BM-21 MBRL
- 4 FROG SSFFR + 12 ext missiles

Sapper Bn

- Mine detection vehicles. Mine clearing ploughs and explosives. Minelayers.
- BTM trenchers BAT Arty support vehicles. Bulldozers.
- River Crossing 18 × PMP 8 TMM/MTU 12 × PTS 6 × GSP Launch.
- Recce BRDM Frogman

AA / Field Arty

- 30 × SA-6
- 18 × 122mm D-30
- 18 × 122mm D-30
- 18 × 152mm SP guns

Tail

- **Medical Bn** Decontamination Treatment and evacuation centre.
- **Technical Support** Workshop vehicles ARVs.
- **Supply Bn** 200 × 5 ton cargo/fuel trucks+trailers
- **Commandant's Service** BRDM, UAZ-69 motor cycles (liaison & traffic control)
- **Rear Depots** Field kitchens. Post Office.

N.B.A. Tank Division has 3 Tank Regiments and 1 MR Regiment; it has no A-Tk guns or Reserve Tank Bn.

for, as explained below, logistics are structured so as to ensure maximum mobility.

A tank battalion, the basic armoured sub-unit, is organised on similar lines, but has no mortars or anti-tank support, and has a slightly larger tail. The tank platoons in the tank battalions of a tank regiment have ten tanks per company, i.e. 31 per battalion. The tank platoons in the tank battalion organic to motor-rifle regiments have four tanks per platoon, i.e. 40 per battalion.

The basis of a motor-rifle regiment is three motor-rifle battalions plus one tank battalion of 40 tanks. In addition a regiment has strong support elements: a strong reconnaissance company equipped with reconnaissance versions of the BMP, BRDM heavy armoured reconnaissance vehicles and motorcycles for reconnaissance and liaison. At least two of the BRDMs will be equipped for reconnaissance in a nuclear, biological and chemical warfare (NBC) environment. Artillery support is provided by an anti-tank company, equipped with Sagger or Swatter ATGWs mounted on BRDM vehicles; an anti-aircraft battery of four ZSU-23-4 multi-barrelled .AA tanks, and four SA-9 infra-red homing missiles mounted in packs of four on BRDM (twin 23-mm cannon, trolley-mounted, are available in some regiments in addition to or instead of the new SA-9); and a field battery or battalion of towed or SP guns. Towed guns (D-30 type) are found in BTR-60-equipped regiments; SP guns in BMP-equipped regiments. Re-equipment of regiments with 18 D-30 or 122-mm M-1974

Top: A battalion forward command and observation post. Regimental and formation commanders often establish similar tactical command posts, leaving most of their staff in rearward HQs.

Above: The first stage in the formation of a heriditary officer elite is provided for by the 9 SUVOROV military boarding schools. Like the former Tsarist cadet academies. these take mainly sons of serving officers.

Right: Such impressive war memorials and cemeteries are features of all Soviet cities, especially in the European USSR. Their function is to engender patriotic emotion and maintain a ''war spirit'' among the people.

Above: An artillery observation post deployed on a particularly open piece of country with little attempt at camouflage or concealment. Parties such as this travel well up with forward troops for rapid reaction.

Below: The Soviets consider lightweight anti-tank weapons, such as the NVA RPG-7 shown here, to be extremely effective if used in sufficient numbers and in conjunction with heavier long-range weapons.

SP guns instead of the original 6 is progressing rapidly.

A tank regiment is a considerably smaller organisation, with only 1,300 officers and men at the most. Its basis is three tank battalions, 95 tanks in all. In the past, tank regiments had no organic motor-rifle troops; but it is now thought that, in the front-line units, at least a company, and in some cases a battalion, of motor-rifle troops is included in the regiment. Artillery support is also absent – the tank regiment has only anti-aircraft artillery for protection, utilising the ZSU-23-4 and SA-9.

Both tank and motor-rifle regiments have engineer mine-clearing and river-crossing support, and decontamination equipment. The light regimental tail provides scanty field recovery and repair facilities and a small medical post as well as cargo and fuel vehicles to resupply the sub-units.

The organisation of the basic all-arms formation, the division, is founded upon three motor-rifle regiments and one tank regiment for motor-rifle divisions, and three tank and one motor-rifle regiment for tank divisions. Recent increases in the numbers of tanks in motor-rifle regiments and divisions have, however, tended to make the motor-rifle division an equally balanced tank and infantry formation, while the tank division remains an armour-heavy formation. Both divisions have strong reconnaissance battalions with a commando-type parachute company for deep penetration; they also have effective battlefield radar and direction-finding equipment, as well as armoured vehicles for ground reconnaissance in conventional and nuclear war. A motor-rifle division alone has an extra tank reserve of some 40–50 tanks.

Both motor-rifle and tank divisions have a considerable amount of artillery in addition to that held by their regiments. Air cover is provided by 24 57-mm towed AA guns and a battalion of SA-6s or SA-8s. A motor-

Above: The Soviets believe that local command of the air is essential to the success of a rapid offensive. The highly mobile SA-6 system provides air cover for a division during an advance and attack.

Left: The SCUD-B is the basic Army and Front level nuclear missile. In war, nuclear warheads will probably be kept under KGB control until nuclear release is given by the political leadership.

rifle division alone has 18 100-mm towed anti-tank guns. Field artillery support is provided by three battalions, each of 18 122-mm guns; in motor-rifle divisions only, one battalion is equipped with 152-mm guns, which are beginning to be replaced by a new 152-mm SP gun.

Eighteen 40-round multi-barrelled rocket launchers and four free-flight surface-to-surface missile (SSM) launchers complete the division's formidable artillery support. The former weapon is ideal for delivering a chemical strike, and the latter a nuclear strike. A division has particularly strong mine-clearing and river-crossing support, much of the equipment it uses having been tried and proven in the Yom Kippur Israeli–Arab war of 1973. The engineers also have fair obstacle-creating ability in the way of mine-laying vehicles and trench-diggers; and chemical defence troops provide good decontamination ability with personnel and vehicle decontaminating equipment.

The division's logistic tail is true to the principle of lightness and flexibility. The

Right: The 'SAGGER' ATGW is the last of the Soviet 1st generation missile systems. It is effective up to 2 km, but requires a high degree of operator skill. Its replacement is the 2nd generation 'SPANDREL'.

Far right: The BM-21 is one of a long line of 'Katyusha' type rocket motors. A battalion of 18 can fire 720 rounds in 30 seconds. It is ideal for counter battery fire up to 10km or delivering volatile chemicals.

Below: The 130mm M1946 was originally a naval gun remounted for field use because of its exceptional range—27km. It is held at Army level for counter-bombardment and long-range engagements.

recovery and repair facilities of the technical support battalion are not extensive and not designed for repairing heavily damaged vehicles. The medical battalion's field hospital is designed to treat 60 bed cases at any time, but provides light treatment or immediate evacuation for many more. The divisional supply transport battalion has the task of carrying fuel and supplies forward to the regiments. Divisional movement is controlled by a strong detachment of traffic police (the so-called 'Commandant's Service') who organise routes and deployment areas and site depots etc.

The organisation of a Soviet army is flexible, with a variable number of divisions of all types. A typical combination might be three tank divisions plus two motor-rifle divisions. An army would dispose of a large amount of artillery, some of which in war would probably be retained for army use, and some of which would be allocated to whichever divisions the army commander thought to be in most need of it. As well as a large number of 122- and 152-mm gun-howitzers, army artillery includes such excellent pieces as the M1943 130-mm field gun with a range of 17 miles, the 180-mm heavy gun with an even greater range, the 160-mm heavy mortar and a variety of multi-barrelled rocket-launchers. An army commander would be extremely unlikely to allot any of his medium-range SS-1C 'Scud' nuclear missiles to a division. An army commander would also have a tank reserve which could be used to strengthen an important axis, and a large amount of engineer equipment to construct more permanent river-crossing sites.

Most of the army's logistic capability is

supplies down to that division's regiments and battalions. Divisional supply is the responsibility of the Army Commander. Not only does this prevent division and lower units from being encumbered with large logistic tails, thus increasing their mobility, it also enables the Army or Front commander to concentrate his supplies more easily on those axes where they will be of greatest value. To the same end now, as in the 1941–45 war, a large proportion of artillery and engineer resources are held not organic to divisions, but as reserves of the operational commander. The same principle applies at strategic level, where the strategic reserves of the high command provide an ability to switch concentrations of support elements from one front to another.

Most of the soft-skinned transport vehicles which will be needed to supply divisions in time of war are under army control. They are not, however, held on strength in peacetime, but in event of war will be mobilised, together with their drivers, from the civilian economy. To diversify his means of fuel supply in an offensive war, the army commander might have units capable of laying tactical fuel pipelines from strategic railheads to forward depots.

In time of war, Soviet Ground Force formations, now organised into Groups of Forces (outside the USSR) and Military Districts (inside the USSR), would be organised as 'Fronts', and several Fronts together would probably be combined in a Theatre of Military Action. For example, the 20 Soviet divisions now forming the Group of Soviet Forces Germany (GSFG) would probably become a Front in war, and along with the Northern (Poland) and Central (Czechoslovakia) Group of Forces

Below: A column of tanks moves forward escorted by its air defence. The tanks are T-72s and the missile-armed vehicle the SA-8 (Gecko), the Soviet equivalent of the French Roland or the British Rapier.

held at high level, because the supply of lower formations is the responsibility of the higher formation. In other words, the logistic tail of a division is not there to keep the division supplied, but to furnish

might be classed as the Central European Theatre.

It is to the Front commander that the Soviet tactical air force (Frontal Aviation) would be subordinated. The Front commander would deploy his air power in co-ordination with his ground forces, allotting it to whichever sector of the battlefield he considered most important. The Front commander has in addition medium-range nuclear missiles ('Shaddock' and 'Scaleboard') which he can deploy as he wishes.

The airborne forces would also come under Front control; but, as a result of the very limited amount of air transport available to drop or air-land troops, and the great vulnerability of large-scale assault groups, the Front commander would probably detach a proportion of the airborne troops allotted to him to armies under his control.

The airborne forces are the elite of the Soviet Ground Forces. There are eight divisions, and all are stationed inside the territory of the USSR in peacetime. The airborne forces are in effect maintained as a strategic reserve of the High Command. They are considered the most reliable of the country's troops, and are chosen to spearhead any major operation. They were used in this way in Czechoslovakia in 1968 and in Afghanistan in 1980. A conscious effort is made by the Soviet authorities to maintain an elitist spirit among these airborne troops by means of a constant propaganda campaign, a special distinctive uniform and a hard and exciting training programme. The airborne forces get the pick of the conscripts, many of whom will have practised parachuting or other military sports with the *DOSAAF* organisation (see Chapter 3) before their conscription.

The Soviet airborne forces are trained to operate in several roles. They could be dropped in small teams by advanced parachuting techniques to operate secretly as reconnaissance and sabotage groups in the enemy rear. Considerably larger units, up to a battalion or larger, might be deployed deep in the enemy rear on suicide missions of strategic importance, such as the destruction of a communications centre or government buildings in a city.

The airborne forces would also be used in the traditional role: they might be landed by aeroplane, parachute or helicopter in the enemy rear to fight conventionally until relieved by the advancing main forces. When used in this manner, there would be no limit to the size of the airborne force deployed; but it is unlikely that the Soviets would fly their men in in more than battalion-size groups because of their vulnerability to counter-strike, especially in nuclear war. The Soviets do insist that to mount any airborne operation of a significant size, local command of the air is essential.

An airborne battalion is organised on similar lines to a motor-rifle battalion: three companies, mortars, anti-tank support and a light tail. However, its equipment scales will vary enormously depending on its role, means of transport and means of landing. Long-range reconnaissance teams of up to a platoon in size would have only the lightest scale of issue: as they would hope to remain undetected, vehicles and heavy kit would be merely an embarrass-

ment. However, battalion groups operating independently in the enemy rear, to exploit rapidly the effect of a nuclear strike or to seize and hold a strategic position in advance of the main forces, would be heavily equipped. The 82-mm mortars, SPG-9 recoilless anti-tank guns and portable 'Sagger' ATGWs and SA-7 AA missiles which are standard equipment in airborne battalions, could be dropped by parachute, followed by 120-mm mortars, ZU-23 twin AA cannon and 85-mm anti-tank field-guns for heavier fire support.

The battalion could also be provided with the BMD – the air-droppable infantry combat vehicle – which would give it a significant offensive capability and extra protection in an NBC environment. This vehicle replaces or supplements the old but effective ASU-57 self-propelled anti-tank gun.

A battalion group equipped with these weapons, operating in the enemy rear, would be quite a formidable force. It could be strengthened still further by helicopter-borne and air-landed equipment, if local mastery of the air could be maintained, and if, in the case of transport aeroplanes, a suitable landing field could be found.

Right: It is now the standard Soviet drill to dismount for an attack except where the defence is very weak. Infantry advance 200m behind the tanks under cover of artillery fire. BMPs follow giving fire support.

Below: Most Soviet front line units now have 18 amphibious 122mm SP guns. However, despite their ballistic computers, batteries often still deploy in the traditional 'line abreast' formation .

The great increase in the number of helicopters in the Soviet Army in recent years now gives a senior Soviet commander the capability to lift several battalion groups with light scales at any one time. The great advantage of helicopters is that ordinary motor-rifle troops can be used with minimal training. This makes it more likely that helicopters would be deployed under divisional control to enable tactical landings to be made in very close support of the leading formations and at very short notice. The equipping of helicopters with heavy armament has made them capable of lending a considerable amount of fire support to any landing party.

Airborne forces, however transported, would have only a limited amount of supplies and ammunition, and would not be expected to operate without support or reinforcement for very long.

The exception is long range diversionary teams of up to 12 men dropped in the enemy rear to carry out a mission of strategic importance, such as the sabotage of a vital installation or the assassination of an important person. Having completed their task, there might be no way for such groups

Below: M-1974 SP guns deploy to cover the advance and attack of a T-55 unit. Effective artillery suppression of the defence is absolutely essential to the success of a Soviet attack.

Bottom: The effect of an APDS hit on an Arab T-62 in the Yom Kippur War; note how the complete turret has been displaced. Soviet tank designers learned a lot from the Arab-Israel wars.

to return or escape. This is just their hard luck; the Soviet High Command is not likely to worry about the loss of a few soldiers if they accomplish a mission of sufficient importance.

Formidable though the airborne forces may appear, however, their role is only subsidiary to, and in support of, the operations of the motor-rifle and tank formations; for it is on the ground that the Soviets consider the war will be lost or won.

A study of the deployment of units and formations brings one to a conclusion that the Soviet High Command envisages two major roles for the Ground Forces, in addition to the responsibility for internal security in the Soviet Union and Eastern Europe, a responsibility which they share with the para-military KGB and MVD troops. Firstly, they must defend the USSR from invasion by land from Western Europe, the Middle East or China, and secondly, they must prosecute a war beyond the Socialist *bloc* with the aim of extending Soviet communist influence to other countries. A closer study of troop dispositions will quickly show that the force level which the Soviet High Command maintains facing China, while adequate to repel any Chinese invasion of the Asiatic USSR, is nothing like sufficient to ensure success in a major invasion of that country. The force level maintained in the European USSR and Eastern Europe, however, is certainly much higher than at present necessary to deter NATO from invading the Soviet Union, and may well be thought sufficient, under the right conditions, to invade Western Europe, defeat the forces of NATO and bring most of Western Europe under Soviet domination.

Above: Surprise is one of the most important of Soviet military principles, and instant combat readiness is the prerequisite for attaining it. Here, soldiers of GSFG practise crash-out procedures.

Right: A unit of GSFG on exercise. Neither the flat Russian plains nor these training areas of East Germany provide the Soviets with practice in operating over hilly or broken country, as in West Germany.

Below: The demands of Soviet Military Doctrine—and the realities of the Russian climate—go to ensure that Soviet equipment is well suited to winter warfare, and that the soldier is well practised in it.

The principles of Soviet military doctrine, and therefore the shape and form of the Ground Forces, are heavily influenced by the geography and economics of the USSR. The country is so vast and the population density (even in European Russia) so low, that the state simply could not bear the cost of Maginot Line-type fortifications along its entire borders, even assuming that this kind of fortification could be made effective nowadays, in areas devoid of natural obstacles. For almost the whole of the European USSR is a vast plain, bounded by the Baltic Sea to the north and the Black Sea to the south, while to the west the plain stretches unbroken to Holland. Eastwards, only the rolling hills of the southern Urals lie between Moscow and the Tien Shan mountains, where the border with China

Above left: Traditional Soviet tactics took no account of undulations in terrain, only of obstacles or natural features commanding the surrounding area. Modern NATO anti-tank tactics are forcing a Soviet rethink.

Left: Unditching drill. In fact, Soviet tanks have excellent soft going capability, yet all carry a log to aid unditching, because they deploy along trenches that most Western tank crews would think impassable.

Below: Soviet success in a European war will depend on their ability to pre-empt NATO deployment. Against a strong defence, this BMP attack could face total failure, even with tank and artillery support.

runs. Only along her mountainous border with China has the USSR made any real effort to create physical defensive lines in strength. Here, the nature of the ground and the composition of the potential enemy army makes static defence an attractive measure for deterrence, and for buying time in the event of attack.

The greatest obstacle to any military operations within the USSR are the massive size of the country and the large rivers which dissect it. Consequently, Soviet military thinking is bound to reckon with these factors, which affect attacker and defender alike, and plan the development of the Ground Forces accordingly.

The size of the Soviet armed forces in peacetime is limited only by the level of the Soviet economy. However, sufficient forces are maintained (a) to deter any possible attacker and (b) to provide sufficient strength for the USSR to repel any surprise attack and (c) to enable the USSR to launch (or to reply to) a surprise attack capable of achieving primary strategic objectives in the opening stages of a war.

It must be emphasised that the 166 divisions of the Ground Forces maintained in peacetime are *merely the framework* of the Soviet Army. Only the 'front-line' divisions in Eastern Europe, the strategically important Airborne Divisions, plus a very few elite divisions in the USSR, are maintained at full strength. All the others—three-quarters of the total number—are maintained at half strength or cadre strength

(⅓ to ¼ strength). The real basis of the Soviet Army's strength lies in its ability to mobilise reservists, men who have recently completed conscription service. Some 1,700,000 conscripts are demobilised into the reserves each year. These men can fill out the under-strength divisions and man the mothballed equipment comparatively quickly, bringing the strength of the Ground Forces up to over 5 million within a few weeks. It is the function of the Military District to accomplish this mobilisation, covertly if possible.

The Soviet Union's experience of being the victim of surprise attack, the geo-strategic features of the country, the military assessment of the features of modern weaponry, and the national and ideological drive to spread her influence—all these are factors which lead Soviet military doctrine to stress the absolute primacy of the offensive as a means of waging war. This lays great value on the seizure of the initiative, the ability to cover large distances at great speed and the achievement of the maximum of effect by manoeuvre, concentration and surprise, together with vigorous fighting to the very depths of the enemy's position.

These principles of military art the Soviets consider to be equally applicable to strategic defence or offence. Thus whether their role is strategically defensive or offensive is of less importance for the training and equipping of the Soviet Ground Forces than might have been thought. Whatever their strategic role, the Soviet Ground Forces are trained and equipped to fight any campaign by offensive means – to seize the initiative by attack or counter-attack and to carry the action to the depths of the enemy's position, so as to bring about his defeat in the shortest possible time. Only in the offensive (or counter-offensive) lies the way to victory; and in event of any major war – certainly in the event of war between capitalist and communist states – the Soviets will aim for nothing less than complete and total victory, irrespective of whether or not they start the war.

The Ground Forces are, therefore, organised, trained and equipped on one overall basic standard pattern to fight one type of war, no matter where and for what they are located; though of course those units stationed in areas where special geographic or climatic conditions appertain will be additionally trained to fight in those particular conditions.

The requirement of mobility and manoeuvrability affects organisation of units and formations, and design of equipment alike. Soviet military doctrine demands that units and formations up to divisional level are not burdened with a cumbersome, mobility-hampering logistic train. The combat vehicles themselves must carry as much as possible in the way of essential fuel and

Above right: An assault river crossing. WP forces place great emphasis on instant amphibious capability in their AFVs, so as to make for a speedy initial crossing. However, steep banks can frustrate exit or entry for wheeled AFVs.

Right: A T-55 and ARV (with large schnorkel) cross a PMP. This assault bridge is quick to lay and lift, and hard to destroy. Advancing divisions will leave bridges down for following units to use.

ammunition, and units have organic to them merely a flexible tail, receiving further logistic support from transport and equipment held by higher formations. The design of Soviet combat vehicles shows clearly that considerations of range, mobility and firepower are given priority over those of protection and crew comfort.

One advantage that highly mobile forces bring is the possibility of concentrating them at chosen points to achieve overwhelming local superiority over an enemy, thus giving them the chance to break through into the depths of his position. Soviet doctrine is to exploit this by firm, centralised control at high level, with stricter subordination of formations than is common in the armies of the Western

Below: A field refuelling point. Although problems remain, logistics are no longer the Soviet army's Achilles heel. Their supply system is now well designed to meet the needs of their offensive doctrine.

Bottom: Fixing a schnorkel to a tank for deep wading. All WP tanks have this useful facility, although the exercise requires great care and suitable crossing sites at rivers or lakes.

alliance. This characteristic is regarded by the Soviet High Command as one of its main strengths, permitting as it does the greatest strategic value to be obtained from a concerted effort.

It might be useful at this point to list the principles of Soviet military art – the means by which doctrine is to be put into practice – as defined by contemporary Soviet strategists and tacticians. As principles, they are equally applicable at both tactical and operational level, and are still largely relevant at the strategic level. In Soviet terminology, 'strategic' means any military action at theatre or national level; 'operation' means activity at Front or Army level; 'tactical' describes the activities of a division or less.

In order of priority these principles are given as:

(1) the achievement of mobility and the maintenance of a high tempo of combat operations;

(2) the concentration of the main effort and the creation thereby of superiority of men and *materiel* over the enemy at the decisive place and time;

(3) surprise;

(4) aggressiveness in battle – no let-up in the attack, break-through and pursuit;

(5) preservation of the combat-effectiveness of one's own troops by
(a) being properly prepared and efficiently organised,
(b) maintaining at all times efficient command and control over one's forces and
(c) maintaining morale and the will to fight in one's troops;

Right: Frog 7 and BM-21. A Soviet division has 4 Frog launchers, carrying up to 1 ton HE, 20 kt nuclear, or chemical warheads. However, their use is controlled by the Army, not the Divisional commander.

Below: The excellent 122mm D-30 will be the mainstay of Soviet gunners until more SP guns become available. This vulnerable style of deployment in line is adopted for the sake of speed and ease of fire control.

The Soviets accept that in modern war a superiority in the order of 3 or 4: 1 at least is desirable if an attacker is to have a good likelihood of success, and that a 7 or 8: 1 superiority is even better because it doubles the chance of a quick victory. However, in key areas where the Soviet Army might be employed, e.g. Western Europe or Soviet Central Asia, the USSR cannot at present achieve even a 3: 1 superiority in men and equipment over the whole front. (While such a superiority is possible on, for example, the flanks of NATO, these areas would not be of major strategic importance to the USSR in the event of a general war, and therefore they are not discussed in detail at this point).

As the third example of an 'operation' above, involving as it does a push along the whole front, would therefore require overall superiority of at least 3: 1 and desirably double that, it is unlikely to be the operation chosen under present conditions for a campaign against China or the central front of NATO.

The other operations, both the encirclement and the attack along axes, do not require overall superiority, but achieve their effectiveness by the attainment of overwhelming local superiority in the order of 8 or 10: 1 to smash through or around the enemy defences, and break through into his 'soft' rear area where they can do a disproportionate amount of damage. While overall superiority in men and equipment is highly desirable for these operations, Soviet strategists do emphasise that if the operations are carried out skilfully, using the proper tactics, success can be achieved by an attacking force equal in size to the defending force or, in extreme cases, even inferior in terms of manpower. (It does seem extremely unlikely that the Soviet Army should even have to consider the likelihood of fighting a European enemy which has superior numbers of men.)

By the speed of the advance into enemy territory that both these operations entail, they do offer the best possible medium for a successful offensive force to penetrate to the economic heart of an enemy nation and occupy or neutralise it, thus bringing the war to a speedy conclusion.

The key to the success of the operations is an effective break-through of the main enemy positions, either directly or around the flank, and it is particularly interesting to study the Soviet principles of military art enumerated above in the light of such a break-through.

A diagrammatic representation of such a break-through, taken from Soviet sources, is given. From a study of information supplied by the many means of reconnaissance available to him, the Front commander will select the area or areas for concentration and break-through, paying particular attention to finding suitable terrain for the movement of large armoured forces. Making every effort to conceal his intentions, he will attempt to achieve surprise, and if possible to catch the enemy before they have even taken up their de-

(6) ensuring that the aim and plan of any operation conform with the realities of the situation, so that neither too much nor too little is attempted;

(7) ensuring the co-operation of all arms of service and ensuring the co-ordination of effort towards achieving the main objectives; and

(8) attempting simultaneous action upon the enemy to the entire depth of his deployment and upon objectives deep in his rear.

The organisation of field units, the design and employment of equipment, and the tactics and operational models in the Soviet Ground Forces all comply with these principles. Thus, units and formations are structured for rapid movement and deployment. A high rate of advance, the ability to concentrate quickly, and constant combat readiness dictate the tactics and training of army units. Fighting vehicles are designed firstly for mobility (which designers translate into reliability, cross country and amphibious performance, *all-round* protection, and self-containment) and secondly for firepower (as the basic ingredient of

'concentration'). Crew comfort comes a long way down the list of priorities.

There are three basic types of 'operation' by which the Ground Forces might seek to implement the requirements of Soviet military art to defeat an enemy such as the NATO forces in Western Europe;

(1) an encirclement: the delivery of two main attacks, or one main and one subsidiary attack, to converge on and encircle the enemy forces, subjecting these encircled forces to assault and bombardment from all directions and preventing their reinforcement while continuing the main offensive deep into the enemy's rear;

(2) an attack along axes: the delivery of one or more frontal attacks on the enemy's defensive position and advancing deep into his rear, to destroy rear installations and reserves moving up, at the same time developing the attack sideways to attack defending forces from the flank or rear;

(3) single concerted thrust to push the enemy back along the whole front and squash him against a natural obstacle such as the sea or a mountain range.

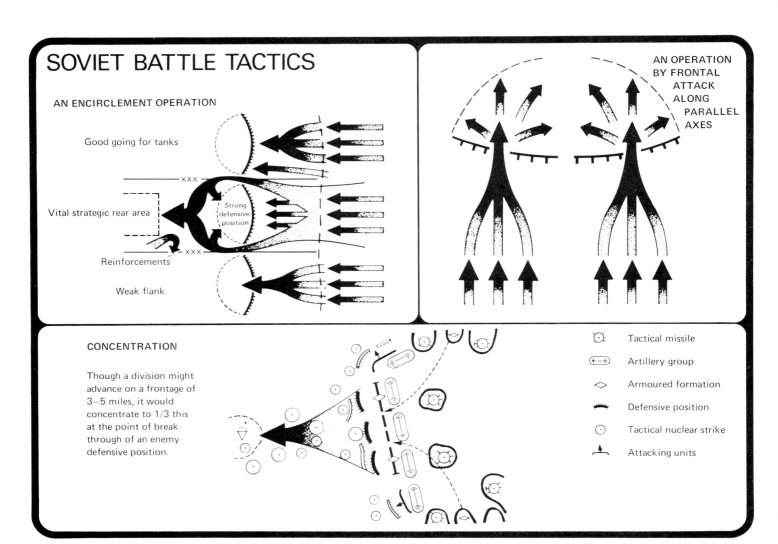

SOVIET BATTLE TACTICS

AN ENCIRCLEMENT OPERATION

Good going for tanks

XXX

Vital strategic rear area

Strong defensive position

Reinforcements

XXX

Weak flank

AN OPERATION BY FRONTAL ATTACK ALONG PARALLEL AXES

CONCENTRATION

Though a division might advance on a frontage of 3–5 miles, it would concentrate to 1/3 this at the point of break-through of an enemy defensive position.

☼ Tactical missile

⊕ Artillery group

◇ Armoured formation

⌒ Defensive position

⊙ Tactical nuclear strike

⚑ Attacking units

Above: The Soviets' bitter experience of attacking well-defended towns in 1944-5 has persuaded them to avoid built up areas wherever possible during an advance as they soak up men, equipment and time.

Left: Recce patrols combing the divisional frontage and flanks, with motorcycles, tanks and APCs, have two express tasks: to locate the enemy defences and to discover routes through and past them.

Right: Only airborne forces, naval infantry and certain selected motor rifle units train in street fighting. Towns are surrounded, split along converging axes, and reduced street by street with flame throwers, tanks, and SP guns.

Far right: Special training in mountain warfare is given to airborne forces, and to those motor rifle and tank formations stationed in mountainous regions.

fensive positions. The four or five divisions of the army allotted the task of accomplishing the break-through, or at least of acting as the first wave of the assault, would approach the appointed area well dispersed in extended march column to concentrate only on the objective itself. As the leading elements of the army reach the enemy positions, they will immediately engage them to test their strength, and to give cover to the following main forces, approaching rapidly, a heavy air and artillery bombardment into the very depths of the enemy's defensive position (with either conventional or nuclear and chemical shells depending on a political decision at higher level) would be laid down very rapidly. On the heels of this the main forces of the army would advance at speed to overwhelm the defences and break through into the flanks or rear of the enemy position. On the nuclear battlefield the actual breakthrough sector would be in the order of 12 to 20 miles per Army. In conventional conditions, the need to destroy the enemy defence absolutely will force the Army Commander to restrict his breakthrough sector to a mere 3 to 5 miles in width. As an Army deploys at least 400 to 600 artillery pieces (guns, mortars or rocket launchers), this will enable the commander to concentrate the fire of over 140 guns on each mile of front, i.e., about one gun's fire for each 15 yards of the artillery barrage.

So as to lessen their vulnerability to enemy counter-strikes, especially under nuclear conditions, the Soviet divisions would deploy in balanced or armour-heavy battle groups of regimental size. These would themselves be divided into three or four battalion groups with a high degree of linear separation – a division might advance on one or two axes on a front of only five or six miles but extended to a depth of up to 30 or more miles. Concentration would be achieved as each successive regimental group was fed into the battle, advancing rapidly in march columns and only deploying when approaching the area of fighting.

Whenever the defenders have created a defensive position in depth, with several lines of fortifications, it is Soviet practice to split their attacking forces into two successive waves or 'echelons'. The task of the first echelon (normally about two-thirds of the total force) is to breach the first line(s) of defence. The second echelon has the responsibility of exploiting this success, and passing on to breach the subsequent lines of defence, bursting out into the enemy rear. When the enemy has taken up a defensive position in one deep belt of strongpoints, without identifiable continuous successive lines, then the Soviet commander will attack in one echelon, maintaining a strong reserve to commit in the area of greatest success. A reserve of about one-ninth of the total force can be retained during a two-echelon attack. At Division or Army level, when the defence is very deep, a further 'mobile group' will be retained as an exploiting force in event of the second echelon being too exhausted on breaking through the defences. The reserve will be committed in the areas of greatest success, *not* in the areas of greatest difficulty.

As a general rule, the Russians never reinforce failure, always success.

The sub-unit, or formation on the march, can best be visualised, in organisational terms, as a huge tadpole of four basic components. The body of the organism (i.e., the main forces of the division as it is in this example), for the purposes of march and attack, can be divided into two basic sections—the first and second echelons. At the head of the first section comes the 'brain'—the commander, with a few personal assistants in his forward command HQ. He makes all the basic outline plans for his operations and personally controls the division at all times, directing the battle from a command-observation post when possible. The command HQ will comprise in all only a few specialised vehicles with AA defence.

Back in the second echelon comes the main headquarters. Here, the Divisional Chief of Staff sits, with the numerous divisional staff officers. They act as the organism's 'central nervous system' completing the detailed planning to 'put the flesh on the bones' of the commander's outline plan. They also relay back to the commander intelligence analysis and planning considerations such as levels of stock remaining. The large size and consequent vulnerability of this HQ element compel

Below left: Regimental forward command HQ on joint WP exercise. Soviet doctrine stresses the need to maintain reliable communications – and to disrupt enemy communications by bombardment or EW.

Below: From FEBA to divisional main HQ, signals go by HF or VHF. From division rearward, radio relay (shown here) is also used. Signals exercises are one of the most common types of joint WP exercises.

SOVIET BATTLE TA

KEY

An apc or apc unit (eg. motor rifle company)

A tank or a tank unit

A gun or artillery unit

Anti-aircraft artillery

(a) Strong recce patrol eg. BRDM BMP T62 motorcycle
(b) & (c) The Vanguard
 (b) Recce vehicle (BRDM)
 (c) Vanguard consisting of a Motor rifle coy (10 apcs) plus a tank platoon (4 tanks)
(d) – (p) Main Forces
 (d) Recce vehicle
 (e) Bn HQ
 (f) SP anti-aircraft guns (2 x ZSU 23-4)
 (g) Tank platoon
 (h) Tank platoon
 (i) Motor rifle coy (10 BMP)
 (j) Motor rifle coy (10 BMP)
 (k) Engineer vehicle
 (l) Artillery platoon 2-3 SP guns
 (m) Artillery platoon 2-3 SP guns
 (n) Rear service vehicles
 (p) Flank guard – (BMP or BRDM
(q) Rearguard – (BMP or BRDM

BATTALION DEFENSIVE POSITION

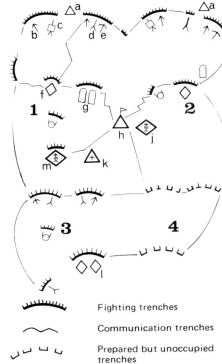

~~~~~~~ Fighting trenches

〜〜 Communication trenches

⊔⊔⊔⊔ Prepared but unoccupied trenches

(a) Observation post
(b) Machine gun
(c) Anti-tank missile launcher (Sagger)
(d) Anti-tank grenade launcher (RPG-7)
(e) Heavy machine gun
(f) Dug in tank
(g) APCs giving fire support
(h) Bn HQ
(j) Anti-aircraft tank (ZSU 23-4)
(k) Medical post
(l) Tanks for counter attack
(m) Mortars

1 & 2 – Company positions – 1st echelon of defence

3 – Company position – 2nd echelon an expected (left flank) axis of enemy attack

4 – Reserve position in case main attack is on right flank

MARCH ORDER

Soviet military map symbols depicting a motor-rifle battalion group on the march. This march order is adopted when an encounter battle is anticipated and rapid deployment will be necessary.

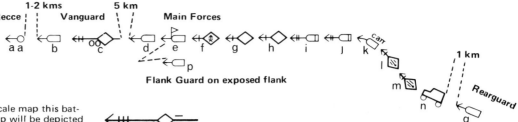

On small scale map this battalion group will be depicted by the symbol

A BATTALION'S DEPLOYMENT FROM THE MARCH TO THE ATTACK -- BASIC DRILL

A Battalion group would normally attack in one line (or echelon) as indicated here, with another battalion group of the same regiment close behind the second wave of the attack.

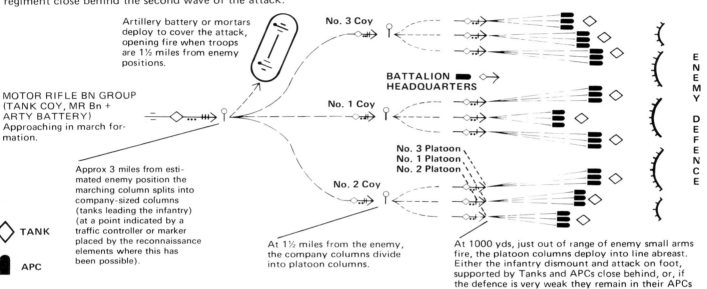

Artillery battery or mortars deploy to cover the attack, opening fire when troops are 1½ miles from enemy positions.

No. 3 Coy

BATTALION HEADQUARTERS

MOTOR RIFLE BN GROUP (TANK COY, MR Bn + ARTY BATTERY) Approaching in march formation.

No. 1 Coy

No. 3 Platoon
No. 1 Platoon
No. 2 Platoon

No. 2 Coy

Approx 3 miles from estimated enemy position the marching column splits into company-sized columns (tanks leading the infantry) (at a point indicated by a traffic controller or marker placed by the reconnaissance elements where this has been possible).

◇ TANK

▮ APC

At 1½ miles from the enemy, the company columns divide into platoon columns.

At 1000 yds, just out of range of enemy small arms fire, the platoon columns deploy into line abreast. Either the infantry dismount and attack on foot, supported by Tanks and APCs close behind, or, if the defence is very weak they remain in their APCs for the assault and fire from them on the move.

ENEMY DEFENCE

The **encounter battle** is a tactic much favoured by the Soviet Army. When the enemy is occupying a prepared defensive position, superiority in the order of 5:1 will probably be needed to destroy him. An encounter battle occurs when Soviet forces, moving forward rapidly, meet an enemy force advancing in a counter move. In such a case it is clearly in the interests of the Soviets, in the role of attacker, to engage the enemy whilst he is still on the move. Thus, battle is between two totally mobile forces, and no time is available for defensive positions to be occupied. This effectively evens the odds, and the Soviets believe that by careful manoeuvre they should be able to overwhelm an opponent of equal size very quickly. This is particularly true if the opponent is equipped with British or US AFVs which are much less suited to this type of battle on the move than are the Soviet vehicles. The stages of an encounter battle are as follows:

The recce elements of the advancing Soviet column locate an advancing enemy and the Soviet advance guard engages the enemy vanguard. As the enemy main forces advance to assist their hard-pressed van, the Soviet main forces abandon their advance guard and execute a flanking manoeuvre under the guidance of their own recce. They are thus able to attack the marching enemy column from the flank, following a short artillery barrage from their attached battery (which would deploy at first contact). Travelling at high speed, the deployed Soviet unit will drive right into the enemy column, and a fierce fire fight at pointblank range will ensue.

The Soviets consider that such an encounter battle is the most decisive means of achieving tactical victory, as the side which is defeated will be totally destroyed; so much so that there is no Soviet drill for recovery from defeat in an encounter battle!

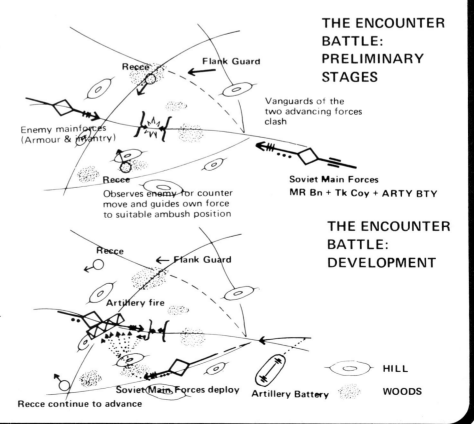

THE ENCOUNTER BATTLE: PRELIMINARY STAGES

Vanguards of the two advancing forces clash

Observes enemy for counter move and guides own force to suitable ambush position

Soviet Main Forces
MR Bn + Tk Coy + ARTY BTY

THE ENCOUNTER BATTLE: DEVELOPMENT

Artillery fire

Soviet Main Forces deploy

Artillery Battery

Recce continue to advance

HILL

WOODS

Soviet tactics and deployment for the offensive

MAIN FRONTAL ATTACK

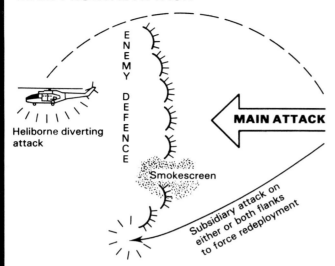

Heliborne diverting attack

ENEMY DEFENCE

MAIN ATTACK

Smokescreen

Subsidiary attack on either or both flanks to force redeployment

A head-on attack is the basic offensive pattern at all levels, from platoon to FRONT. The speed and consequent surprise attending the employment of this form of attack should outweigh its obvious disadvantages as long as the enemy can be effectively forestalled in his defensive deployment. Attempts will be made to overthrow the stability of the defence by ground or airborne attacks on the enemy flank or rear to distract his attention, disrupt movement of supplies or reserves, and cause panic. The offensive can be launched in one or two echelons (depending on the structure of the defence), and against a strong defensive line, the offensive will take the form of a classic breakthrough (see page 154). Against a strong, well prepared defence, a purely conventional head-on attack might well fail.

PRINCIPLES OF CONTROL WITHIN A FORMATION

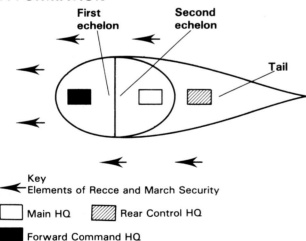

First echelon

Second echelon

Tail

Key
← Elements of Recce and March Security

☐ Main HQ   ▨ Rear Control HQ

■ Forward Command HQ

Soviet units and formations in the advance move in a pattern designed to facilitate speedy reaction, deployment, and command and control. The analogy to a 'tadpole' is useful to explain this. The advancing unit (or formation) does not spread out across the width of its allotted boundaries but it does recce across the width. The first half of the tadpole's 'body' is the first echelon, comprising about two-thirds of the teeth armies. At the head of the main forces marches the unit commander in his small forward C.P. The second half of the body is the 2nd echelon, with the rest of the teeth armies, plus the main HQ and staff. The 'tail' is the unit logistic train on wheels, feeding its supplies to the teeth as the unit goes along. When the tail has dried up, supplies are replenished by the *next higher formation*.

BYPASSING

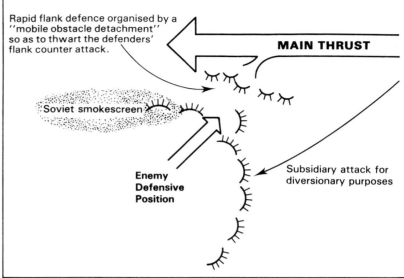

Rapid flank defence organised by a "mobile obstacle detachment" so as to thwart the defenders' flank counter attack.

MAIN THRUST

Soviet smokescreen

Enemy Defensive Position

Subsidiary attack for diversionary purposes

ENVELOPMENT

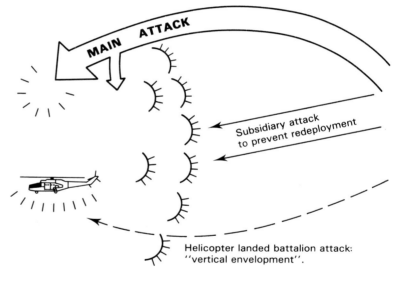

MAIN ATTACK

Subsidiary attack to prevent redeployment

Helicopter landed battalion attack: "vertical envelopment".

PRINCIPLES OF MARCH AND MARCH SECURITY

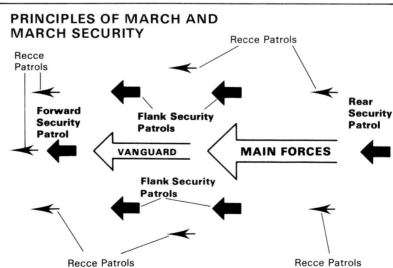

Recce Patrols

Recce Patrols

Forward Security Patrol

Flank Security Patrols

Rear Security Patrol

VANGUARD   MAIN FORCES

Flank Security Patrols

Recce Patrols

Recce Patrols

In the preferred Soviet option of a high speed offensive to achieve deep penetration into the enemy country so as to accomplish his rapid political collapse, great emphasis is placed on any tactic which avoids delay. Where a strong defensive position exists, it will be Soviet preference to avoid this if possible, and to exploit flanking areas of weakness. Thus the defending divisional or corps commander might find himself bypassed, with major enemy formations behind him advancing towards the national centres of political or economic power. At the lower tactical level, the commander of a battalion's defended area might be faced with a similar problem as the vanguard of the Soviet regiment passes him by to assault the rear. When the danger of counter-attack by the defender is high, the Soviet commander will throw out a rapid defensive screen on the threatened flank. A Soviet division creates a "mobile obstacle detachment" of minelayers and anti-tank weapons to this end.

To protect the advancing forces and to avoid their unnecessary deployment (see page 154) or to give adequate warning of any need to deploy, the following principles are applied. The recce advances across the whole frontage of its parent unit with the jobs of discovering enemy locations and ways around them, then continuing to advance. Five-man recce groups cannot be expected to determine the *strength* of an enemy, so the main forces are encircled by march security patrols of some strength (the frontal MS patrol is normally an infantry company plus tanks and engineers, the flank patrols—a strong platoon each). These patrols attack the enemy and by doing so force him to betray his strength and the true extent of his positions. This sacrifice establishes whether either the vanguard or the whole main forces need to deploy, or whether they can both afford to bypass the enemy if routes permit, or whether envelopment manoeuvres, etc, are feasible.

In a subsidiary attack to the defenders' front, smoke, EW, and other means of deception will be employed by the Soviet commander in an attempt to fool the defence as to the location, direction, and timing of his main effort. Whereas in *bypassing* this effort is aimed at *avoiding* the defence, in *envelopment* the Soviet advance, having passed the forward positions, turns in to hit the defenders' flank or rear, and to pass into the position from behind. An envelopment can be single (one main thrust) or double (a divided main thrust) and can have the assistance of an air or heliborne assault landing within the defensive zone ('vertical envelopment') if local air superiority can be achieved.

When an offensive is maintained with two main thrusts designed to *converge*, the result is the *encirclement* of part or all of the enemy force. The principles and methods of encirclement at operational or tactical level are the same as at the strategic level (see page 154).

Top: Officer cadets on field training. Cadets do 3-4 years at an all-arms or special-to-arm military college. This equips them for all command positions up to battalion commander or equivalent.

Above right: An officer of the Political Directorate (GLAVPUR) delivers a lecture during an exercise. Indoctrination is a regular feature of Soviet service life.

Above left: The battalion commander directs the battle. Recently, serious doubt has been cast upon the ability of the average sub-unit officer to organise the combined-arms attack the Soviets prefer.

Below: It is impossible to overestimate the role of the commandants' service during operations. They organise all movement up to and on the battlefield, mark the routes, and direct advancing columns at all stages.

it to deploy well to the rear of the battle area.

The third basic section of the organism is the rear or 'tail'. Like the tadpole's tail, this is a mobile appendage of the division, containing just enough to nourish the division. It is not responsible for, nor is it big enough for, keeping the division supplied ad infinitum from Army or Front level stocks. As has been explained, it is the responsibility of the higher command to supply the lower. Consequently, the divisional tail is responsible for supplying the division's regiments and battalions. Divisional re-supply is done by the Army tail. The tail is controlled by a staff officer from a rear control HQ behind the fighting troops.

Several senior divisional staff officers will travel with a subordinate HQ (e.g., a regimental HQ), forming in effect an

alternative command HQ in case the divisional commander's HQ is knocked out.

The fourth basic section of the organism is the reconnaissance and march security elements. These can be likened to the eyes and the scales of the organism. Although the division on the march and in the attack will probably not deploy across the whole of its frontage within boundaries, it will recce this area by sending out small two-three-vehicle patrols ahead, on the flanks and in the rear. The task of these patrols is two-fold. Firstly, they are to find the enemy; secondly, they are to recce routes through and past enemy positions and penetrate into the enemy rear.

When these patrols alone are insufficient to ascertain enemy strengths, the forces of march protection will be deployed to attack the enemy and discover his strengths and positions by drawing his fire. One regiment of the division will provide a vanguard battalion and forward and flank march security patrols of company and platoon strength, respectively. The main forces are thus preceded and surrounded not only by recce elements but by stronger combat groups, whose task is (a) to deal with minor opposition, thus making it unnecessary for the main forces to deploy on every occasion that the enemy is sighted, and (b) to attack an enemy either for the purposes of gathering information that the recce has been unable to get or so as to distract him and give the main forces time and space to deploy to the attack in safety.

Speed of advance is achieved by march in column, when not in direct contact with enemy troops. The axes of the advance will be planned to make the best possible use of good ground for rapid movement and good road networks. A division would advance probably on two axes, up to two miles apart. Although the divisional front of responsibility might be up to 10 miles wide, the division would not be spread out over the whole distance, but concentrated over perhaps only one-third of this, with reconnaissance and flank protection sub-units covering the extra ground.

The division would march in regimental groups (motor-rifle or tank regiments plus

Above: A pre-dawn briefing for the crews of a Mi-8 helicopter unit. Soviet helicopter crews are well trained in night operations and could mount a surprise attack which would open hostilities in any future war.

Right: GSFG training. Helicopters are used to land troops in the enemy tactical rear to divert the defence or to seize a crucial objective such as a bridgehead—provided local mastery of the air can be attained.

Below: Signallers in support of a bridgehead. Surprise assaults in the enemy rear help destroy the stability of the defence and hasten the enemy's political collapse, aiding a quick end to the war.

elements of divisional artillery and engineers), each of which would deploy a strong battalion as an advance guard, and even further forward or on threatened flanks strong companies as march security patrols. Reconnaissance patrols would scout the area in front of and between the marching units. Each marching battalion would attempt to keep just over one mile distant from its neighbour to avoid presenting a juicy nuclear target.

Soviet tactical drills

The Tactical Commander, having identified the strength and location of his enemy, will, according to Soviet tactical doctrine, have a choice of options. These are:

1. *The bypassing*, whereby he will attempt to avoid engaging the enemy. He will employ a diversionary attack for deception purposes, and will deploy a diffusion screen on his flank to give protection.

2. *The envelopment*, whereby the main forces will attempt to outflank the enemy, delivering their main blow to his flank or rear rather than his front. A small scale frontal attack, timed to coincide with the main blow, is designed to divert the defenders' attention and prevent their redeployment. A two-pronged attack to the flanks or rear is known as a 'double envelopment'.

3. *The frontal attack*, whereby the main weight of the attack falls on the front of the defences. At the same time as or just before the main attack, a subsidiary flank attack will be put in to divert the defenders' attention and make them redeploy.

4. *Encirclement*, whereby the aim of the Soviet commander will be to avoid engagement with his main forces as much as possible, and to surround the defenders with his first echelon. While the defence is slowly being reduced the Soviet second echelon will continue to its next objective.

During an offensive, commanders at each level will normally be given a primary and ultimate objective to achieve by a given time.

Soviet tactical doctrine lays great stress on the desirability of speed and rapid manoeuvre, and emphasises that it far preferable not to have to attack a prepared enemy defence, where the attacker needs superiority of forces, but rather to attack his troops while the latter are still on the march. This tactic is known as the encounter battle. When the reconnaissance units of the advancing Soviet forces give warning of an enemy force advancing towards them, the Soviet advance guard will engage the enemy advance guard, and the Soviet main forces would then hope to manoeuvre and, deployed in platoon columns 100 yards apart, to attack the advancing enemy in the flank while still on the move, giving him no chance

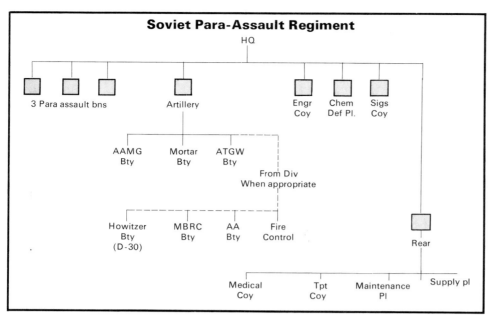

Soviet Para-Assault Regiment

HQ

- 3 Para assault bns
- Artillery
  - AAMG Bty
  - Mortar Bty
  - ATGW Bty
  - From Div When appropriate
    - Howitzer Bty (D-30)
    - MBRC Bty
    - AA Bty
    - Fire Control
- Engr Coy
- Chem Def Pl.
- Sigs Coy
- Rear
  - Medical Coy
  - Tpt Coy
  - Maintenance Pl
  - Supply pl

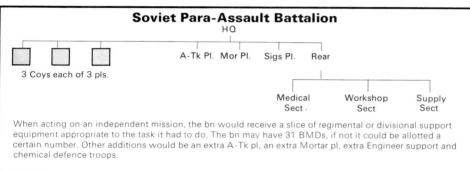

Soviet Para-Assault Battalion

HQ

- 3 Coys each of 3 pls.
- A-Tk Pl.
- Mor Pl.
- Sigs Pl.
- Rear
  - Medical Sect
  - Workshop Sect
  - Supply Sect

When acting on an independent mission, the bn would receive a slice of regimental or divisional support equipment appropriate to the task it had to do. The bn may have 31 BMDs, if not it could be allotted a certain number. Other additions would be an extra A-Tk pl, an extra Mortar pl, extra Engineer support and chemical defence troops.

to prepare a defence. Thus the odds would be even in a very fluid battle, and by dint of careful planning, surprise and the attacking of the enemy along the whole depth of his formation at the same moment, the Soviet forces would hope to wrest a victory without numerical superiority.

The attack directly from the march is the basis of all Soviet tactical deployments and is not employed just as a hasty measure. However, if this attack fails, but Soviet troops do not withdraw, then an 'attack from close contact' will be launched on the enemy. This, however, is an unpopular tactic and, on the fluid battlefield of the 1980s, not one which is likely to be common.

Because of their experience in the last war, the Soviet forces put great emphasis on their ability to cross water obstacles quickly. Much of their equipment is amphibious and Soviet tanks have a deep wading capability. The army is well equipped with a very comprehensive range of excellent combat engineer bridges and ferries, and Soviet units spend a great deal of time training for this phase of war. Tactics for fording water obstacles are, firstly, to try and reach the river or canal before the enemy has prepared his defensive line along it, and to cross rapidly, deploying from the line of march towards a suitable section of the river in APCs, with tanks schnorkelling where possible. Narrow rivers will be crossed by tank-launched assault bridges.

If the rapid crossing fails, or the river line is heavily defended, then the Russians will mount a 'crossing with careful preparation'. This involves fording the obstacle on a

Above: Trained for any mission in every terrain and all climates, the 8 airborne divisions are the spearhead of the Soviet armed forces. They are the first troops to be employed in any major crisis or conflict.

Left: A Soviet airborne battalion with BMD would be a great threat to NATO's rear. Military aviation could drop only one-eighth of the forces at once: Aeroflot would land others on fields and roads.

broad front under cover of smoke and heavy artillery fire.

A very important phase of war begins for the Soviet Army as soon as the enemy defence is broken. This is the pursuit. By pushing on after a withdrawing enemy and constantly harrassing him, the Soviets hope to prevent his establishing a second line of defence, or taking refuge in a town or in difficult terrain. As a general rule, the Soviet Army will seek to avoid getting involved in towns or cities, which eat up scores of troops and significantly favour the defence.

The spread and dynamism of modern war has increased the importance of certain traditional Soviet tactics designed to hit the enemy in the flank and rear. By striking here, rather than against the teeth, the Soviets hope to encompass the collapse of the defenders, and to be able to penetrate to and neutralise the key political centres of the enemy country. Thus, a rapid political victory might be achieved before the enemy teeth armies were completely defeated.

A mixed armour and mechanised unit with engineer and artillery support may be formed and despatched into the enemy rear through a gap in the defence. Such a unit

may be tasked with carrying out a 'raid', i.e., penetrating deep into the rear with the objective of destroying a target of vital importance, even at a cost of total loss. Alternatively, it might be tasked as a 'forward detachment' whose job is to seize an objective in advance of the attacking forces, such as a defile or river crossing place, so as to facilitate the high speed of their offensive. A 'flanking detachment' has the task of getting past the defence and launching a surprise blow to the enemy from a flank or from the rear. A 'reconnaissance detachment' will seek to reconnoitre the depths of the enemy defences. All these minor formations use the standard march and deployment tactics as do the main forces when putting in a conventional attack.

Operations in the enemy rear will also be carried out by troops of the airborne forces, and motor rifle troops transported by helicopter. Small teams from the elite 'diversionary brigades' will be dropped or otherwise inserted into the enemy rear areas to identify key targets (nuclear weapons, radars, HQs, etc.), and to guide heavier assaults or strikes in. These teams will also resort to sabotage and diversion if they find the opportunity. Battalion-sized para drops will be made to secure key areas, attack important targets, etc. A battalion of motor rifle troops might be lifted by helicopter and landed just to the rear of the defenders to put in a surprise attack from behind, coordinated with a main blow on the forward position.

At all stages of the offensive, the Soviets place a great deal of reliance on their artillery to neutralise the defence and engage enemy batteries. Their formations are

equipped with very large quantities of artillery, about half of which is self-propelled and armoured. In a conventional war, non-nuclear artillery becomes exceptionally important, because suppression of the latest anti-tank missiles is essential if the advance is to proceed at a high speed.

This in itself creates problems, however, because the higher the rate of advance the less time there is for an effective barrage. For this reason the Soviets now supplement their artillery with helicopter gunships.

Although the Soviet Ground Forces consider fighting a war only by means of the offensive and counter-offensive, they by no means ignore the tactics of defence, accepting that enemy counter-attacks might well throw them on to the defensive at very short notice. A diagram of a classic Soviet defensive position is also shown. Of particular significance is the positioning of the defence in two echelons, with good communication and flank cover, and the massing of a mobile counter-offensive force to meet the enemy should he break through, and to seize the initiative and counter-attack at the first possible moment.

Such tactics as are described above are extremely demanding of an army, and necessitate not only a high degree of co-ordination and control and well trained officers and men, but also first-class units and formations suitably organised and equipped to fight such highly intensive mobile engagements. As our study of the Soviet Ground Forces has shown, in organisation, equipment and training they do indeed attempt to fulfil these operational requirements and this is why they differ in

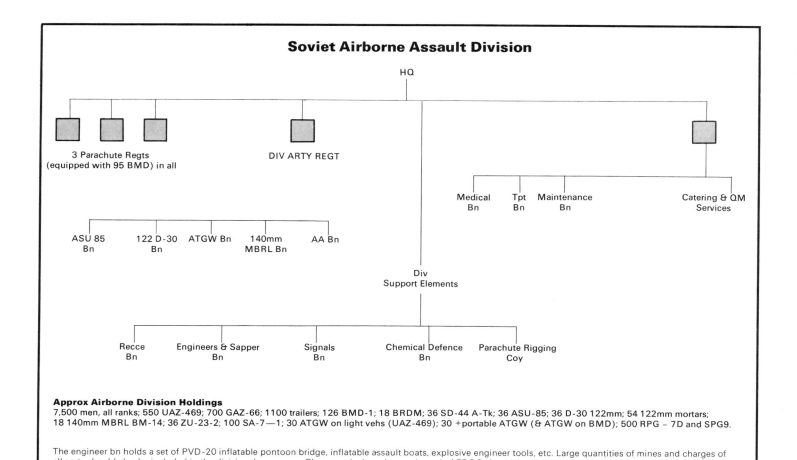

Soviet Airborne Assault Division

HQ

3 Parachute Regts
(equipped with 95 BMD) in all

DIV ARTY REGT

Medical
Bn

Tpt
Bn

Maintenance
Bn

Catering & QM
Services

ASU 85
Bn

122 D-30
Bn

ATGW Bn

140mm
MBRL Bn

AA Bn

Div
Support Elements

Recce
Bn

Engineers & Sapper
Bn

Signals
Bn

Chemical Defence
Bn

Parachute Rigging
Coy

Approx Airborne Division Holdings
7,500 men, all ranks; 550 UAZ-469; 700 GAZ-66; 1100 trailers; 126 BMD-1; 18 BRDM; 36 SD-44 A-Tk; 36 ASU-85; 36 D-30 122mm; 54 122mm mortars; 18 140mm MBRL BM-14; 36 ZU-23-2; 100 SA-7—1; 30 ATGW on light vehs (UAZ-469); 30 +portable ATGW (& ATGW on BMD); 500 RPG – 7D and SPG9.

The engineer bn holds a set of PVD-20 inflatable pontoon bridge, inflatable assault boats, explosive engineer tools, etc. Large quantities of mines and charges of all sorts should also be included in the divisional weaponry. Photographs have been released of FROG-4 vehicles being air landed, but whether this actually occurs, and whether such weapons are held on the divisional strength is not known.

several marked respects from the armies of many NATO states.

Weapons of mass destruction

All the tactics and operations discussed so far are seen by the Soviets as being equally applicable to wars fought in a conventional environment or using weapons of mass destruction (the Soviet term for nuclear and chemical weapons). In conventional conditions, greater concentration is possible than in conditions where nuclear weapons might be used, and a slower overall rate of advance would be expected on a non-nuclear battlefield: 15–20 miles per day instead of 25–30 miles.

The Soviets have a very significant capacity for fighting with weapons of mass destruction. They are known to hold stocks of persistent and non-persistent chemical agents for their artillery. The BM-21 multi-barrelled rocket-launcher is an ideal weapon for rapid delivery of a non-persistent chemical agent, for example hydrogen cyanide or a nerve gas such as sarin. Persistent chemical agents could be delivered by air strike or long-range artillery to targets such as airfields which the Soviets might want to deny to the enemy but not to destroy. Soviet commanders at field level and above are taught to regard the use of chemical weapons as a matter of course – simply a weapon available to them which will be used

Right: Soviet tactics and equipment are designed for both the conventional and the contaminated battlefield. However, NBC suits are clumsy and tiring, and standard of personnel training is often low.

Above: Chemical defence troops in a routine exercise using an ARS-12U decontamination bowser. The Soviet Army possesses chemical weapons and considers their use in war to be highly probable.

Right: A soldier in full NBC protective gear uses a radiac monitor to check the radiation levels on contaminated equipment. NBC training in Soviet and WP forces is frequent and realistic.

when tactical and meteorological conditions permit.

Although political considerations are likely to determine whether or not battlefield nuclear weapons are used, if they are released, then they too are simply regarded for tactical terms as replacing a large artillery barrage; and commanders must expect to take their use in their stride. Whether their battlefield systems will in fact be capable of dealing with nuclear devastation on a large scale is impossible to say, but the Soviets certainly pay more than lip service to the necessity for planning for such an eventuality. All reconnaissance units in the Ground Forces have elements specially equipped for duty in contaminated areas. Each soldier has protective clothing, a respirator and a personal decontamination kit. Decontamination sprays are held at company level and above, and divisions have complex mass decontamination equipment such as the TMS 65 – a jet engine mounted on a lorry which sprays activated bleach slurry to decontaminate armoured fighting vehicles (AFVs).

The Soviet Ground Forces are also widely equipped with passive and infra-red night-vision devices and battlefield surveillance radar, although many Western specialists consider these to be less effective than some possessed by NATO forces. Soviet doctrine insists that pressure on the enemy must be maintained at night, but it is unlikely that the advance would be continued at daytime pace. Cover of darkness would be used for the consolidation of positions, moving up of supplies and preparation for resumption of the advance at first light. River crossings would probably be attempted at last light, and bridges built and crossed at night wherever possible to enable attacks to be launched from bridgeheads before dawn. Certain operations, such as deep-penetration paratroop or heliborne assaults,

might, of course, wait for darkness because the protection it affords outweighs the difficulties of operating in the dark.

The Soviets do not maintain units solely for warfare in special conditions such as desert, mountain and snow. The entire army is expected to be able to fight in all climatic conditions – and in view of the extremes of climate in the USSR this is hardly surprising. Those units stationed in mountainous or desert areas practise the same tactics and operations with the same equipment as does the army as a whole. Tactics will be adapted to accommodate the difficult conditions where necessary, but in practice Soviet units seem to make few concessions to difficult terrain.

Chemical warfare

One area in which, it is generally agreed, Soviet military technology leads the West is chemical warfare. From the establishment in

the 1920s, with German help, of a gas warfare school, the USSR has continued to develop her CW capability. Chemical weapons are considered a most effective means of waging war; indeed, the USSR sees herself as being particularly vulnerable to their strategic use.

Along with nuclear weapons, chemical and bacteriological weapons are classed by the Soviets as "weapons of mass destruction". Although bacteriological warfare is under international interdict, there is no doubt that the USSR has conducted a great deal of research in this sphere too.

The Soviet Armed Forces of today are trained to accept the use of chemical weapons as a matter of course. Soviet officers make an intensive study of the special conditions of chemical warfare on their Staff courses. Chemical phases are included in all large Ground Forces exercises and many Naval ones, and are a major feature of most Civil Defence exercises.

Army Weapons

Bill Gunston

The Soviet Union

Total armed forces	Active 4.9 million; reserve 9 million.
Ground Forces Command	1.9 million active regular and conscripted troops (KGB troops 375,000, including border guards, Ministry of Interior troops 200,000, Construction troops 250,000). The USSR is divided into 16 Military Districts and Soviet troops abroad are formed into 4 'groups of forces'. In peacetime, teeth arms are organised in divisions of 3 types: 118 Motor Rifle Divisions; 47 Tank Divisions; 8 Airborne Divisions.
There are 3 stages of combat readiness	
First category	over 75 per cent manned with full equipment scales
Second category	50-75 per cent manned with full scales of fighting vehicles but not necessarily of the latest type
Third category	35-50 per cent manned with 50-75 per cent equipment scales plus 'mothballed' obsolescent equipment.
First category equipment scales	*Tank Divs:* 325 tanks; 170 combat APCs; 98 battle reconnaissance vehicles; 96 guns, rocket launcher vehicles or heavy mortars, plus 60 AA missile vehicles or radar controlled gun systems; 4 FFR (FROGs) 21 heavy anti-tank weapons.
	Motor Rifle Divs: 260 tanks; up to 372 combat APCs; 125 battle reconnaissance vehicles; 144 field guns; rocket launcher vehicles or heavy mortars; 60 AA missile vehicles or radar-controlled gun systems; 4 FFR (Frogs); 81 heavy anti-tank weapons.
	Airborne Divs: 102 BMD combat vehicles; 30 ASU-85 SP guns; 36 field guns; 15 battle reconnaissance vehicles.
Second category equipment scales	*Tank Divs:* 310 tanks, less AA defence.
	Motor Rifle Divs: 215 tanks; 312 combat APCs; less AA and anti-tank weapons.
Third category equipment scales	These vary to accommodate stockpiling requirements. Combat ready vehicles usually comprise 75 per cent of Second Category scales.

Deployment

Divisions	Tank	M.R.	Air	
Group of Soviet Forces (Germany)	10	10	—	All Category 1
Central Group of Forces (Czechoslovakia)	2	3	—	All Cateogry 1
Northern Group of Forces (Poland)	2	—	—	All Category 1
Southern Group of Forces (Hungary)	2	2	—	All Category 1
European USSR (Moscow, Leningrad, Kiev, Odessa, Belorussian, Baltic, Carpathian Military Districts)	23	36	4	All airborne: Cat 1 / Tank and MR: 35% Cat 1 / 35% Cat 2 / 30% Cat 3
Southern USSR (N. Caucasus, Trans-Caucasus and Turkestan Military Districts)	3	19	2	All airborne: Cat 1 / Tank and MR: 35% Cat 1 / 35% Cat 2 / 35% Cat 3
Central USSR (Volga and Ural Military Districts)	1	5	—	All Cat 3
Eastern USSR (Central Asian, Siberian, Transbaikal and Far Eastern Military Districts and Mongolian Peoples Republic)	7	5	1 or 2	Airborne div(s): Cat 1 / Tank and MR: 35% Cat 1 / 30% Cat 2 / 35% Cat 3

Major Weapons and Equipment

			Estimated Totals
Tanks:	T-72, T-64, T-62, T-55, T-54		42,000
APC'S and AAICVs:	BMP, BMD, PT-76, BRDM, BTR-60, BTR-40, BTR-152, MTLB		41,000
Artillery:	152 and 122mm SP guns, 180mm, 152mm, 130mm, 122mm field guns; 122mm, 140mm, 200mm, 240mm, multi-barrelled rocket launchers;		20,000
	120mm, 160mm, 240mm, heavy mortars, Spigot, Spandrel, Spiral 57mm, 73mm, 82mm, 85mm, 100mm, 107mm anti-tank guns and Snapper, Sagger and Swatter anti-tank guided weapons.		8 to 10,000
AA Artillery:	23mm, 57mm; towed AA guns; ZSU-23-4 AA SP guns; 85mm, 100mm, 130mm emplaced guns; SA-7 (hand held), SA-4, SA-6, SA-7, SA-8, SA-9, SA-11 mobile AA missiles.		6 to 7,000 (excluding SA-7)

Per Annum Production Rates 1974-75 (USSR only)	Tanks 2,600	Artillery 1,400	APC/AAICV 3,700	
Frontal Aviation (Under Ground Forces Control)	*Helicopters:*	Hind, Hip, Hook, Hound (under Divisional and Army Control)		1,800
	Fixed wing aircraft	Total: 6,000 aircraft — 1,000 fighters, 2,000 fighter bombers — 3,000 strike aircraft. Grouped in Tactical Air Armies, one with each of 12 border Military Districts and European Military Districts in USSR, and one with each Group of Forces abroad. Largest is 16 TAA with GSFG. Approx. 4,200 aircraft in Europe and European USSR and 1,800 in Central and Eastern USSR.		
	Aircraft:	Mig-25, MiG-27, MiG-23, Su-17/20, Su-24, MiG-21, Su-7, MiG-19, MiG-17, Yak-28, Il-28, An-12 EW.		

Non-Soviet Warsaw Pact Countries

In recent years the improvement in the quality of equipment supplied by the USSR to her Warsaw Pact Allies has been tremendous. In addition, several Warsaw Pact Nations, most notably Czechoslovakia, have developed their own armaments industries. The table below shows the priority allotted to Non-Soviet Warsaw Pact (NSWP) armies for quality/quantity of equipment supplied by the USSR. (The figures indicate total equipment to date, not during year in question.)

	1963	1967	1971	1976
1	POLAND } equally	CZECH	POLAND	POLAND
2	CZECH } equally	POLAND	CZECH	E. GERMANY
3	BULGARIA	HUNGARY	HUNGARY	CZECH
4	HUNGARY	BULGARIA	E. GERMANY	BULGARIA
5	ROMANIA	E. GERMANY	BULGARIA	HUNGARY
6	E. GERMANY	ROMANIA	ROMANIA	ROMANIA

The low positions of Czechoslovakia and Hungary on the list reflect the large amount of equipment produced for these armies in Eastern European arms factories. In effect, of all East European armies, only Romania's was not fully modernised by early 1976. The improvement in the East German Army's equipment holdings was most marked of all the Warsaw Pact Armies.

East Germany (DDR)

Total Armed Forces	140,000 MOD troops, 48,000 Border troops, 25,000 Ministry of the Interior troops, 500,000 Territorial Workers Militia, 250,000 Reserves (active),	
Ground Forces	102,000	
	Along with Romania, E. Germany is the only Warsaw Pact country in the short (18 months) conscription period (usually 2 years) 4 Motor Rifle Divs; 2 Tank Divs. organised into Northern (V), Southern (III) Military Districts, the Tank Divs in each case being located close to the Polish border (see maps); 2 airborne battalions. All at full or 75 per cent strength.	
Weapons and Equipment	*Tanks* T-62, T-55, T-54, T-34	2,500
	OT-65, PT-76, BRDM, BTR 40 Recce vehicles	

	APCs/AAICVs	BMP, BTR 60, BTR 50, BTR 152, APCs	
	Artillery	76mm, 85mm, 100mm, 122mm, 130mm, 152mm, Czech RL-70, MBRL, 120mm mortars;	

Snapper, Swatter, Sagger, ATGM; and 57, 82, 85, and 100mm A-Tk guns
Frog-7 and Scud B Tactical Surface-to-Surface missiles (SSMs);
ZSU 57-2 and ZSU 23-4 SPAA guns and S60 57mm AA guns; SA-7 missiles

Recently, East Germany has begun to buy equipment from Czechoslovakia, in addition to heavy equipment made in the GDR under licence. There are, however, no AFVs of native design.

Frontal Aviation 90 Mi-1, Mi-4, Mi-8 helicopters, 500 FGA aircraft (MiG-17, MiG-21, MiG-23 and Su-7), 34 Transport aircraft
The airborne battalions rely on Soviet aircraft or Civil aviation for transport.

Poland

Total Armed Forces 298,000 MOD troops, 80,000 Territorial Defence Troops (inc. Border Guards), 350,000 Volunteer Militia, 500,000 Reserves

Ground Forces 212,000

5 Tank Divs.; 8 M.R. Divs.; 1 Airborne Div.; 1 Marine Div.; a large percentage at full strength. Qualitatively and quantatively the strongest Non-Soviet Warsaw Pact Army.

Weapons and Equipment	*Tanks:*	T-62, T-55, T-54, JS-III	4,200
	Battle Recce Vehicles	PT-76, BRDM, FUG	800 +
	APCs	OT-62, TOPAZ, OT-64, SKOT	
	Artillery	76mm, 85mm, 100mm, 122mm, 152mm, guns; 85 and 100mm SP assault guns; 122 and 152mm modern SP guns; 122mm and 140mm MBRL; 120mm mortars.	
		80 Frog 7 and Scud B SSMU.	
		76, 82, 85, 100mm A-Tk guns.	Total 2,000
		ASU-57 and ASU-85.	
		Snapper, Sagger, ATGW.	
		ZSU 57-2 and ZSU 23-4 AA guns.	
		57, 85mm and 100mm AA guns.	
		SA-6, SA-7, SA-9 AA missiles.	
	Frontal Aviation	130 Mi 2, 4, 8, helicopters, 645 FGA aircraft — Mig 17/19/21/23, Su-7, Su-20,	

60 Transport aircraft can transport about ¼ of Airborne strength.
Almost all APCs are domestically produced with Czechoslovakia. Many other items of equipment are bought from Czechoslovakia or licence-built in Poland.

Hungary

Total Armed Forces 103,000 MOD Troops, 20,000 Border Guards, 60,000 Volunteer Militia, 110,000 Reserves

Ground Forces 88,000 conscript and regular

1 Tank Div., 5 Motor Rifle Divs.

Weapons and Equipment	*Tanks:*	T-62, T-55/54, T-34	1,700
	Battle Recce Vehicles:	BTR 40, PT-76, OT-65, FUG	2,200
	APCs	BTR 50, BTR 60, OT62	
	Artillery:	76, 85, 100, 122 and 152mm guns; 122mm and 140mm MBRC; 120mm and 160mm heavy mortars; 57, 82, 85 and 107mm A-tk guns; Snapper and Sagger ATGW.	700
		Frog 3/4/5 and Scud A SSM; S60 and ZSU 57-2 AA guns; 85 and 100mm AA guns and SA-7.	
	Danube flotilla:	10 gunboats; 6 landing craft.	
	Frontal Avaition	30 Hook and Hound helicopters; 120 FGA Aircraft — MiG 15/17/19/21;	

A large percentage of Hungary's AFVs are the light domestically produced battle/recce vehicles such as the OT-65 and FUG.

Bulgaria

Total Armed Forces 150,000 MOD troops, 20,000 Ministry of Interior troops and Border Guards, 12,000 Construction troops, 150,000 Volunteer militia, 280,000 Reserves

Ground Forces 120,000 conscript and regular

8 Motor Rifle Divs.; 5 Tank regiments; 1 Airborne regiment; 35 per cent at cadre strength (20 to 30 per cent manned and all equipment). Due to the mountainous terrain, Bulgaria does not deploy Tank Divisions, but alone amongst Warsaw Pact Armies deploys her armour with her infantry.

Weapons and Equipment	*Main tank force:*	T-55/T-54 — approx 2,000. A few training units with T-62 plus approx 150 T-34 tanks; 600 PT-76 and BRDM and BTR-40 Recce vehicles: 2,000 BTR-60, BTR-50 and OT-62 (Topaz) APCs.
		1,000 Artillery pieces, rocket launchers and mortars, inc. 100mm, 122mm, 130mm, 152mm towed guns and 120mm mortars; 30 Frog 3/4/5 and 20 Scud A missiles; 57mm, 76mm, 85mm anti-tank guns; Snapper and Sagger ATGW; ZSU 23-4, S-60 AA guns and SA-7; plus a large stockpile of older artillery pieces.
	Frontal Aviation	36 Mi-4 Hound helicopters; 72 MiG-17 FGA aircraft; 12 MiG-21; 12 MiG 15; 12 Il-28 reece aircraft; approx 20 older type transport aircraft.

The army relies on the Soviet air forces or its own civil air fleet to transport its Parachute Regiment.

Czechoslovakia

Total Armed Forces 210,000 MOD troops, 20,000 Ministry of the Interior Border Guards, 120,000 Voluntary militia/CD, 305,000 Army reserves

Ground Forces 161,000 Conscript and regular

5 motor Rifle Divs.; 5 Tank Divs.; 1 Airborne Regiment; (35 per cent at Cadre strength).

Weapons and Equipment	*Tanks:*	T-62, T-55/54	3,300
	APCs:	OT-65 O/FUG Recce; OT-62 Topaz OT-64 Skot APCs.	2,000
	Artillery:	85mm, 100mm, 122mm, 130mm, 152mm towed guns; 122 SP; RM-70, RM 132 multiple rocket launchers; 120mm mortars; 72 tactical SSM (Frog 4/5, Scud); Snapper, Sagger and Swatter ATGW; 57mm, 82mm, 85mm SP, 100mm, 107mm anti-tank guns; 23mm, 30mm, 57mm, 85mm AA guns; 30mm and ZSU SP AA guns; SA-7.	
	Frontal Aviation	220 Hook, Hound, Harc helicopters; 370 FGA aircraft, inc. MiG 15, MiG 21, SU-7 and domestically produced trainers/close support aircraft.	

Almost all the Czech Army's APCs are domestically produced (and in conjunction with Poland and Hungary), as is much of her artillery. Other heavy equipment is built under licence, including the 122mm SP gun. The RM-70 40 barrelled rocket launcher is an improvement on the Soviet BM-21. There is also a complete range of excellent Czech small arms and infantry anti-tank weapons.

Romania

Total Armed Forces 167,000 MOD troops, 45,000 Border troops and Ministry of Interior troops, 700,000 Volunteer militia, 500,000 Reserves

Ground Forces 139,000
(16-months National Service Period)

Romania is the only Warsaw Pact country to have reduced its defence expenditure over the past 5 years, and her army is deficient in many items of modern equipment. There is little domestic production of AFVs. The BTR-60 has recently been produced under licence.
2 Tank Divs.; 8 Motor Rifle Divs.; 2 mountain regiments; 1 Airborne battalion (40 per cent at full strength; 60 per cent at 50 to 30 per cent strength.)

Weapons Equipment	*Tanks:*	T-55/T-54, T-34	1,800
	Battle Recce vehicles:	BTR-40, PT-76, OT-65	300
	APCs:	BTR-50, 60, 152; OT-810, 62.	
	Artillery:	76mm, 85mm, 100mm, 122mm, 130mm, 152mm guns; 85mm and 100mm obsolescent SP guns; 120mm mortars; 132mm Czech MBRL; Frog 4, Scud A SSM; 57mm, 85mm, 100mm A-Tk guns; Snapper and Sagger ATGW; ZSU 57-2 SPAA guns; 37, 57 and 100mm AA guns.	
	Frontal Aviation	12 Hound helicopters; 180 FGA aircraft — MiG 15/17/19/21; 30 Transport aircraft (II-14 and II-18).	

ARMOURED VEHICLES

Despite all the developments of modern weapon technology, the Russians still consider the tank to be the most suitable instrument of their offensive. The Soviet commitment to the tank remains total, and much of their weapons systems development since the war has aimed at giving other arms the same mobility, protection and firepower that the tank forces possess. It is recognised that today, on a battlefield saturated with guided weapons, the tank cannot survive alone, even in large numbers. Consequently all units and formations are to a greater or lesser extent comprised of 'combined arms' which afford each other mutual protection. This does not mean that all Soviet fighting formations tend towards the same composition, however. The Russians still maintain tank-heavy formations, convinced that these formations are the best sort for rapid thrusts deep into the enemy's position, delivering a "shock" blow so as to precipitate his rapid military and political collapse.

T-72

Main battle tank
Combat weight: 39·3 tons (40,000kg).
Length: (Gun to front) 29·5ft (9·02m).
Length: (Hull) 20·46ft (6·35m).
Width: 10·03ft (3·375m).
Height: (To cupola) 7·41ft (2·265m).
Engine: Water-cooled diesel of about 700bhp.
Armament: 125mm smoothbore gun firing fin-stabilised APFSDS and HEAT ammunition, with automatic loader; one 7·62mm coaxial machine-gun and one 12·7mm remote-controlled DShK AAMG.
Speed: 50mph (80km/h).
Range: 310 miles (500km).
Armour: Maximum about 120mm, possibly of modern 'special' material resistant to shaped charges.

Considerable confusion was caused in the West over the correct designation of the MBTs which followed the T-62. This has at last been resolved and it is now clear that there are two quite distinct designs: the T-64 and the T-72. The latter is a developed version of T-64, with revised suspension and a slightly different turret It is also suggested in some quarters that T-72 is constructed of a new type of armour, which is resistant to shaped charges, similar to that developed in Britain ('Chobham' armour). The principal visible difference between the two tanks is that T-72 has six large road wheels whereas T-64 has six rather small road wheels which are quite unlike those on any other Soviet MBT.

T-72 is armed with a 125mm gun, which is fitted with a fume extractor. The gun fires APFSDS, HE or HEAT rounds, and it is thought that an integrated fire control system (IFCS) is installed. The IFCS would relieve both commander and gunner of some of their tasks and would also significantly increase the probability of a first-round hit.

T-72 was put into production in 1974 and was in service with the Soviet Army shortly after. It is now in production in several State armament factories in the Soviet Union and may also be produced in Poland and Czechoslovakia as well. Current production is running

at some 2,000 MBTs per year and all front-line divisions in the Warsaw Pact should soon be equipped with this excellent vehicle.

A special command version of T-72 exists, which carries additional communications equipment in place of the 12·7mm machine-gun. When stationary a 10 metre mast can be erected. This tank is designated T-72K.

The successor to T-72, the T-80, has already completed trials and should be entering production soon, keeping the USSR in the forefront of MBT design.

Above: The neat and compact lines of the T-72 are displayed in a Moscow parade. The 125mm calibre gun is the world's most powerful tank gun.

Below: A T-72 of the Tumansky Guards Division is inspected by French generals. The 125mm fin-stabilised ammunition is on display and the dozer-blade can be seen. The skirting plates defeat HEAT warheads.

T-64

Main battle tank
Combat weight: 39·3 tons (40,000kg).
Length: (Gun to front) 29·5ft (9·02m).
Length: (Hull) 20·46ft (6·35m).
Width: 10·03ft (3·375m).
Height: (To cupola) 7·41ft (2·265m).
Engine: Water-cooled diesel. 700bhp.
Armament: 125mm smoothbore main gun, firing fin-stabilised APFSDS and HEAT ammunition; automatic loader. One 7·62mm coaxial machine-gun. One 12·7mm remote-controlled DShk AAMG.
Speed: 50mph (80km/h).
Range: 310 miles (500km).
Armour: Maximum about 120mm.

Western military commentators have suggested that the T-62 has proved to be less than satisfactory, and it is certainly true that the tank has not been exported on the scale of T-54/55, nor has it been produced in the Polish and Czechoslovakian tank factories. A new experimental tank was running in the late 1960s which was designated M-1970 in the West; this mated the T-62 turret and gun to a new hull with six small road-wheels and return rollers. The production version, designated T-64, had the M-1970 hull and suspension, the 115mm smoothbore gun from the T-62 and a completely new turret and automatic loader, and a crew of three. A few years after entering service a modification programme was carried out to fit the new 125mm gun to all existing T-64s, while all new production vehicles have the 125mm as standard.

The 125mm gun is a smoothbore weapon, firing armour piercing, fin stabilised, discarding sabot (APFSDS), high-explosive anti-tank (HEAT) (also fin-stabilised), and high explosive rounds. Forty rounds are carried, the usual mix being 12 APFSDS, 6 HEAT and 22 HE. The automatic loader has enabled the Soviet Army to reduce the crew to three, an interesting step in an army not short of manpower, and which saves 95 men in every tank regiment.

The engine and transmission are mounted at the rear of the T-64, the engine being a new design of water-cooled diesel. Initial reports credited this with a power output of 1,000bhp, but a more realistic figure of 700—760bhp is now quoted.

The salient features of this fine MBT are the very powerful gun and the reduction in crew by 25 per cent. This latter step must make Western armies re-examine their long-standing adherence to the four-man crew, especially as their manpower problems are so much more acute than the Soviet Army's. The T-64 also illustrates the Soviet philosophy of step-by-step development, which has kept it in the forefront of tank design.

Above: The T-64 MBT fitted with a 125mm smoothbore gun. Alone among modern Soviet MBTs this tank is fitted with small road-wheels; it was also the first since the 'heavies' to be fitted with return rollers.

Below: An overhead view of a T-64 showing the storage boxes around the turret for MG ammunition.

T-62

Main battle tank
Combat weight: (Fully stowed, no crew) 36.93 tons (37,500kg).
Length: (Gun to front) 30ft 8in (9488 or 9770mm).
Length: (Gun to rear) 22ft (6705mm).
Width: 11ft (3352mm).
Height: 7ft 11in (2400mm).
Engine: V-2-62 vee-12 watercooled diesel, 700hp.
Armament: U-5TS 115mm smooth-bore gun, 40 rounds, APFSDS, HEAT, HE, one 7.62mm (co-axial) with 2000 or 3500 rounds.
Speed: Up to 34mph (50km/h).
Range: Typically 310 miles (500km).
Armour: Up to 100mm, mantlet up to 170mm.

The Soviet designers found the existing (T-55) tank design almost impossible to better. The T-62 follows exactly the same formula but with a slightly bigger hull housing more power and some extra equipment, and with an outstanding smooth-bore gun firing fin-stabilising ammunition. The bigger gun, with evauator well back from the muzzle, is an identification feature, as are the close-spaced three front pairs of road wheels (the opposite of T-54/55). The commander's cupola is cast integral with the turret, and equipment includes full active IR, NBC protection and deep schnorkel for wading. Since 1973, eight years after T-62 entered service, these tanks have been updated with laser rangefinders and a 12.7mm AAMG. In 1977 a new version of T-62 was revealed with six large roadwheels and return rollers similar to the new T-72.

T-62 seems only to have been a success with the Soviet Army and it will remain in front-line service with them until replaced by the T-72 (now in service) or T-80 (under development).

Major faults: poor gearbox, liability to shed tracks, thin armour, vulnerable ammunition and fuel storage, poor crew operating conditions.

Above: The T-62 introduced the formidable 115mm smoothbore gun with its APFSDS ammunition. The tank itself, however, was not an outstanding success and is replaced by T-64/72.

Right: A T-62 on a realistic looking exercise. This picture shows the length of the main gun, together with the excellent ballistic shape of the turret. The tracks are easily shed, however.

T-54, T-55

Main battle tank and derived vehicles
Combat weight (fully stowed, no crew): About 35·9 tons (36,500kg).
Length: (Gun to front) 29ft 7in (9020mm).
Length: (Gun to rear) 21ft 7in (6570mm).
Width: 10ft 9½in (3265mm).
Height: 7ft 10in (2380mm).
Engine: T-54, V-2-54 vee-12 water-cooled diesel, 520hp; T-55, V-2-55 vee-12, 580hp.
Armament: D-10T, D-10TG or D-10T2S 100mm gun (T-54, 34 rounds, T-55, 43 rounds; 7.62mm SGMT or PKT machine gun (co-axial) with 3000 rounds; T-54 also one 12.7mm DShK with 500 rounds for AA use, and one 7.62mm SGMT (bow).
Speed: 30mph (48km/h).
Range: T-54, 250 miles (400km); T-55, 310 miles (500jm).
Armour: Up to 100mm, mantlet up to 170mm.

The Soviet tank designers found it hard to improve on the T-34/85, the T-44 of 1945 introducing an improved chassis but having the old turret. In 1947 the T-44 chassis reappeared with a new elliptical turret mounting a 100mm gun, and the resulting T-54 became the standard Soviet-bloc battle tank (much faster and more compact than Western tanks, but cramped inside). There were seven main production versions, some built in Poland, Czechoslovakia and China. The T-55, built in even greater numbers, appeared in 1961. This has slightly more power, a revised turret with more ammunition and no AA gun, and very tall snorkel tube for deep wading. Most tanks of these series have been progressively fitted with IR night equipment, stabilized gun and provision for NBC-contaminated environments. They are used by all Warsaw Pact armies, in tank, bridgelayer, flame-thrower, mine-clearing, recovery and dozer versions, and also by about 25 other countries.

Major faults: as for T-62, plus obsolescent main armament.

Above: This early version of T-54 does not have a fume extractor on the muzzle, but is still in service with the Warsaw Pact.

Left: The fume extractor at the top of the picture shows the 23mm sub-calibre device fitted to T-55s to reduce training costs.

Lower left: A T-54 on exercise in one of the western Military Districts of the USSR. It is carrying three large fuel drums to give extended range on an approach march.

Below: A T-55 with an obsolescent 100mm gun. It would have little effect on NATO tanks, but would destroy APCs and SPs.

PT-76

PT-76 (three models) amphibious light tank and derivatives
Combat weight: (No crew) 13·78 tons (14,000kg).
Length: (Gun to front) 25ft 0in (7625mm).
Length: (Gun to rear) 22ft 7in (6910mm).
Width: 10ft 5in (3180mm).
Height: 7ft 5in (2260mm) (early models, 2195mm).
Engine: V-6 six-in-line water-cooled diesel, 240hp.
Armament: 76mm gun (D-56T, multi-slotted muzzle brake, PT-76-I; D-56TM, double-baffle brake plus bore evacuator, Model II; unknown gun designation, plain barrel, Model III), 40 rounds; 7·62mm SGMT (co-axial), 1,000 rounds.
Speed: 27mph (44km/h) on land; 7mph (11km/h) on water.
Range: 155 miles (250km) on land, 62½ miles (100km) on water.
Armour: Usually 11–14mm.

Since it appeared in 1952 this large, lightly armoured but highly mobile vehicle has appeared in at least 15 different guises, and been built in very large numbers. The basic PT-76 (PT-76B when fitted with stabilized

gun) is still the most numerous reconnaissance tank of the Warsaw Pact armies. To swim, the twin hydrojets at the rear are uncovered and clutched-in, and a trim board is folded down at the front. Smokelaying equipment is standard. The 76mm ammunition is the same as for the M-1942 (ZIS-3), SU-76 and T-34/76. The PT-76 is used by at least 17 countries outside the Warsaw Pact. Its basic design of chassis is used in the ASU-85, SA-6 Gainful SAM vehicle, BTR-50, FROG-2/-3/-4/-5, GSP bridger, M-1970, OT-62 APC, Pinguin, PVA and ZSU-23-4. In front-line Soviet divisions, the PT-76 is now almost completely replaced by a recce version of the BMP.

Right: Three PT-76 reconnaissance tanks demonstrating their amphibious capability. These vehicles have served the Soviet Army for some 28 years, but are now being phased out and replaced by a reconnaissance version of the BMP-1 APC. The PT-76 hull is rather bulky in order to achieve buoyancy; many weapons use this chassis.

BMD

Air-portable fire support vehicle
Combat weight: (without crew) Estimated 8.86 tons (9000kg).
Length overall: 17ft 4½in (5300mm).
Width overall: 8ft 8in (2640mm).
Height overall: (excl. crew or aerials) 6ft 0in (1850mm).
Engine: Possibly a V-6, of about 280hp.
Armament: Turret identical to BMP, with 73mm low-pressure smooth-bore gun with auto-loading, from 30-round magazine, 7.62mm PKT co-axial, and 'Sagger' missile on launch rail. In addition, two 7.62mm PKT in mounts in front corners of hull.
Speed: estimated at least 53mph (85km/h) on land, 6mph (10km/h) in water.
Cruising range: Estimated 250 miles (400 km) on land.
Armour: Probably 20mm.

First seen in a Moscow parade in November 1973, this trim little fire support vehicle is yet another of the 'quart a pint pot' vehicles developed primarily for the large and important Soviet airborne forces. Though such aircraft as the An-22 could easily carry the BMP, it was judged the same capability could be built into a smaller and lighter APC capable of being airlifted in greater numbers and more readily dropped by parachute. At first styled 'M-1970' in the West, the BMD (Boyevaya Machine Desantnaya) has a crew of three and carries six airborne infantry in open seats in the back, and not inside like the slightly larger BMP. It operates in water by hydrojet propulsion like the PT-76. It is probably most correctly classified as an airborne infantry combat vehicle.

Above right: The BMD is a lightweight APC designed specifically for the parachute troops, utilising the same turret as the BMP, and carrying 3 crew and 6 passengers.

Right: The compact design of this small APC is clearly shown, together with the 73mm low-pressure gun and the Sagger anti-tank missile. BMDs were among the Soviet vehicles used to invade Afghanistan.

ASU-57

Airborne assault gun
Combat weight: 3.4 tons (3455kg).
Length: (Gun to front) 16ft 4½in (4995mm).
Length: (Excl. gun) 11ft 5in (3480mm).
Width: 6ft 10in (2082mm).
Height: (Shield down, no AA) 3ft 10in (1180mm).
Engine: M-20E four-in-line water-cooled gasoline, 55hp.
Armament: Ch-51M 57mm gun, 30 rounds.
Speed: 28mph (45km/h).
Range: 155 miles (250km).
Armour: 6mm.

The Soviet Union was the pioneer of the modern air-borne army which, so far as technology allows, lacks nothing. Great efforts have been made to build up an air-portable capability which includes even self-propelled heavy firepower. The ASU-57 was the first of these purpose-designed vehicles, and since 1957 it has been in large-scale service with Warsaw Pact powers. To get the weight down to a scarcely credible value it is extremely lightly armoured, and is mainly of light alloy. The engine is derived from that of the Pobeda family car. Large transport aircraft or helicopters can carry several, the former delivering via parachutes with retro-rockets ignited just above impact. The gun has the same ammunition as other Soviet ATk 57mm, and traverses 12° with rate of fire up to 10 rds/min. The original Ch-51 had a long 34-slot muzzle brake. Six airborne troops can ride as passengers behind the regular crew of three. It is now being replaced by the BMD.

Below left: ASU-57 was designed to give Soviet parachute divisions a highly mobile anti-tank defence. The vehicle weighs only 3.35 tonnes (3.3 tons) fully loaded, and carries a crew of 3. The gun is the Ch-51M 57mm and fires both HE and anti-tank shells; maximum AT range is 1,200m.

Below: Soviet parachute troops removing an ASU-57 from its air-dropping pallet. Each Soviet parachute regiment has a company of nine ASU-57 which can be held centrally or detached to parachute battalions as tactics demand.

ASU-85

Airborne assault gun
Combat weight: Loaded 13·78 tons (14,000kg).
Length (Gun horizontal ahead) 27ft 10in (8490mm).
Width: 9ft 2½in (2800mm).
Height: (Excl. IR etc.) 6ft 11in (2100mm).
Engine: V-6 six-in-line water-cooled diesel, 240hp.
Armament: Improved SD-44 85mm gun, 40 rounds; 7·62mm PKT (co-axial).
Speed: 27mph (44km/h).
Range: 162 miles (260km).
Armour: Up to 40mm.

Much tougher and heavier than the ASU-57, this formidable vehicle became possible with the advent of the Mi-6 and Mi-10 helicopters and (for fixed-wing drop) high-capacity multi-chute and retro-rocket systems. The ASU-85 was first seen in 1962 and is widely used by the Soviet, Polish and East German airborne divisions. Though the chassis is based on the PT-76 it is not amphibious. The gun has 12° traverse and fires up to 4 rounds a minute. Above the NBC-sealed and armoured roof are a large IR night-fighting light for the gunner, aligned with the gun, and a smaller one on the right for the commander. Since 1973 other target-acquisition and ranging aids are reported to have been retrofitted to these useful anti-armour vehicles.

Right: An ASU-85 emerging from an An-12 Cub transport aircraft. This vehicle is more of an assault gun than just an anti-tank weapon and 18 are held in the ASU battalion of each airborne division.

BMP

Infantry combat vehicle and derivations
Weight: Empty, 11.32 tons (11,500kg); laden in combat, 12.5 tons (12,700kg).
Length: 22ft 2in (6750mm).
Width: 9ft 9in (2970mm).
Height: Over hull, 4ft 10in (1470mm); over turret IR light, 6ft 6in (1980mm).
Engine: V-6 six-in-line water-cooled diesel, 280hp.
Armament: 73mm smooth-bore gun, 40 rounds; AT-3 ('Sagger') ATGW launcher; 7.62PKT (co-axial), 1000 rounds.
Speed: Land, 34mph (55km/h); deep snow, 25mph (40km/h); water 5mph (8km/h).
Range: 310 miles (500km).
Armour: Mainly 14mm.

When it appeared in 1967 the BMP was thought in the West to be what the West's own armies needed: a true MICV (mechanised infantry combat vehicle). Significantly smaller than the West's own APCs, it has considerably greater firepower. The eight troops have multiple periscopes and can, in theory, fire on the move. Like the crew of three (the commander is also the leader of the troop squad), they have NBC protec-

Above: The BMP is an outstanding design which has now been in service for 13 years, with no sign yet of a successor. The Soviets have, however, revised their use of APCs.

Below: BMPs of the East German army on parade. The infantrymen can fire through the three ports on each side of their compartment; there are two more in the doors.

ACRV-2

Armoured command and reconnaissance vehicle
Combat weight: Loaded 13 tons (13.21 tonnes).
Length: 20.83ft (6.35m).
Width: 9.18ft (2.8m).
Height: 7.55ft (2.3m).
Engine: Model IZ-6, 6-cylinder diesel; 200hp
Armament: Nil.
Speed: 34.2mph (55km/h).
Range: 248 miles (400km).

It has long been customary for Soviet commanders at regimental and divisional level to position themselves right forward, in a vantage point from which they can observe the essential parts of the battlefield. During an advance this has involved the hasty siting and construction of a chain of command posts, usually dug in, although rarely with overhead protection. This small headquarters comprises the commander, his artillery officer, an engineer, radio operators, and a tiny defence element. The detailed command of the division or regiment is exercised by the chief-of-staff, operating from a main headquarters somewhat further back.

This procedure is clearly most effective on the plains of western Russia where the terrain is open and flat, and visibility is excellent. In central and western Europe, however, the country is rolling, densely wooded in some places, and heavily urbanised in others. It is, therefore, debatable as to whether the Soviet commanders will achieve very much by being so far forward.

However, it is quite clear that they intend to try to operate in this fashion, and the latest evidence to this effect is the appearance of the ACRV-2, a large armoured command and reconnaissance vehicle.

No technical details of this interesting vehicle have yet been made public, but it is obviously based on the chassis used for the SA-4 (Ganef) surface-to-air guided-missile system. The ACRV-2 has seven road wheels with the engine and drive sprocket at the front of the vehicle. The driver and vehicle commander are right at the front, leaving a large compartment for the commander, his staff, and radio sets. On the roof is an observation cupola fitted with periscopes and an electronic viewing device.

The ACRV-2 is replacing the command versions of previous APCs: BTR-152, BTR-60PU and BTR-50PU, and illustrates the growing tendency in the Soviet Army to develop specialised vehicles, although an effort is made to utilise common components wherever possible. ACRV-2 also demonstrates the Soviet adherence to the philosophy of attack, with all current vehicles being highly mobile, amphibious, and with built-in NBC protection.

These command vehicles play a crucial role in the headquarters deployment drills. Soviet HQs are usually sited near the principal axis of advance, with vehicles in groups. Photographs of Soviet forces on exercise

Above: ACRV-2 seen here in silhouette is one of the latest Soviet armoured vehicles and is designed to give divisional and regimental commanders a mobile command post capable of keeping pace with forward troops.

suggest that the general standard of camouflage and concealment is mediocre, although this may be prompted by a theory that the HQ will move before any retaliatory strike can be made. The Commandant's Service which provides the route guides is also responsible for guarding HQs.

Soviet Army communications systems seem, in general, to be less sophisticated than those in the West. This is certainly not due to any lack in technical capability, and their very simplicity increases their chance of survival on the modern battlefield. Like most modern armies the Soviets constantly discuss cutting down on the size of their tactical headquarters, e.g., Front, division, but little ever seems to be actually achieved.

---

tion in the pressurised and filtered hull. The new 73mm gun has a smooth bore and fires fin-stabilised HEAT ammunition at eight rounds per minute with the aid of an automatic loader. The missile launcher above the gun carries one round with three more loaded manually from racks inside. In addition, one SA-7 Grail launcher is carried inside the vehicle. The BMP is amphibious, with scoops on the tracks and rear water-deflector plates to give thrust. Since 1970 the sharp bow has been made more prominent, which has improved swimming behaviour. In 1975 a variant was seen with the troop compartment replaced by a rear-positioned turret carrying a battlefield radar. A reconnaissance version is rapidly replacing the ageing PT-76. The radar version is equipped with only a machine-gun for main armament; the recce version lacks an ATGW, but carries observation equipment as well as its 73mm gun in an enlarged turret. The BMP's extreme vulnerability in the face of a strong defence was amply demonstrated in the 1973 Arab/Israeli war. Soviet tacticians have consequently concluded that BMP units must always have close support from tanks, engineers and particularly artillery.

Above right: The new reconnaissance version of the BMP crossing a river. Note the trim board and the more-than-adequate freeboard which ensure good flotation.

Right: The line drawings show the sleek, functional lines of the BMP. As with their ships, the Soviets cram more firepower onto their APCs than does the West.

Below: Two BMPs on winter training. The wrap-round glass windscreen for the driver is an unusual concession to crew comfort, normally rated low in priority.

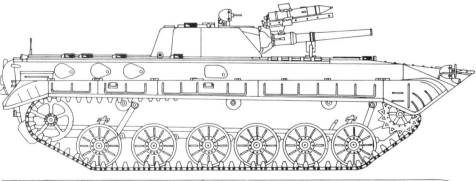

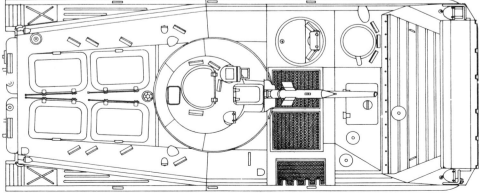

MT-LB

Multi-role tracked vehicle
Weight: (Empty) 11·71 tons (11,900kg).
Length: 21·17ft (6·454m).
Width: 9·35ft (2·85m).
Height: 6·12ft (1·865m).
Engine: YaMZ 238 V6-cylinder engine diesel, 240hp.
Armament: 7·62mm PKT machine-gun.
Speed: 38·2mph (61·5km/h).
Range: 248 miles (400km).

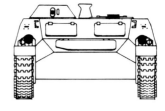
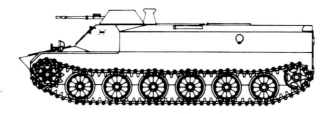
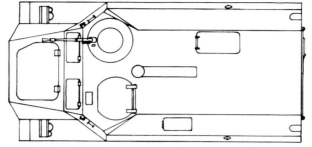
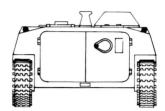

This vehicle was first seen in 1970 and was designated 'M-1970 armoured personnel carrier', although it was also sometimes described mistakenly as the GT-T carrier. It is now known that the correct designation is MT-LB. The hull is of all-welded steel construction, with the engine between the crew and passenger compartments. There are two rear doors and hatches over the passenger compartment. There is one firing port in each door and one on each side of the passenger compartment. Sole vehicle weapon is one 7·62mm machine-gun, turret-mounted. The vehicle is amphibious and is propelled in the water by its tracks.

It is of considerable interest that the Soviet Army has felt the need to develop another vehicle when the BMP was already in existence. However, the latter has only ever been seen as an APC, command vehicle or radar vehicle, while the MT-LB serves as APC (3 crew plus 10 infantry), command vehicle, artillery command post, artillery tractor, cargo carrier, minelayer and radio vehicle. This is clearly a useful and versatile machine, and is probably cheaper than using the sophisticated BMP.

Above right: The MTLB multi-purpose vehicle is now in service in some numbers as an APC, command post, cargo carrier, artillery control, and gun tractor.

Right: The MT-LB in the APC role. Although it is about the same size as the BMP (and seems to be of less sophisticated design), it accommodates two more men.

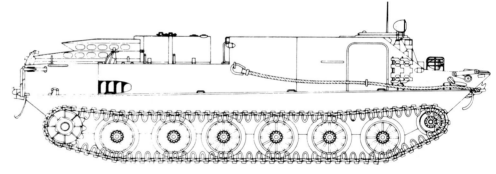

BTR-50

Amphibious tracked APC and variants (data for PK)
Combat weight: (Loaded) 14·27 tons (14,500kg).
Length: 23ft 3in (7080mm) (not 6910mm as commonly reported).
Width: 10ft 3in (3140mm).
Height: (Excl. gun) 6ft 6in (1980mm).
Engine: V-6 six-in-line water-cooled diesel, 240hp.
Armament: 7·62mm SGMB, 1,250 rounds (see text for variations).
Speed: Land, 27mph (44km/h); water 6¼mph (10km/h).
Range: Land 162 miles (260km).
Armour: Up to 10mm.

Based on the amphibious PT-76 chassis, the BTR-50 was first seen in 1957 as the open-topped BTR-50P. The most common version is the 50PK with armoured roof, though these cannot transport the artillery (usually 57, 76 or 85mm) transported and fired aboard the original open model. Normal load is two crew and 10 troops. Variants include the -50PA with 14·5mm KVPT or ZPU-1, the -50PU command vehicle with extremely elaborate navigation and communications equipment, and small numbers of special-purpose modifications used for such tasks as carrying ECM (countermeasures). In front-line Soviet units, the BTR-50 has been replaced by the BMP but it is still found in very large numbers in second-line units and in almost all other Warsaw Pact armies.

Above right: The BTR-50 was a hastily produced conversion of the PT-76 to give a tracked, protected APC for motor rifle troops in a tank division. Infantry travel in the forward compartment and must 'debus' over the sides; there are no doors.

Right: The Czechs built a modified version of the BTR-50PK designated OT-62, which has higher road speed and range, and is a much better vehicle. This OT-62 is operated by the Polish Marines, having been landed from a 'Polnochniy' class tank landing ship.

BTR-60

Armoured personnel carriers and derivatives
Combat weight: Loaded: -60PK, 9·82 tons (9980kg);
-60PB, 10·14 tons (10,300kg).
Length: 24ft 10in (7560mm).
Width: 9ft 3in (2818mm).
Height: -60PK, 6ft 9in (2055mm); -60PB, 7ft 7in
(2310mm).
Engine: Two GAZ-49B six-in-line water-cooled
gasoline, 90hp each.
Armament: See text.
Speed: Land, 50mph (80km/h); water, 6¼mph
(10km/h).
Range: 310 miles (500km).
Armour: -60PK, 10mm; -60PB, 14mm.

First seen in November 1961, the BTR-60 family of armoured personnel carriers is impressive and is widely used in Warsaw Pact forces and has been exported to at least ten other countries. The large hull is boat-shaped for good swimming and to deflect hostile fire. It runs on eight land wheels, all powered and with power steering on the front four. Tire pressures are centrally controlled at all times. The twin rear engines can be switched to drive waterjets. The basic BTR-60P has an open top or canvas hood, and carries two crew plus 16 troops. Typical armament is a 12·7mm and from one to three 7·62mm SGMB or PK. The BTR-60PK has an armoured roof, carries 16 passengers and has a single 12.7 or 7.62mm gun. The PB has a turret with co-axial 14.5mm KPVT and 7.62 PKT (the same turret as on the BTR-40P-2) and carries 14 troops. There is a special version for platoon and other commanders, with extra communications (BTR-60PU). BTR-60P is the standard amphibious APC for the Soviet marines.

Above: The BTR-60 eight-wheeled APC has been a most successful design, having served in the Soviet Army since 1960. The basic APC has been used in the Motor Rifle divisions: the first —BTR-60P—had an open roof; the second (shown here) had proper overhead armour —BTR-60PK; while the third version, BTR-60PB, had a turret with a 14.5mm machine-gun.

Below: A platoon of BTR-60Ps coming ashore during amphibious training. The Soviet Army has made a particular point of giving as many of its tactical vehicles as possible an amphibious capability. This is achieved without recourse to flotation screens as in many Western vehicles, and preparation time is usually less than 60 minutes.

Left: Inside a BTR-60PK. It all looks tranquil enough but, in fact, with 14 passengers on a long journey (especially cross-country) conditions would soon be most unpleasant.

Below: A BTR-60PB Forward Air Control Vehicle. There are special antennas on the roof, with additional generator to power the extra communications equipment. Infra-red headlights are on the glacis plate.

BTR-40/BRDM-1 and -2

BTR-40 family, BTR-40P (BRDM) family and BTR-40PB (BRDM-2)

Combat weight: -40, 5·2 tons (5300kg); -40P, 5·5 tons (5600kg); -40PB, 6·89 tons (7000kg).
Length: -40, 16ft 8in (5000mm); -40P, 18ft 8in (5700mm): -40PB, 18ft (5750mm)
Width: -40, 6ft 3in (1900mm); -40P, 7ft 6in (2285mm): -40PB, 7ft 8½in (2350mm).
Height: -40, 5ft 8½in (1750mm); -40P, 6ft 3in (1900mm); -40PB, 7ft 7in (2310mm).
Engine: -40, GAZ-40, six-in-line water-cooled gasoline, 80hp; -40P, GAZ-40P, 90hp; -40PB, GAZ-41, vee-eight, 140hp.
Armament: Most, 7·62mm SGMB, 1,250 rounds; PB has 14·5mm KPVT turret, 500 rounds.
Speed: -40, 50mph (80km/h); -40P, land 50mph (80km/h), water 6mph (9km/h); -40PB, land 62mph (100km/h), water 6¼mph (10km/h).
Range: -40, 404 miles (650km); -40P, 310 miles (500km); -40PB, 465 miles (750km/h).
Armour: All 10mm.

The wartime GAZ-63A 4×4 truck was developed into the BTR-40 scout car which went into production in 1951. Large numbers of many versions are still serving, but from 1959 many were replaced by the amphibious BTR-40P (BRDM), which has central tire-pressure control and two pairs of retractable mid-wheels for rough ground and trench-crossing. Again there are many versions, some carrying either 'Snapper', 'Swatter' or 'Sagger' ATGW (anti-tank guided weapons). All have hydrojet water propulsion. In 1966 appeared BTR-40PB, also called BTR-40P-2 and BRDM-2, which has a modified hull, more power, gun turret (same as on the BTR-60PB) and advanced overland navigation system. Unlike similar designs of other Warsaw Pact forces it has a single waterjet (not twin). Two important versions respectively mount six AT-3 'Sagger' ATGWs and quad or octuple launchers for the SA-7 surface-to-air missile.

Above right: The side view shows the basic BRDM-2 reconnaissance vehicle, which is sometimes known as BTR-40PB or -40P2.

Right: A closed-down BRDM-2 patrols a heavily rutted track in western Russia. The turret is identical to that fitted to the BTR-60PB APC, mounting a 14.5mm MG.

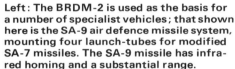

Left: The BRDM-2 is used as the basis for a number of specialist vehicles; that shown here is the SA-9 air defence missile system, mounting four launch-tubes for modified SA-7 missiles. The SA-9 missile has infra-red homing and a substantial range.

Below: This version of the earlier BRDM-1 is a specialised radiological and chemical reconnaissance vehicle. Its equipment includes an automatic flag dispenser above the rear nearside wheel.

152mm M-1973

Self-propelled gun
Weight: 24·6 tons (25,000kg).
Length: 25·52ft (7·78m).
Width: 10·49ft (3·2m).
Height: 8·92ft (2·72m).
Engine: Water-cooled diesel, 500hp.
Speed: 31mph (50km/h).
Armament: 152mm.
Elevation −3° to +65°.
Traverse: 360°.
Projectile mass: (HE) 96·0lb (43·6kg).
Muzzle velocity: (HE) 2,149ft/sec (655m/sec).
Maximum range: 18,920 yards (17,300m).

The Soviet Union continued to use exclusively wheeled artillery for many years after Western armies had begun the process of converting to self-propelled (SP) weapons. This was somewhat surprising in view of their emphasis on rapid and flowing advance for which the SP gun is, of course, ideal. Nor can the innate conservatism of Soviet artillerymen be blamed, since they have been so innovative in other fields. However, whatever the reason, they are now making up for lost time and have produced two sturdy, effective and relatively uncomplicated weapons, the 152mm M-1973 and 122mm M-1974.

The first to appear was the M-1973 152mm, which comprises the 152mm D-20 elevating mass (qv) mounted in a large turret and placed on the same chassis as that used by the SA-4 Ganef (qqv). The only noticeable modification to the tube is the addition of a fume-extractor to keep the turret clear of toxic gases. Like so many Soviet AFVs the M-1973 is fully amphibious.

It is suggested in some reports that a nuclear shell has been developed for this gun, with a 0·2KT warhead. It is also reported that an SP version of the 180mm gun is also under development.

Above: The 152mm M-1973 self-propelled gun mounts the barrel of the D-20 towed gun/howitzer on a modified Ganef chassis, a typical example of the economy of effort and expense often achieved by Soviet designers. There is a battalion of 18 of these effective SPs in a tank division, but none so far in motor rifle divisions.

Below: A proud artilleryman salutes as his battalion passes the reviewing stand in Red Square. The double-baffle muzzle brake and the fume extractor of the 152mm tube are well in evidence; the gun fires HE, armour piercing and chemical shells, with a maximum range of 18,000 metres. A 203mm SP may appear shortly.

122mm M-1974

Self-propelled howitzer
Weight: 19·68 tons (20,000kg).
Length: 23·94ft (7·3m).
Width: 9·85ft (3·004m).
Height: 7·93ft (2·42m).
Engine: V-6, six-in-line, water-cooled diesel, 240hp.
Speed: 31mph (50km/h).
Armament: 122mm.
Elevation: −5° to +60° (approx).
Traverse: 360°.
Projectile mass: (HE) 48lb (21·8kg).
Muzzle velocity: (HE) 2263ft/sec (690m/sec).
Maximum range: 16,732 yards (15,300m).

The second of the new range of SPs to appear is the 122mm M-1974. This is also a straightforward combination of the 122mm D-30 elevating mass with a new turret, and mounted on a modified PT-76 chassis (there is an additional roadwheel making seven in all). The piece appears to be a modified version of the D-30 field howitzer, but, as with the 152mm SP, with the addition of a fume-extractor. The turret is very low compared with Western SPs and there is only one hatch (for the commander), suggesting that an automatic loader is fitted. Some 40 rounds are carried, a mixture of HE and anti-tank rounds (HEAT, which can penetrate up to 460mm of armour in the direct-fire mode). Like the 152mm M-1973 this is an effective weapon designed to fit into the Soviet concept of fast-moving advances.

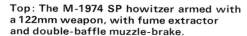

Top: The M-1974 SP howitzer armed with a 122mm weapon, with fume extractor and double-baffle muzzle-brake.

Above: A 122mm M-1974 is repaired in the field, with a maintenance crew dropping in a new YaMZ-238 V-6 diesel engine; this develops 240hp at 2100rpm.

Left: M-1974 SPs on parade. The main armament is a modified version of the 122mm D-30 towed howitzer with a range of 16,738 yards (15,300m).

Below: M-1974 SPs on exercise in winter conditions. The normal camouflage scheme has been modified with white paint.

ARTILLERY AND ANTI-TANK WEAPONS

'Without effective suppression of the defender's anti-tank weapons, no high speed advance can hope to succeed.' Thus state the most authoritative Soviet tacticians, and it is to the artillery that the main task of suppression falls. For the suppression of lines of fortification in the path of the advancing troops, Soviet gunners prefer a complex rolling barrage. When the defence is organised on a belt of strong points, each strong point will be engaged by concentrations of fire. The phases of bombardment during what could be considered typical Soviet attack are:
1. Preparatory, before the attack starts.
2. Supportive, during the attack.
3. Accompanying—guns actually accompany the attacking troops into the depths of the defence to give close and immediate fire support.

Nowadays, helicopter gunships (Hind, Hip) are employed with exactly the same role in support of the attack, but from the air.

Counter battery bombardment, and bombardment of key targets deep within the enemy position are the other very important tasks of artillery. In the Soviet concept of artillery are included not only field guns and howitzers, but also mortars, missiles and multiple rocket launchers such as BM21.

It is not surprising that a military doctrine which allots such importance to the tank should seek to provide for sufficient means to destroy enemy tanks. In Soviet eyes, the very best anti-tank weapon is another tank. Failing that, the ATGM is their preferred weapon as it combines long range, accuracy, destructive power and mobility. In all these features, it is considered superior to conventional guns. The latest Soviet ATGM systems (AT-4, 5 and 6) are all semi-active homing or semi-auto guided, making operator control much simpler. Man-portable versions (AT-3 and AT-4) are used by motor rifle and airborne subunits, all other versions are on armoured vehicles and deployed in subunit or unit strengths.

Field guns, such as the D-30, have an effective anti-tank capability up to 1000m, and an anti-tank gun, the T-12, is still in service with a similar range. The advantages of a gun are rate of fire and the fact that once the weapon is fired, no amount of counter measures will deflect it if it has been well aimed.

For close range protection the Soviet soldier has the SPG-9 recoilless gun and the RPG-7 grenade launcher. The latter is held in particularly large numbers and is very effective when used en masse. An improved weapon is under development.

180mm S-23

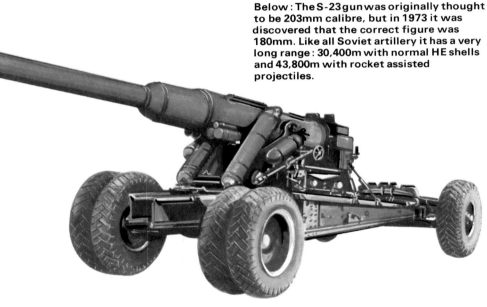

Below: The S-23 gun was originally thought to be 203mm calibre, but in 1973 it was discovered that the correct figure was 180mm. Like all Soviet artillery it has a very long range: 30,400m with normal HE shells and 43,800m with rocket assisted projectiles.

Field gun
Weight: Firing; 20.07 tons (21,450kg).
Length: Travelling, 34ft 5in (10,485mm).
Width: Travelling, 9ft 10in (2996mm).
Elevation: −2° to +50°.
Traverse: ±22°.
Projectile mass: (HE) 194lb (88kg).
Muzzle velocity: (HE) 2,600ft/sec (790m/sec).
Maximum range: 29,250m.

The S-23 gun is currently the largest piece of ordnance in the Soviet inventory. For several years it was thought to be 203mm calibre, but some examples were captured by the Israeli Army in 1973 and it was learnt that a mistake had been made and that they are actually 180mm. They are easily recognisable by their large size, the method of mobility with the barrel hauled back out of battery, and the pepper-pot muzzle-brake. The S-23 is towed by the large tracked artillery tractor designated AT-T.

As is usual with Soviet artillery it has a very good range (30,400m), but this can be stretched even further by the use of a rocket assisted shell which has a maximum range of 43,800m.

The S-23 is normally held in Frontal regiments, but, in line with normal Soviet practice, will then be allotted to one of the first echelon divisions.

There are three known projectiles. The HE shell weighs 88kg (194lb) and there is thought to be a nuclear round with a 1KT yield. There is a concrete 'blockbuster' round, and it would seem logical, from

known Soviet practice, that there should be a chemical shell as well. However, unlike virtually all other Soviet artillery there is not an anti-tank round for this gun. Rate of fire is approximately one round per minute.

As recorded elsewhere on these pages there has been a definite move in the Soviet Army in the past few years towards self-propelled artillery. Divisional artillery

regiments are now virtually completely re-equipped with the M-1973 155mm SP and the M-1974 122mm SP. There have been rumours in the Western Press that the Soviet Army has started development of a 203mm SP, but it would seem more in line with previous practice if they were to take the quick and cheap method and mount the S-23 on an SP chassis.

152mm D-20

Field gun
Weight: Firing 5.56 tons (565kg).
Length: Travelling, 26ft 8½in (869mm).
Width: Travelling 7ft 8½in (2350mm).
Elevation: −5° to +45°.
Traverse: ±45°.
Projectile mass: (HE) 96.0lb (43.6kg).
Muzzle velocity: (HE) 2,149ft/sec (655m/sec).
Maximum range: 18km.

Standard heavy artillery, the D-20 is a powerful 6-inch weapon which replaced the M-1937 (ML-20) of the same calibre used during World War II. The massive barrel has a large double-baffle muzzle brake and semi-automatic sliding-wedge breech giving a rate of fire up to 4 rds/min despite the use of separate-loading variable-charge case-type ammunition. The D-20 is used by the Soviet Union, Hungary and East Germany.

Below: The 152mm D-20 gun-howitzer. This was introduced in 1955 to replace the 152mm M-1943 (D-1), and is normally to be found in the artillery regiments at Front and Army level (usually 18 guns per regiment).

130mm M-46

Field gun
Weight: Firing 7·57 tons (7,700kg).
Length: (Travelling) 38·47ft (11·73m).
Width: (Travelling) 8·04ft (2·45m).
Elevation: −2·5° to +45°.
Traverse: 50°.
Projectile mass: (HE) 73·6lb (33·4kg).
Muzzle velocity: (HE) 3050ft/sec (930m/sec).
Maximum range: 29,700 yards (27,150m).

There is no doubt that the Soviet artillery designers lead the world in producing simple, effective and reliable guns, and with greater range for a given calibre than any other nation can achieve. Typical of the many excellent wheeled artillery pieces is the 130mm M-46, which first appeared publicly in 1954, and which is still one of the most powerful of its type in the world.

As with all other Soviet indirect-fire weapons the M-46 is also supplied with an anti-tank round (actually APHE) which will penetrate 230mm of armour at 1,000m range. The HE round has a range of 27,150m, which is only bettered in the West by the American 175mm M-107 and the new 155mm M-198 with a rocket-assisted shell.

Also, like many other Soviet guns, this equipment is in service around the world in at least seventeen countries.

Right: 130mm M-46 field guns on parade. This gun fires a 33.4kg HE shell to a maximum range of 27·15km, a very good performance when compared with Western artillery. (The US M109 155mm, for example, fires a 43g shell to a range of only 14.6km). This weapon is in service with many countries in the Soviet bloc and has been exported to Egypt, Finland, India, Iraq, Iran, Nigeria and Yugoslavia. It is also built in China as the Type 59. The tracked tractor carries the crew of nine.

122mm D-30

Field howitzer.
Weight: Firing 3·1 tons (3150kg).
Length: Travelling 17ft 8½in (5400mm).
Width: Travelling 6ft 5in (1950mm).
Elevation −7° to +70°.
Traverse: 360°.
Projectile mass: (HE) 48·1lb (21·8kg).
Muzzle velocity: (HE) 2,264ft/sec (690m/sec).
Maximum range: (HE) 15,300m.

This howitzer, of 121·9mm (4·8in) calibre, typifies the dramatically advanced and effective design of the latest Soviet artillery. It is towed by a large lunette lug under or just behind the muzzle brake, with its trails folded under the barrel. To fire, the crew of seven rapidly unhitch; lower the central firing jack (lifting the wheels off the ground) and swing the outer trails through 120° on each side. The gun can then be aimed immediately to any point of the compass. The barrel is carried under a prominent recoil system, has a semi-auto vertically sliding wedge breechblock, and fires cased but variable-charge, separate-loading ammunition. The D-30 is the basic field gun of the Soviet Army, and is used throughout the Warsaw Pact. In addition to conventional or chemical shells, it fires a fin-stabilised non-rotating HEAT shell from its rifled barrel, giving it a formidable direct fire capability against armour.

100mm M-1955 and T-12

Anti-tank and field guns (data for M-1955).
Weight: Firing 2.95 tons (3000kg).
Length: Travelling, 28ft 7in (8717mm).
Width: Travelling, 5ft 2½in (185mm).
Elevation: −10° to +20°.
Traverse: ±14°.
Projectile mass: (APHE) 35lb (15.9kg).
Muzzle velocity: (APHE) 3,280ft/sec (1000m/sec).
Maximum range: (HE) 15,400m.

One of the most widely used guns of the Warsaw Pact ground forces, these long-barreled (56 calibres) weapons have high muzzle velocity and can fire HE, APHE or HEAT ammunition. Fixed ammunition is used, which with the semi-automatic, vertical-sliding wedge breechblock gives a practical rate of fire of 7 to 8 rds/min. The M-1955 is lighter than the old M-1944 (D-10) and runs on single tyres. It has box-section split trails, twin recoil cyclinders behind the shield, and a prominent 'pepperpot' muzzle brake. The later T-12, which has replaced the M-1955 in many Soviet and E. German units since 1968, is a smooth bore weapon firing fin-stabilised ammunition of much improved effectiveness. The most obvious difference is that the muzzle brake does not taper and is only fractionally larger in diameter than the barrel. Usual towing vehicle is the Zil-131, Zil-157 or AT-P tracked tug, all of which carry the crew of seven and other personnel.

Above right: 100mm T-12 anti-tank gun. The USSR is virtually the only country still developing anti-tank guns of the traditional type. The T-12 is to be found in the Anti-Tank Battalion of Motor Rifle Divisions, with usually 18 per battalion.

Right: M-1955 100mm field guns. This gun was the predecessor of the T-12 and its primary task is as an anti-tank weapon, although an HE shell is available.

Below left: The 122mm D-30 entered service in 1963 and is an excellent weapon. It is towed by the muzzle, but when deployed the wheels are lifted off the ground and it stands on its three trail legs. The breech, seen clearly in this picture, is of the vertical, sliding wedge type and is semi-automatic in operation.

Below: An official Soviet picture of the D-30 in action with the towing attachment and multi-baffle muzzle-brake clearly shown. Maximum range with HE is 15.3km, and like all Soviet field guns the D-30 also fires anti-tank shells.

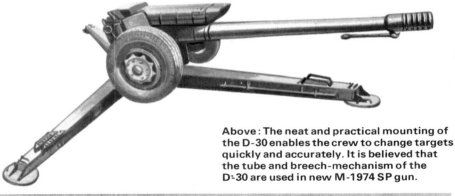

Above: The neat and practical mounting of the D-30 enables the crew to change targets quickly and accurately. It is believed that the tube and breech-mechanism of the D-30 are used in new M-1974 SP gun.

85mm D-44 and SD-44

Anti-tank and field guns.
Weight firing: (D-44) 3,804lb (1725kg); (SD-44) 4,961lb (2250kg).
Length travelling: (D-44) 27ft 4in (8340mm); (SD-44) 27ft 0in (8220mm).
Width travelling: (Both) 5ft 10in (1780mm).
Elevation: (Both) −7.° to +35°.
Traverse: ±27°
Projectile mass: (HE) 21·0lb (9·5kg); (HVAP) 11·0lb (5kg).
Muzzle velocity: (HE) 2,598ft/sec (792m/sec); (HVAP) 3,379ft/sec (1030m/sec).
Maximum range: (HE) 15,650m.

Variously designated D-44, D-48 or M-1945, the 85mm divisional gun is one of the most widely used in the Soviet ground forces. The gun is the same as in the T-34/85 tank and M-1944 AA weapons, and is also used in the SU-85 and ASU-85 assault vehicles. It fires various kinds of fixed ammunition at 15 to 20 rds/min, with the usual semi-automatic vertical-sliding wedge-type breech. The muzzle brake is a double baffle. To enable this gun to drive itself about the battlefield it can be fitted with an auxiliary engine, becoming the SD-44. The M-72 two-cylinder 14 hp engine is mounted on the hollow left trail, in which is its fuel; the right trail carries ready-ammunition. The SD-44 is completed by the driver's seat and steering on a large trail wheel.

Right: The D-44 gun uses the same barrel as the T-34 tank and is now only to be found in the anti-tank battery of parachute regiments. Shown here is the SD-44 with a 14hp engine on the left trail.

RPG-7V

Anti-tank rocket launcher
Weight firing: (Excluding projectile) 15.42lb (7kg).
Length: (Without projectile) 38½in (990mm).
Calibre of tube: 40mm.
Calibre of projectile: 85mm.
Mass of projectile: 4.95lb (2.25kg).
Muzzle velocity: 984ft/sec (300m/sec).
Effective range: (Moving target) 300m.

Standard anti-armour weapon of Soviet infantry, the RPG-7V replaced an earlier weapon derived from the World War 2 German Panzerfaust which merely fired the hollow-charge projectile from a shoulder-rested tube. RPG-7V fires a new projectile which, a few metres beyond the muzzle, ignites an internal rocket to give shorter flight-time, flatter trajectory and better accuracy. The HEAT or HE warhead has improved fuzing, the HEAT round penetrating to 320mm (12·6in) of armour. The optical sight is frequently supplemented by the NSP-2 (IR) night sight. There is also a special folding version used by airborne troops; designated RPG-7D.

Above: The RPG-7V is a small, light anti-tank weapon with a big 'punch'. The PG-7 grenade is percussion fired, the rocket motor igniting after 10 metres.

Below: A Soviet infantryman in a somewhat precarious firing position in open country takes aim with his RPG-7V.

122mm BM-21

Rocket launcher (40 rounds).
Weight: One rocket, 101lb (45·9kg); launcher, 7,718lb (3500kg); vehicle, launcher and 40 rounds, 11·3 tons (11,500kg).
Length: Rocket 8·99ft (2740mm); vehicle, 24ft 1in (7350mm).
Calibre: 4·8in (122mm).
Engine: (Vehicle) ZIL-375 vee-8 gasoline, 175hp.
Speed: (Vehicle) 47mph (75km/h).
Launcher: Elevation 0° to +50°.
Traverse: ±120°.
Time to reload: 10min.
Maximum range: (Rocket) over 15,000m.

An important multi-rocket system which first appeared in November 1964, the BM-21 uses a smaller-calibre rocket than any other of its era, and can thus fire a greater quantity (40). It is the first rocket system carried by the outstanding Ural-375 truck, which among other attributes has exceptional cross-country capability. The rockets are fired in salvo, or 'rippled' in sequence or selected individually, always with the vehicle parked obliquely to the target to avoid blast damage to the unprotected cab. The BM-21 is used by the Soviet ground forces and by those of several other Warsaw Pact nations except Czechoslovakia (which uses its rather similar M-51). The BM-21 is ideal for delivering non-persistent chemical agents. Czechoslovakia produced a much improved version (called RM-70, also used by E. Germany) which carries a palletised reload, effectively doubling its rate of fire.

Above: The BM-21 multiple rocket launcher comprises a 40-tube pallet mounted on a rotating platform, carried by a Ural-375 6x6 truck. There are 18 BM-21s in each tank and motor rifle division.

Above: The crew of a BM-21 receiving orders. The vehicle is parked obliquely to prevent damage to the unprotected cab.

Left: BM-21s firing. The rockets can be fired individually, in 'ripple', or in salvo; their effect is devastating.

Below: A battery of BM-21s in the archetypical Soviet artillery deployment, lined up in a row in the open. BM-21 is the most widely used rocket launcher.

240mm BM-24

Rocket launcher (12 rounds).
Weight: one rocket, 248lb (112·5kg); launcher, 5,995lb (2720kg); loaded launcher on ZIL-157, 9·35 tons (9500kg); loaded launcher on AT-S tractor, 15 tons (15,240kg).
Length: Rocket, 46½in (1180mm); ZIL truck, 22ft 4in (6800mm); AT-S tractor, 19ft 2½in (5870mm).
Calibre: 9·5in (240mm).
Elevation: 0° to ±45°.
Traverse: ±105°.
Time to reload: 3—4min.
Maximum range: 11,000m.

The Soviet 240mm rocket is a spin-stabilized weapon of relatively short and fat shape, packing a tremendous punch but having short range for its calibre. One of its standard carriers is the ZIL-157 truck, on which is mounted an open-frame launcher of welded steel tube, with two rows of six rounds. Another is the AT-S tracked vehicle, found chiefly in armoured units, on which is mounted a different 12-round launcher of the tube type. The truck-mounted frame launcher is used by many countries, but the AT-S installation is believed to be used only by the USSR (designated BM-24T).

Above: Soviet BM-24 rocket launchers captured from the Arabs are paraded in Israel after the 1973 war. The 240mm rockets have a maximum range of 11,000m.

MORTARS

Mortars are a very effective way of bringing heavy fire to bear rapidly and accurately, and their light weight and simplicity of operation make them ideal for use by the infantry. The Soviet Army has always been very enthusiastic about mortars, using them in vast numbers. They have also developed some very large calibre mortars, including 160mm and 240mm, whereas the largest normally encountered in Western armies is 120mm. These very large Soviet mortars have such long barrels that the traditional method of loading by dropping the bomb down the tube cannot be used, and the mortar must be 'broken' like a shotgun and the bomb inserted in the base of the barrel. One of the main characteristics of mortars is their mobility, resulting from their light weight, simple construction and the ease with which they can be broken down into one-man loads. The Soviet mortars are either man-portable, or are towed by vehicles. Interestingly, there does not appear to have been any attempt to mount mortars in APCs as is done by the United States in the M113 and the British in the FV 432.

The lethal area of a mortar bomb is virtually circular due to its nearly vertical angle of descent. This makes it very effective against troops in the open, while the addition of a VT fuze to achieve an air burst makes it almost as effective against dug-in troops. Current

140mm RPU-14

Rocket launcher.
Weight: One rocket, 87·3lb (39·6kg); launcher (loaded) 2,646lb (1200kg).
Length· Rocket, 43in (1092mm); launcher (tubes horizontal) 13·2ft (4·0m).
Calibre: 5·5in (140mm).
Elevation: 0° to ±45°.
Traverse: ±15°.
Time to reload: 4min.
Maximum range: 10,600m.

The 16-tube RPU-14 140mm rocket launcher is used only by the Soviet Airborne troops, with 18 held in the Artillery Battalion of the Airborne Division. First seen in 1967 the lightweight launcher uses the same chassis as the M-1943 57mm anti-tank gun.

Right: The RPU-14 multiple rocket launcher was developed specially to give parachute divisions some heavy and mobile firepower. There are 16 tubes firing 39.6kg rockets to a maximum range of about 10km.

Above: The 240mm mortar, M-240, is one of the largest ever produced and was first seen in November 1953. It is thought to be still in service; details are unknown.

Left: A 120mm M-1943 mortar is brought into action by its crew. It has a maximum range of 5,700 metres.

Below left: An officer checks the sight setting on a M-1943 120mm mortar. Mortar fire is used to suppress enemy defensive positions to cover an attack.

Below left: Mortars are particularly useful for mountain troops, and the M-107 was developed specially for animal transport.

Below: An M-160 160mm mortar emits a large amount of 'flash' during a night-firing exercise. Two-three rounds can be fired per minute to a maximum range of 8km.

mortars are not, however, of any use against mobile targets such as APCs, or armoured vehicles. It is possible that some form of terminal guidance may be developed which, combined with an armour-piercing warhead, could give the mortar an anti-tank capability. There has been no evidence so far of any such developments by the Soviet Army, however.

The principal models currently in service with the Soviet Army are:

M-1937 (42/43) 82mm, which is now-found mainly in parachute and mountain battalions.

M-1943 120mm, a very efficient model, mounted on wheels, and firing a 15.4kg bomb to a maximum range of 5,700 metres. There is a company of six in all motor rifle and parachute battalions.

M-160 160mm, a breech-loading weapon which fires a 41.5kg bomb. It was widely used in motor rifle divisions, but, as far as is known, is now confined to mountain units.

M-240 240mm, a massive weapon, firing a 100kg bomb. Scale of issue is not known.

The USSR has exported its mortars to many armies all over the world, and the lighter models have been found in use with many revolutionary armies.

AIR DEFENCE WEAPONS

Command of the air space over their own forces is considered by the Soviets as an essential prerequisite for a successful offensive. The Soviet army has what is perhaps the most comprehensive range of air defence weapons of any army in the world. Close in air defence of troops is provided by fire from small calibre weapons —the 12.7mm and 14.5mm machine guns in AFVs, the ZU-23AA multiple machine gun, and also from the SA-7 missile, which is held at company level.

Unit protection is provided by a mix of SA-9 and ZSU-23-4 mobile systems, and at formation level a mix of SA-6 and SA-8 provide both low and medium level cover.

S-60

Towed anti-aircraft gun
Weight: 4·42 tons (4,500kg).
Length: (Travel) 27·88ft (8·5m).
Width: (Travel) 6·74ft (2·054m).
Elevation: −4° to +85°.
Traverse: 360°
Projectile mass: (HE) 6·17lb (2·8kg).
Muzzle velocity: (HE) 3280ft/sec (1,000m/sec).
Maximum range: (Horizontal) 13,123 yards (12,000m).
Effective range: (Vertical) 13,120ft (4,000m).
Rate of fire: (Effective) 70rpm.

This is still the most widely used anti-aircraft (AA) weapon in use in the field armies, with a scale of 24 per division, although it is being replaced by either SA-6 Gainful or SA-8 Gecko. The towed gun is radar-controlled and can be used in either an anti-aircraft or anti-tank role.

The towed version of this gun is used by some 30 armies. A self-propelled version, mounting two guns in a large square turret, has been developed.

Right: A 57mm S-60 AA gun deployed for action. This towed gun is widely used at the moment, but is being rapidly replaced by self-propelled guns and by missiles. Typical holdings have included 24 in tank and motor rifle divisions and 18 in parachute divisions. Practical rate of fire is some 70 rounds per minute and effective ceiling is 4,000 metres. A self-propelled version, designated ZSU-57-2, has two 57mm guns mounted in a large open-topped turret on a tracked chassis.

ZU-23

Towed twin 23mm automatic AA gun
Combat weight: 950kg.
Length: 15ft (4.57m).
Width: 6ft (1.83m).
Height: 6ft 11 ¾in (1.87m).
Ammunition: HEI, API.
Muzzle velocity: 3182ft/s (970m/s).
Rate of fire: 800—1000 cyclic per barrel, 200 rounds per minute per barrel practical.
Effective range: AA-2, 16,400ft (5000m); anti-tank, 22,995ft (7000m).

The twin 23mm ZU-23 is in service throughout the Warsaw Pact. It is a fully automatic weapon with a high rate of fire, but lacks any provision for radar control, and can, therefore, only be used in clear weather conditions.

Ammunition is fed from two large, box-type magazines located outboard of the trunnions, each of which contains 50 rounds of ammunition in a belt. Maximum anti-aircraft range is 16,400ft (5000m), but the effective ceiling is 8,200ft (2500m).

These weapons are normally deployed in six-gun batteries, with one battery per motor-rifle and parachute regiment.

Four of these cannon, modified for water-cooling, are used in the ZSU-23-4 (see next page), and a single-barrel towed version also exists, although it is not often seen. Like most Soviet weapons the ZU-23 has an anti-tank capability, firing an armour-piercing shell.

Right: A ZU-23 twin anti-aircraft cannon surrounded by soldiers from various Warsaw Pact armies. Although still widely used at the moment this weapon is being super-seded in the Soviet Army by self-propelled AA guns and missiles. Many have been exported to countries in the Warsaw Pact and to Third World nations.

ZSU-23-4

Quad self-propelled AA gun system
Combat weight: 13·78 tons (14,000kg).
Length: 20ft 8in (6300mm).
Width: 9ft 8in (2950mm).
Height: (Radar stowed) 7ft 4½in (2250mm).
Engine: V-6 six-in-line water-cooled diesel, 240hp.
Armament: Quadruple ZU-23 23mm anti-aircraft, 1,000 rounds.
Speed: 27mph (44km/h).
Range: 162 miles (260km).
Armour: 10mm.

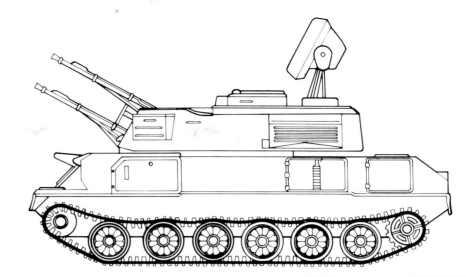

Extremely dangerous to aircraft out to a slant range of 6,600ft (2000m), the ZSU-23-4 is a neat package of firepower with its own microwave target-acquisition and fire-control radar and crew of four in an NBC-sealed chassis derived from the amphibious PT-76. Each gun has a cyclic firing rate of 800 to 1,000rds/min, and with liquid-cooled barrels can actually sustain this rate. The crew of four comprise commander, driver, radar observer and gunner, and there is plenty of room in the large but thin-skinned turret. Gun travel is unrestricted in traverse, and from −7° to +80°. First seen in 1955, this vehicle is used throughout Warsaw Pact armies where it is popularly named Shilka. ZSU-23-4 was tested under battle conditions in the 1973 Arab-Israeli War where it proved to be one of the most effective low-level air defence systems. However, its radar suffers from 'clatter' when trying to deal with targets below 200ft (60m).

Above right: The ZSU-23-4 is a typical Soviet weapon, marrying a quadruple 23mm cannon mount derived from the ZU-23 to a Gainful chassis, with a valve-technology fire control and target acquisition system. These simple steps have produced a cheap and very effective weapon.

Right: The ZSU-23-4 is issued on a scale of four per motor rifle and tank regiment, giving 16 per division. They are used to protect columns on the line of march, and would normally be expected to operate in pairs. The practical rate of fire is about 200 rounds per minute per barrel, fired in 50 round (per barrel) bursts.

12.7mm DShK-38

Heavy machine gun.
Weight: (Basic gun) 75lb (34kg).
Length overall: 62½in (1588mm).
Ammunition: All standard Soviet 12·7mm, in 50-round metal-link belt (in most installations fed from box).
Muzzle velocity: (API) 2,822ft/sec (860m/sec).
Effective range: (Horizontal) 1500m; (slant) 1000m.
Rate of fire: (Cyclic) 550–600rds/min.

This old gas-operated weapon is still used in great numbers in many applications. The basic Degtyarev-Shpagin model is the M-1938/46, of post-war vintage, but the basic design is earlier. Most DShK guns in land forces are carried on a two-wheel chassis, which increases total weight to 368lb (167kg), whose trail legs can be extended to form a tall tripod for AA use. Other examples are found on many Soviet armoured vehicles, including several types of tank and APC, primarily as an AA weapon with day and night optical sighting.

Right: Perhaps the most widespread use of the 12.7mm DShK-38 machine-gun is as the air defence weapon on armoured fighting vehicles. It is used on all Soviet tanks from the T-54 up to and including T-72. Designed by the famous Degtyarev with a Shpagin feed mechanism the original version was designated DShK-38. After the war the complicated feed was replaced by a much simpler Degtyarev system and this modified gun is designated DShK-38/46. This is still effective, firing 575 rounds per minute and with an effective range of some 2,000 metres. On T-54/T-55 the commander must fire the AAMG as shown in this picture but T-72 has remote control.

SMALL ARMS AND PERSONAL EQUIPMENT

The Soviet Army has an excellent range of small arms, and a good scale of personal equipment. Although a high degree of standardization exists, there are, of course, different scales of issue for different branches of the armed forces. For example, the Airborne Forces have their own range of combat tools, portable saws, bivouacs, etc. The AFV crews carry the folding stock versions of the AKM and AK-74 weapons. A sound moderator is available for the AKMs. Clothing scales differ depending on the unit's location and the time of year. Winter clothing is, as should be expected, of a very high standard.

7.62mm PK

General-purpose machine gun.
Weight of basic gun: (Bipod) 19·8lb (9·0kg); (tripod) 36·3lb (16·5kg).
Weight of ammunition box: With 100-round belt, 8·58lb (3·9kg); 200-rd belt, 17·6lb (8·0kg); 250-rd belt, 20·6lb (9·4kg).
Length: (Gun) 45·7in (1173mm); (on tripod) 49·5in (1270mm).
Ammunition: Soviet 7·62 rimmed Type 54R, propellant charge 3·11g.
Muzzle velocity: 2,755ft/sec (840m/sec).
Effective range: 1000m.
Rate of fire: (Cyclic) 650 rds/min.

Above: The basic PK machine-gun with a heavy fluted barrel, weighing some 9kg.

Though a hotch-potch of other weapons (mostly the Kalashnikov AK-47), the PK family is an excellent series of weapons which can be described as the first Soviet GPMGs (general-purpose MGs). Unlike almost all other Soviet rifle-calibre weapons except the sniper's rifle it fires the long rimmed cartridge with over twice the propellant charge of the standard kind. It is a fully automatic gas-operated gun with Kalashnikov rotating bolt, Goryunov cartridge extractor and barrel-change, and Degtyarev feed system and trigger. The PKS is the PK on a light tripod for sustained or AA firing. The PKT is a solenoid-operated version without sights, stock or trigger mechanism for use in armoured vehicles. The PKM is the latest service version with unfluted barrel and hinged butt rest, weighing only 8·39kg (18½lb); in a tripod it becomes the PKMS. The PKB has stock and trigger replaced by a butterfly trigger for pintle mounting on armoured vehicles (but the standard PK and PKM can be fired from the ports of, say, a BMP).

Right: A Polish soldier with a PK machine-gun, but with a slightly different flash-hider from that shown above.

7.62mm RPK

Light machine gun.
Weight: With box magazine (loaded) 12·4lb (5·6kg), (unloaded) 11·1lb (5·0kg); with drum magazine (loaded) 15·0lb (6·8kg), (unloaded) 12·4lb (5·6kg).
Length overall: 41in (1040mm).
Ammunition: Standard M43 (M-1943).
Muzzle velocity: 2,411ft/sec (735m/sec).
Effective range: 800m.
Rate of fire: (Cyclic) 600rds/min.

Standard Soviet LMG, the Kalashnikov RPK is essentially an AK-47 assault rifle with a longer and heavier barrel, bipod, different stock and two larger-capacity magazines, a 40-round curved box and 75-round drum. At any time regular AK or AKM magazines can be clipped on instead. Compared with the Degtyarev RPD of the immediate post-war era the RPK is much lighter and handier, cheaper and more versatile. Like the AK series it is gas-operated, with rotating bolt, and having selection for full or semi-automatic fire. It is often seen fitted with the NSP-2 (IR) night sight.

Above right: The current Soviet light machinegun is the RPK, designed by Kalashnikov. There is no provision for changing the barrel which limits its sustained fire capability to about 80 rounds per minute. The magazine takes 40 rounds.

Right: A reconnaissance detachment on an M-72 motor-cycle combination. The soldier in the sidecar is armed with an RPK light machine-gun, fitted with the 40-round long magazine. There is also a 75-round drum magazine which is apparently used only in the early stages of battle.

7.62mm AK and AKM

Above: Designed by Kalashnikov, the AK series is the most successful post-War rifle, serving throughout the world.

Assault rifles.
Weight: AK (loaded magazine) 10·58lb (4·8kg), (empty magazine) 9·47lb (4·3kg); AKM (loaded magazine) 8·0lb (3·64kg) (early version 8·4lb, 3·8kg), (empty magazine) 6·93lb (3·14kg) (early version 7·3lb, 3·31kg).
Length overall (no bayonet): AK-47 (either butt), 34·25in (870mm); AKM, 34·5in (876mm).
Ammunition: Standard M43 (M-1943).
Muzzle velocity: 2,345ft/sec (715m/sec).
Effective range: (semi-auto) 400m; (auto) 300m.
Rate of fire: Cyclic, 600rds/min; auto, 90rds/min; semi-auto, 40rds/min.

Produced in greater quantity than any other modern small arms, the Kalashnikov AK and AKM can fairly be claimed to have set a new standard in infantry weapons. The original AK-47 came with a wooden stock or (for AFV crews, paratroopers and motorcyclists) a folding metal stock. It owed much to German assault rifles, and like them uses a short cartridge firing a stubby bullet. A gas-operated weapon with rotating bolt (often chrome-plated), it can readily be used by troops all over the world of any standard of education, and gives extremely reliable results under the most adverse conditions. Versions with different designations have been licence-produced in at least five countries, and it is used in about 35. The standard Soviet military weapon today is the AKM, an amazingly light development making extensive use of plastics and stampings, and with a cyclic-rate reducer, compensator and other improvements. Either rifle can have luminous sights or the NSP-2 IR sight. Another fitment is a new bayonet which doubles as a saw and as an insulated wire-cutter.

Below: Soviet soldiers firing their AKM rifles during an assault. Kalashnikov's brilliant design is short, light, easy to handle, reliable and accurate – just the qualities the infantry require.

5.45mm AKS-74

The success of the United States Armalite AR-15 (M-16) rifle firing the 5.56mm round in the 1960s led most armies to review their rifle designs. In the West some very curious weapons have appeared together with sound designs such as the British 4.85mm Individual Weapon, and there is intense competition to win the order for the next NATO standard rifle. The USSR appeared, however, to be satisfied with the AK series which gave excellent service both in the Warsaw Pact armies and with many revolutionary forces.

In the mid-1970s there was considerable curiosity in the West as to whether Soviet small arms designers would follow the tendency towards a smaller calibre, but for a long time there was no evidence of any activity. Then, suddenly in the usual Russian way, Soviet parachute troops appeared on a Moscow parade carrying a totally new weapon which had passed through design, tests, troop trials and into production without a word leaking to the West. No official data has yet been published, so the following must be regarded as provisional.

The rifle is designated AKS-74 and is of 5.45mm calibre, ie, slightly smaller than the US round. The external appearance of the rifle suggests that it is a Kalashnikov design, possibly based upon the well-proven AKM. The cylinder at the end of the barrel could be a flash eliminator, but is more likely to be a muzzle-brake, which would indicate a very high velocity bullet. The plastic magazine and hollow butt indicate major efforts to save weight, which are confirmed by the ease with which it is carried.

Right: The new 5.45mm AKS-74 assault rifle was first revealed to the West in this parade in Moscow. The rifle is shorter and lighter than the AKM and there are some indications that it may fire a very high velocity bullet with a good performance.

7.62mm SVD

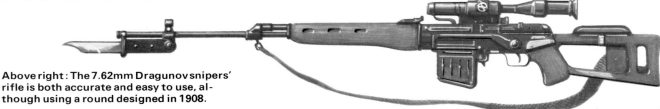

Above right: The 7.62mm Dragunov snipers' rifle is both accurate and easy to use, although using a round designed in 1908.

Sniper rifle
Weight (with PSO-1 sight): (Loaded magazine) 9·95lb (4·52kg); (empty magazine) 9·4lb (4·3kg).
Length (no bayonet): 48¼in (1225mm).
Ammunition: Long 7·62mm rimmed, Type 54R, 3·11g propellant charge.
Muzzle velocity: 2,725ft/sec (830m/sec).
Effective combat range: 800m.
Rate of fire, semi-auto: 20rds/min.

The Dragunov SVD sniper's rifle is a thoroughly modern, purpose-designed weapon, though it uses the same 54R ammunition as the old 1891/30 sniper's rifle and the RK series of GPMGs. It is reported that users are issued with selected batches of ammunition to increase accuracy. A gas-operated semi-automatic rifle, the SVD has the Kalashnikov rotating-bolt breech but a completely new trigger system, barrel and 10-round magazine. The muzzle has a flash suppressor and a recoil compensator to hold the barrel near the target. The PSO-1 sight is 370mm (14½in) long, and comprises a ×4 optical telescope with rubber eyepiece, integral rangefinder, battery-powered reticle illuminator, and IR sighting for use at night.

RKG-3M Anti-tank hand grenade

Weight: (Fuzed) 2·34lb (1070g).
Length: (Before firing) 14½in (362mm).
Diameter of head: 2·19in (55·6mm).
HE charge: 1¼lb (567g).
Fuze: Impact.
Typical range: Up to 20m.
Armour penetration: 165mm.

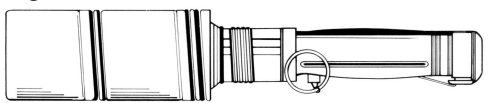

The standard hand-thrown anti-armour grenade of the Warsaw Pact forces is the RKG-3M, a stick-type weapon which is stabilised in flight by a fabric drogue. The warhead is of the High-Explosive Anti-Tank (HEAT) type, otherwise known as a 'hollow-charge'. The original RKG-3 had a steel conical liner in the warhead, but this has been replaced in the -3M by a more efficient copper liner; this change increased armour penetration from 125mm to 165mm.

The drogue is stowed in the handle but is ejected when the grenade is thrown, thus completing the arming process. The grenade should land as near to 90° to the armour plate of the target as possible to achieve maximum effect, and the drogue is designed to ensure that this happens.

This type of anti-tank grenade has been developed as a direct result of the Soviet experiences in World War II, where battles frequently became so desperate that grenade-armed tank-killing parties were essential to success. Whether such tactics would stand any chance against modern tanks, especially those fitted with 'Chobham-type' armour, is questionable. Grenades such as the RKG-3M would, however, certainly be effective against APCs and other more lightly armoured vehicles. Certainly the RKG-3M was used in the 1973 Yom Kippur war with considerable success.

Above right: The AKG-3M anti-tank grenade has a HEAT warhead and has been shown to penetrate 165mm of armour.

Right: This soldier ambushing a modern tank with an RKG-3M grenade appears to be suicidal, but such tactics were employed by the Soviet Army in World War II with some success. The range must be close for a hit.

RGD-5

Hand grenade
Weight: (Fuzed) 0·68lb (310g).
Length: 4½in (114mm).
Diameter of body: 2¼in (56mm).
HE charge: 3·85oz (110g).
Fuze: 3—4sec delay.
Effective fragmentation radius: 25m.

Probably the most widely used hand grenade of the Warsaw Pact forces, the RGD-5 comprises an HE charge in a serrated frag liner, enclosed in a body of thin sheet steel. The fuze is the same UZRG type used in earlier Soviet grenades, but the RGD-5 is much more compact and can be carried in greater quantity and thrown further.

Right: The RGD-5 hand-grenade is a neat and easily handled weapon containing 110 grammes of TNT. Normal throwing range is some 30 metres.

ENGINEERING EQUIPMENT

Soviet engineers are a most important arm, serving several essential tasks. They, too, have a comprehensive range of exceptionally well developed equipment, which falls conveniently into several categories.

River Crossing

Assault bridging is provided by the MTU tank launched bridges, by the TMM scissors bridge and by the PMP pontoon bridge. These enable Soviet forces to span virtually any type of water obstacle. In addition, the GSP and PTS ferries serve to carry individual items of hardware across a river. It must be remembered that, in addition, a very large proportion of Soviet AFVs can swim with little nor no preparation, and tanks can schnorkel when conditions are right. The airborne forces have an inflatable lightweight pontoon bridge, the PVD-20.

Obstacle Clearing

Large areas of destruction will be commonplace in nuclear war, and not uncommon in conventional conditions. The IMR combat engineer tractor is designed for rubble and tree clearance. Dozer blades can be fitted to tanks to supplement the efforts of standard dozer-tractors. Graders are available for road making. In addition there are large quantities of engineering tools held in stock—power saws and drills, plus the associated generators.

Trenching

This is not just of significance in defensive positions, but even in attack the Russians recognise the value of digging-in where possible. The BTM and MDK 2M are most effective rapid trenching machines. Excavators are available for digging-in HQs and the like, and a range of explosive tools give rapid cratering and hole digging capability.

Mine Laying and Mine Clearing

The ability to lay mines rapidly so as to thwart a counter attack, or for the protection on a likely line of enemy attack, is provided by the GMZ armoured tracked minelayer. Mines are also laid by hand-fed chute. The Soviets have not yet demonstrated remotely delivered or cassette mines.

Mine detectors are issued on a wide scale, but are of limited value in view of the trend towards plastic mines. In addition to hand-held devices, an induction coil apparatus can be attached to the front of a VAZ469 for road clearing. The Russians still place a lot of reliance on the individual sapper with a prodding stick. The primary means of mine clearance is by plough (KMT) or a combination of roller and plough, attached to tanks leading the assault. Explosive hose is used to breach known minefields, and is towed behind a ploughing tank, winched across, or fired by rocket from a tank or APC. Behind the assault forces, the lanes will be properly cleared and widened by hand-laid "Bangalore torpedoes".

Engineer Support

Engineers are responsible for other supporting tasks, for which they carry appropriate equipment. These include power supply, water supply, construction of fortified positions, etc.

RIVER CROSSING

Top: A KrAZ-214 (6x6) truck lowers a section of a TMM (heavy mechanised bridge) into position. Normally a maximum of four spans is laid, giving a 40 metre bridge.

Above: Soviet sappers assembling sections of a PMP bridge. It was this type of bridge that was used to successfully by the Egyptian Army to cross the Suez in 1973.

Above right: A GSP heavy amphibious ferry. The cabs of the two vehicles can just be seen between the two pontoons on the right. The left and right units are not interchangeable.

Right: A platoon of tanks crosses a PMP bridge, which is being held in place by BMK-150 bridging boats. Even heavier bridges can be built to take railways.

continued on next page

continued

Right: The MTU-20 armoured bridgelayer is based on the T-55 chassis. The bridge can span a gap of up to 18 metres and takes loads of up to 60 tonnes. It is launched horizontally as shown here.

Below right: The MT-55 armoured bridgelayer was developed in Czechoslovakia, but has been adopted by other countries, including the USSR. Spanning gaps of 16 metres, the bridge is launched vertically.

Left: Another example of how the USSR is preparing for a speedy advance is the GSP ferry, one unit of which is shown here entering a river. The pontoon on top of the vehicle is swung over in the water, whereupon two units link up to form one ferry. Maximum load is 52,000kg, the weight of the now obsolescent T-10 heavy tank. The hull of the GSP is filled with plastic foam which both increases bouyancy and also minimises the effects of enemy fire. Loaded speed in water is 4.8mph(7.7km/h).

OBSTACLE CLEARING

Right: The recently-introduced IMR – the Soviet Army's combat engineer tractor. It is based on the T-55 MBT chassis, but the turret has been replaced by a heavy-duty crane on a fully rotating mounting. The jib of the crane is telescopic and is fitted with a pair of grabs which are used to remove trees. The crane operator has an armoured cupola from which he can operate without exposing himself to enemy fire. This picture shows the rear of the vehicle with its unditching beam. At the front is an hydraulically operated dozer blade. In an army where speed of advance is the basis of all tactical thought, the ability of the engineers to open routes is of paramount importance and a whole range of specialised vehicles have been developed to meet the General Staff's needs. IMRs form the core of 'Route Opening Detachments' whose task is to move ahead of the main body in an advance and clear any obstructions which have been reported by reconnaissance troops. This is especially important following a nuclear strike.

TRENCHING

Below: The MDK-2 ditching machine is based on the AT-T artillery tractor. Its task is to dig weapon pits for guns and vehicles and the ditching machine is carried behind the cab in a horizontal position until it is required for work when it is lowered until vertical. The cutters operate at 90° to the direction of travel of the vehicle and can displace a maximum of 300cu. m. per hour, depending, of course, on the type of soil.

Below: The BTM digging machine has a similar cab and chassis to the MDK-2, but the digger itself operates in the same direction as the vehicle. It produces a narrow trench some 0.8 metres wide at a speed of about 1000 metres per hour (depending on the nature of the soil). A further development of this vehicle – the BTM-TMG – is designed to dig trenches in frozen ground, which it can do at a speed of about 100 metres per hour.

Below: Yet another engineering vehicle based on the AT-T chassis is the 25-tonne BAT Tractor/Dozer shown here. The dozer blade is carried swung back across the top of the crane, but when needed for use it is swung over the top of the cab and then is used as a normal blade. A variety of special-purpose attachments are available. The crane has a rotating jib which can only be used when the dozer blade is in the forward operating position

MINE CLEARING AND LAYING

Right : The Soviet Army has numerous methods of mechanical mine-clearing and this hazardous task will only be carried out manually if the tactical situation leaves no alternative. These men are operating in two-man teams; one has an IMP mine-detector and the other an old-fashioned 'prodder'. The IMP is designed to detect mines with even the tiniest metal components, eg, the fuse in a plastic mine. The IMP can also be used up to three feet under water.

Below : Air-landed troops clear the landing zone of mines. The leading soldier has a modified UMIV-1 detector with a new hexagonal head in addition to the usual small square head. Behind him lies a second man with a 'prodder'. Clearing mines in this fashion is very slow and would probably only be undertaken to clear nuisance minefields or to maintain silence. Clearing an LZ as shown here is not very realistic.

Above : A most critical aspect of offensive operations planned by the Soviet Army are river obstacles, of which there are many in Western Europe. Almost every conceivable preparation has been made to overcome this including the development of the many specialised equipments shown in these pages. Other plans include the use of divers, such as shown here, who work in pairs and who carry out reconnaissance of deep wading sites. They ensure that the underwater 'going' is reasonable and also clear any mines or other obstacles.

Left : Another aspect in which much development effort has been expended is in minelaying. One of the products is the GMZ armoured minelayer shown here. At the rear of the vehicle is a minelaying plough which is swung out to follow behind, making a furrow into which mines are led by a chute. The vehicle is a development of the Ganef surface-to-air missile launcher. Three or four GMZs are held in a divisional engineer regiment and their main task is the rapid laying of anti-tank minefields.

REAR SERVICE EQUIPMENT

Repair and Maintenance

Soviet equipment is specifically designed so as to require minimum maintenance in the field. Combat units carry little in the way of repair facilities, but at formation level there is considerable capacity for light repair. Soviet principles of operation demand that damaged equipment is collected in assembly points, and repair facilities move to these locations. Equipment is not evacuated backwards as a general rule. The repair trains, with comprehensively equipped workshop vehicles and a limited range of spares, will concentrate on mending these vehicles which are least damaged and can be returned to the battle. Badly damaged equipment will be cannibalised to this end if necessary.

Medical Services

These work on the same principles as vehicle repair, i.e., medical facilities will be moved to the areas of greatest casualties, not vice versa. Without a vast influx of civilian personnel, the Medical Services could never hope to deal with the mass casualties of nuclear war, and even conventional war will stretch their capacity. Subunits have orderlies trained in first aid, and battalions maintain dressing stations. Primary medical assistance is given at regimental level, and proper treatment at division. The principle is to give treatment at any stage of the chain when it is possible, given the nature of the wound. The aim is to return as many men to the field of battle as quickly as possible. Casualty evacuation is done by returning logistics vehicles and a few special ambulances. A large proportion of the medical staff in war time would be women.

Transport

There are not sufficient vehicles in the peace time Soviet Army to provide for its road transport needs in war. Vehicles must be mobilized from the civilian economy. However, as the same vehicles are used by farms and factories as are used by the army, there is not such a problem as might be thought. The basic army trucks are the ZIL 131 and the URAL 375 with trailers. The cross country ability of these vehicles, with their automatic tyre deflating systems, is unparalleled. There is in addition a whole range of heavier vehicles, including the massive KAMAZ, and several lighter vehicles, the UAZ-66 one-tonne and the UAZ 469 $\frac{1}{4}$-tonne "jeep". Virtually all the mid-range and large transport vehicles have NBC cab filtration. Transport priorities which are strictly maintained, are ammunition and fuel. POL constitutes over half of the Soviet's logistic load on the battlefield. Ninety per cent of all ammunition, stores and food for the battlefield is now palletted, and fork lift trucks are available to move it. Strategic transport still relies heavily on the rail network.

Fuel Supply

A great deal of fuel goes in road bowsers, especially near the front line. Strategically, fuel is moved by train. From railhead to forward dump there is available, in addition to road transport, a field pipeline system, the PTM. With pumping stations every 10 to 12km, formed by clipped sectioned lengths of 150mm diameter aluminium pipe, the troops of the army's pipelaying corps can lay up to 30km per day behind a field army. The pipeline is laid on the surface by semi-automatic laying machines towed by heavy tractors.

Fuel dumps nowadays take the form of clusters of pillow tanks of various sizes. These are easy to conceal and have the advantage that they can be loaded into ordinary flat multi-purpose trucks instead of ammunition. A truck so loaded can carry more fuel than a fuel bowser.

REPAIR AND MAINTENANCE

Right: A scene familiar to all soldiers as a vehicle mechanic supervises the recovery of a ditched truck, although the technique of using a dummy axle is unusual. The Soviet Army does not place too great an emphasis on recovery and repair because of its plan for a very short war and rapid movement.

Below: A welder at work in a field workshop. Only quick and simple repair work is envisaged because of the time factor, and equipment requiring major repairs will be ditched or cannibalised.

Below right: Not an enviable job as a Soviet Army tank crew replaces a tank track in very cold conditions. Emphasis is placed on operator maintenance and repair.

MEDICAL SERVICES

Right: The general principle used for medical evacuation is that higher formations collect from the lower, ie, regiment collects from battalion, division from regiment, and so on. Here two GT-T over-snow load carriers have been pressed into service as temporary ambulances.

Below: An army mobile field hospital.

TRANSPORT

Above left: The standard work-horse of the Soviet Army for many years was the GAZ-69 ½ tonne 4x4 field car. This one belongs to an airborne unit and is towing a twin ZU-23 anti-aircraft cannon.

Left: A ZIL-135 (8x8) 10 tonne truck is followed by a massive MAZ-543 (8x8) 15 tonne cargo carrier.

Above: ATS-59 artillery tractors towing guns through the snow, the vehicle crews communicating with each other by means of flags. The Soviet artillery uses a very large number of tracked tractors of various types, which gives them a great degree of mobility and flexibility, although it must also lead to a considerable maintenance liability. This last is eased somewhat by commonality of parts and spares.

FUEL SUPPLY

Right: A platoon of T-54A tanks refuels at a depot during Exercise Dnieper in 1967. Not shown are the pillow tanks containing the fuel supply.

FIELD BAKERIES

Below: Bread is an essential part of the Soviet soldier's diet and is baked at field bakeries such as this. It is ironic that with the constant inability of the Soviet agricultural system to produce sufficient grain for the nation's needs the Soviet Army may well feed on American grain!

NUCLEAR, BIOLOGICAL AND CHEMICAL WARFARE

NBC warfare, sometimes alternatively called CBR (chemical, biological, radiological), plays a central role in all Soviet planning. As far as published information seems to indicate, the Soviet ground forces are more fully equipped for such warfare than any other in the world.

Means of Delivery.

All Soviet artillery pieces of 122mm calibre and over can be used to deliver persistent and non-persistent chemical agents, but in practice, the most likely weapon for the delivery of non-persistent agents is the BM-21. The density of fire of this area saturation weapon makes it ideal for this purpose. A battery of six such weapons could deliver 240 chemical shells to a target area in a few seconds. Persistent agents would most likely be delivered by the long-range D-74 122mm and M-46 130mm guns. Agents of both types can be delivered by aerial bombs or spray tanks from FGA aircraft of the Tactical Air Armies. Chemical warheads might well be used together with conventional explosives to delude the defender.

Agents.

The Soviet Union is known to hold stocks of several kinds of chemical warfare agents. These include:
Hydrogen cyanide compounds which cause rapid respiratory failure, but disperse very quickly. One contamination by this agent renders most types of gas mask and vehicle filter useless.
Nerve agents, developed from insecticides by German scientists during the last war; the most important of these are known by code letters—GA(Tabun), GB(Sarin), GD(Soman) and VX. Small amounts of these agents inhaled or absorbed through the skin cause malfunction of the nervous system and rapid death. These agents can be used in the persistent and non-persistent forms. Some nerve agents can be countered by antidotes or injections, but it is thought that the latest Soviet compounds may well prove difficult, if not impossible, to counter with present medicines.
Blistering Agents—developments of the mustard gas used so effectively in World War I. These are very persistent and produce incapacitating blisters and the vapour, if inhaled, causes death.

It is known that the Soviets maintain stocks of CW agents ready for use, and it is assumed that these

Right: It appears that every soldier in the Soviet Army is issued with a respirator and chemical protection suits. This man is using a detector to assess contamination levels.

Below: A closed-down T-62 drives through a cleansing spray delivered from a modified aircraft turbo-jet engine. This expedient is effective, if expensive on fuel.

would be issued to army formations as the result of a high-level political decision. All army units have the capability of delivery CW attacks, and divisional artillery recce is tasked to provide meteorological data for divisional staffs to plan their employment. In addition to this offensive capability, all army units and formations, unlike Nato armies, have integral chemical recce and defence elements for detection of contamination and marking of contaminated areas, and for mass decontamination of vehicles and personnel (see diagrams showing structure of motor rifle divisions). Every Soviet soldier has his individual NBC protective clothing and a decontamination kit, and all modern Soviet AFVs are capable of operating in a contaminated environment.

There are several types of Soviet NBC reconnaissance vehicles to detect and warn of contamination, at least 17 types of decontamination vehicle for vehicles, terrain and buildings, and nine types of mobile decontamination station for personnel and clothing. Some of these vehicles carry steam boilers whose output is automatically doped with an additive such as formaldehyde or ammonia. Others are tankers equipped with multiple sprays with special nozzle attachments, discharging alkali or other emulsions or fogs.

The smaller drawing shows the BRDM-rkh reconnaissance vehicle equipped with two sets of automatic emplacers for a total of 40 warning flags. The vehicle explores the boundaries of an infected zone and marks the limits by the 40 bright flags, each automatically driven into the ground by a firing chamber and propulsion cartridge. The larger illustration shows the TMS-65 decontamination vehicle, used for the mass cleansing of vehicles and large items such as radars and missiles. The 6×6 Ural-375E chassis carries a VK-1F turbojet engine and operator cabin, with swivelling and elevation controls. Tanks on the chassis and a towed trailer supply jet fuel and additive decontaminants, delivered by the jet over a line of infected equipment (either the latter or the TMS-65 can be driven past the other).

Once such a uniform is in general use, it will reduce considerably the impediments to the employment of chemical weapons on the battlefield. All Soviet soldiers carry an extremely effective kit of prophylactic antidotes which render harmless at least their own chemical agents, and probably anything the West has. It must be assumed, therefore, that in any major conflict the Soviet Ground Forces will use chemical weapons as a matter of course.

Above: A BRDM-1 reconnaissance vehicle is decontaminated using a hand-held spray by a soldier from a chemical defence unit.

Below: These men are not surrendering, but are passing through a chemical decontamination shower!

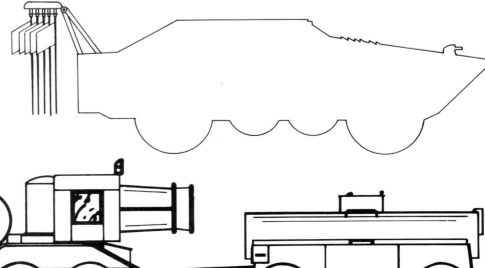

Right: The BRDM-1 rkh is specifically designed for chemical reconnaissance. The flags are used to mark cleared lanes.

Below: The TMS-65 comprises a turbojet mounted on a Ural-375 truck chassis. The trailer contains liquid decontaminant.

The Soviet Strategic Rocket Forces

Strategic superiority is both difficult to define and to achieve under contemporary circumstances. However, the USSR has acquired a strategic capability which is not just more than sufficient to deter an attack upon the Homeland, but which will also enable the leadership to support an aggressive global policy. Contemporary Soviet strategists appear to assume that a nuclear war can be won especially since the fractionalisation of warheads now enables a single launch vehicle to destroy several enemy nuclear systems, thus making a pre-emptive strike an attractive military option.

Dr. James E. Dornan, Jr.

No one today would challenge the assertion that the development and deployment of a substantial strategic nuclear striking force by the Soviet Union constitutes one of the decisive turning points of contemporary international history. The growth of Soviet strategic strength has altered the very structure of world politics, transforming the USSR from a self-proclaimed 'encircled fortress', surrounded by predatory capitalist states, into a global superpower, capable not only of dealing effectively with challenges to immediate Soviet interests but also of projecting its power and influence on a world scale. In the process, the Soviet diplomatic style and the pattern of Soviet behaviour in world politics has been substantially changed as well. The bluff and bluster of the

The ultimate symbol of Soviet military power is this intercontinental ballistic missile, blasting off from its silo. The Soviet Union possesses sufficient nuclear weapons to destroy every vestige of animal life on earth *twenty times over.*

Khrushchev era has been replaced by a new self-confidence and assertiveness, as the USSR manipulates client states in every major strategic region of the world and otherwise behaves as if the world correlation of forces has indeed shifted in its favour. Although the recent massive increases in Soviet strategic strength are a product of the procurement programmes of the last decade – indeed, the Strategic Rocket Forces (*Raketnye Voiska Strategicheskogo Naznacheniya* or Rocket Troops of Strategic Designation) themselves were not created as a separate branch of the Soviet armed forces until 1960 – their origins lie in the Stalinist era, and in particular in the strategic situation by which the USSR was confronted at the close of World War II.

The origins of strategic power

It is worth recalling at the outset that Soviet military doctrine and practice – unlike, for example, that of the United States – has always stressed the necessary connection between military power and politics, and in particular the impact of Soviet arms upon the course of the world revolution. In the years immediately following the 1917 Revolution, Soviet theorists attempted at length to develop a set of principles for translating military power into political gains, and in particular for profiting from the expected collapse of the capitalist governments in Western Europe.

World War II was taken by Soviet thinkers as confirmation of the view that the maintenance of a powerful military capability was essential if the socialist camp was to fend off the forces of counter-revolution and exploit emergent political weaknesses in the capitalist camp.

Nevertheless, after World War II the USSR confronted an entirely new military situation: the need to prepare for a possible conflict with an adversary which was not accessible by land, as Russia's traditional enemies had been, and which moreover was accustomed – and possessed the capability, most dramatically in the form of nuclear weapons – to utilise power at great distances from its homeland. While the precise manner in which Stalin viewed the world of 1945 remains a matter of scholarly debate, there is general agreement on his specifically military concerns. The USSR faced the need to deter the US from reacting vigorously to hostile political moves emanating from Moscow and from attempting to exploit political unrest in Eastern Europe; more generally, Stalin saw the need to usher the USSR safely through the period in which it would be vulnerable to Western strategic nuclear strength. His immediate solution was to emphasise, both operationally and in his declaratory policy, the continuing significance of land power, represented by mass armies defending a territorial heartland and operating on interior lines of supply and communications – the traditional Russian form of military power. Concretely, he may have consciously decided, as Thomas Wolfe has suggested in his *Soviet Power and Europe, 1945–1970*, to make Western Europe a kind of 'hostage' to ensure US good behaviour by deploying large forces with a substantial offensive capability in the satellite nations and in the Western USSR. In any case, Soviet land

power became the counterpoise to US strategic strength.

At the same time, Stalin made substantial efforts to acquire both nuclear weapons and long-range delivery systems. A nuclear weapons research programme had been begun in the USSR as early as 1942. The first Soviet graphite reactor went into operation in December 1946, and, following several public claims that Soviet scientists had solved the problem of the atomic bomb, the first known atomic device was tested on 29 August 1949. Nearly four years later, the USSR exploded its first thermo-nuclear device.

Soviet development of delivery vehicles, although lagging somewhat behind accomplishments in the nuclear weapons field, also proceeded at a steady pace. USSR rocket technology originated in the early 1940s. Short-range tactical rockets were utilised freely in area bombardments during the final campaigns against the Axis in World War II. After the war the USSR took over large stocks of the German V-2 rockets, the type which had been used against London, and put captured German scientists to work on more advanced systems. By 1947 a small number of SS-1 'Scunner' SRBMs (short-range ballistic missiles) – essentially improved V-2s – had been deployed. The initial Soviet nuclear delivery vehicles, however, were aircraft suited mainly for use against European targets: Tu-4 'Bull' piston-engined medium bombers copied from four US B-29s which had made emergency landings in the Far East during World War II, and Il-28 'Beagle' light jet bombers. (The Tu-4 could, of course, have reached the US on a one-way mission or with air refuelling, but the Soviets did not develop a capability for the latter until the late 1950s.) Development of intercontinental bombers was also begun in the late 1940s. Moreover, although the creation of the long-range missile force has often been credited in Soviet historiography to Khrushchev, an ICBM (intercontinental ballistic missile) research programme apparently was established at Stalin's direction in 1948 as a follow-on to the work on the V-2 types. (The commander of the Soviet rocket forces, Marshal N. I. Krylov, has stated that research and development on long-range missiles started in the early postwar years.) Only one additional rocket of significance was deployed during the Stalinist years, however; this was the SS-2 'Sibling' SRBM, which embodied some improvements in range and reliability over the SS-1

Thus although it is probably in the main correct to conclude – as have most Western and Soviet writers – that Stalin did not adequately grasp the strategic and political implications of the new technology, such criticisms should not be pushed too far. Although his stress on the 'permanent operating factors' of war and on old doctrines and strategies generally, as well as the commanding position which he assigned to the army within the Soviet military hierarchy, helped to prolong the pre-eminence of a continental military outlook in Soviet strategic thinking, Stalin's public depreciation of the significance of nuclear weapons was a reasonable response to Soviet military weakness. And his declaratory policy was in any case belied by his decisions to expend a substantial portion of Soviet R & D (research and development) resources on modern nuclear weapons and delivery systems – decisions which laid the foundation for the Soviet strategic programmes of the Khrushchev and Brezhnev years and the rise of the USSR to a position of no less than strategic parity with the US.

The Khrushchev period

The death of Stalin and the rise to power of Georgi Malenkov set off a lengthy debate among Soviet theorists about the impact of the new weapons on war and international politics. Several prominent thinkers, including General N. A. Talenski, argued that the nature of war itself had been transformed by nuclear weapons and modern long-range delivery systems, and that the traditional advantages enjoyed by the USSR, stemming from geographic location and physical size, were by themselves no longer sufficient to ensure victory in the event of a major conflict with the West. A new doctrine was needed, in their view, which took into account the now-transcendent importance of strategic surprise; several leaders, including General Talenski, appeared to advocate a pre-emptive attack by the USSR in the event that an assault on the homeland appeared imminent. Above all, the USSR, in the view of Stalin's critics, had to be prepared to fight a nuclear war. Malenkov, on the other hand, in a series of 1954 speeches, appeared to take the position that a new war would mean the destruction of civilization, Soviet as well as Western. He moreover stated that when both sides possessed an adequate strategic nuclear force, there would exist a state of mutual deterrence; under such conditions, local and conventional wars were far more likely than general nuclear war.

The position of Malenkov and his supporters was bitterly opposed by Molotov, Bulganin, Marshal Zhukov and other prominent generals, and ultimately by Khrushchev; and Malenkov was forced from office in February 1955. The new Bulganin–Khrushchev duumvirate immediately set out to shape a new military doctrine and to reorganise the Soviet high command. Generals loyal to Khrushchev were eventually placed in key positions, and the new strategy emphasised preparation for nuclear war. The development of modern weapons continued, and in some areas was accelerated. The SS-3 'Shyster' MRBM (medium-range ballistic missile), like its predecessors essentially an improved V-2, entered service in 1955, and was publicly displayed in Red Square on 7 November 1957. Moreover, the jet Mya-4 'Bison' and the turbo-prop Tu-95 'Bear' long-range strategic bombers had been publicly displayed in 1954 and 1955 respectively, and the Tu-16 'Badger' medium jet bomber was ready to enter the operational inventory. A modest force of the former was eventually deployed, along with some 1,300 'Badgers' assigned to both the strategic and naval air arms. (It was the July 1955 Moscow Air Show which gave rise to the widespread fears in the West that a significant 'bomber gap' had developed, putting the West at a serious strategic disadvantage in dealing with the USSR. But apparently the Soviets

SOVIET STRATEGIC MISSILE TEST CENTRES AND RELATED FACILITIES

A: Kapustin Yar (48.4°N, 45.8°E). Early test centre for short and medium-range ballistic missiles: Soviet V-2, Shyster/Sandal, Skean. ABM tests with two-stage SL-8 fired towards Sary Shagan. Small Cosmos satellites since 1962.

B: Tyuratam (45.8°N, 63.4°E). Test centre for ICBMs launched to target areas Kamchatka Peninsula and central Pacific; small impact area for short/medium range missiles angled

NE. Cosmos photo-reconnaissance (52°, 65° incl.), SIS, ocean surveillance, FOBS, etc.

C: Plesetsk (62.9°N, 40.1°E). ICBM base (e.g. 65 × SS-13). Military meteorological satellites, Cosmos photo-reconnaissance (63°, 65°, 73°, 81° incl.), military comsats, early warning, ferret, multiple navsats (74° and 83°) SIS target.

D: Moscow. Galosh ABM defence site. Four complexes with 16

launchers apiece and associated radars.

E: Severomorsk. Major submarine base near Murmansk including Delta class submarines firing SS-N-8 SLBM's.

F: Barents Sea. Firings of SS-N-8 SLBM's from submarine to impact central Pacific (stellar-inertial guidance), October 1974.

G: White Sea. Firings of SS-N-8 from submarine to impact near Kamchatka

ABM, anti-ballistic missile; SIS, satellite interceptor system; FOBS, fractional orbit bombardment system; ICBM, inter-continental ballistic missile; SLBM, sea-launched ballistic missile.

*Operational ICBM silos have been reported in various sectors of the Soviet Union, e.g. north-west USSR, Ural Mountains, Eastern Siberia; IRBM sites in Western USSR and central Asia covering Europe and Middle East, Eastern Siberia (near the border with Mongolia) covering the whole of the People's Republic of China. Some Scrooge and Scamp mobile launchers in West and East.

MILITARY DISTRICTS AND MAJOR FLEETS

1, Leningrad. **2,** Baltic (Riga). **3,** Belorussian (Minsk). **4,** Moscow. **5,** Carpathian (L'Vov). **6,** Odessa. **7,** Kiev. **8,** N. Causasus (Rostov-on-Don). **9,** Transcaucasus (Tbilisi). **10,** Volga (Kuybyshev). **11,** Urals (Sverdlovsk). **12,** Turkestan (Tashkent). **13,** Central Asian (Alma Ata).

14, Siberian (Novosibirsk). **15,** Transbaikal (Chita). **16,** Far Eastern (Khabarovsk). **Fleets:** (I) Northern (Murmansk). (II) Baltic (Kaliningrad). (III) Black Sea (Sevastopol). (IV) Pacific Ocean (Vladivostok).

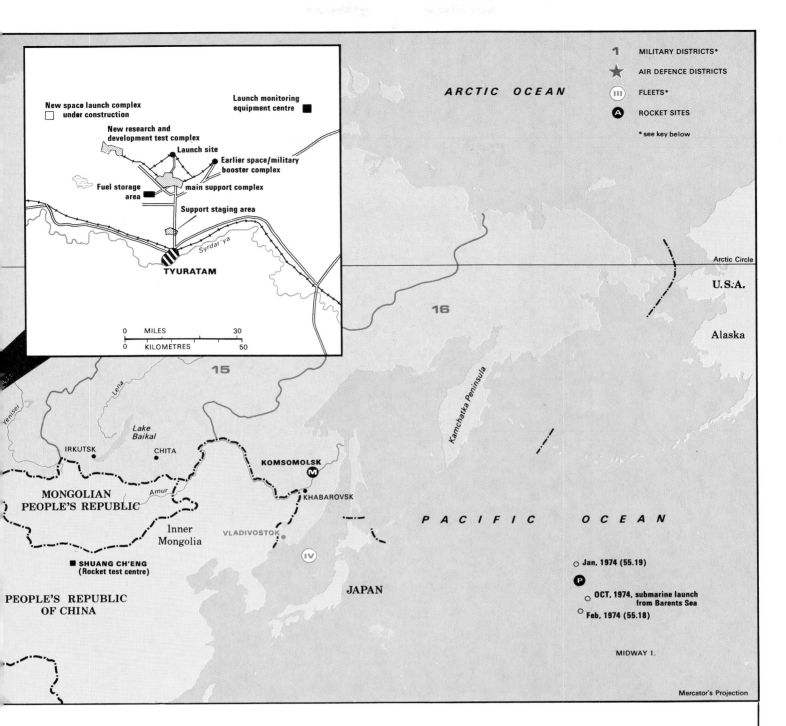

New space launch complex
under construction

Launch monitoring
equipment centre ■

New research and
development test complex

Launch site

Earlier space/military
booster complex

Fuel storage
area

main support complex

Support staging area

Syrdar'ya

TYURATAM

MILES 0 30
KILOMETRES 0 50

1 MILITARY DISTRICTS*
★ AIR DEFENCE DISTRICTS
ⓘ FLEETS*
Ⓐ ROCKET SITES
* see key below

ARCTIC OCEAN

16

Arctic Circle

U.S.A.

Alaska

15

Yenisei
Lena

Lake Baikal

IRKUTSK CHITA

KOMSOMOLSK Ⓜ

KHABAROVSK

MONGOLIAN PEOPLE'S REPUBLIC

Amur

Inner Mongolia

VLADIVOSTOK

Ⓘⱽ

Kamchatka Peninsula

PACIFIC OCEAN

JAPAN

SHUANG CH'ENG
(Rocket test centre)

PEOPLE'S REPUBLIC OF CHINA

○ Jan. 1974 (55.19)
Ⓟ
○ OCT. 1974, submarine launch
from Barents Sea
○ Feb. 1974 (55.18)

MIDWAY I.

Mercator's Projection

Peninsula, February 1974.
H: Novaya Zemlya. Major nuclear test centre; impact area for ICBM's launched from Soviet operational silos.

J: Semipalatinsk. Underground tests of ABM warheads (20-200 KT); kill mechanisms for ABM and SIS including (?) high-energy lasers and

charged particle beams.

K: Severodvinsk. World's largest submarine yard, near Archangel, building Delta-class nuclear-powered submarines.

L: Gorki. Submarine yard building nuclear-powered Charlie-class vessels able to launch eight SS-N-7 missiles whilst submerged.

M: Komsomolsk. Second major submarine yard, on Amur River in Soviet Far East.

N: Sary Shagan. Anti-ballistic missile test centre including long-range ABM SH-4 and never high-acceleration ABM in Sprint class.

P: Pacific target areas: (a) SS-19 ICBM Jan. 1974 from Tyuratam; (b)

SS-18 ICBM Feb. 1974; (c) SS-N-8 SLBM Oct. 1974 from Delta 2 class submarine, Barents Sea.

Chinese facilities
a. Lop Nor nuclear test centre 40°20'N, 90°.10'E.
b. Shuang-Ch'eng-tze rocket test centre 41°N, 100°E.

flew the same squadrons of 'Bisons' and a few 'Bears' repeatedly past the viewing stand, leading Western observers to conclude that the USSR had embarked on a large-scale build-up of heavy bombers. It has been observed that this air show was 'one of the most successful peacetime military demonstrations of modern times'.)

The technical shortcomings of the 'Bison' and 'Bear' may have influenced Khrushchev's decision not to procure them in large numbers, but in retrospect it seems probable that he simply decided to leap-frog into the missile age. The first full-range test of a Soviet ICBM, involving an early version of

the SS-6 'Sapwood', took place on 26 August 1957; production began almost immediately. War-head production had also been proceeding rapidly. (It has also been suggested that war-head production outran that of strategic delivery systems, enabling these war-heads to be deployed in Europe, this in turn making possible the manpower reductions in the Soviet armed forces of the Khrushchev period.) Extensive nuclear weapons tests were carried out in 1958 and again in 1961, when a 58MT (megaton) weapon was exploded. In 1959 a further development of the 'Shyster', the SS-4 'Sandal' MRBM, entered deployment. With

its relatively high reliability, a maximum range of 1,200 statute miles, and a 1MT war-head capability, the 'Sandal' quickly became a standard IRBM (intermediate-range ballistic missile) in the Soviet armed forces; 500 or so remain in service at present, deployed both in the western USSR and along the Sino-Soviet border. (Early versions of the SS-4 were radio-command guided, but later models incorporate inertial guidance. The 'Sandal' was one of the two types of Soviet missiles deployed in Cuba late in 1962.) The SS-5 'Skean' IRBM (intermediate range ballistic missile), followed two years later. Similar in appearance to the SS-3 and SS-4, but without fins, the 'Skean' has a range of 2,300 miles. About 100 were deployed, some in underground silos; most remain in service. Although generally said to mount a 1MT war-head, the SS-5 has also been reported to carry a large war-head in the 5–10MT range.

The seemingly rapid Soviet progress in the strategic weapons field undoubtedly helped stimulate Khrushchev to undertake another re-examination of Soviet strategic doctrine during the late 1950s. Apparently persuaded by Western behaviour at the Geneva Conference of 1955, by the lack of US action during the Hungarian revolution in 1956, and by the vacillating Western response to his 'rocket diplomacy' during the Suez crisis and the Turkish-Syrian tensions of late 1957 that there was little chance that the West would initiate military hostilities against the USSR, he decided to rely on a 'minimum deterrence' posture both to ensure Soviet security and as the basis for an adventuresome political strategy against the West. In his assessment of world political trends at the 21st Party Congress in January 1959, he delivered his famous pronouncement that war was no longer 'fatalistically inevitable', not because the West had become more kindly disposed toward the socialist camp, but because a decisive shift in the world correlation of forces had occurred in favour of the communist world. In Khrushchev's view, the West would be increasingly deterred in the future from offering vigorous resistance to communist political initiatives. The advance of socialism was thus assured.

In a subsequent speech on defence issues, delivered before the Supreme Soviet on 14 January 1960, he developed this theme at greater length, and also set forth the principal elements of his military doctrine. Nuclear explosives and rocket weapons, he stated, had become the decisive factors in modern war. Under these conditions, although the USSR would of course be able to survive and triumph in any future war, no matter what the circumstances, the first phase of a future global conflict might well be crucial. War, he said, 'would start in the heart of the belligerent countries: there would not be a single capital, not a single major industrial or administrative centre, not a single strategic area which would not be subjected to attack, not only in the first days but in the first minutes of the war.' The USSR, he continued, must therefore reorganise its military forces to take account of these factors. In the future, the most important component of the Soviet armed forces would be the Strategic Rocket Forces; research, development and procurement of the most modern rocket weapons would consequently be stepped up substantially. There would be corresponding cuts, Khrushchev concluded, in conventional forces, particularly in the army.

On 7 May 1960, when the Strategic Rocket Forces were elevated to the status of an Armed Service, on a par with the Ground, Air, Air Defence and Naval Forces, under the command of Marshal K. S. Moskalenko, the shift in Soviet doctrine away from a purely continental, land power strategy to one which took fully into account the revolutionary impact of the new weaponry was completed. All offensive missiles with a range of more than 1,000 kilometres (620 statute miles) were assigned to the Strategic Rocket Forces (missiles of lesser range, designated as 'operational-tactical' missiles in Soviet terminology, are assigned to the Ground, Air, and Naval Forces). Work on the second generation ICBMs by 1960 was already far advanced; the first of these, the SS-7 'Saddler', about which little is known even today although nearly 200 have been deployed, began to enter service late in 1961; the SS-8 'Sasin', like 'Saddler' a two-stage storable liquid-fuel ICBM with a 5MT war-head and a range of nearly 7,000 miles, entered deployment two years later.

Nevertheless, Soviet ICBM progress was not nearly as rapid as Khrushchev had expected during the heady days of the first 'Sputnik' launchings. From the time of the first tests in late 1957 to mid-1961, only a handful of ICBMs was actually deployed; Western intelligence sources credited the USSR with only 10 operational SS-6s as of late 1959. It is now clear that technical complications with the 'Sapwood' were primarily responsible for the slow development rate. Electronics difficulties and problems with the non-storable liquid fuel system led to extremely poor accuracy and low reliability; moreover, the missile required 'soft' emplacement (unprotected against nuclear explosion) in above-ground launching pads and a lengthy pre-launch preparation period. (It has been suggested that one motive for Khrushchev's exaggerated claims for Soviet progress in strategic weaponry during the 1959–1960 period was to conceal from the West his decision not to deploy extensively the first-generation SS-6.)

After the Cuban missile crisis, the deployment pace quickened somewhat. Moskalenko was succeeded by Marshal S. S. Biryuzov in 1962. The Soviet ICBM total had reached 200 by the time of Khrushchev's ousting, with perhaps one-third of these second-generation 'Saddlers' and 'Sasins'. Many of the latter were deployed in dispersed and 'hardened' (protected against nuclear explosion) launchers. An entirely new generation of ICBMs was in the development stage. By this time also MRBM and IRBM deployments had reached their peak of perhaps 750, all of them SS-4 'Sandal' and SS-5 'Skean' types. The Strategic Rocket Forces now consisted of 110,000 men, under the command of Marshal N. I. Krylov, who succeeded Biryuzov in 1963. (Too much is made of the Cuban crisis as a motive for the post-1962 Soviet missile build-up. Khrushchev's retreat in the face of the US ultimatum certainly helped to strengthen Soviet resolve to catch up with the United States as quickly as possible, but it certainly does not by itself explain the size of the Soviet deployments in the late 1960s.) But the unsatisfactory outcomes of the Cuban affair and the campaign against Berlin made it clear that, despite the pronounced shift in doctrine, resources and deployment from conventional to strategic forces which Khrushchev instituted, he had failed to develop a military posture sufficient to support the assertive political strategy he desired. Along with difficulties in the domestic economy for which he was also held accountable, his

Above: The SS-14 (Scamp) system comprises a Scapegoat IRBM mounted on a tracked launcher. The missile has a range of 2,500 miles and many are facing China.

Below left: SS-9 (Scarp) was the USSR's largest operational ICBM until the SS-18 entered service in the mid-1970s. Although 288 of these missiles were once deployed, only a few now remain in service.

Below: SS-15 (Scrooge) on parade in Moscow on 7 November 1965, the only time it has ever been seen. Although once reported to be deployed in the Far East it is now uncertain that SS-15 entered service.

strategic failures helped bring about his political demise.

From inferiority to parity plus

Throughout the 1950s and early 1960s there were numerous indications that Khrushchev's ideas on military strategy and on the appropriate force posture for the USSR were encountering opposition within the Soviet military bureaucracy. His decision to accord primacy to nuclear weapons and strategic missiles was one of the issues on which he encountered particularly sharp criticism, and after he was retired his successors once again altered Soviet doc-

trine. His 'single option' strategy was modified, and his apparent belief that all wars between the socialist and capitalist camps must inevitably and quickly escalate to the holocaust level was gradually – if subtly – modified. At the same time, Brezhnev and Kosygin jettisoned the 'minimum deterrence' strategic posture on which Khrushchev, in part out of necessity, based his activist foreign policy between 1958 and 1962.

Generally speaking, the policies of the Brezhnev era have been directed toward improving the global power position of the Soviet Union. This meant that the USSR had to improve substantially its position in the strategic balance *vis-à-vis* the US, and develop the capability to project its military power and political presence into the farthest reaches of the globe. It is of course the former that concerns us here. Shortly after assuming power the regime made the decision to accelerate considerably the missile procurement programme set in motion during Khrushchev's last years, and by late 1966 deployment of two third-generation ICBMs – the SS-9 'Scarp' and the SS-11 'Sego' – was proceeding at the rate of one every two days.

The 'Scarp', the earliest version of which appeared in 1965, is a particularly impressive weapon; it is approximately 35 metres long and 3 metres in diameter, with a throw-weight (payload) of at least 12,000 pounds. The 'Mod 1' and 'Mod 2' versions carry single large war-heads of up to 25MT. The Soviets also begain testing in 1966 a fractional orbital bombardment (FOBS) version of the SS-9, designed to deliver its weapon from a satellite before completing a single orbit; the SS-9 was also tested later in a depressed trajectory mode.

The SS-11 'Sego', which followed in 1966, is, like the 'Scarp', a three-stage missile using a storable liquid propellant; early versions carried a single war-head in the 1–2MT range. Due to unimpressive accuracy the 'Sego' has from the start been regarded as a soft-target, or 'countervalue', weapon. It has been deployed in large numbers – approximately 960 of the 'Mod 1' and 'Mod 2' were in position by 1973, most in underground silos constructed in a broad belt 250 miles wide and 3,000 miles long, beginning east of Moscow and ending near Chita, east of Lake Baikal. The SS-10 'Scrag', another very large ICBM, was shown in Moscow parades beginning in 1965; it was apparently not deployed, however, and may have been a prototype or transition missile presaging the later SS-18. Also in this period the first Soviet solid-fuel missile, the SS-13 'Savage', reached the deployment stage, along with an IRBM variant using the upper two stages, the SS-14 'Scapegoat'. (The SS-14, when considered with its associated erector/transportation system, is known as 'Scamp'.) These missiles were beset with various technical difficulties, however, and were deployed only in small numbers, beginning in 1968. The earliest Soviet multiple re-entry vehicles (MRVs) were also tested in 1968 (unlike the more sophisticated multiple independently-targeted re-entry vehicles, or MIRVs, MRV war-heads cannot be directed at widely separated targets).

By early 1970 the USSR had passed the US in numbers of operational ICBMs (see Chart 1). By February 1970, 275 SS-9s had been deployed, with a combination of war-head yield and accuracy sufficient to cause concern in the United States and elsewhere that the Soviets were on the verge of acquiring a hard-target capability against the US Minuteman ICBM force. Finally, early in 1970 a 'Mod 2' version of the SS-11, with a more accurate re-entry vehicle, was tested.

The Strategic Rocket Forces by now numbered some 350,000 men. They had become the most widely publicised component of the Soviet armed forces within the USSR. The commander-in-chief of the Strategic Rocket Forces always takes precedence over the other service commanders-in-chief, regardless of actual rank. High position in the Strategic Rocket Forces, in fact, seemed increasingly a path to even greater prominence: after the death of Defence Minister Malinovskiy in 1967, there were rumours that Marshal Krylov was a leading candidate for the position, and in the autumn of 1970 Colonel-General N. N. Alekseyev of the SRF was made a Deputy Defence Minister, and apparently put in charge of co-ordinating all strategic weapons development programmes. When Krylov died in May 1972, his one-time deputy, General V. F. Tolubko, became commander of the Strategic Rocket Forces.

By the time of SALT-1, then, the Brezhnev regime had more than achieved its initial objectives of 1964. The 1972 Interim Agreement on Offensive Weapons permitted the USSR to complete deployment of all ICBM (and SLBM, or submarine-launched ballistic missile) launchers under construction as of 1 July 1972; strategic missile-launcher levels were frozen at that level.

The Soviets were thus guaranteed a substantial advantage over the United States – no less than 1,408 to 1,054, depending on how many of its older missiles each side chooses to trade in for new SLBMs – in numbers of ICBM launchers. Each side was also allowed to upgrade qualitatively its missile force; thus the long-anticipated Soviet development of MIRV war-heads would not be restricted. Nor were any limits imposed on the USSR's emergent 'cold launch' or 'zero stage' technology, by which ICBMs are propelled from their silos by compressed gas and ignited above ground. The latter development is particularly significant, in that it obviates the need for extensive shielding inside the silo, thus permitting both the deployment of much larger missiles per silo and reasonably rapid re-use of the silo itself. When coupled with continued Soviet progress in the modernisation of their Air, Naval and Ground Forces, the strategic advantages guaranteed the USSR at SALT-1 meant that they had achieved no less than military parity with the US – a fact which was widely acknowledged by Western experts.

It was the hope of the United States government that the SALT-1 agreement would stabilise the strategic competition between the superpowers. The more advanced technology of the American strategic forces was said to compensate for any disadvantages by the Soviets under the accord. The willingness of the USSR to accept severe constraints on deployment of a missile-type ABM (anti-ballistic missile) system, some commentators argued, indicated that the Soviets might be moving towards acceptance of an 'assured destruction' strategic posture and away from the 'war-fighting' doctrine implicit in much past Soviet military thinking. On this basis,

it was suggested, *détente* might over a time become more than a slogan.

It soon became clear, however, that the Soviets intended to exploit fully the opportunities for further force improvements provided them under the SALT-1 accord. Their strategic force build-up since 1972 has proceeded at a pace which former US Defense Secretary Schlesinger termed 'unprecedented in its breadth and depth'. In the mid-1970s the Soviets tested and deployed a 'MRVed' version of the SS-11 'Sego', with more accurate re-entry vehicles. Then an entire new generation of ICBMs was tested and deployed: SS-17, a solid-fuel weapon using 'cold-launch' technology and carrying four 200KT MIRVs; SS-19, a 'hot-launch' missile with a volume 56% greater and a throw-weight four times more than that of the SS-11 it replaces, with 6 MIRV, on the Mod. 1 version; and finally the giant SS-18, a 'cold-launch' vehicle carrying either a 25MT warhead or ten 600KT MIRVs. All three have new bus-type post-boost vehicles and war-heads with higher re-entry speeds for greater accuracy. The silo-hardening programme for these missiles also continues and some reports have suggested that the latest silos have been hardened to withstand over-pressures

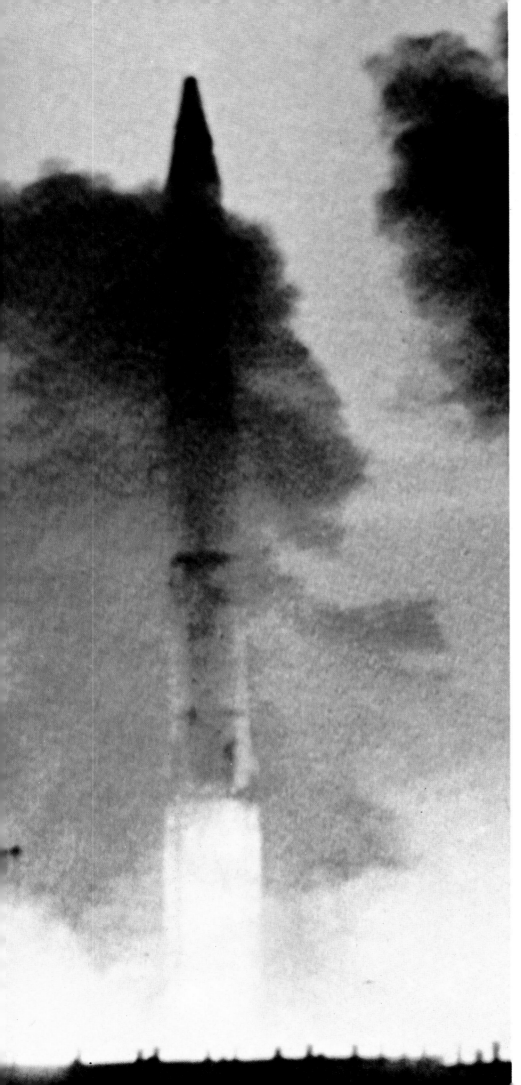

in excess of 3,000 pounds per square inch.

SS-20, a two-stage version of SS-16, has been extensively tested and is being deployed as a mobile IRBM system to replace the aging SS-4 and SS-5. There are, however, no indications that the Soviets are satisfied with these fourth-generation missiles and the US Secretary of Defense revealed in early 1978 that they were known to be developing four new fifth-generation missiles.

SALT-II was negotiated painfully over an eight-year period, starting with a framework agreed by President Ford and Mr Brezhnev at Vladivostok in November 1974 and culminating with the meeting between President Carter and (the by then) President Brezhnev in Vienna in mid-1978. In outline, SALT-II would result in a limitation of 2,400 strategic nuclear delivery vehicles six months after ratification, reducing to 2,250 by the end of 1981. Within this ceiling there would be three sub-limits affecting numbers of MIRVed land- and sea-based ICBMs, bombers with ALCMs, and ALBMs.

The major factors affecting the Soviet rocket forces include the scrapping of some 300 strategic launchers to come down to the 2,250 ceiling. They would also not be able to exceed an 820 MIRV ICBM sub-limit. An added complication is that, it has been agreed that once a missile has been tested with MIRV all missiles of that type will count against the 820 ceiling; therefore all single-warhead SS-17, -18 and -19 ICBMs will be regarded as MIRVed. The Soviets would also not be able to deploy more than 308 SS-18, and (as with the USA) they would only be allowed to develop one new ICBM by the end of 1985 and even that would not be permitted to be more powerful than SS-19. A further restriction on the Soviets would be that SS-16 could not be further tested, nor could it be put into service. Land-based ICBMs would also be limited to ten MIRVs, the number currently carried by SS-18.

Following summit agreement the USA needed Congressional approval and this seemed just possible, despite many reservations, when the USSR invaded Afghanistan in December 1979 and President Carter withdrew SALT-II from Congressional consideration as a reprisal.

It may be, as some commentators have suggested, that the USSR remains obsessed with a 'more is better' approach to weapons procurement, and that neither Soviet political nor military leaders are acting on the basis of a master plan to achieve strategic superiority over the US. Strategic superiority, as has often been pointed out, is in any case both difficult to define and to achieve under contemporary circumstances. But there can be no doubt that the Soviets have acquired a strategic capability not only more than sufficient to deter any attack on the USSR, but one which may also enable them to support the sort of aggressive global political strategy which Krushchev attempted 20 years ago.

Soviet military use of space

When aircraft were first used for military purposes the sky seemed to be a neutral area, and in the early days of World War I opposing reconnaissance machines would fly past each other with pilots exchanging no more than a friendly wave. As the influence of aircraft upon the land battle came to be appreciated, however, the waves soon changed to bullets and war in the air has ensued ever since. Unfortunately, the same process is being repeated today in space. The USA and USSR have both become increasingly dependent upon their various satellite systems, which are both technically superior to older means of reconnaissance and communication, and also much more economical. The Limited Test Ban Treaty (1963), the Outer Space Treaty (1976) and the Anti-Ballistic Missile Agreement (1972) imposed certain restrictions upon the signatories, but none bars the use of anti-satellite (ASAT) systems.

Reconnaissance satellites

The reconnaissance satellite programme represents the largest proportion of Soviet military launches and started on 26 April 1962 with the launch of Cosmos 4. This remained in orbit for three days and carried camera equipment aboard an unmanned Vostok spacecraft, the use of proven hardware enabling the programme to be undertaken quickly and reliably and avoiding the sort of bad luck which dogged the US Discoverer.

The rate of launches accelerated through the mid-1960s, finally stabilising at some 30 per year. Unlike US satellites all these Soviet missions are recovered and they are fitted with a self-destruct device which is actuated if it is thought that they will land in non-Soviet territory. A new reconnaissance satellite has been under development since 1975 and is believed to use a modified Soyuz spacecraft. The first was Cosmos 758 (5 Sept 1975), but this exploded after 20 days in orbit and some later craft in this series have also failed for various reasons. There are about two flights a year, each with a duration of some 30 days. The most advanced Soviet reconnaissance satellite is a military version of the Salyut space station, which has a capability equivalent to the US Big Bird.

Satellites used for electro-magnetic surveillance missions are known as 'ferrets' and the Soviets use two distinct types. The smaller 'ferrets' are launched about four times a year for general surveys and larger craft are then used for detailed examination; the latter are launched at a rate of about one per year.

The Soviets have concentrated on ocean surveillance systems to compensate for their lack of overseas bases from which to mount reconnaissance flights by aircraft. Cosmos 198 (December 1967) was the first in a series of large ocean surveillance satellites and development continued slowly until 1974 when the system became operational. Satellites are launched into a 174 by 162 mile (280 by 260km) orbit and one distinctive feature is that two satellites are launched within a few days of each other. Both carry a powerful radar which can locate ships in any weather condition. The complete satellite is 45ft (14m) long and 6.4ft (2m) in diameter, with a nuclear reactor about 19.3ft (6m) long containing 110lb (50kg) of enriched uranium (U^{235}). Once the satellite has completed its mission (usually 60 to 70 days) the reactor package is boosted by an on-board rocket into a higher (589 mile

Chart 1: Historical Comparison of USSR and USA ICBM Strengths, *1960–1980*

	1960	*1961*	*1962*	*1963*	*1964*	*1965*	*1966*	*1967*	*1968*	*1969*	*1970*
USSR	35	50	75	100	200	270	300	460	800	1,050	1,300
US	18	63	294	424	834	854	904	1054	1054	1054	1054

	1971	*1972*	*1973*	*1974*	*1975*	*1976*	*1977*	*1978*	*1979*
USSR	1510	1550	1575	1590	1599	1527	1477	1400	1400
US	1054	1054	1054	1054	1054	1054	1054	1054	1054

Sources: The Military Balance, 1969–70, and *1979–80*; and Ray S. Cline, *World Power Assessment* (Washington, DC: Center for Strategic and International Studies, 1975), p. 57.

Chart 2: Characteristics of Soviet Strategic Missiles, *1980*

Type	Number Deployed	Year Initially Deployed	Max. Range (statute miles)	No. of Reentry Vehicles	Warhead Yield	Throw-weight in 1,000 lb.[1]	Est. CEP (nautical miles)[2]
SS-4 Sandal	500	1958	1,200	I	1MT	n.a.	n.a.
SS-5 Skean	90	1961	2,300	I	1+MT	n.a.	n.a.
SS-7 Saddler	170[3]	1962	6,900	I	3MT	3.0	1.5
SS-8 Sasin	39[3]	1963	6,900	I	5MT	3.0	1.5
SS-9 Scarp (Mod. 1 & 2)	100[4]	1965	7,500	I	18–25MT	12–15	0.7
SS-9 Scarp (Mod. 4)		1971	7,500	3 MRV	5MT	12–15	0.5
SS-11 Sego (Mod. 1 & 2)	500[6]	1966	6,500	I	1MT	1.5–2	0.7
SS-11 Sego (Mod. 3)	66[6]	1973	6,500	3 MRV	500KT	1.5–2	0.5
SS-13 Savage	60	1969	5,000	I	1MT	1.0	0.7
SS-14 Scapegoat[7]	—	1968	2,500	I	1MT	n.a.	1+
SS-16[8]	n.a.	1978	6,300	I	1+MT	2.0	n.a.
SS-17	100	1975	6,500	4 MIRV	200KT	6.0	0.3
SS-18 (Mod. 1)	50	1974	6,500	I	18–25MT[9]	16–20	0.3
SS-18 (Mod. 2)	150+	1976	5,700	10 MIRV	600KT	16–20	0.25
SS-18 (Mod. 3)	n.a.	1978	6,500	I	n.a.	na.[10]	n.a.
SS-19 (Mod. 1)	425	1974	6,500	6 MIRV	200KT	7.0	0.25
SS-19 (Mod. 2)		1977	6,500	I	n.a.	n.a.[10]	0.25
SS-20	120	1977	3–4,000	3 MIRV	150KT	1.2	n.a.

Sources: *The Military Balance, 1979–80*; Ray S. Cline, *World Power Assessment* (Washington, DC: Center for Strategic and International Studies, 1975); *Jane's Weapon Systems, 1979–80*.

1 Throw-weight is the total weight (warheads, guidance systems, penetration aids, etc) that can be delivered over a given range. Throw-weight will be less than that shown at maximum range.

2 CEP = Circular Area of Probability, and are drawn from various sources.

3 The Soviets began phasing out the older ICBMs, as specified in SALT-I, in the mid-1970s, in order to increase the number of SLBMs beyond those deployed or under construction as of July 1972 and numbers deployed may now be lower than those shown here.

4 SS-9 silos are being converted for SS-18, and SS-9 is being phased out of service.

5 The SS-9 Mod. 3 was the Fractional Orbital Bombardment System (FOBS) and has never, as far as is known, been deployed.

6 Includes approximately 100 deployed within MRBM/IRBM fields. Many SS-11 silos have been converted to receive SS-17 and SS-19 missiles.

7 The SS-14 consists of the upper two stages of SS-13. It is a mobile system mounted on a tracked launcher and numbers cannot be estimated.

8 There has been only one test flight of SS-16 since 1975 and none has been deployed. This missile is specifically banned under SALT-II, although this treaty has not yet been ratified.

9 There have been reports that SS-18 (Mod. 1) has been deployed with a 50MT warhead, but this has never been substantiated.

10 SS-18 (Mod. 3) is reported to mount a lighter and more accurate re-entry vehicle than Mod. 1.

11 The SS-20 consists of the upper two stages of the SS-16 plus a Post-Boost Vehicle.

(950km)) circular orbit. Although known since the early 1970s, this satellite system only really came to public attention in January 1978 when the reactor on Cosmos 954 failed to separate and crashed in north Canada, causing much international concern.

The Soviets also use a smaller non-nuclear 'ferret' for ocean surveillance, which is placed in a 279 by 273 mile (450 by 440km) orbit, ie, somewhat higher than the nuclear-powered version. The first of these was Cosmos 699 (Dec 1974) and one is launched each year, between pairs of the nuclear satellites. In the wake of the Cosmos 954 debacle the Soviet ocean surveillance programme underwent a review. None was launched in 1978, but in April 1979 a resumption was signalled by the launching of two of the non-nuclear type, and it could be these that the US Secretary of Defense was referring to when he credited the USSR

with the capability of targetting US ships at sea.

Ideally early warning (EW) satellites should be in geosynchronous orbit, but, because of the distance of the launch sites from the Equator, Soviet EW satellites are placed in elliptical 12-hour orbits 310 by 24,800 miles (500 by 40,000km). The first was Cosmos 174 (Aug 1967) and the second Cosmos 174 (Dec 1968), but there were no more similar flights until Cosmos 520 (Sep 72). Launches then followed at a rate of one per year until 1977 when three were launched, indicating the achievement of operational status. Cosmos 775 (Oct 1975) was placed in geosynchronous orbit and may be the first of the second generation EW satellites.

C³ satellites

The Soviet military communications satel-

Right: An SS-4 (Sandal) IRBM being lifted by its transporter/erector for installation in the launch silo. This liquid-fuelled missile attained some notoriety in November 1962 when it was at the heart of the Cuban crisis and the confrontation between the USSR and the USA. SS-4 was the first operational Soviet missile to use storable liquid propellants, burning red-fuming nitric acid (RFNA) and kerosene. Although it was first deployed in 1958 the SS-4 remains in wide-scale service with the Strategic Rocket Forces and is reportedly deployed facing China in some numbers.

Below: A remarkable picture of an SS-9 test, with Multiple Re-entry Vehicles (MRVs) entering the Earth's atmosphere. The bright streak at the top shows the booster parts burning-up, while the prominent streaks below are the MRVs which would contain the weapon payload. The streaks are caused by the heat generated by re-entry into the atmosphere and disappear during cooling. The bottom three objects are associated with the payload and therefore have a similar spatial relationship.

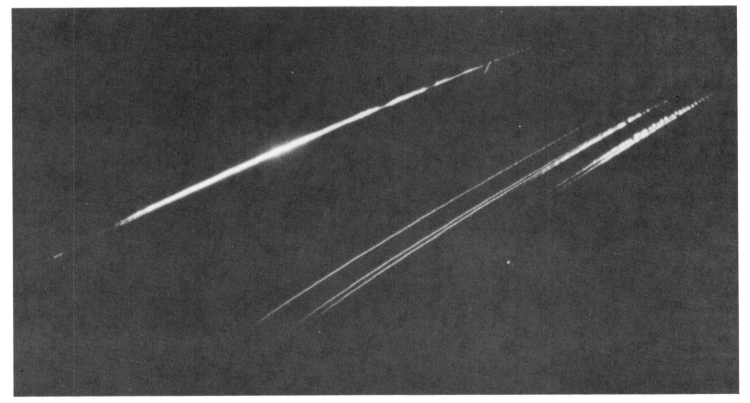

lites (COMSATS) fall into three groups. For point-to-point communications the Soviet armed forces use the Molniya 1, which flies a 25,300 by 300 mile (40,800 by 470km) elliptical orbit, allowing some eight hours' coverage during each pass. About three of these are launched per year interspersed with the later Molniya 2 and 3 series. They carry speech, telegraph and television circuits.

Another type of satellite is used to store information for short periods and then transmit it back to Earth. These are used when real-time transmission is not necessary. Eight are put into orbit at a time, with launches occurring two or three times a year; approximately 30 are operating at any one time. The third type of Soviet COMSAT is reputed to be used to record data from clandestine sensors and secret agents and then replay it to receiver stations on the

satellite's next pass over the USSR.

The Soviet navigation satellites are very similar to the US 'Transits', and, like them, went through distinct phases before becoming operational in 1971. About five are launched per year.

In contrast to the US, the USSR was slow to fly weather satellites, the first not being launched until 1967. Three operational military satellites are maintained in orbit 90° to 180° apart, passing over a given area at intervals of 6 to 12 hours.

Anti-satellite interception

At a time of deepening tension an opponent's satellite systems would make very tempting targets and the sudden destruction of the opponent's satellite-based command, communications and intelligence gathering systems would confer major advantages on the aggressor. In the USA studies of such a

concept were started in 1959 but dropped in late 1962. In October 1967, however, the USSR began testing a satellite interceptor system and their first successful interception was achieved on 20 October 1968. Cosmos 248—the target—had been launched the previous day carrying instruments to report on the miss-distance and Cosmos 249—the interceptor—was launched on 20 October. It first made several orbital adjustments to achieve an eccentric orbit and then made a fast fly-by of the target, finally destroying itself.

In the first series (1968–71) seven successful interceptions were made. Then, in 1971, a new launch vehicle was used and all except one of the interceptions followed the pattern of the earlier missions. The exception was the interception of Cosmos 400 by Cosmos 404 in April 1971. The latter was manoeuvred into a near co-orbit resulting in

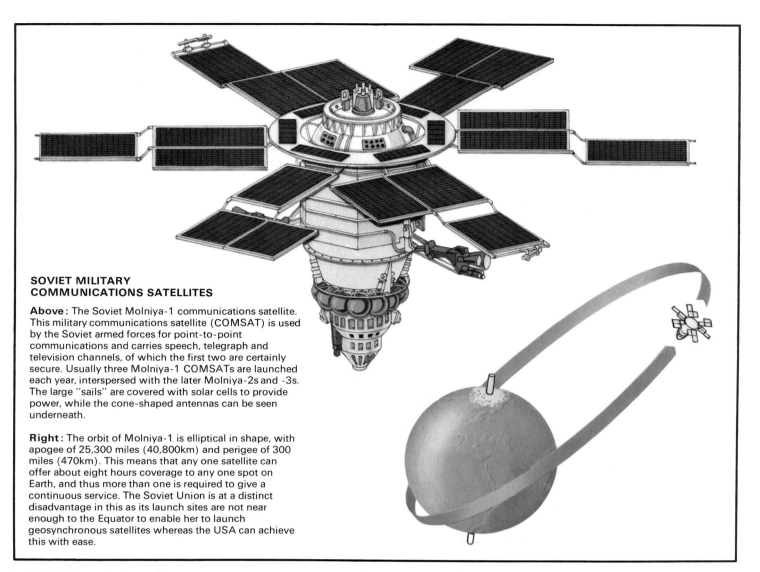

SOVIET MILITARY COMMUNICATIONS SATELLITES

Above: The Soviet Molniya-1 communications satellite. This military communications satellite (COMSAT) is used by the Soviet armed forces for point-to-point communications and carries speech, telegraph and television channels, of which the first two are certainly secure. Usually three Molniya-1 COMSATs are launched each year, interspersed with the later Molniya-2s and -3s. The large "sails" are covered with solar cells to provide power, while the cone-shaped antennas can be seen underneath.

Right: The orbit of Molniya-1 is elliptical in shape, with apogee of 25,300 miles (40,800km) and perigee of 300 miles (470km). This means that any one satellite can offer about eight hours coverage to any one spot on Earth, and thus more than one is required to give a continuous service. The Soviet Union is at a distinct disadvantage in this as its launch sites are not near enough to the Equator to enable her to launch geosynchronous satellites whereas the USA can achieve this with ease.

Left: A close-up of the correcting drive unit of the Molniya-1 COMSAT, used to ensure correct alignment in space.

a slower fly-by of the target and was then de-orbited over the Pacific. There was a break in Soviet interceptor flights between 1971 and 1976 and then they were resumed with Cosmos 804 intercepting Cosmos 803. The next test in April involved a new technique: Cosmos 814 was launched into orbit, but then fired an on-board engine almost immediately and went into a 'pop-up' trajectory. It made a fast fly-by of the target (Cosmos 803) and then re-entered over the Pacific. The entire mission took less than one orbit and the intention of this new flight profile was to reduce the time during which the satellite under attack could take evasive action. There were eight further missions in this second series of tests, which showed that the Soviets now had the ability to destroy reconnaissance, ferret and navigation satellites. This, not surprisingly, caused deep concern in Washington and in 1979 the US DoD reported to Congress that the USSR '... has an operational ASAT interceptor that could be used against some of our (US) critical satellite systems. Not only are they improving their orbital ASAT interceptor, but they are also engaged in other programs, including activities which appear to be ASAT related.'

In June 1978 the US and USSR began discussions in Helsinki to seek to limit

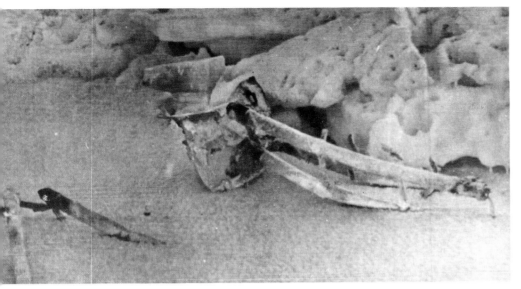

Left: This wreckage, found in Canada's North-West Territory, is believed to be part of the Soviet Cosmos-954 which crashed in January 1978.

Centre left: The USAF duty operator watching a visual display of the track of the Soviet Salyut-5 space mission.

Bottom left: A present-day laser beam can burn its way through metal, if focussed to a point. Such implements cannot yet be used in space, but Soviet research has alarmed the US DoD.

ASATs, and discussions are continuing in Vienna, although progress in this very complex area is bound to be slow. Any such agreement could, however, only follow on from SALT 2 and so the decision of President Carter to withdraw the draft treaty from Congressional consideration in January 1980 as a reprisal for Soviet aggression in Afghanistan is bound to have a 'knock-on' effect and will slow progress in the ASAT area even further.

For the future, speculations centre on a 'sci-fi' array of weaponry, particularly energy beams; either a chemical laser or a charged-particle beam. Such a weapon would be ideal for the killer-satellite role; it would not need to co-orbit nor even to approach the target closely, and could also engage multiple targets. Whether they are built or not depends not so much upon technological considerations as on political and strategic factors. Such a system could not only be used against satellites but also against ICBMs, attacking them as they leave the Earth's atmosphere during the boost phase and thus before they got anywhere near their targets. This is described in the USA as a 'benign weapon', in that it can only be used to destroy missiles or satellites and not cities or people.

Both the USA and the USSR are working on such systems, the American one being designated 'Sipapu', an American Indian name for 'sacred fire'. This is a charged particle beam for use against ICBMs; the technical principles are clearly understood, but factors such as cost, range, power requirements or effectiveness could still prove to be insuperable.

One report suggests that the intensity level needed to destroy an ICBM 4,000 miles distant could be produced by a chemical laser: either a 2 Megawatt laser using a 33ft (19m) mirror or a 5 Megawatt laser using a 13ft (4m) laser.

The Soviet Union has poured vast sums of money and effort into the space programme for its armed forces and has obtained as a result a very sophisticated and effective capability. Comparisons with the USA are difficult because the two countries' strategic needs are different, while the USSR's space programme is bound to be influenced by its infelicitous geographical location which deprives it of the ability (at any rate with existing technology) to launch geosynchronous satellites with ease. Further, the Soviets tend to launch single-mission vehicles whereas the USA apparently prefers multi-mission vehicles. However, the Soviet capability and its continuing programme are awesome and it is certainly well ahead in the ASAT field which just might give it an edge in the opening days of World War III.

Soviet Missiles

Bill Gunston

The following section gives information and often revealing illustrations of most of the major missiles (and rockets) used by the Soviet armed forces today. Some of the weapons are obsolete, not in production, or even in use by Warsaw Pact forces by now, but they have been included for their usefulness in giving pointers to the development of later-generation weapons. Other missiles that may have been developed by the Soviet Union have been excluded since in many cases the available information on them is based so much on mere conjecture that to have repeated it would have served no useful purpose. The weapons have been arranged by main function.

AIR-TO-AIR: TACTICAL

AA-2 Atoll

Dimensions: Length (IR) 9ft 2in (2.8m), (SARH) about 9ft 6in (2.9m); diameter 4.72in (120mm); span (early canard) 17.7in (450mm), (tail and later canard) 20.9in (530mm).
Launch weight: Typically 154lb (70kg).
Range: About 4 miles (6.4km).
Unlike most Russian weapons this AAM is beyond doubt a copy of a Western original, the early AIM-9B Sidewinder. When first seen on 9 June 1961, carried by various fighters in an air display, it was almost identical to the US weapon. Since then it has followed its own path of development, and like Sidewinder has diversified into IR and SARH versions. Body diameter is even less than that of Sidewinder, and so far as is known all models have the nose-to-tail sequence of AIM-9B. The 13.2lb (6.0kg) warhead is a BF type with smooth exterior. Believed to be designated K-13A or SB-06 in the Soviet Union, several early versions have been built in very large numbers as standard AAM for most models of MiG-21, which carry two on larger adapter shoes (which house the seeker cooling system in later models) on the underwing pylons. Licence production by the MiG complex of Hindustan Aeronautics has been in progress since the early 1970s, and it is generally believed there is also a Chinese version. Other users include all Warsaw Pact air forces, Afghanistan, Algeria, Angola, Cuba, Egypt, Finland, Iraq, North Korea, Syria and Vietnam. Since 1967 there have been later sub-types called AA-2-2 or Advanced Atoll by Nato. Some reports ascribe these designations to the SARH versions, but the consensus of opinion is that there are IR and radar versions of the first-generation missiles, in various sub-types, and IR and radar versions of the Advanced model. Several photographs indicate that later models have quite different control fins. These fins are driven in opposite pairs through 30°, and the later fin is unswept, has a cropped tip and greater area and is fitted after loading on the launcher. Like AIM-9 versions, IR missiles have hemispherical noses transparent to heat, and radar versions slightly tapered noses that appear opaque. Current carriers include all later fighter MiG-21s, with four missile shoes instead of two, and the MiG-23S swing-wing fighter which also carries later AAMs. Various versions have also been seen on MiG-17PFU fighter-trainers, in place of AA-1. All AA-2 models have plenty of combat experience in the Middle East, SE Asia and over India/Pakistan. Early results were not impressive. The pilot's aural buzz, which changes to an increasingly urgent warbling as the missile seeker locks-on and range closes, could not be relied upon as proof of subsequent homing. Today's missiles are probably more reliable, and it is assumed an all-aspect IR seeker is now also in service.

AA-3 Anab

Dimensions: Length (IR) 157in (4.0m), (SARH) 142in (3.6m); diameter 11.0in (280mm); span 51.0in (1.3m).
Launch weight: About 606lb (275kg).
Range: Probably at least 20 miles (32km).
This second-generation AAM was the first large long-range all-weather missile to reach the PVO, which it did at about the time dummy examples were displayed carried by an early Yak-28P interceptor at Tushino at the 1961 Soviet Aviation Day display. At that time it was at first thought by the West to be an ASM, but gradually it was identified as a straightforward AAM carried in both IR and SARH versions, usually one of each. The carriers are the Yak-28P in all versions except trainers, Su-11 and Su-15. All these aircraft have the radar called Skip Spin by Nato, a much more capable installation than those associated with the earlier AAMs and probably derived from the Scan Three fitted to the Yak-25. Believed to be designated RP-11, it operates in I-band between 8690/8995 MHz at peak power of 200 kW, with a PRF of 2700/3000 pps and pulse-width of about 0.5 microsec. It is assumed that CW illumination is proved for missile homing. AA-3 has large rear wings indexed in line with cruciform canard controls, and solid propulsion is assumed. Aerodynamics may be dervied from AA-1, though as there appear to be no wing control surfaces it is probable that the canards can be driven as four independent units for roll control. There is no information on either type of homing head; the motor has a single central nozzle, and may have boost/sustainer portions, and the warhead is amidships, with a proximity fuze. An AA-3-2 Advanced Anab has been identified since 1972, but how it is 'advanced' has not become public. Anab was used by several WP air forces but was not exported, and since 1975 has been progressively replaced by AA-7.

AA-4 Awl

Dimensions: Length 17ft (5.2m); diameter 12in (305mm); span 6ft (1.8m).
Launch weight: About 880lb (400kg).
Range: Possibly 62 miles (100km).
In the mid-1950s the Soviet Union took great interest in the British and American attempts to develop a fully active AAM, and by about 1958 had begun work itself, using unknown radar homing guidance. Virtually no information is available on the weapon beyond what can be deduced from the inert test vehicles carried at the 1961 Aviation Day display at Tushino under the wings of the large twin-engined Mikoyan prototype codenamed Flipper. (This aircraft sired the I-75F swept-wing interceptor with AA-3 Anabs and the single-engined world-speed-record breaker Ye-166.) Codenamed Awl by Nato's ASCC, the missiles were exceedingly large and superficially rather crude vehicles, with cruciforms of wings and fins of almost rectangular shape indexed in line on a large tubular body with a conical nose. There has been speculation that this missile, designated AA-4 by the DoD, was a two-stage device, the rear fins separating with the boost motor to leave a shorter missile that manoeuvred at hypersonic speed by body lift. Data are very approximate.

AA-5 Ash

Dimensions: Length (SARH) about 217in (5.51m), (IR) 205in (5.21m); diameter 12in (305mm); span 51in (1.3m).
Launch weight: both about 860lb (390kg).
Range: (SARH, author's estimate) about 40 miles (64km), (IR) about 13 miles (21km).
This large AAM was developed in 1954-59 specifically to arm the Tu-28P long-range all-weather interceptor, and genuine missiles were seen carried by a development aircraft of this family at the 1961 Aviation Day display at Tushino. Early versions of Tu-28, at first mistakenly reported as Blinder but corrected to Fiddler, carried two of these missiles on underwing pylons. So far as one can tell, they were SARH guided, associated with the Big Nose radar of the carrier aircraft, a very large and powerful I-band radar which had no counterpart operational in the West until the AWG-9 of 1974. The missile is matched to the radar in

Above: A MiG-21 with two AA-2 Atolls (or K-13A). These are infra-red homing although an advanced version is radar-homing.

Right: AA-3 Anabs (probably of the so-called 'advanced' type) arming a Flagon-F, the latest version of the Sukhoi Su-15 interceptor.

scale, being larger than any Western AAM. For many years Western estimates of AA-5 range were ludicrously low, but they are creeping up and may now be about half the true value for the radar version. Early Tu-28s are thought to have entered PVO service soon after 1961, filling in gaps around the Soviet Union's immense frontier. By 1965 the Tu-28P was being armed with the newly introduced IR version of this missile. This aircraft has four under-wing pylons carrying the IR version, with Cassegrain optics behind a small nose window, on the inners and the SARH model, with opaque (usually red-painted) conical nose on the outers. Early versions of MiG-25 Foxbat interceptor were also armed with this missile, usually one of each type. It is not known whether these aircraft also had Big Nose or an early model of Fox Fire radar. Ash has been reported to have served with most other WP air forces, but as no nation except the Soviet Union has used either of this missile's carrier aircraft the report appears to be false. This large weapon remains in the inventory.

AA-6 Acrid

Dimensions: Length (SARH) 248in (6.3m), (IR) 232in (5.9m); diameter 15.7in (400mm); span 88.6in (2.25m).
Launch weight: (SARH) about 1,874lb (850kg), (IR) 1,433lb (650kg).
Range: (SARH) 62 miles (100km), (IR) 15.5 miles (25km).

Largest AAM in the world, this awesome weapon family was designed around 1959-61 originally to kill the B-70 Valkyrie (which instead was killed by the US Congress) and entered PVO service as definitive armament of the Mach 3.2 MiG-25 'Foxbat A' interceptor. With four missiles, two IR-homers on the inner pylons and two SARH on the outers, this aircraft is limited to Mach 2.8. (It is, of course, totally a straight-line aircraft at such speeds, and in its original form was not intended for any kind of close encounter with hostile aircraft. Since 1975 developed versions with many changes have emerged able to withstand about +6g at Mach 2 and armed with AA-6 and AA-7 missiles.) Like the Tu-28, the MiG-25 was intended to detect targets at long range, using the Markham ground-air data link to give a cockpit display based on ground surveillance radars, switching to its own Fox Fire radar at about 100 miles' (160km) range. This equipment, likened to an F-4 AWG-10 in character but greater in power, includes CW aerials in slim wingtip pods to illuminate the target for the SARH missiles, which could probably lock-on and be fired at ranges exceeding 65 miles (100km); both peak-pulse/CW power and receiver-aerial size are considerably greater than for any Sparrow and closely similar to AWG-9/Phoenix. The IR version has much shorter range, though there is no reason to doubt that current Soviet technology is increasing IR fidelity as is being done elsewhere. Acrid has a large long-burning motor, giving a speed generally put at Mach 4.5 (the figure of 2.2 in one report is nonsense) and manoeuvres by canard controls, with supplementary ailerons (possibly elevons) on all four wings. The latter have the great area needed for extreme-altitude interception, for the B-70 cruised at well over 70,000ft (21km); but early Acrid missiles did not have look-down capability. Soviet films suggest that, when the range is close

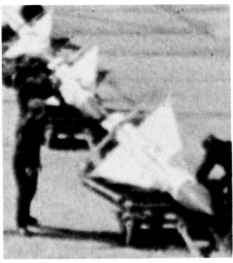

Above: A MiG-25 Foxbat-A interceptor with four AA-6 Acrids, SARH outboard, IR inboard. AA-6 is the world's largest AAM.

Right: AA-5 Ash missiles about to be mounted on Tu-28P long-range interceptors. These are of the IR-homing type.

enough, it is usual to follow national standard practice and ripple missiles in pairs, IR closely followed by SARH. The two homing heads are different in shape, as in the case of AA-5 which AA-6 probably replaces. No missiles of this family has been seen on any carrier aircraft except the PVO MiG-25.

AA-7 Apex

Dimensions: Length (SARH) 177in (4.5m), (IR) 166in (4.22m); diameter 10.2in (260mm); span 55.1in (1.4m).
Launch weight: (SARH) 705lb (320kg), (IR) slightly less.
Range: (SARH) 30 miles (48km), (IR) 12 miles (20km).

Standard medium-range AAM of the MIG-23S in all except export versions, this intensely interesting missile is large and apparently formidable. It has a unique configuration with three sets of aerodynamic cruciform surfaces, all indexed in line. It appears to be roll-stabilized by tail controls and to manoeuvre by the canards, but it is possible that in extreme manoeuvres both front and rear sets work together. Combined with a flight Mach number of 3.5 this could give unprecedented manoeuvrability. The central wings do not appear to carry movable surfaces. Predictably, Apex is issued in equal numbers of both SARH and IR versions, the homing heads having the usual distinctive forms. Most MiG-23S carry one of each type on their wing-glove pylons, leaving the body pylons for other stores. Twin Apex are also sometimes carried on each outer pylon of the MiG-25, though it is not known what overall mix of SARH/IR missiles is preferred. One report states that this family of missiles can be carried by the 'MiG-21' but no version of this aircraft appears to be compatible with the SARH Apex which is matched with High Lark radar. It is assumed that this missile replaces AA-3. It became known in the West in 1976. It is assumed that this missile is for use mainly at low/medium altitudes and has look-down/look-up capability. One report suggests a warhead of 88lb (40kg). Data are, of course, estimates.

AA-8 Aphid

Dimensions: Length (SARH) 84.6in (2.15m), (IR) 78.7in (2.0m); diameter 5.1in (130mm); span 20.5in (520mm).
Launch weight: 121lb (55.0kg) (possibly SARH heavier, IR lighter).
Range: (SARH) 9.3 miles (15km), (IR) possibly slightly less.

In contrast to its wealth of formidable large long-range AAMs, the PVO never had a good dog-fight weapon until this neat missile entered service after 1975 with the MiG-23S. Aerodynamically it appears to be a baby Acrid, though vastly different in scale. The canard controls are of very low aspect ratio and apparently rectangular (though some representations show a curved leading edge/tip). These surfaces are very close to the nose, and are driven by control impulses from either of the two usual types of homing seeker. It is suggested by Western drawings that there are the usual differences in head geomertry. MiG-23S can carry one of each type on the body pylons, replacing Atoll. It is not yet known if AA-8 can be carried by the MiG-21, the VTOL Yak-36 or by attack aircraft such as the MiG-27, Su-19 or Hind-D helicopter. One report gives warhead weight as 13.2lb (6kg).

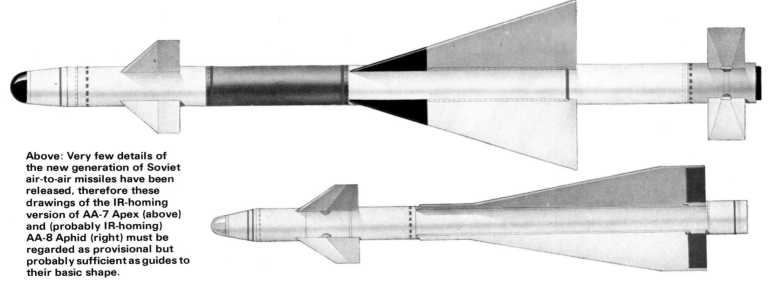

Above: Very few details of the new generation of Soviet air-to-air missiles have been released, therefore these drawings of the IR-homing version of AA-7 Apex (above) and (probably IR-homing) AA-8 Aphid (right) must be regarded as provisional but probably sufficient as guides to their basic shape.

AS-2 Kipper

Dimensions: Length 31ft (9.4m); span 16ft (4.9m).
Launch weight: In the region of 11,000lb (5,000kg).
Range: Estimated at 132 miles (212km).

First seen at the 1961 Soviet Aviation Day display, this large ASM has a more advanced aeroplane configuration than AS-1 and is considerably larger, the Tu-16 Badger-C carrying one missile on the centreline recessed into the weapon bay. Propulsion is by a single turbojet, possibly a Lyulka AL-5 of 11,023lb (5,000kg) thrust, in a short pod underslung at the rear. In appearance this missile faintly resembles Hound Dog, but is utterly different in mission, it being intended to attack moving targets with large radar signatures. Guidance probably duplicates that of AS-1: the inference has been that the missile was launched in the general direction of a known target, flying on autopilot and possibly steered from time to time by radio command either from the launch platform or from another aircraft, possibly at a lower level but closer to the target. At a distance of about 19 miles (30km) the missile's own seeker, either active radar or passive seeker, would lock-on to the target and home the weapon on to it. The AS-2 merely increases flight performance and payload. The warhead is conventional and very large. Cruising speed has generally been estimated at Mach 1.2, at high altitude, with a final dive on target at over Mach 2.

AS-3 Kangaroo

Dimensions: Length 49ft 1in (14.96m); span 22ft 6½in (9.00m).
Launch weight: About 22,045lb (10,000kg).
Range: full payload to 404 miles (650km).

This missile was also disclosed at the 1961 Soviet Aviation Day display, when one was carried low overhead by a Tu-20 (Tu-95) Bear bomber. This particular installation was probably a full-scale model to prove aircraft compatibility; the vehicle lacked many features seen in the actual missile, and a streamlined white nose appeared to be a temporary fairing forming part of the aircraft. This fairing is absent from some of the so-called Bear B and C carrier aircraft, many, if not all, of which belong to the AV-MF, the Soviet Naval Air

Force. The missile is aerodynamically similar to Mach 2 fighters of the mid-1950s, and could well have been based on the Ye-2A Faceplate by the Mikoyan bureau. This was powered by a Tumansky R-11 two-shaft afterburning turbojet rated at 11,244lb (5,100kg), and this fits the missile perfectly. AS-3 has exactly the same wing, circular nose inlet, small conical centrebody, long instrument boom at the bottom of the nose, identical aerodynamic controls and the same fuselage structure, and the ventral fin at the rear resembles that of the earlier Mikoyan Ye-50 prototype. The tips of the tailplane have anti-flutter pods similar to those flown on the MiG-19 fighter but not fitted to Ye-2. AS-3 is commonly described as 'operational since 1960' but was not seen in service until 1963. The main puzzle is how it steers itself to its target, because though it is easy to see how radio command/autopilot guidance could carry it up to 180 miles (290km) from the launch aircraft, despite cruising at Mach 2 with full afterburner, the ultimate range is put by the DoD at 350n.m., or 404 miles (650km), far beyond the visual horizon and implying subsonic cruise. A nuclear warhead is assumed, and this suggests inertial or preprogrammed guidance against cities, ports and similar large fixed targets. A few of these giant ASMs are thought still to be operational.

AS-4 Kitchen

Dimensions: Length about 37ft (11.3m); span about 8ft (2.4m).
Launch weight: About 15,432lb (7,000kg).
Range: Probably about 186 miles (300km), cruising at about Mach 2.

Yet another disclosure at the 1961 Soviet Aviation Day fly-past was this much more advanced and highly supersonic ASM, carried recessed under the fuselage of one of the ten Tu-22 Blinder supersonic bomber/reconnaissance aircraft that took part. This aircraft, dubbed Blinder B by Nato, had a larger nose radome, and other changes, as have several other Tu-22s seen in released photographs. Most aircraft of this sub-type have the outline of the AS-4 missile visible on their multi-folding weapon-bay doors, but the missile appears seldom to be carried today and in any case most remaining Tu-22s are of other versions, serving with the ADD and AV-MF. The missile itself has

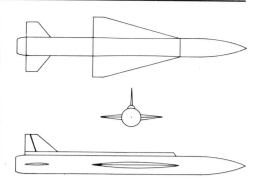

Above: This three-view of AS-4 Kitchen outlines its slender-delta wings and cruciform tail. The missile is highly supersonic.

slender-delta wings, a cruciform tail and, almost certainly, a liquid-propellant rocket. Prolonged discussion in the West has failed to arrive at any degree of certainty concerning the guidance, though the general consensus is that it must be inertial, possibly with midcourse updating by a Tu-95 or other platform. A homing system is obviously needed for moving targets such as ships. Both versions of the swing-wing Tu-26 Backfire multi-role platform are believed to have carried this missile, probably in AV-MF service.

Below left: The fast-diving AS-2 Kipper anti-shipping missile, as formerly carried by the Tu-16 Badger-C. It has a swept-wing configuration.

Bottom left: Resembling a Fitter interceptor, an AS-3 Kangaroo is released from the underbelly of a Tu-95 Bear-C. Few are thought to be in use.

Below: There seems to be a light on the left wing-tip of this AS-4 Kitchen slung beneath a low-flying Blinder-B. AS-4 has also armed Backfire-A and -B.

Above: A Soviet-supplied combination: Egyptian Air Force Tu-16 Badger-G carrying AS-5 Kelt missiles with nose radomes and tail-warning radar. Egyptian bombers launched a number of AS-5s against Israeli targets in the 1973 October war.

Left: A Tu-16 with an AS-6 Kingfish under the left wing. This highly-accurate missile is thought to be carried in pairs by Backfire-B for stand-off strike against land targets from high and low level, and it is also possible that it has an anti-shipping role.

AS-5 Kelt

Dimensions: Length about 32ft 1in (9.78m); span 15ft 7in (4.75m).
Launch weight: About 10,580lb (4,800kg).
Range: Widely reported to reach 200 miles (320km).

First seen in a released photograph of September 1968, showing one of these missiles under the wing of a Tu-16, AS-5 is based on the airframe of AS-1 and some may even be rebuilds. In place of the turbojet and nose-to-tail duct there is a rocket with extensive liquid-propellant tankage. In the nose is a large radome. Superficially the nose and the underbody fairing appear to be identical to those of SS-N-2 Styx and AS-5 thus is credited with the same choice of active radar or passive IR homing, having cruised to the vicinity of the target on autopilot, with initial radio-command corrections. By the early 1970s deliveries are thought to have exceeded 1,000, all of them carried by the so-called Badger G. This launch platform has the same pylons as the Badger B, and the broad nose radome of Badger C. In the early 1970s about 35 of these aircraft, plus missiles, were supplied to the Egyptian air force, possibly with Soviet crews and specialist tradesmen. In the Yom Kippur war in October 1973 about 25 missiles were launched against Israeli targets. According to the Israelis 20 were shot down en route, at least one by an F-4; five penetrated the defences. A supply dump was one of the targets hit, but at least two AS-5s homed automatically on the emissions from Israeli radar stations. All the missiles were released at medium height of some 29,528ft (9,000m), reaching a speed of about Mach 0.95; in the denser air at low level speed fell to about 0.85.

AS-6 Kingfish

Dimensions: Length in the region of 35ft (10.7m); span about 8ft (2.4m).
Launch weight: In the neighbourhood of 11,000lb (5,000kg).
Range: Varies from about 404 miles (650km) at high altitude to 155 miles (250km) at sea level.

At first thought to be a development of AS-4, this completely new missile was gradually re-assessed as the first Soviet ASM publicly known that offers precision guidance over intercontinental ranges. It is still largely an enigma in the West, but is believed to have a very large fuselage with pointed nose, low-aspect-ratio delta wings and quite small aircraft-type tail controls. Propulsion is almost certainly by an advanced integral ram-rocket, and key features of AS-6 are much higher flight performance and dramatically better accuracy than any previous Soviet ASM. It clearly reflects vast advances in inertial guidance and nuclear-warhead design, and it is generally believed to possess terminal homing, either by active radar, area-correlation or some passive method. Development appears to have been protracted, and though reported prior to 1972 was still not in wide service in 1975, though by 1977 it was carried under the wings of both the Tu-16 (sub-type unknown) and Tu-26 Backfire. User services certainly include the AV-MF and possibly the ADD. Launched at about 36,000ft (10,973m) the missile climbs rapidly to about 59,000ft (17,983m) for cruise at about Mach 3. It finally dives on its target, the warhead yield being estimated at 200 kT.

AIR-TO-SURFACE: TACTICAL

AS-7 Kerry

One of the more puzzling gaps in the immense array of Soviet airpower has been any type of tactical ASM. Even today this missile, about which little is known, is often reported as an interim type. It is said to have a solid rocket motor, radio command guidance, conventional warhead, range of about 6¼ miles (10km) at Mach 0.6, launch weight of 2,645lb (1,200kg) and to be launched at heights between 1,000 and 10,000ft (300-3,000m). The chief carrier is said to be the Su-19, and certainly a weapon of this size would be a problem for some earlier FA (Frontovaya Aviatsiya) aircraft. There is no reason to doubt that tactical ASMs roughly equivalent to Bullpup and other early Western missiles have been tested in the Soviet Union for 25 years, but none has apparently entered service.

AS-8

As yet not publicly associated with a Nato reporting name, this is said to be a 'fire and forget' missile to be carried by all Soviet attack helicopters, such as the Mi-24 Hind-D. Described as similar to the American Hellfire, it is reported to have a solid rocket motor, passive radiation seeker (Hellfire has a seeker that homes on laser radiation) and range of 5-6¼ miles (8-10km) at a flight Mach number of 0.5-0.8. IOC was apparently achieved in 1977 when AS-8 missiles began to appear on Mi-24 units in East Germany.

AS-X-9, AS-X-10 and ATASM

The AS-X-9 is described as an anti-radiation missile, launched from Su-19 and other FA attack aircraft. Assumptions are that it has a solid rocket motor, large conventional warhead, passive radiation seeker of unknown sophistication, and a range of 50-56 miles (80-90km).

The AS-X-10 is reported to be an EO-homing ASM, with supposed solid rocket motor, conventional warhead, and range of about 6¼ miles (10km) at Mach 0.6-0.8.

The Advanced Tactical ASM is believed to be a larger version of AS-X-10 with inertial or command mid-course guidance and EO-homing over the last part of its mission of up to 25 miles (40km) at high-subsonic speed. Presumably it will become AS-X-11 to the DoD and receive a Nato codename.

SA-1 Guild

Dimensions: Length about 39ft 5in (12m); diameter 27.6in (700mm); span about 110in (2.8m).
Launch weight: About 7,055lb (3,200kg).
Range: One British estimate is 20 miles (32km).
First seen in the Red Square parade in November 1960, this SAM system was an incredible technical achievement, both in technology and in sheer scale. Development must have begun immediately after World War I, because this system—called SA-1 by the DoD and given the Nato reporting name 'Guild'—is estimated to have been in operational service in 1954, earlier than any other SAM apart from the Swiss RSC family. The main radar, called Yo-Yo by Nato, is a tour de force: it has six rotating aerials, covering an arc of 70° in both azimuth and elevation, and uses flapping-beam techniques to track more than 30 targets simultaneously. The peak power is estimated at at least 2 MW, on a frequency of some 3GHz (E/F-band, the old S-band). For this and other reasons the DoD has always regarded this system as part of the Soviet Union's fixed strategic defences, though the missile itself has invariably been seen on the articulated transporter, with ZIL-157 type tug, which brings reloads to the (never seen) launcher. The missile is very large, yet has usually been credited with a rather poor flight performance, partly because it is thought to have no separate boost motor. Main propulsion is officially described as liquid-propellant. Control is by cruciforms of powered canard fins and cropped-delta rear wings each with an elevon or aileron. There appears to be a nose radar, and active homing would be entirely in keeping with this remarkable weapon. Guild has never been exported, and since the 1960s its numbers are assumed to have been dwindling from a peak of many hundred batteries.

SA-2 Guideline

Dimensions: Length 35ft 2in (10.7m) (varies with sub-type); diameter (boost) 27.5in (700mm), (missile) 21.6in (500mm); span (boost) 86.6in (2.2m), (missile) 66.9in (1.7m).
Launch weight: Typically 5,070lb (2,300kg).
Range: Up to 31 miles (50km).
For uniformity the Western designations of this system are given, though after capture of large numbers by Israel from 1967 onwards there are few secrets left and the Soviet designation is reported to be V75SM, the missile alone being (in one version) V750 VK. Unlike SA-1 this weapon system is quite normal in design, and it has for 20 years been perhaps the most widely used missile system of any kind in the world. Unlike SA-1 it was planned as a general-purpose land-mobile system, though the complete system is very bulky and weighs over 100 tons. First put into production in about 1956, this system has ever since been subjected to updating and improvement. The original basic missile comprised a shapely weapon with a cruciform of cropped-delta wings towards the rear, a cruciform of small fixed nose fins and a third cruciform of powered control fins at the tail, all indexed in line. In tandem was a solid boost motor with four very large delta fins, again indexed in line, one opposite pair of which had trailing-edge controls for initial roll-stabilization and gathering into the guidance beam. The missile rode on a ZIL-157 hauled articulated trailer from which it was pulled backwards on to a large rotatable launcher incorporating many system-items and elevated to about 80° before firing, with blast deflector positioned at the rear. The boost burned for 4.5 sec, the acid/kerosene sustainer then burning for a further 22 sec. Apart from surveillance radars and Side Net heightfinders, the standard radar, called Fan Song by Nato, operates in A/B (E/F) or D/E (G) bands, locked-on to the target to feed data to the computer van. The latter set up the launcher and, after liftoff, used a UHF link to pass steering commands to the missile, which had to be centred in the guidance beam within 6 sec if it was not to fall out of control. The warhead was a 286.6lb (130kg) charge with an internally grooved heavy casing. Various impact, command and proximity fuzes were used. Subsequently there have been too many modifications to follow, involving radar, guidance, control, warhead, fuzing and, above all, ECCM. Very extensive combat experience in the Middle East and South East Asia forced numerous changes on top of an existing programme of new versions. The first externally evident change was introduction of cropped delta nose fins instead of rectangles. The latest family, first seen in 1967, have larger white-painted warheads (said to be nuclear), no nose fins and no boost control surfaces. Most effort has gone into the radars, called Fan Song A to G in seven distinct types with track-while-scan elements and a sawtooth-profile flapping Lewis scanner backed up by various parabolic dishes. Once exceeding 4,000, SA-2 launchers in the Soviet Union are rapidly running down. Other users included Aghanistan, Albania, Algeria, Bulgaria, China, Cuba, Czechoslovkia, Egypt, East Germany, Hungary, India, Iraq, North Korea, Libya, Mongolia, Poland, Romania, Syria, Vietnam and Yugoslavia. A naval version is SA-N-2.

Below: SA-3 Goa SAMs which are widely used by Warsaw Pact countries. Radars used in their launch and control are 'Flat Face' (acquisition) and 'Low Blow'.

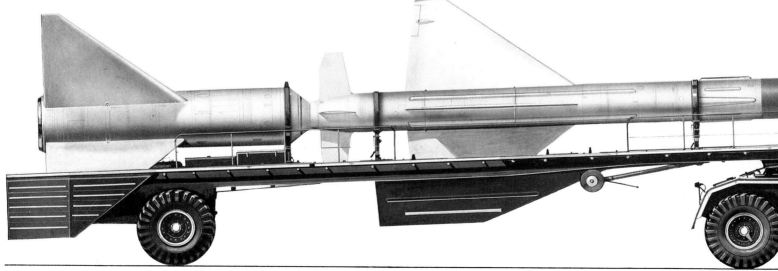

SA-3 Goa

Dimensions: Length about 22ft (6.7m); diameter (boost) 27.6in (700mm), (missile) 18.1in (460mm); span (boost) 59in (1.5m), (missile) 48in (1.22m).
Launch weight: About 882lb (400kg).
Range: Up to 18 miles (29km).

The medium-altitude partner to SA-2, this equally aged system is widely used by the Soviet Ground Forces, Navy and many other countries. The missile is carried in pairs on ZIL-157 family tractors, mounted direct on the vehicle and not needing a trailer. The inclined ramps also serve as launchers. The same installation has been seen on three tracked chassis, and in Yugoslavia a quad installation is standard. When associated with the SA-2 this missile is fired from a power-rotated twin launcher elevated to 75°. Radars used in this system include P-15 Flat Face, a UHF acquisition set with superimposed parabolic aerials and range to about 155 miles (250km), and Low Blow, a target-tracking and missile-guidance radar of up to 53 miles (85km) range with mechanically scanned trough aerials at 45°. SA-3 and SA-2 batteries can also have early warning from P-12 Spoon Rest radars. SA-3 has a large tandem boost motor with giant rectangular fins which spread out through 90° at launch, a solid sustainer, fixed rear wings with ailerons on two opposite surfaces, and powered nose control fins. The warhead weighs 132lb (60kg). Details of guidance must

be fully understood in the West, but have not been published. Terminal homing is provided, almost certainly by semi-active means, and Low Blow can steer up to two missiles simultaneously to the same target, with unspecified means of overcoming ECM. This missile is used by Cuba, Czechoslovakia, Egypt, East Germany, Hungary, India, Iraq, Libya, Peru, Poland, Soviet Union, Syria, Uganda, Vietnam, Yugoslavia and, in SA-N-1 form, several navies.

SA-4 Ganef

Dimensions: Length 29ft 6in (9.0m); diameter 31½in (800mm); span 102in (2.6m).
Launch weight: About 3,968lb (1,800kg).
Range: To about 47 miles (75km).

First displayed in the Red Square parade on May Day 1964, this impressive long-range SAM is part of every Soviet Ground Forces combat army, to provide AA defence in great depth against targets at all speeds and altitudes. Fully mobile and amphibious, the SA-4 system moves with the advancing forces in nine batteries, each comprising three launch vehicles, one loading vehicle and one Pat Hand radar. Three of the batteries move forward about 6½ miles (10km) behind the most forward elements, and the other batteries follow some 9⅓ miles (15km) further back. All are ready to fire at all times. The basic missile has four solid boost motors and a kerosene-fuelled ramjet sustainer

giving great speed and manoeuvrability to the limits of its considerable range. Missiles are put on targets initially by Long Track mobile surveillance radar (reported variously as operating in E-band and I-band and having very long range, most unlikely with I-band) and the widely used H-band Pat Hand provides command guidance and semi-active homing, the missile's receiver aerials being dipoles projecting ahead of the wings. It is persistently reported that this missile can also be used in the tactical surface-to-surface role, though how it is guided in this role has not been explained. It is typical of Soviet defence funding that a completely new tracked amphibious vehicle was developed to carry both the twin missiles ready for launch and the pair following close behind as reloads. Unlike previous Soviet SAMs this missile has its fixed fins indexed at 45° to the moving wings. There is a large conventional warhead. SA-4 was deployed briefly in Egypt around 1970. It is standard with the Soviet Ground Forces and is gradually being issued to other Warsaw Pact armies beginning with East Germany and Czechoslovakia.

SA-5 Gammon

Dimensions: Length about 54ft 1½in (16.5m); diameter (boost) about 44in (1.1m), (missile) about 33½in (850mm); span (main wings) 156in (3.96m).
Launch weight: About 22,046lb (10,000kg).
Range: Estimated at 155 miles (250km).

One of the largest SAMs ever developed, this missile was first seen in Red Square in November 1963, when the commentator called it an 'anti-missile missile'. At once dubbed 'Griffon' by Nato, it has since become generally known as Gammon. Capability against an ICBM is clearly limited, but the exceptional speed and range of SA-5 certainly makes it useful against many other types of missile and all aircraft. It does not travel with the Soviet Ground Forces but instead is the longest-ranged anti-aircraft missile of the ZA-PVO, the 'zenith rocket troops of the air defence of the homeland'. This missile is launched singly from a trainable fixed launcher, but in parades it rides on a special articulated trailer, pulled by a Ural 357S tug, a separate crane being needed to transfer missiles to launchers. The target-tracking and missile-guidance radar is Square Pair, a large and powerful set believed to have been in use since 1964 but apparently still almost unknown by the West. Square Pair is said to be associated with Back Net or Barlock surveillance and Side Net heightfinder radars. These provide data on distant targets, allowing Square Pair to bring the missile to the correct block of airspace. Then the missile's own active radar, with a dish at least 24in (600mm) diameter, homes the missile to the target. SA-5 is believed to have third-stage propulsion for the separated warhead and terminal guidance system. Control for most of the trajectory is by cruciform rear fins, with ailerons for roll control. SA-5 was also known as the Tallinn system, because it was originally seen deployed near the Estonian capital. Today about 1,200 launchers are thought to be operational in many areas of the Soviet Union; no SA-5 installations have been reported from other countries. Warhead is thought to be nuclear, and is certainly nuclear in supposed improved models—associated with a mobile phased-array ABM radar—observed on test from Sary Sagan in 1972.

Top of page: Two SA-4 Ganef missiles are carried in a vertically staggered pair on tracked amphibious launch vehicle. Launch is by automatic system including 'Long Track' surveillance radar.

Left: SA-5 Gammons are seen at the back of this section of a parade. They are believed to be the largest conventional SAMs ever to have gone into service. Their launcher has not been seen.

Left: The SA-5 Gammon on its transport vehicle (not launcher). The red-painted nose contains the active radar, and the warhead (immediately behind) is believed to incorporate third-stage motor to steer to final interception. The missile was formerly called 'Griffon' by NATO.

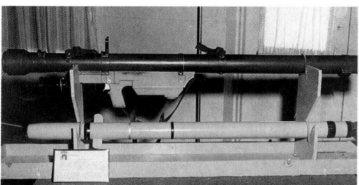

SA-6 Gainful

Dimensions: Length (with rocket nozzle) 20ft 4in (6.2m); diameter 13.2in (335mm); span (wings) 49in (1,245mm), (tail) 60in (1,524mm).
Launch weight: 1,213lb (550kg).
Range: To 37 miles (60km) against high-altitude target, half as much at low altitude.

Seen in Red Square on 7 November 1967, and many times since, this outstanding SAM system appeared to be misinterpreted by Western observers, even the ramjet inlet ducts merely being described as 'prominent fairings'. Suddenly in the Yom Kippur war in 1973 Israeli combat aircraft began to tumble out of the sky like ninepins, and SA-6 acquired an instant reputation for destroying its target no matter what the latter tried in the way of manoeuvres or ECM. The whole system is mobile, air-portable and amphibious, being mounted on modified PT-76 chassis. A fire unit comprises three vehicles each with triple launchers, a loading vehicle and a Straight Flush radar vehicle. Each Soviet Ground Force army deploys five such batteries, three keeping 3 miles (5km) behind the front line and the other two filling the gaps 6 miles (10km) further back. Various radars, notably Long Track, provide early warning and preliminary target data. In Egypt the van-mounted P-15 Flat Face has been deployed with SA-6 units, both in parades and in the field. But the key guidance radar is Straight Flush, which has two major turret-mounted aerials and provides several functions. The top dish tracks the chosen target with a 1° H-band (7.7-8 GHz) pencil beam, and guidance commands are transmitted to the missile in I-band (8.5-9 GHz), with frequency agility over a wide spread. Terminal semi-active homing is CW, to which Israel in 1973 had no antidote except generally useless chaff. The missile is a beautiful design, with integral ram/rocket propulsion since urgently copied in the West. The solid boost motor accelerates the missile at about 20g to Mach 1.5, burns out and the nozzle is jettisoned. The case then becomes a ramjet, with a larger nozzle, fed with ram air from the four ducts and with hot gas from a solid-fuel generator, which continues acceleration to a steady speed of about Mach 2.8. Control is by cruciform centrebody wings and fixed rear fins with ailerons for roll control and carrying command/beacon aerials. The 176lb (80kg) warhead normally has impact and proximity fuzes, with IR fuzing a source of argument in the West. Users include Bulgaria, Czechoslovakia, Egypt, Iraq, Libya, Mozambique, Poland, Soviet Union, Syria and Vietnam.

SA-7 Grail

Dimensions: Length 53¼in (1.35m); diameter 2¾in (70mm).
Launch weight: (missile alone) 20.3lb (9.2kg).
Range: Up to 6¼ miles (10km).

Originally called Strela (arrow) in the West, this simple infantry weapon was originally very similar to the American Redeye, and suffered from all the latter's deficiencies. These included inability of the uncooled PbS IR seeker to lock on to any heat source other than the nozzle of a departing attacker—with the single exception of most helicopters which could be hit from the side or even ahead, if the jetpipe projected enough to give a target. The basic missile is a tube with dual-thrust solid motor, steered by canard fins. The operator merely aims the launch tube at the target with an open sight, takes the first pressure on the trigger, waits until the resulting red light turns green (indicating the seeker has locked on) and applies the full trigger pressure. The boost charge fires and burns out before the missile clears the tube. At a safe distance the sustainer ignites and accelerates the missile to about Mach 1.5. The 5.5lb (2.5kg) warhead has a smooth fragmentation casing and both graze and impact fuzes. This is lethal only against small aircraft, and in the Yom Kippur war almost half the A-4s hit by SA-7s returned to base. Height limit is still widely given as 4,921ft (1,500m), but in 1974 a Hunter over Oman

Top left: SA-6 Gainful SAMs revealed in an Egyptian military parade to mark the first anniversary of the Yom Kippur war. SA-6s were very effective against low-flying Israeli strike aircraft.

Above left: A captured SA-7 Grail: the missile is the slim grey tube with flick-out fins. Launcher is above it.

Above: The original SA-7 Grail, here in the hands of a Soviet artilleryman, is a limited weapon, similar to US Redeye.

was hit at 11,500ft (3,505m) above ground level. An improved missile has been in production since 1972 with augmented propulsion, IR filter to screen out decoys, and much better guidance believed to house a cryogenic cooler in a prominent launcher nose ring. There are probably 50,000 missiles and nearly as many launchers, large numbers of them in the hands of terrorists all over the world. Users include Angola, Bulgaria, Cuba, Czechoslovakia, East Germany, Egypt, Ethiopia, Hungary, Iraq, North Korea, Kuwait, Libya, Mozambique, Peru, Philippines (Muslim guerrillas), Poland, Romania, Soviet Union, Syria, Vietnam and PDR of the Yemen. A small-ship version is SA-N-7.

Right: The very impressive SA-8 Gecko SAMs revealed in Red Square in 1975. The whole system is air-portable and amphibious. Four rounds are carried on a rotatable launcher, plus an estimated 12 in reload magazines. Two missiles are normally launched simultaneously at one target. The missile is believed to have infra-red homing.

Above: Side and front views of SA-8 Gecko system. Each pair of missiles has its tracking aerial, and the large dish in the centre is the target-tracking radar.

SA-8 Gecko

Dimensions: Length 10ft 6in (3.2m); diameter 8.25in (210mm); span 25.2in (640mm).
Launch weight: About 419lb (190kg).
Range: Probably up to about 8 miles (13km).

A surprise in the 7 November 1975 Red Square parade was a dozen completely new vehicles each carrying quadruple launchers for this advanced and highly mobile system which was rather incorrectly called 'the Soviet Roland', and it was almost certainly derived from SA-N-4. Despite its great size the 6 × 6 amphibious vehicle is air-portable in an An-22, and carries missiles ready to fire. Inside the body, or hull, are an estimated eight further missiles, enough for two reloads. Towards the rear of the vehicle is the rotatable and elevating quad launcher, surmounted by a folding surveillance radar probably operating in F-band at under 4 GHz. Between this installation and the cab is a large guidance group comprising a central target-tracking radar, two missile guidance-beam radars, two command-link horns for gathering, an optical tracker and an LLLTV and telescopic sight. All the radars have flat-fronted Cassegrain aerials, the main set being a J-band (13-15 GHz) tracker with a range of about 15½ miles (25km). Each guidance aerial has a similar but smaller geometry, with limited azimuth movement; below each is the command link horn. After careful study semi-active radar homing has been judged unlikely and it is believed all SA-8 missiles have IR homing. The missile has small fixed tail fins, small nose canard controls, a radar beacon and external flare. The dual-thrust solid motor gives very high acceleration to a burn-out speed greater than Mach 2, the average speed in a typical interception being about Mach 1.5. It is believed missiles are fired in pairs, with very short time-interval, the left and right missile-tracking and command systems operating on different spreads with frequency-agility in the I-band to counter ECM and jamming by the target, with TV tracking as a back-up. The warhead weighs about 110lb (50kg) and has a proximity fuse. So far as is known SA-8 is used only by the Soviet Ground Forces, in extreme forward areas.

SA-9 Gaskin

Dimensions: Length 71in (1.8m); diameter 4.33in (110 mm); span (fins are not retractable) 11.8in (300mm).
Launch weight: 66lb (30kg).
Range: Several miles/km.

First seen in the November 1975 Red Square parade, installed in BRDM-2A amphibious scout cars, this light SAM system was at once assumed to use a missile similar to a scaled-up SA-7. In all examples so far seen the apparently simple vehicle carries little but four launch boxes (sometimes only the outer pair are fitted) on an elevating and rotating mount which for travelling can fold the boxes down on to the rear decking where

Right: In one of the few SA-9 Gaskin photographs, only the outer pair of four launcher boxes is carried; both crew members are standing .

protective grills can be clipped around the sides. There appears to be no radar, optical sight or other target acquisition or tracking system, though obviously one must be fitted. It is assumed that targets are acquired by radars in other vehicles which tell-off individual SA-9 operators by radio and may even slew the launcher automatically. Thereafter it is assumed that the operator sights visually and uses a small control panel with red/green lights to launch single, twin or all four missiles. In 1977 there were reports of BRDM-2A vehicles fitted with a new turret with a radar, almost certainly closely related to (or identical to) the Gun Dish used with the ZSU-23-4 Shilka AAA vehicle. Shilka has always been installed in the amphibious tracked PT-76 chassis, and this NBC-sealed vehicle would be ideal for SA-9 because it could carry missiles, radar and reload missile boxes whereas the four-wheeler is cramped. SA-9 is used by Warsaw Pact forces and Egypt, and is believed to be used by Syria, Iraq and possibly Iran. Data are approximate estimates.

SA-10

Dimensions: Length said to be 23ft (7m); diameter 17¾in (450mm).
Launch weight: Possibly 3,300lb (1,500kg).
Range: Between the figures cited below.

As yet not associated with a public Nato name, and probably more correctly called SA-X-10, this new SAM system is still little understood in the West and has been the subject of conflicting and often silly reports. The few things that seem to be agreed are that

it has exceptional flight performance, uses CW radar and is intended to kill cruise missiles. It therefore needs low-level capability and guidance against manoeuvring targets with extremely small radar signatures. The DoD announced the existence of SA-10 in October 1977, saying it might be in operational services in 'seven to eight years'. In 1978 two journalists claimed that the SecDef had privately told Congress it could be in service 'by the end of 1978'. This was hotly denied by the DoD, which nevertheless a few weeks later publicly stated that the first deployment could be in 1979. Range is given as '50km' (31 miles) in some reports and as 2,000 n.m. (3,700km) in others. Some reports announce that the Soviet Union would need '500 to 1,000' of these missiles, while in others the figures are '5,000 to 10,000'. In each case the cost of such deployment is put at '$30 billion'. Most reports aver that a single-stage rocket gives 100g acceleration, which is possible provided that the range is nothing like 2,000 n.m. Cruising speed is generally put at Mach 5, and the missile is said to have terminal homing by active radar; the CW set is presumably the airborne radar used for terminal guidance, though it could apply to both radars.

ABM-1B Galosh

Dimensions: Length about 65ft (19.8m); diameter (fins folded) 101in (2.57m).
Launch weight: About 72,000lb (32,700kg).
Range: About 200 miles (322km) reported, probably several times greater, but accurate figures have not been revealed. *continued on next page*

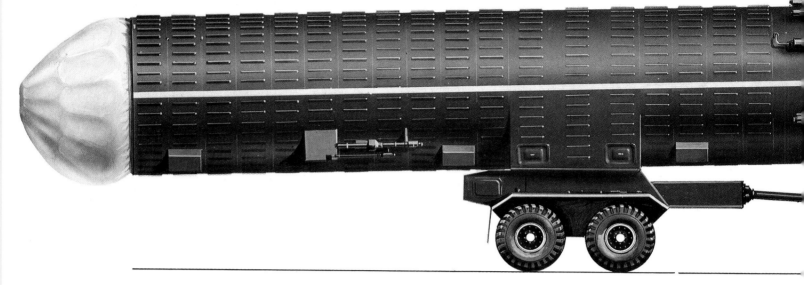

Originally called SA-7 by the DoD, a designation later applied to the shoulder-fired Grail, this system is the only ABM in operational use in the world. It uses a large conical multi-stage missile first seen (or rather not seen) in its tubular container in the Red Square parade of November 1964. This was the first showing of the MAZ-543 eight-wheel tug, which has since become standard for towing many ICBMs on separate trailers, the tug accommodating numerous crew-members. With Galosh the missile travels in a ribbed tubular container pivoted above the rear wheels and with its own powered truck further back. With this missile no attempt is made to carry extra crew in the tug. The missile travels base-first, the open front of the container revealing four first-stage nozzles. The other end of the container was covered by a fabric shroud attached over a light framework until 1969, when a light rigid convex end-closure apparently of plastic material was substituted. It is assumed that the travel container is mounted vertically in an underground silo and used as the launcher, the missile going through the top closure, with the tail fins unfolding beyond the tube. There are thought to be three propulsion stages

and a thermonuclear warhead with a yield of several megatons (one report says 2-3 MT). The SALT I treaty allowed the Soviet Union to deploy 100 ABM launchers, and in the late 1960s eight extensive ABM complexes were started in areas around Moscow. These were to be fed with early-warning data by the first of the Hen series of gigantic ABM radars, Hen House. This was described by Dr John S. Foster, Director of DoD Research & Engineering in 1970, as 'like three football fields lined up end-to-end and standing on their sides . . . to provide . . . the same radar coverage that the US will have some eight years from now if all the Safeguard program is completed' (which, of course, it was not). Hen House installations are remote from Galosh sites, for example near Irkutsk in Siberia, in Latvia and near the Barents Sea. The Galosh sites themselves each contain two large battle-management radars of the Dog House or Cat House phased-array type, four Triad (Try Add) engagement radars including Chekhov target/missile trackers, and 16 launch silos. Dog House became operational around 1968 and has a range of some 1,750 miles (2,816km). Each complex also has large

computer installations and other supporting services. In the event only four complexes (16 launchers) have been completed, but ABM research continues 'on a massive scale'. Flight testing of an improved SH-4 Galosh missile was reported in 1976, with a manoeuvrable bus which can 'loiter' while incoming warheads are separated from chaff and decoys, restarting its propulsion several times and then homing for the kill. Since 1976 the Soviet Union has also been building OTH radars said by DoD to be 'on a scale much greater than anything we have ever considered deploying'.

Anti-SRAM

As yet not associated with a public Nato or DoD designation, this system has been persistently reported since 1974. It is said to be mobile, despite incorporating a powerful C-band PAR (said to be called X-3 in the United States). The missile has launched acceleration of about 100g to speed greater than Mach 5. No data.

SURFACE-TO-AIR: SEA

SA-N-1 Goa

Data: As for SA-3 Goa.
So far as one can tell from poor-quality photographs this SAM system for large ships uses a missile identical to the land-based SA-3, but almost every other part of the system is completely different. So far as Western observers can tell the basic installation is standardized, with a two-deck magazine for 20 reload missiles, assembled with tandem booster and stored vertically, which progress on railed trolleys to the vertical hoist which loads them on to the launcher set to 90° elevation. The launcher has twin rails on a stabilized mounting and can be driven by powerful servos to the

azimuth and elevation of the associated radar. The latter is known to Nato as the Peel Group, and like most Soviet shipboard radars is of instantly distinctive appearance with four solid-reflector ellipsoidal dishes, a large pair with axes vertical and horizontal and a small pair with axes vertical and horizontal. It is thought the large aerials, probably G/H-band, are for searching the sky in the direction indicated by the surveillance radar (usually Head Net) and locking-on to the target, thereafter commanding the small pair, thought to be I-band, which provide precision tracking and missile guidance. The installation of magazine, loader, launcher and radars is fitted both fore and aft in the four Kresta I cruisers and 19 Kashin/Kashin-Mod destroyers. The four Kynda cruisers have one system forward, while the eight Kotlin-SAM and seven Kanin destroyers each have one system aft. A further Kotlin-SAM, Warsawa, serves with the Polish Navy, and in 1978 SA-N-1 was identified on a new Indian frigate design.

SA-N-2

Data: As for SA-2.
A single ship, the ageing cruiser Dzerzhinski, was around 1969 rebuilt with X turret replaced by a major installation for what appears to be a unique ship installation using the SA-2 Guideline (V750VK) SAM. The installation appears to occupy most of the considerable space between the aft funnel and Y turret. The stabilized twin launcher is quite unlike land launchers for this missile and has the launch rail above the missile. Ahead of the launcher is a hangar-like building which probably encloses the reload system. Ahead of this is the Fan Song E radar group, which almost certainly posed problems on a ship (especially in rough weather) and may have been the main reason for abandoning further SA-N-2 installations. Between the funnels is the only known installation on a ship of the High Lune nodding HFR (height-finder radar),

Below: SA-N-1 aboard a Kashin-Mod destroyer. Below right: Boost fins not quite fully deployed at the launch of a Goa.

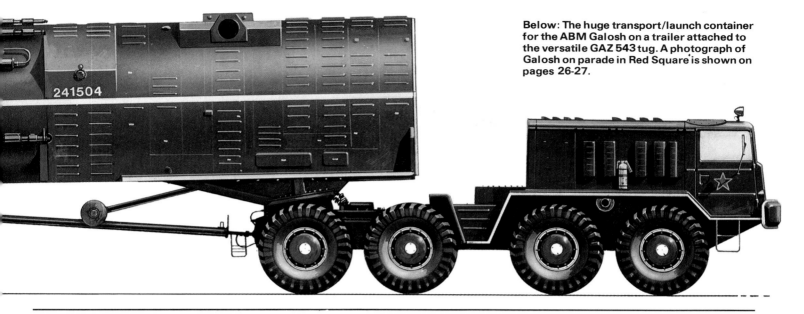

Below: The huge transport/launch container for the ABM Galosh on a trailer attached to the versatile GAZ 543 tug. A photograph of Galosh on parade in Red Square is shown on pages 26-27.

thought to be related to the land-based Cake series HFRs, which provides necessary height information. The performance of this missile is thought to be comparable to the land based version.

SA-N-3 Goblet

Data: not yet known in West.

When the ASW cruisers (helicopter carriers) *Moskva* and *Leningrad* were first seen in 1967 their SAM launchers were described as 'similar to Goa'. A little later they were described as 'of an improved Goa type' but by the mid-1970s, when SA-N-3 was widely used in cruisers, it was belatedly recognised that the SAM system of these ships bears virtually no resemblance to SA-N-1 Goa at all. In all ships so far seen with this weapon system the installation appears to be the same, and to comprise: below-decks magazine for about 24 reload rounds; vertical reload mechanism with two pairs of lifts to four hatches so that by swivelling 180° between each reload the launcher can double its rate of fire (compared with SA-N-1, for example); modern twin-rail launcher which, as it appears to have no gyro-stabilization, suggests highly positive missile gathering and guidance; the extremely large and powerful Top Sail 3-D surveillance radar; and the intensely interesting Head Light Group of SAM radars. Like SA-N-1's Peel Group this installation comprises two large (G/H-band?) aerials and two small (probably I-band), but Head Light dishes are circular open mesh, and larger. There seems to be little similarity to the Straight Flush radars of the SA-6 Gainful SAM, apart from one possible equality in wavelength, but since 1973 there has been prolonged speculation in the West that SA-N-3 Goblet uses the SA-6 Gainful missile, or a near-relative. The SA-N-3, an obviously successful and formidable area-defence weapon, is fitted to the two ships mentioned (two installations forward), the big *Kiev* and other *Kuril* class multi-role carriers (one forward), the five (or six) new *Kara* class cruisers (one forward, one aft) and the ten *Kresta II* cruisers (one forward, one aft).

Above: Close-up of *Moskva*'s SA-N-3 launchers and associated twin 'Head Light' guidance radars.

Left: Heavily retouched 'official' photograph of the SA-N-2 installation on the ageing *Dzerzhinski* cruiser.

SA-N-4

Data: assumed similar to SA-8 Gecko.

As yet not publicly associated with a Nato reporting name, this is the standard short-range shipboard SAM system of the Soviet Navy. It has been installed in over 100 vessels of all sizes and sold to foreign customers, though details are still tantalisingly sparse in the West. Not until the appearance of the land-mobile SA-8 Gecko with its near-identical radar group could some definite form be added to the bare externals of ship-radar bin and launch bin. N-4 was first seen in the late 1960s installed in the foredeck of the *Grisha* corvettes, and soon afterwards in the new *Krivak* destroyers and two converted *Sverdlov* cruisers: *Admiral Senyavin* appeared in 1972 with an N-4 installation built into the top of a helicopter hangar (which with the landing pad replaced X and Y turrets) and *Zhadanov* had just an N-4 installation above a large deckhouse in place of X turret. The handsome *Krivaks* have one installation forward and one aft, while in

1973 the *Nikolayev*, first of the almost futuristic *Kara* class cruisers, showed an N-4 installation on each side amidships. With this system not even the launcher or radar need be visble; in each case the whole assembly is normally retracted inside a circular bin closed by a lid. All that was seen by Western observers until 1976 was the Pop Group radar and sight system, and even this was often hidden inside its deckhouse bin under two sliding lids. Pop Group was first noticed on a *Nanuchka* small missile boat, and after further sightings was recognised as a high-speed target- and missile-tracking radar group, almost certainly supplemented by optical and TV sight systems, able to guide the N-4 missile and the twin 30mm gun turret(s) usually mounted close by. In 1976, when the *Kiev* (and, presumably other *Kuril* carriers) was seen to have three N-4 installations, a photograph became available showing the launcher of a corvette in the raised position. It is described as a twin launcher, but in fact could carry four Gecko-size boxes. The first overseas user is India, whose *Nanuchkas* have the system installed.

SA-N-7

Data: presumed as for SA-7.

This is the DoD designation of the version of SA-7 Grail used aboard all the chief classes of missile boat and MTB (motor torpedo boat) for close-range AA protection. So far as is known the missile and launch tube/sight are identical with the improved form of SA-7, and it is strange that the SA-9 Gaskin vehicle-mounted system should not be used. In most installations the tube is pivoted to the superstructure at a convenient place and aimed by hand in the usual way. N-7 has been seen on all recent *Osa I* and *II* missile boats and *Shershen* torpedo boats, which are also used by certain Arab countries.

Below: Close-up of the SA-N-4 system aboard a Krivak-class cruiser which passed through the English Channel in 1973. A is the bin housing the missile, and B is the associated 'Pop Group' guidance radar and optical sight head.

SS-8 Sasin

Dimensions: Length 80ft (24.4m); diameter 9ft (2.74m).
Launch weight: About 169,753lb (77,000kg).
Range: About 6,500 miles (10,460km).
For many years after this ICBM was first seen in a Moscow parade, in 1964, American official literature invariably linked it with SS-7 in such a way as to imply a technical similarity between the two systems. In fact the only links were geographical; the few SS-8s were apparently all emplaced at existing SS-7 sites. Technology is more akin to that of SS-5, though on a larger scale. Sasin is very nearly of the same diameter as Saddler, though it is shorter. The storable liquid propellants are probably RFNA/kerosene, and control is almost certainly by four large jet vanes which were removed from the examples seen in 1964. These (two) missiles also had large circular covers over the base of the first stage, though it would be unwise to jump to the conclusion that this stage has one large thrust chamber. The second stage has prominent fairings over what are probably separation motors. Each stage has an external instrument conduit along the top of the tank sections. The warhead yield is estimated at 5 MT, and guidance is inertial. In the 1964 parade the transporter was of great interest, the new 8 × 8 tug of MAZ-537 ancestry pulling an articulated trailer with three axles, suggesting that the missile can travel with its tanks already filled. Number deployed is arguable: one US estimate of 209 SS-7 and -8 together was interpreted as 100 + 109, but the correct 1975 figure was apparently 190 + 19. The 19 have now been deactivated and replaced by SLBMs.

Below: The SS-8 Sasin was first seen in a Red Square parade in 1964, although it is thought to have been deployed a year earlier.

Bottom: Containers of the most menacing SS-11 Sego ICBMs which have been targetted on strategic sites in the West for well over 14 years. There are three versions, all widely deployed.

SS-9 Scarp

Dimensions: Length (Mod 2) about 118ft (36m); diameter about 10ft 2in (3.1m).
Launch weight: About 418,871lb (190,000kg).
Range: (Mod 2) over 7,456 miles (12,000km).
On 7 November 1967 the Soviet Union struck a chill of fear into Western observers by trundling through Red Square some of the first of these mighty missiles, then easily the biggest and most capable of any mass-produced weapon in history. Development started as a far more capable successor to Sapwood around 1959, with two tandem stages, storable liquid propellants and a clean single-tube configuration. Probably RFNA/kerosene are used, and the first stage has a ring of six fixed thrust chambers, plus four gimbal-mounted verniers behind fairings around the skirt, which control the trajectory and trim the cutoff velocity at stage separation. The second stage has tankage of the same diameter but tapers to a very large blunt RV. The latter has its own post-boost propulsion, making three stages in all. Extremely long and accurate flights in 1963-65 disturbed the Americans, and when deployment in giant underground silos began in 1965 this missile was causing as much alarm as the Foxbat 2,000 mph aircraft. Subsequently five stages of development were identified by the DoD: Mod 1, the original ICBM, with the first-generation silo and warhead of about 20 MT; Mod 2, the main production SS-9 with 25 MT warhead, then the largest on any missile; Mod 3, flown over depressed-trajectory missions, sacrificing range to reduce enemy radar warning time, and also over planned FOBS missions, the first being Cosmos 139 on 25 January 1967 and later followed by many others mostly at an orbital inclination of 49.5°; Mod 4, with three MRVs, used for tests in 1969-70 and 1973 with the three warheads impacting with the same spread as the three silos of a typical USAF Minuteman complex; and Mod 5, flown from Tyuratam with satellite-killing warheads against orbital targets put up from Plesetsk by a series of SS-5-derived launch vehicles. By 1975-6 there were 313 SS-9 silos operational with the RVSN, but, as the even bigger SS-18 takes over, these missiles are being withdrawn and used in trials and training programmes.

SS-11 Sego

Dimensions: Length about 62ft 4in (19m); diameter about 8ft (2.44m).
Launch weight: In the neighbourhood of 105,820lb (48,000kg).
Range: Estimated at 6,525 miles (10,500km).
Like SS-7 this missile has never been positively identified in any public parade, though in the 1973 October Revolution parade MAZ-537A 8 × 8 tugs drove past pulling a new articulated trailer carrying extremely plain drum-like containers of the appropriate size. To the public in Western nations neither 'SS-11' nor 'Sego' means anything, yet this is the ICBM that for 14 years has most greatly and universally menaced every Western capital and all other important industrial centres from silos west and east of the Urals. The numbers deployed have been so great as to keep American photo-interpreters constantly busy watching the updating and other changes at silos all round the peripheries of the Soviet Union. The missile is a little longer than the USAF's Minuteman, but much fatter and carries a much greater payload. Study of the supposed SS-11 containers led to discussion of the cold-launch technique and some reports imply or even announce that this is a feature of the SS-11 system; the author doubts this, and does not believe the container goes into the silo. There are two stages of storable-liquid propulsion, the first having four gimballed chambers. The so-called Mod 1 missile has a single RV with a reported choice of two warheads, one 500 kT and the other a thermonuclear device of 20-25 MT. After prolonged testing this achieved IOC in 1966, and by the 1972 SALT I agreement filled 970 silos, with 66 more being built. Mod 2 is reported as being a non-operational test vehicle. Mod 3 is the first Soviet ICBM to have MRV, the first three-warhead test being detected in 1969. At least 60 of the Mod 3 were in silos in early 1978, the yield being put at 3 × 300 kT. The SS-11 is being replaced by SS-17 and -19.

SS-13 Savage

Dimensions: Length about 65ft 7in (20m); diameter of first stage 5ft 7in (1.7m).
Launch weight: About 77,160lb (35,000kg).
Range: Over 5,000 miles (8,000km).
This was almost certainly the first large Soviet missile to have solid propulsion; it has three stages linked by open Warrengirder trusses, each having four TVC nozzles. It was developed in parallel with SS-11, though it is smaller and more akin to Minuteman III. Shown in the 9 May 1965 parade, it reached IOC in 1968 and about 60 have since been in RVSN service around Plesetsk. SS-11 has much greater payload and accuracy, and SS-13 development appears to have ceased prior to 1970. No MRV version is known (despite some reports), yield of the single warhead being estimated at 1 MT. The two upper stages are thought to form SS-14, and there has been speculation that SS-13 itself has been deployed in a mobile role. Successor is SS-16.

SS-14 Scapegoat (Scamp)

Dimensions: Length about 35ft 5in (10.8m); diameter of first stage 4ft 7in (1.4m).
Launch weight: In the neighbourhood of 26,455lb (12,000kg).
Range: About 2,485 miles (4,000km).
For some unaccountable reason the Nato co-ordinating committee has seen fit to allocate two names to this weapon: Scapegoat for the missile itself and Scamp for the complete package inside its container riding on a rebuilt IS-3 tank chassis, with eight small road wheels on each side. All previous Soviet mobile missiles have a single code name, and the use of two causes needless confusion. To make things more involved, the missile is superficially identical to the two upper stages of SS-13 Savage, apart from small changes to the warhead which Western observers think may have lower yield. Classed as an IRBM, it in fact has greater range and can be regarded as a mobile land-based Polaris A3. Such a weapon can be driven to countless concealed sites all round the Soviet frontier. There were many hundreds of IS-3 chassis available, some of them ex-

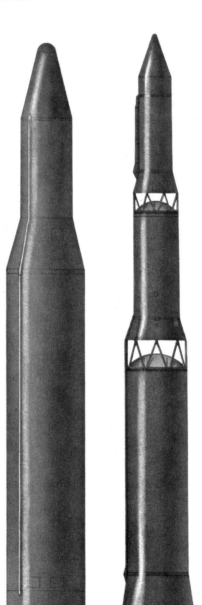

Above: The Red Square parade of November 1965 revealed for the first time the enormous SS-15 Scrooge ICBM casing and tracked carrier, although the true nature of the missile has kept Western experts guessing. Exactly how the missile is launched is also puzzling.

Right: A training deployment in a forest area for the SS-14 Scamp system (Scapegoat being the name of the missile portion.) US satellites, though having difficulty tracking these mobile systems, have spotted them near the Chinese border.

Frog carriers, and the impossibility of satellite surveillance of so mobile a system results in 'unknown' appearing beside Western estimates of the number deployed. Soviet films show the way the 'Iron Maiden' container is elevated, opened and lowered back on the carrier which then drives off to control the launch.

SS-15 (XZ) Scrooge

Dimensions: Length estimated at about 60ft (18.3m); diameter of first stage assumed 5ft 7in (1.7m).
Launch weight: Probably about 61,828lb (28,000kg).
Range: Estimated at over 3,107 miles (5,000km).
First seen in the November 1965 Red Square parade, this is the largest mobile weapon system in the world to have been seen publicly. The tracked chassis, of IS-3 ancestry with 16 road wheels, carries a very large tubular container which elevates vertically but cannot open to release the missile. It is sized to fit a shortened SS-13, and most observers agree that this missile is the most likely answer, but how it is launched is unknown. Cold launch is not possible, and the assumption is that the tube is used to protect the still-attached carrier and is not recovered after firing. With the carrier driven to a distance the tube would stand on the supporting surface and the efflux would all pass up the interior. Neither answer seems satisfactory, neither is the gross vehicle weight of some 132,275lb (60,000kg) a happy situation. Another puzzle is why, after ten years as 'SS-15', this system is now called 'SS-XZ'' in most American literature. Around 1970 it was accepted that this system was operational near the Chinese frontier around Buir Nor. Scrooges in the western Soviet Union could be targeted throughout Western Europe and the UK, even if (as has been suggested) the first stage is shorter than that of SS-13.

SS-8 Sasin

SS-9 Scarp

SS-11 Sego

SS-13 Savage

SS-16

Dimensions: Length about 65ft 7in (20m); diameter about 5ft 7in (1.7m).
Launch weight: Probably about 79,365lb (36,000kg).
Range: Over 5,592 miles (9,000km).

Four new missile systems were in flight test in the early 1970s, all embodying completely new techniques and much more 'unstoppable' than their predecessors, and all were timed to reach IOC in 1975. Of these SS-16 (then called SSX-16, because of its development status) is the only one with solid propulsion. It is universally regarded as a much superior replacement for SS-13, similar in size (the DoD said it is 'slightly smaller' but the Pentagon artwork and desk-top models show it rather larger) but with such superior motor performance as to give greater range despite a considerably heavier warhead. Until mid-1978 all operational SS-16s were believed to carry a single

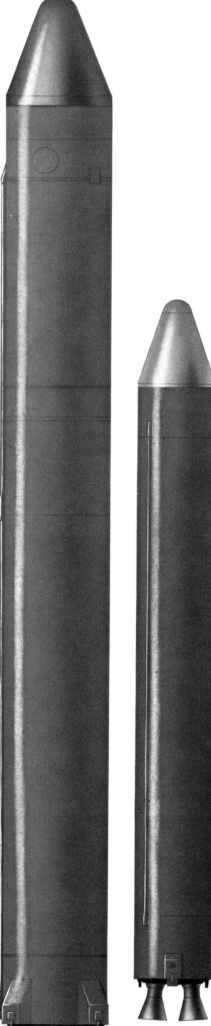
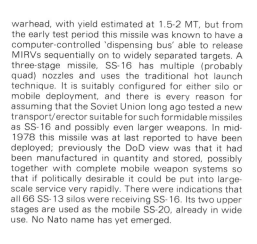

warhead, with yield estimated at 1.5-2 MT, but from the early test period this missile was known to have a computer-controlled 'dispensing bus' able to release MIRVs sequentially on to widely separated targets. A three-stage missile, SS-16 has multiple (probably quad) nozzles and uses the traditional hot launch technique. It is suitably configured for either silo or mobile deployment, and there is every reason for assuming that the Soviet Union long ago tested a new transport/erector suitable for such formidable missiles as SS-16 and possibly even larger weapons. In mid-1978 this missile was at last reported to have been deployed; previously the DoD view was that it had been manufactured in quantity and stored, possibly together with complete mobile weapon systems so that if politically desirable it could be put into large-scale service very rapidly. There were indications that all 66 SS-13 silos were receiving SS-16. Its two upper stages are used as the mobile SS-20, already in wide use. No Nato name has yet emerged.

SS-17

Dimensions: Length about 80ft (24.4m); diameter about 8ft 3in (2.5m).
Launch weight: In the order of 143,300lb (65,000kg).
Range: Over 6,214 miles (10,000km).

Again not yet associated with a Nato reporting name, this ICBM was first seen in flight test in 1972. Together with SS-19, which is almost certainly a competitive design to act as a spur and insurance, this extremely formidable missile is a successor for SS-11, and is now installed in many former SS-11 silos. Unlike all previous Soviet missiles known in the West, SS-17 has cold-launch ejection, with great advantage to the silo and also conferring an increase in ultimate range. Compared with SS-11 this missile has similar calibre but much increased length, the first stage being particularly long. Storable liquids are used, and an American model shows fairing ducts past the tanks of both stages (this would not affect cold launching, which uses a piston or sabot to blow the missile out). Early testing features three MIRV warheads, and this is the first Soviet MIRVed ICBM in service. The warhead is estimated to weigh twice as much as that of SS-11, and the Mod 1 missile in operation since 1975 has four heads estimated at over 200 kT each (the 1978 DoD Secretary's Report says 4 × 600 kT). Mod 2 has a single RV of very high yield which, in conjunction with reported outstanding accuracy, gives SS-17 the capability of backing up SS-18 as a counter-force weapon. Deployment has been slower than the Soviet Union could have achieved, but over 70 were operational by August 1978.

SS-18

Dimensions: Length about 121ft 4in (37m); diameter about 10ft 6in (3.2m).
Launch weight: About 485,000lb (220,000kg).
Range: Estimated at 7,456 miles (12,000km); Mod 3, greater.

Again as yet devoid of a NATO reporting name, this is the missile that has demolished almost all the West's bargaining power and ability to deter aggression. The largest missile in the world, its appearance was not unexpected as a modern successor to SS-9; but nobody in the West was prepared for its frightening accuracy, which, in conjunction with by far the most formidable warhead(s) in history, renders any practical degree of hardening a waste of effort. The DoD view is that this chilling capability has been demonstrated 'four to five years earlier than expected'. SS-18 is cold-launched from a silo of new design, though this is often installed at existing SS-9 launch complexes. There are two stages of storable-liquid propulsion and separate computer-controlled post-boost propulsion for the RV or MIRVs. Throw-weight is estimated at 30 per cent greater than for SS-9, and this is multiplied in effectiveness dozens to hundreds of times by the truly remarkable guidance accuracy which in recent (1977-8 flights) has averaged about 180m. According to DoD the Minuteman force is vulnerable as soon as large-warhead CEP is brought within 370m. The Mod 1 SS-18, which reached IOC in 1974, has a single RV with a yield estimated at 25 to 50 MT, and most of the 80+ missiles deployed in mid-1978 are thought to be of this type. Probably any of them could be converted to Mod 2 standard, which has eight MIRVs with a yield put at 2 MT each (another estimate is eight to ten of 1 MT, but eight was the number invariably seen on the

SS-16

SS-17

SS-19

SS-18

intensive Mod 2 test programme in 1975-6). Mod 2 entered service in 1976, but at a low rate of deployment. Mod 3 has a single RV, lighter and more accurate than Mod 1 and giving even longer range. SALT I permits the Soviet Union to deploy 310 of these terrifying weapons.

SS-19

Dimensions: Length about 88ft 6in (27m); diameter 8ft 3in (2.5m).
Launch weight: Estimated at 171,958lb (78,000kg).
Range: Over 6,214 miles (10,000km).
The competitive partner to SS-17, this ICBM again has no known Nato reporting name, despite the estimate of several hundred already deployed. One report suggests SS-19 is "less advanced technically" than SS-17, but one should not undervalue this missile. It gets results at least as impressive as SS-17, albeit by being fractionally larger. According to one report (*Jane's Weapon Systems*) SS-19 is hot-launched, but most DoD and other literature is agreed on cold launching. Again, the British annual, whose sources are excellent, refers to 'a refinement of the traditional Soviet "fly the wire" technique' (whatever that means), whereas other reports indicate pure inertial guidance in an advanced form. The DoD emphasize the complete success of SS-19 flight testing and in 1977 commented 'We are convinced . . . that the SS-19 is clearly intended to achieve high accuracy; the Soviet designers have done everything right to attain that goal'. The two stages, both with parallel tanks that fill the silo as completely as possible, use storable liquids; and the American plastic display model of this missile shows twin gimballed chambers projecting completely below the first-stage skirt, an unprecedented feature in a Russian ballistic missile and one that suggests the cold-launch sabot thrusts on the airfrme above the chambers. Mod 1 SS-19, first deployed in 1974, has six MIRVs with an individual yield estimated in 1977 at 400-500 kT per head and in 1978 at 800 kT to 1 MT. Mod 2 has flown with a single super-accurate high-yield RV, but is not known to have reached IOC. In mid-1978 about 250 Mod 1 were in service, and it looks as if most of the 1,000-odd SS-11 silos are soon going to be occupied by this ICBM.

SS-20

Dimensions: Length about 34ft 6in (10.5m); diameter 55in (1.4m).
Launch weight: Probably about 28,659lb (13,000kg).
Range: (3 × 600 kT), 3,542 miles (5,700km), (reduced payload) 4,660 miles (7,500km).
Based on the two upper stages of SS-16, this extremely useful mobile missile has much greater range, higher payload and greater accuracy than the DoD had predicted, and it is already being deployed at what could well be a considerable rate—though surveillance is next to impossible. In his annual statement in 1977 the DoD Secretary said SSX-20, as it then was, had 'a range of 2,000n.m. (3700km) but this could be extended to 3,000n.m. (5560km) either by the addition of a third stage or off-loading MIRVs'. By 1978 the range estimates had jumped to the figures given in the data. Moreover, SS-20 poses other problems for SALT surveillance and negotiations because it falls outside the range provisions of such an agreement yet, by fitting an SS-16 first stage, it becomes an exceptionally powerful ICBM. Compared with the older weapons it replaces, such as SS-4 and -5, it is mobile, easily concealed, is fired from a tracked vehicle which can be rapidly reloaded, carries three MIRVs of 500-600 kT each and has accuracy of some 750m CEP when firing from a pre-surveyed site. Initial deployment was in mid-1978 predicted at 300-400 launchers plus reloads.

SSX-22

This designation is probably applied to one of the 'fifth generation' of Soviet long-range missiles which for several years have been under development (SS-21 being a tactical rocket). In his 1978 Statement the DoD Secretary announced 'Flight testing of one or two of these missiles could begin at any time, with others following in the 1980s'. With four known 'fifth-generation' systems the DoD numbers thus probably extend to SSX-25. A sobering picture for the West, which has not deployed a single new ICBM system since 1963 and has no IRBM of any kind other than the 18 French SSBS.

SURFACE-TO-SURFACE: LAND TACTICAL

Frog series

Understood to be an acronym for 'Free Rocket Over Ground', Frog refers to a family of unguided, spin-stabilised artillery rockets armed with nuclear, chemical or conventional HE warheads and intended to lay down a devastating blanket fire on battlefield and rear-area deployments of troops and armour. Mounted on a tracked launch vehicle (IS-3), the first to enter service (1957) was Frog 1, with an estimated range of 20 miles (32km). Frog 2, a smaller rocket with a range of 7.5 miles (12km), was deployed the same year. Neither is thought to be in service with Soviet or Warsaw Pact forces.

Frog-3

Dimensions: Length 34ft 5½in (10.5m); diameter 15¾in (400mm); warhead diameter 21½in (550mm).
Launch weight: About 4,960lb (2,250kg).
Range: About 25 miles (40km).
The oldest of the family believed to be still in service, this was first seen in the 1960 parade and was the first to have tandem two-stage propulsion, each motor having a central nozzle surrounded by a ring of 12 smaller nozzles. At launch, both front and rear motors fire together, the front efflux being canted out to avoid destruction of the rear. The whole rocket impacts on target. Around 1970, Western literature agreed on a nuclear or conventional warhead weighing 551lb (250kg) but by 1975 this estimate had changed to a figure of 992lb (250kg). Carrier remains the PT-76 chassis.

Frog-4

Launch weight: Estimated at 4,409lb (2,000kg).
Range: About 31 miles (50km).
This weapon system appears to differ from Frog-3 only in that the rocket has a slim warhead the same diameter as the motor tube.

Frog-5

Dimensions: Length about 29ft 10½in (9.1m); diameter 21½in (550mm).
Launch weight: Estimated at 6,614lb (3,000kg).
Range: About 34 miles (55km).
At first (1964) this was thought to be merely a Frog-4 with a conical nose. Later study showed that in fact the whole missile was increased in diameter to that of the Frog-3 warhead; in fact it is a fair guess that Frog-5 is a Frog-3 with a fatter but slightly shorter motor.

Above: A Frog-3 being readied for launch. Some photographs of the rocket in action show that a forward ring of thrusters fires at the same time as the 'first stage' motor as the rocket leaves the ramp. First introduced about 1960, Frog-3 is still believed to be in service.

Below: A wintry scene showing Frog-3 unguided artillery missiles on the move on the PT-76 chassis. Although elderly, these weapons are effective up to about 25 miles. They carry nuclear or conventional (high explosive) warheads, with some reports suggesting chemical warheads also being fitted.

Frog-7

Dimensions: Length 29ft 6½in (9.0m); diameter 23.6in (600mm).
Launch weight: About 5,511lb) 2,500kg).
Range: At least 37 miles (60km).

Nato observers use "Frog-6" to identify a dummy rocket used in training, so Frog-7, first seen in 1967, is next and also the last in the family. Like all Frogs from -3 onwards it has a central sustainer and ring of peripheral boost nozzles (there are 20 of the latter), but there is only one stage of propulsion. The airframe is cleaner, the fins larger, motor performance higher and the launcher a plain girder rail with quicker elevation and limited traverse. There are thought to be speed brakes for range adjustment, but details of the necessary radar (doppler) tracking and radio command system are unknown. The carrier vehicle is the ZIL-135 wheeled prime mover, with an on-board crane for rapid reloading and cross-country performance as good as a PT-76 except for lack of amphibious capability. Large numbers of Frog-7 are in use with all WP members as well as Egypt, Iraq, N Korea, Syria and possibly other countries.

SS-1 Scud

Dimensions: Length 36ft 11in (11.25m); diameter 33.5in (850mm).
Launch weight: Scud-A, about 12,125lb (5,500kg); Scud-B 13,888lb (6,300kg).
Range: Scud-A, about 50-93 miles (80-150km); Scud-B 100-175 miles (160-280km).

The Scud medium range missiles are battlefield support weapons designed to strike at targets such as marshalling areas, major storage dumps and airfields behind enemy lines. Warheads can be nuclear, chemical (persistent) or conventional HE. The original Scud-A version (first seen 1957) was thought to

Above right: A Frog-7 on the march on its ZIL-135 transporter. This is the last Frog, although some guesses link the new SS-21 with the designation Frog-9.

Right and below: SS-1 Scud-A battlefield support missiles having been set on their launchers at surveyed sites. The weapon is designed to strike at targets such as marshalling areas, major storage dumps and airfields behind enemy lines.

combine radio command of propulsion cutoff and gyro-stabilized guidance and to have no trajectory control after motor cutoff. It remained in Soviet operational service until at least 1972.

Scud-B is estimated to be 1ft 7½in (0.5m) longer and to have greater range (see data), and the propellant tanks appear to have been transposed. It was first seen in 1962 on the IS-3 chassis, with the steel-tube ladder round the tip of the missile suitably extended. In 1965 Scud-B made its appearance on the new MAZ-543 articulated eight-wheel prime mover, which is lighter and faster than the heavy tracked chassis. This carries a completely new erector/launcher much neater than that originally used. Soviet Ground Forces erector/launchers have numerous features not seen in the other Warsaw Pact Scud systems, probably betokening nuclear warheads which have not so far been permitted to other WP forces or export customers. The Scud-B erector/launcher is totally unlike that of Scud-A; there is extensive new equipment, large double calipers to grip the upper end of the missile, and redesigned structure, but the prominent ladder that extended up each side of the earlier weapon to meet above its nose is absent. Guidance of Scud-B is by simple strapdown inertial system, steering as before via refractory vanes in the motor efflux, the fins being fixed. There does not seem to be any fine adjustment of cutoff velocity, and it is not known if the nuclear or conventional warhead separates before starting the free-fall ballistic trajectory. Resupply missiles are towed tail-first on an articulated trailer attached to a ZIL-157V, with a Ural-375 truck-mounted crane (Type 8T210) to swing the missile on to the lowered erector/launcher. Crews

are trained to operate from points of maximum concealment, eg, heavily forested areas, to avoid detection. After a missile is fired the transporter is immediately driven to a new location to avoid a counterstrike and the vehicle is reloaded from the support vehicle. Certainly the time taken to set up and fire Scud-B is much less than the hour of Scud-A, and End Tray radar is used for radio-sonde (radio-equipped balloon) tracking for upper-atmosphere data.

SS-1C Scud-B is widely deployed by all WP armies, and by Egypt, Iraq, Libya and Syria. The Syrian Army was reported to have flown a Scud 155 miles (250km) in November 1975, but in the Yom Kippur war two years earlier three Scuds fired by Egypt all apparently missed their targets in Sinai. Persistent rumours of a Scud-C with range of 280 miles (450km) have not been confirmed.

SS-12 Scaleboard

Dimensions: Length 37ft 9in (11.5m); diameter 43in (1.1m).
Launch weight: Probably about 17,636lb (8,000kg).
Range: Estimated at up to 500 miles (800km).

First reported in Western literature in 1967, this mobile ballistic missile almost comes into the strategic category, because it can menace Western Europe from WP soil and is universally agreed to have a warhead in the megaton range. Yet in many ways it is similar to Scud-B; it is little different in length, rides on an erector/launcher mounted on an MAZ-543, and almost certainly has similar strapdown simplified

Above: A Scud-B about half-way through the 60-second elevation procedure. Launching is from its small platform, usually from concealed areas.

Above: A Scud-B on its MAZ-543 launcher/erector. This is a specially adapted version of the 8 x 8 cargo truck, and offers good cross-country capability.

Below: The SS-1 Scud-B missile is shown both on its transporter/erector and separately above it. Reloading is carried out by mobile crane.

Above: The SS-12 Scaleboard on its MAZ-543 transporter/launcher make a compact unit. The missile travels in a metal casing which is also raised into the firing position before launch.

Right: Elevating the SS-12 ready for launching. Note that it is still in its casing. Photographs of the missile itself have not been released.

inertial guidance. One of the few obvious differences, apart from the much greater missile diameter, is that the erector/launcher is in the form of a ribbed container, split into upper and lower halves, which protects the weapon from the weather while it is travelling. It is possibly shock-mounted, and the container may even offer limited protection against nuclear attack.

Though there are clear illustrations of the complete weapon system on the march, or elevating for firing, the missile itself remains almost unknown, and the data are little more than the best guesses of Western intelligence. It is reasonable to assume that there is a single rocket engine burning storable RFNA/UDMH. Steering may be by refractory jet-deflector vanes, but a later method would be desirable for maximum range. The Soviet Ground Forces enjoy a wealth of superb purpose-designed vehicles, and the MAZ-543 transporter/launcher is one of the best. A beautiful exercise in packaging, it is powerful, highly mobile on rough ground, air-conditioned for extremes of heat or cold, and has automatic regulation of tyre pressure from the driver's cab on the left side. The right front cab is the launch-control station, as in the Scud-B system. The rest of the launch crew sit in the second row of seats in line with the rear doors on each side. Some related vehicles are amphibious.

Like all Soviet tactical missiles Scaleboard is intended for "shoot and scoot" operation. But it is too large for snappy reloading and in any case this needs the services of one, if not two, additional vehicles. Resupply missiles are carried in their own ribbed casings, with propellant tanks empty, and even with fast pressurized-gas transfer the fuelling process must take about a quarter of an hour. The likelihood is that the Soviet Ground Forces already have a detailed itinerary of pre-surveyed firing sites offering good concealment throughout Western Europe. So far as is known, this powerful thermonuclear weapon serves only with the Soviet Union.

SS-21

Data: Not known.

This is the US designation for the new battlefield rocket being introduced by Soviet Ground Forces. No Nato name has yet been published. Details are speculative, though a variety of types of warhead is a foregone conclusion. This may be the weapon often reported as "Frog-9", but this is a guess.

SSC-1B Sepal

Data: assumed as for SS-N-3.

This is the land-based version of the large, formidable and widely deployed shipboard cruise missile called by Nato SS-N-3 Shaddock. Sepal is thought to use an identical missile, though this assumption may be unjustified. As it rides inside a large cylindrical container, making the ZIL-135 family prime mover look like a tanker truck, little has been seen of it in Red Square parades; photographs with the rear lid raised reveal the expected Shaddock back-end with ventral fin, rocket boost motor on each side and large air-breathing cruise-engine nozzle covered by a plate. At each end the container has a full-diameter closure, swung open on to an upper ring by remote-control actuators on the left side. These could allow a cruise turbojet to be started prior to opening the rear lid for the launch, but this is speculation. The whole container is elevated to a suitable angle by two large jacks prior to launch in a forward direction across the prime-mover cab. Wings unfold in the first second or so of free flight. Western observers have concluded that Sepal uses the same airframe as Shaddock but with rather more versatile guidance. IR-homing has often been associated with this land-based weapon, but not with Shaddock. Radio command, mid-course up-date and terminal radar homing seem to be common to both. So far as is known, Sepal serves only in the anti-ship role, not for overland missions. Each battalion is said to have 15 to 18 launchers, plus reloads.

SSC-2A Salish

Data: assumed similar to Samlet.

Derived from the pioneer long-range ASM known to Nato as AS-1 Kennel, this and its close relative Samlet (below) are not fully understood. Both use the Kennel-based airframe, which is that of a miniature first-generation swept-wing jet fighter and clearly dates from the late 1940s at the time the MiG-15 was coming into production. The cruise engine is a simple small turbojet, of unknown type, fed from a plain nose inlet, and the wings fold upwards for easy ground handling. Launch is from an elevating ramp under the thrust of a single rocket booster with down-canted nozzle. Photographs showed both fixed and mobile launchers, as well as large quantities of ground-support equipment. Salish is obsolescent, and is believed to be withdrawn from combat duty with Soviet Ground Forces. Several observers believe it was an overland tactical missile, presumably with radio command guidance to a predetermined map location. If so, the small radome above the inlet remains an enigma.

SSC-2B Samlet

Dimensions: Span about 23ft (7m); diameter 47in (1.2m).

Launch weight: Estimated at 6,614lb (3,000kg).

Range: Estimated at 124 miles (200km).

Compared with Salish, this missile has a larger nose radome, electronics pod above the fin and other smaller changes. The consensus of opinion is that it is a coast-defence missile, with active homing against ships. Semi-active homing has also been reported, and the Sheet Bend radar has been seen on vehicles at Samlet sites, but this could not give effective guidance against over-the-horizon targets which Samlet is capable of reaching. Of course, this weapon system may be associated with air- or ship-based mid-course guidance. In addition to the Soviet Union, Samlet has been seen in service with Polish coast-defence forces and in Cuba and Egypt, usually operated by naval personnel. It is believed still to be operational with all recipients.

Top: Transporter/launcher for the SSC-1B Sepal mobile cruise missile, the land-based version of SS-N-3 Shaddock. The end closures have been swung up to their top rests.

Above centre: An unconvincing photograph apparently showing SSC-2A Salish on a flimsy launcher which appears to be resting on the ground. The missile is probably withdrawn from combat units by now.

Above: The launch crew of the Red Banner Northern Fleet scramble to fire and SSC-2B Samlet from its launcher. This and the SSC-2A Salish are derived from the AS-1 Kennel air-to-surface missile, which was the first such missile to be seen in Soviet service (in the 1950s). Samlet is reported to have been used as a coastal defence weapon by the Soviet Navy (replacing the old 130mm coastal gun) in stations from the Baltic to the Pacific.

AT-1 Snapper

Dimensions: Length 44.5in (1,130mm); diameter 5.51in (140mm); span 30.7in (780mm).
Launch weight: 49.05lb (22.25kg).
Range: 7,546ft (2,300m) at 199 mph (320km/h).

The first-generation Soviet anti-tank missile was not only much in evidence in the July 1967 Middle East war but numerous examples were captured by the Israeli army and so it soon became well known in the West. At that time it was carried in a quad mount on the GAZ-69 4 × 4 car, the missiles travelling nose-up and the whole launcher being cranked down for use, with a further crank to train it in the required direction, facing to the rear. Oddly, each missile was fired from an overhead guide rail, and two bent tubes at the rear contained sockets to which the guidance wires for that missile had to be screwed prior to launch. If necessary the launcher could be fired by an operator up to 165ft (50m) distant. The missile, actually believed to be 3M6 and dubbed Shmell (Bumblebee), was called AT-1 in the West and codenamed Snapper. It has four large wings, a single-charge solid motor and 11.5lb (5.25kg) hollow-charge warhead with penetration of at least 13.8in (350mm). The missile is spin-stabilized, the operator sighting optically on the tracking flares on the tips of the horizontal wings and steering with plastic-insert spoilers on all four wings, the vertical wings having additional outboard spoilers for roll control. By 1970 the usual carrier in WP armies was the BRDM amphibious scout car which can have a retractable triple mounting. Users have included Afghanistan, Bulgaria, Cuba, Czechoslovakia, East Germany, Egypt, Hungary, Jugoslavia, Mongolia, Poland, Romania, Soviet Union and Syria.

AT-2 Swatter

Dimensions: Length 35.5in (902mm); diameter 5.9in (150mm); span 26.0in (660mm).
Launch weight: 55lb (25kg).
Range: 7,218ft (2,200m) at 335 mph (540km/h).

This much more advanced missile has also seen action in the Middle East and been captured by Israel, yet as far as published information is concerned Western

observers cannot make up their minds on the most basic features. Things which are not in dispute are that it is carried on a quad launcher on the BRDM, and has a cruciform of rear wings, all fitted with control surfaces which are probably elevons and two carrying what look like tracking flares, an internal solid motor with oblique nozzles between the wings which fires it off a launch rail of surprising size (so there is no high-thrust booster), and a hemispherical nose, behind which are two small fin-like projections. Most observers flatly state that wire guidance is not used, and in the author's opinion it never was used with this weapon. Others insist the opposite, while another source describes 'Swatter A' with wires and 'Swatter B' without. There seems little doubt it is command guided by radio, which facilitates deployment from the various versions of Mi-24 tactical helicopter, and, it is believed, the AV-MF Ka-25. Air applications are thought to be of an interim nature, pending availability of AS-8. The remaining puzzle is the nose, which suggests IR terminal homing, possibly in conjunction with the two small 'foreplanes'. In mid-1978 this was pure speculation, though an IR seeker head is not impossible with a hollow-charge weapon. The warhead in this case has never been described in the West, but is said to penetrate 19.7in (500mm). Users include WP countries, Egypt and Syria.

AT-3 Sagger

During the Middle East war in October 1973 two-man teams of Egyptian infantry opened what looked like small suitcases and inflicted casualties on Israeli battle tanks the like of which had seldom been seen on any battlefield. Ever since, the little missile codenamed Sagger by Nato has been treated with great respect, though it is still a simple device with no tube launcher or any guidance other than optical sighting and wire command. Called Miliutka in the Soviet Union, it was first seen in a Moscow parade in May 1965. Since then it has been seen on BRDMs (six-round retractable launcher topped by armoured roof), BMP and BMD (single reloadable launcher above the main gun) and Czech SKOT (twin reloadable rear launcher). The Mi-24 Hind A helicopter can also carry this missile on its four outboard launchers, presumably firing from the hover or at low forward speeds. The missile is accelerated by a boost motor just behind the warhead with four oblique nozzles, and flies on a solid sustainer with jetevator TVC for steering. There are no aerodynamic controls, but the small wings can fold for infantry packaging. A tracking flare is attached beside the body, and it is claimed that an operator can steer to 3,281ft (1,000m) with unaided eyesight, and to three times that distance with the magnifying optical sight. The Western estimated penetration of 15.75in (400mm) for the 6lb (2.72kg) warhead is almost certainly a considerable underestimate. Users include the WP armies and Afghanistan, Algeria, Angola, Egypt, Ethiopia, Iraq, Jugoslavia, Libya, Mozambique, Syria, Uganda and Vietnam, and probably at least five further countries.

Above left: In the foreground is an AT-2 Swatter installation on a BRDM-1 amphibious scout car with, behind it, the AT-1 Snapper also on BRDM.

Top: The standard triple installation of AT-1 Snapper on BRDM-1 (BTR-40P) as used by most WP armies. It is a first-generation wire-guided anti-tank missile no longer produced.

Above: An Israeli photograph of a captured AT-3 Sagger being test-fired. The 'suitcase' packs were for use by soldiers lying prone and were very effective against Israeli tanks.

Left: While rather (understandably) 'foggy', this photograph does show the sighting system at the side of the five AT-5 Spandrel missile launchers on the BRDM-2 vehicle. The missile itself has not yet been shown in public.

Below: Spandrel tubes on display. There is a suggestion that man-portable and helicopter versions are probable.

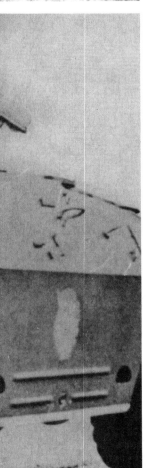

AT-4 Spigot

Code-named Spigot by Nato, this is a high-performance infantry missile fired from a tube and generally similar to Hot. In early 1979 available evidence suggested that it is a man-portable version of AT-5. It probably needs a team of at least three to operate.

AT-5 Spandrel

Allotted the Nato reporting name of Spandrel, this is the tube-launched system first seen on BRDM-2 armoured cars in the Red Square parade of 7 November 1977. Each vehicle has five tubes in a row, on a trainable mount amidships. The tube resembles that of Hot and has a blow-out front closure and flared tail through which passes the efflux from the boost charge. This blows the missile out prior to ignition of its own motor. Folding wings, SACLOS guidance via trailing wires and general size similar to Hot seem reasonable, but the suggested range of 4km appears optimistic. The Group of Soviet Forces in Germany is thought in 1979 to have replaced all its Swatter and Sagger missiles with Spandrel.

AT-6 Spiral

This missile, code-named Spiral by Nato, is believed to be a large laser-guided weapon able to demolish any AFV. It is believed to be standard on the Hind-D helicopter and may also be fitted to the laser-equipped Soviet battle tanks. The suggestion that it is based on the SA-8 SAM appears unlikely.

SS-N-6 Sawfly

Dimensions: Length 42ft 8in (13.0m); diameter about 71in (1.8m).
Launch weight: About 41,887lb (19,000kg).
Range: Mod 1) 1,491 miles (2,400km), Mods 2 and 3) 1,864 miles (3,000km).
This third-generation SLBM shows a totally fresh approach and when it was first seen in the November 1967 parade it posed several problems to Western observers. Geometrically superior to N-5 in that it has the optimum shape to fill a launch tube, N-6 was at first thought to have solid propulsion but has now come to be regarded as a storable liquid missile, almost certainly N_2O_4/UDMH. In its public appearances it has been towed by a Navy/Marines MAZ-537 tractor on a massive articulated trailer which appears to carry the missile with tanks full. The 1st stage appears to be very large, accounting for more than 75 per cent of the total launch weight, with four vectored nozzles. There is no cold expulsion device attached to the missile, and this undoubtedly is part of the launch installation in the Y (Yankee) class submarines which since 1967 have been the carriers of N-6 in service. These formidable nuclear-propelled vessels are considerably larger than any US Navy submarines yet in service, but their hull diameter is still well short of the length of the N-6 missile whose launch tube accordingly project nine feet (2.74m) into a large deck casing. Unlike earlier Soviet FDM submarines the Yankees at least avoid the gross projection of the missile into the sail (bridge-fin) and the standard vessel accommodates 16 launch tubes, the same number as the US Navy Poseidon and Polaris vessels. Clearly the N-6/Yankee combination was the first SLBM system the Soviet Union judged worthy of all-out effort, and from the mid-1960s most of the capacity at the gigantic yards at Severodvinsk and Komsomolsk, assisted by Severomorsk and Gorkii, was devoted to building Yankees at a rate that topped eight per year. A total of 34 were commissioned, representing 544 missiles in tubes, and total N-6 production is put by the MoD at about 1,000.

Three versions are known in the West, believed to be inter-changeable. Mod 1, the original with bluff RV and full-length instrument conduit, has a warhead estimated at 1 to 2 MT. Mod 2, seen on test in 1972 and deployed from 1973, has 'improved propulsion' giving a substantial increase in range (see data). The

DoD states that Mod 2 could hit 'any part of the United States' from the 100-fathom (600ft, 183m) contour offshore. Mod 3, which closely followed Mod 2, has three RVs, not independently targeted. According to the DoD Mod 3 still does not have sufficient combination of yield and accuracy to hit very hard targets, but it would be devastating against cities. It was thought in late 1978 that all N-6 at sea were then of Mod 3 type. Production of N-17 had then already begun as a replacement.

SS-N-8

Dimensions: Length believed to be about 56ft (17m); diameter, variously reported as 79in (2m) and 'same as N-6'.
Launch weight: About 88,183lb (40,000kg).
Range: Observed up to 5,717 miles (9,200km).
In 1971 this missile began an apparently extremely successful flight test programme from a single rebuilt Hotel submarine, the so-called H-III vessel. The N-8 quickly demonstrated a range of 4,847 miles (7,800km), which the Chairman of the JCS, then Gen George S. Brown, said exceeded by at least 1,864 miles (3,000km) the range of any SLBM existing elsewhere. It introduced 'a totally new problem' into Western defence planning. The impact of subsequent testing, from October 1974, when N-8 demonstrated ranges exceeding 5,717 miles (9,200km), on full-range missions from the Barents Sea to a target area in the central Pacific, can thus be imagined. This missile, which at first was vainly hoped in the West to be merely an improved N-6, completely outperforms the Trident C-4 which has not reached the US Navy by 1980. So far no Nato name for N-8 has leaked out, and most details of its design are assumptions. It is believed to be a two-stage storable-liquid missile, and stellar-inertial guidance, unusual in a ballistic vehicle, is said to give CEP to about 1,312ft (400m). This, combined with estimated warhead yields, put N-8 at least in the class of the pre-Mk 12 Minuteman, though the Soviet Union has such a mass of pinpoint high-yield ICBMs that it has no need to use N-8 as a counterforce weapon. Considerably larger even than N-6, this

Below: One of the most recent SS-N-6 SLBMs displayed. The transporter has no provision for handling the missile.

Above: The SS-N-6 Sawfly SLBM. It is fitted in the casing abaft the fin of Yankee class submarines (right).

missile needed the largest submarines ever built to carry it, the D (Delta) class. Even with a hull diameter at least as large as the Yankees the missile length is such that the launch tubes project about 25ft (7.5m) into a giant box aft of the sail. In the Delta I class of about 18 boats the overall length is estimated at 450ft (137m) and the number of launch tubes 12. In 1976 Delta II submarines entered service, with an extra 50ft (15m) section increasing the number of tubes to 16; there are at least eight of these. In mid-1977 a Delta III was seen at sea, with a staggering further increase in length to about 600ft (183m) and 20 or 24 tubes (opinions differ on the number). Several D IIIs were operational in 1980. The missile also exists in at least three forms: Mod 1 has a single 1-2 MT warhead; Mod 2 has three RVs of unknown yield; Mod 3 has three manoeuvrable independently-targeted RVs, the first to enter Soviet Navy service.

SS-NX-12

Data: unknown.
Identified on the foredeck of Kiev, the first of the Kuril class multi-role platforms, this long-range cruise missile is regarded as a successor to N-3 Shaddock and to be compatible with the shipboard magazines and handling systems of the earlier missile. On Kiev there are four twin launchers of a new type, associated with a railed deck handling system and with a crane on the right side of the deck apparently used to bring missiles aboard. Reloading the tubes from below-deck magazines appears to be completely mechanised. The new radar carried in a retractable mounting in the ship's bows, thought to operate in the E/F-band, is generally associated with this missile, which is expected to be a rocket-launched ramjet or turbojet cruise weapon with a range that could be as great as 1,864 miles (3,000km). Speed is generally put at 'transonic'; it will probably be either Mach 0.9 or over Mach 2. The seemingly obvious propulsion would be a ram-rocket matched to a speed of Mach 2.5-3.

SS-NX-13

Data: unknown.
This SLBM appears to be a clever way of evading SALT limitations on the number of strategic missiles that may be deployed. Though similar in size to SS-N-6 and deployed aboard Yankee class submarines, it is reported to be an anti-ship weapon and thus does not count for the purpose of totalling 'strategic' missiles. It is almost certainly an N-6 with different guidance and warhead to give a depressed trajectory and range of 466-621 miles (750-1,000km). Initial target information is believed to be supplied by satellite, which puts the missile into a trajectory giving a near miss. At a range of some dozens of kilometres a terminal homing system with look-down capability (radar, IR or EO) locks-on and steers the RV to impact. The US Navy has suggested that Standard 2 with a nuclear warhead might be able to intercept the relatively slow (said to be Mach 4) RV.

SS-NX-17

Data: unknown.
This is believed to be the first Soviet SLBM to use solid propellant. Prototypes were seen on flight test from land launch tubes in 1975, and testing at sea from submarines was expected to begin in 1977-78. It is reported as a two-stage missile with a PBPS, the first

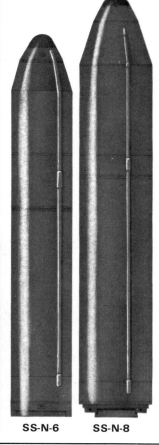

on a Soviet SLBM, though only a single RV was detected on early flight tests. Curiously, dimensions have been given as about 36ft 3½in (11.06m) long and 65in (1.65m) diameter, which does not make NX-17 readily compatible with existing Y or D class launch tubes (though in 1978 the SecDef said one Y boat was testing NX-17 missiles). Several unofficial stories circulating in the West describe a new class of missile submarine under construction at Severomorsk, said to be called the *Typhoon* class by Nato; if this is so, it is a departure from the consistent use of phonetic-alphabet names, T being Tango. The DoD said in 1977 that no Soviet SLBM platform was known beyond the *D-III*, though other observers continue to insist on a completely new, even larger class. NX-17, however, has been positively identified and was expected to enter service, probably in rebuilt *Yankees*, in 1979-80.

SS-NX-18

Data: unknown.
Yet another impressive new SLBM, first seen on flight test a few weeks later than NX-17 in 1975, this is reported as a storable-liquid weapon with a PBPS and, in most tests seen by late 1977, two MIRVS. Land launch-tubes were used many times in 1976, but in November of that year NX-18 first flew from a submarine, in the Beloye More (White Sea) to target off Kamchatka. All evidence to date suggests that NX-18 is the most formidable SLBM yet, with estimated length of 46ft 3in (14.1m) and diameter of 71in (1.8m), similar to the projected Trident D5 but about a decade earlier in timing, and with a range of at least 5,903 miles (9,500km) with advanced MIRVs and penaids.

SS-N-6   **SS-N-8**

Left: Smaller of the two SLBMs is SS-N-6. Diameter is thought to be about the same. Far left: Foredeck of *Kiev*, showing two of eight SS-NX-12 launchers.

SURFACE-TO-SURFACE: SEA TACTICAL

SS-N-2 Styx

Dimensions: Length about 20ft 6in (6.25m); diameter 29½in (750mm); span 9ft 2in (2.8m).
Launch weight: About 5,511lb (2,500kg).
Range: Up to 26 miles (42km).
This simple cruise missile is certainly the most widely used and probably most numerous missile in its class at present. It has also seen action in three wars. Entering service with the Soviet Navy in 1958-9, it was subsequently supplied to many nations and was used in anger in the wars between Egypt and Israel in 1967 (when these missiles sank the destroyer *Eilat*) and 1973, and between India and Pakistan in 1971. N-2 has an aeroplane configuration, with stubby delta wings and tail and a fat bluff-nosed body. Despite this it appears to have rocket propulsion, take-off being under the thrust of a large ventral booster, jettisoned after burnout, and the small sustainer in the tail maintains a speed of around Mach 0.8. In the nose there appears to be a guidance radar, and the consensus of opinion is that the missile is either command guided or flies on autopilot and height lock until its seeker head detects and locks-on to the target. There is abundant evidence of progressive updating of the missiles and launchers over the past 20 years, and most observers believe either or both radar or IR homing may be used by different models of this missile. Some sources use the designations SS-N-2A and -2B to differentiate the supposed original version and a later type with IR homing. The warhead is a linear or polygon charge weighing about 882lb (400kg). Soviet-built missile systems are still being built and over 1,200 are accounted for by the pioneer missile FPB classes, the two-missile *Komar* (Mosquito) and four-missile *Osa* (Wasp), as used by the Soviet Union, Algeria, Bulgaria, Cuba, Egypt, Finland, East Germany, India, Indonesia, Iraq, Jugoslavia, North Korea, Libya, Morocco, Poland, Romania, Somalia, Sri Lanka, Syria, Vietnam and South Yemen. In addition China has its own production line of a derived missile deployed not only on FPBs but also on two destroyer classes and in coast-defence installations (Soviet pictures imply a coast-defence role for N-2, but not convincingly).

Right: An SS-N-2 being hoisted aboard a Soviet Navy Komar class missile boat.

SS-N-3 Shaddock

Dimensions: Length about 42ft 8in (13m); diameter about 39in (1m); span possibly 6ft 10in (2.1m).
Launch weight: About 9,920lb (4,500kg).
Range: Up to 528 miles (850km), though 124 miles (200km) is thought optimum.

Though dating from the same time-frame as the N-1 and N-2 (design about 1951, development and flight-test 1954-57, operational 1958), N-3 Shaddock is vastly more formidable and even today could deliver crushing blows over very great distances. This missile was put into the inventory in ever-increasing numbers and has greatly assisted development of a range of later weapons.

The missile itself is launched from a cylinder of various forms, normally sealed by a cover plate at both ends. Different launch tubes used by the land-based version (SSC-1) have revealed basic information on the configuration. The large body has a pointed nose and internal turbojet or ramjet sustainer (details of the air inlet are unknown in the West); underneath are two solid boost motors which are jettisoned after burn-out, when the short-span wings unfold. There is a ventral fin but no horizontal tail, and the inference is that there is either a foreplane as on Regulus II or elevons on long-chord wings. Cruising speed is certainly beyond Mach 1, a common guess being Mach 1.4; the author sees Mach 2.2 as more attractive. The warhead is either nuclear or conventional of 3,000lb (1,360kg) or over.

Shaddock, quite apart from its Sepal relative, certainly exists in numerous sub-types with different guidance and other changes. Several of the earliest installations were on submarines, and in their haste to deploy this missile the Soviet planners, with total disregard for expenditure, quickly brought into service a succession of quite different installations. The first aboard the *W*-class submarine was dubbed *Whiskey Twin Cylinder* by the West: two Shaddock tubes were installed in an elevating frame completely proud of the rear deck casing, making for an acoustically disastrous submarine. Then followed *Whiskey Long Bin:* a batch of *W*-class were cut in two and given a long amidships section with new conning tower housing four fixed launch tubes. Then came the 16 diesel-engined *J (Juliet)* class, each with a much better installation of two twin launchers which could be elevated from a flush position in the decking. The final scheme was seen in the *E 1 (Echo I)* class nuclear boats, with three such twin launchers, and the 27 really impressive *Echo II* class with four twin launchers. None of these submarines carries suitable guidance equipment, and it has been assumed that mid-course guidance for their missiles is provided by aircraft. These submarines were all in operation by 1963, with 318 launchers in all.

In 1962 the *Kynda* class cruisers appeared, obviously designed around this missile system and carrying two quad launchers with an unknown number of reload rounds rammed in from adjacent deckhouses (how much credence can be placed on a Warsaw pact illustration showing missiles like cartridge cases and shells is doubtful). Each launcher can train through about 25° and elevate to 30°. These ships bristle with radars, with Head Net A for surveillance and the distinctive Scoop Pair to guide the Shaddocks until they disappear over the horizon. In 1967 *Kresta I* cruisers appeared, with two twin launchers abeam the bridge and elevating but fixed in azimuth. *Kresta I* cruisers carry a Ka-25 Hormone A helicopter, but the use of this for target acquisition or missile guidance remains conjectural.

SS-N-7 Siren

Data: unknown.
Called Siren by Nato, this puzzling missile is almost entirely unknown in the West. So far as is known, it is carried only by the *C* class (*Charlie*) submarines, first delivered from Gorki in 1968. While equipped with eight ordinary torpedo tubes of full 21in (533mm) calibre, these vessels do not use these for the missiles which occupy a quite separate eight-round (4 × 2) launcher which can be elevated from the foredeck. Practically nothing is known of N-7 beyond the supposition that it needs a launcher larger than a 533mm tube. (Suggestions that it is derived from N-2 Styx appear ridiculous.) One report (*Flight International*, 1978) suggests a length of 22ft (6.7m) and diameter of 20-21.5in (500-550mm) and while repeating various other estimates of range at around 34 miles (55km) suggests a flight speed of Mach 1.5. One might have expected a speed of either Mach 0.9 or 2, but not in between? The important feature is that N-7 has a dived-launch capability, though at what depth is

Above: One of many forms of installation which Soviet designers have tested for the SS-N-3 Shaddock cruise missile, the Whisky 'Twin Cylinder' class submarine (converted from conventional Whiskys in the late 1950s) must have been noisy when it dived.

Below: Launch of a Shaddock from a surfaced submarine, as shown on a Soviet propaganda film. Apart from submarines, SS-N-3s have been installed on other vessels, such as Kynda and Kresta 1 class cruisers, and the missile is thought to be the fore-runner of SS-N-12s.

unknown. Taken in conjunction with the very high nuclear-driven performance of *C* class submarines, and the little-known *P (Papa)* class that probably also carries this missile, one is driven to conjecture on how these vessels find their targets and how the missiles are guided. It is universally assumed that no outside assistance is needed, in other words the submarines and the missile system form an organic complete system.

SS-N-9

Dimensions: Length less than 29ft 6in (9m).
Though it is conceivable that the *Papa* class nuclear submarines carry this weapon, its only definite application is the outstanding *Nanuchka* class missile boat, sometimes classed as a corvette, which has been in production since 1969. Much larger and steadier than the N-2 boats, *Nanuchkas* carry a triple launch box for this missile on each side. Dominating these ships is the radome-enclosed surveillance radar code-named Band Stand (not Slim Net as first reported), which almost certainly serves a mid-course guidance function. Details of the missile are pure supposition, other than limits on size. Assumptions include flick-out wings, air-breathing or rocket propulsion with emphasis on the latter, radar or IR homing guidance and range of up to 68 miles (110km) at Mach 0.8. It is noteworthy that *Nanuchkas* sold to India carry N-2 or N-11 missiles, not N-9.

SS-N-11

Data: unknown.
Apparently developed from N-2 Styx, this is undoubtedly a much newer SSM of greatly enhanced performance, though similar in size. *Jane's Weapon Systems* expects performance to be 'similar in terms of range and speed', but the developments in propulsion technology in the past 20 years have been dramatic, as have those in structures and, to a lesser degree, in aerodynamics. Guidance is today miniaturized, and may be expected to show advances over N-2, though N-11 has been widely exported, in one case as a substitute for N-7 Siren. N-11 has always been seen in a distinctive drum launcher, with sloping conical muzzle door. it was first deployed on the *Osa II* class missile boats, with four rounds each facing ahead. Four *Kildin* destroyers have been re-reconverted to have four N-11 missiles facing aft around the rear funnel, two twin gun turrets taking the place of the SS-N-1 SSM launcher. By 1967 *Kashin* class destroyers, advanced gas-turbine ships only about 8-11 years old, were appearing with a similar installation. Export customers include India, Finland and Iraq.

Below: SS-N-3 Shaddock launchers on a Kresta 1 class cruiser. The launchers can be raised for firing but not trained.

Above left: Soviet-supplied Egyptian Osa class missile boat armed with short/medium range SS-N-2 Styx.

Above: A Nanuchka class missile boat with triple launchers for SS-N-9s each side of the bridge structure.

Soviet ASW systems

Though the Soviet Union has a vast array of torpedoes and ASW rocket launchers, little is known of its ASW missile systems. The *Moskva* and *Leningrad* ASW cruisers each have a large twin launcher on the foredeck whose projectiles had not, at the time of writing, been seen in the West. The main ASW missile, thought to be fired from this launcher and possibly also from the 'SS-N-10' tubes of all the latest cruisers, is called SS-N-14 by the DoD. It is believed to be a winged drone carrying an ASW torpedo or nuclear depth charge to a range of about 23 miles (37km). An even blinder guess is an ASW rocket, called FRAS-1, said to have a range with nuclear warhead of 18.6 miles (30km). Yet another ASW weapon that appears to be little more than supposition is SS-N-15, a high-speed missile fired from *Victor*-class nuclear attack submarines and credited with a range against hostile submarines of 24.8 miles (40km).

The Forces of The Warsaw Pact

A cursory examination of the Warsaw Pact suggests that it has much in common with NATO. Nothing could be further from the truth, for the Warsaw Pact is designed to ensure the primacy of the Soviet Union in eastern Europe and is rigidly controlled from Moscow. Within the forces of the Pact, organisation, tactical doctrine, equipment training and language are all standardised — they are Russian. Nevertheless there are stresses and the USSR is forced to consider views of other Warsaw Pact members. Some members' reliability in a war not of their choosing is questionable.

In recent years the Soviet Union and other Warsaw Pact nations have vastly increased their capability of projecting power beyond their borders with the use of transport aircraft, troop-carrying warships and aircraft carriers (in the case of the Soviet Union).

Professor John Erickson

Now twenty-five years old, the Warsaw Pact (also referred to as the Warsaw Treaty Organisation: WTO) was born of the Treaty of Friendship, Co-operation and Mutual Assistance "done in Warsaw on May 14, 1955, in one copy each in the Russian, Polish, Czech and German languages, all texts being equally authentic": Article 11 (1st Paragraph) stipulated that the Treaty should remain in force initially for twenty years and for a further ten years, provided that "Contracting Parties" do not one year before the expiry of the Treaty present "a statement of denunciation" to the Government of the Polish People's Republic. So it is that, with Albania the sole legal defector during the past decade, the Warsaw Pact can soldier on well into the 1980s.[1]

At first sight and simply on an inspection of the texts of the North Atlantic Treaty (April 4, 1949) and the enactment of the Warsaw Pact, it might appear that both alliance systems are basically similar and generally equivalent. Such appearances are, however, deceptive. Perhaps the major difference is that the Atlantic Alliance was (and remains still) an association of independent sovereign states, a voluntary association only confirmed after many weeks of lively parliamentary debate, while the Warsaw Pact came into being at the behest, indeed at the command, of the Soviet Union pursuing its own political and strategic purposes. The immediate stimulus to the Warsaw Pact derived from the Paris Agreements (October 1954), whereby the Federal Republic of Germany acceded first to the amended Brussels Treaty and then to NATO itself on May 5, 1955: the signature of the Austrian State Treaty on May 15, 1955, which placed a time limit of ninety days on the stationing of Soviet troops in their "lines of communication" role in Hungary and Rumania, also injected urgency into furnishing a new set of legal justifications for the presence of Soviet forces in East-Central Europe. Finally, in spite of the complex network of bilateral mutual aid treaties between the Soviet Union and separate east European states (dating back in several instances to World War II days and regularly renewed to make them operative right up to the present time),[2] these particular agreements could not of themselves promote, much less embody a sense of unity or collective identification with Soviet interests: it was the function of the Warsaw Pact to do precisely that, ensuring at the same time Soviet predominance.

Again, there is superficial similarity in the structures of NATO and the Warsaw Pact, but the reality is altogether different. In the Warsaw Pact, the Political Consultative Committee is formally required to meet twice a year under the rotating chairmanship of each member nation (holding the chair for a year at a time): the Permanent Commission was also established to frame recommendations on foreign policy on a joint basis. Both of these agencies are physically located in Moscow, but in spite of formal stipulations the Political Consultative Committee has met only irregularly and infrequently, while the Permanent Commission seems more often than not to be by-passed .in favour of bilateral consultation: (in contrast, the NATO Council of Permanent Representatives with its numbers drawn from member nations convenes at least once a week). In full session, the Political Consultative Committee is made up of the First Secretaries of the individual Communist parties, heads of governments, together with foreign and defence ministers: a joint secretariat under the direction of a Soviet Deputy Foreign Minister is attached to the Committee. In March 1969, in the wake of the Soviet invasion of Czechoslovakia and no doubt in response to the severe strains within the Pact, hurried re-organisation set up the Committee of Defence Ministers, which includes the Soviet Defence Minister as well as the six east European Defence Ministers within this body defined as "supreme military organ of the Warsaw Pact": previously these same east European Ministers had been directly subordinated to the Commander-in-Chief of the Joint Armed Forces.

The military organisation of the Pact consists of a Joint High Command, charged with "the direction and co-ordination of the Joint Armed Forces": this organisation was

Below: The non-Soviet members of the Pact add considerable numbers of men and equipment. But, would these Polish soldiers, for example, loyally follow the USSR in an aggressive war against the West?

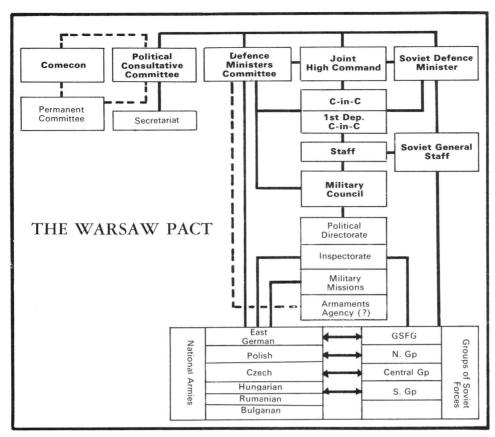

THE WARSAW PACT

brought into existence as early as May 14, 1955 (and thus actually *preceded* the ratification of the Pact itself as required under Article 10). The Commander-in-Chief of the Joint Armed Forces heads the Joint High Command, which also includes the Joint Armed Forces Staff and the Military Council—in line with standard Soviet military practice—which meets under the chairmanship of the Commander-in-Chief together with the Chief of the Staff and permanent military representatives from the East European armed forces. In 1960 the functions of the Staff were enlarged to include competence in preparing training exercises, manoeuvres and war-games: simultaneously senior East European officers were appointed to this command group, though the key command positions continue to be held by Soviet officers, as has always been the case.

The present Commander-in-Chief of the Warsaw Pact is Marshal of the Soviet Union V. G. Kulikov, who has held this post since January 1977 and took the place of the deceased Marshal Yakubovskii. In the same way, Army General A. I. Gribkov became First Deputy C-in-C and Chief of the Joint Armed Forces Staff in November 1976, also in succession to the late Army General Shtemenko. Within the Staff General Gribkov also has his deputies, First Deputy Chief Colonel-General S. F. Romanov and

Left: All is friendly on the surface, but just how reliable would these Warsaw Pact generals be in war? from Left: Generals Coman (Romania), Dzurow (Bulgaria), Hoffman (German Democratic Republic), Dzur (Czechoslovakia); Marshal Ustinov (Soviet Defence Minister); and Generals Jaruzelski (Poland), Castro-Ruz (Cuba) and Czinege (Hungary). (Cuba is not a member of WP.)

Below left: Two Czechoslovak conscripts manning a rocket launcher. From time to time the USSR proposes a supra-national force, but other pact members protest.

Top right: A Soviet-designed 'Shershen' class fast torpedo boat of the East German Navy on firing exercise in the Baltic. East Germany is usually assessed to be the most dependable of the USSR's allies.

Below: A T-62 tank drives ashore from a Labo-class landing craft of the East German Navy. The Soviet Union, Poland and East Germany have powerful amphibious forces in the Baltic, intended for assault landings against NATO.

and Deputy Chiefs Colonel-General A. A. Dement'ev, Lieutenant-General I. D. Krystev, Lieutenant-General Ye. I. Malashenko and Vice-Admiral F. I. Savel'ev (all Soviet officers). In addition, the Inspector-General of the Pact is a senior officer, Lieutenant-General Ye. Ye. Pastushenko, who has held this post since 1970.

The Warsaw Pact does not have its own Pact air defence organisation and air defence is integrated into the Soviet national air defence command (*Protivovozdushnoi oborony strany: PVO Strany*) which is presently directed by Air Marshal A. I. Koldunov (appointed in July 1978 to replace Marshal Batitskii). A Soviet Deputy Commander/*PVO Strany* acts as the "air defence commander" for Eastern Europe and he is responsible for the six main air defence districts in the Pact area, in addition to the ten air defence districts in the USSR proper, all of which include early warning systems, radars, fighter/interceptor forces

and SAMs (surface-to-air missiles), with the local Pact air forces being responsible for the air defence of their own air space though under general Soviet control and within the context of Soviet operational requirements.

Two other arrangements are worth mention. The first concerns the "Soviet representatives" (associated with the Joint High Command) to the several Pact members, located in each capital and responsible for the Soviet military missions attached to non-Soviet armies, navies and air forces. These appointments have more than nominal significance, for example, that of Army General I. E. Shavrov as "Soviet representative" to the German Democratic Republic (DDR), replacing Colonel-General Tankayev and almost certainly indicating an "upgrading" of the DDR in Soviet and Warsaw Pact esteem. (At the same time, these officers must be distinguished from Soviet Military Attachés proper and from the KGB and other intelligence officers assigned throughout eastern Europe to co-ordinate intelligence activities and to supervise operations: Soviet KGB-Bulgarian co-ordination is an illuminating instance of this type of "division of labour".) The second institution or body is the Warsaw Pact *Technical Committee*, seemingly concerned with the overall co-ordination of arms production and the supply of equipment, joint procurement and the supervision of east European military industry: it may also be concerned with improving joint logistics facilities, including rail networks, road links and a common transport pool.

Thus, in origin, structure, military organisation and development the Warsaw Pact differs substantially from NATO, and nowhere more than in the political and military preponderance of a single power, in this case the Soviet Union: the Soviet Union itself contributes some sixty per cent of the

first line forces of the Pact, it is the sole nuclear power within the political directorates unchallenged and unchanging, while its military grip is supplemented by multiple bilateral treaties. Finally, Soviet security in the widest sense is served since the Pact also facilitates control of the internal security (and latterly the political evolution) of the Soviet Union's allies in eastern Europe: no better example of this has been provided by the invasion of Czechoslovakia, which checked internal reform and also served, as far as the Soviet Union's allies at large were concerned, *pour encourager les autres*.

Warsaw Pact combat forces: organisation, strength, deployments

Soviet forces deployed forward in east-central Europe have never at any time in the past thirty years fallen below the level of 25 to 26 divisions and presently stand at the equivalent of 31 to 32 divisions (5 to 6 divisions having been added to the forward order of battle as a result of the invasion of Czechoslovakia in 1968). The Soviet deployment comprises four "Groups of Forces" based in East Germany, Poland, Czechoslovakia and Hungary. Group Soviet Forces Germany (GSFG) consists of five Army HQs (2nd Guards Tank, 3rd Shock, 20th Guards, 8th Guards and 1st Guards Tank Army) with twenty divisions (ten tank, ten motor-rifle plus one artillery division) totalling 370,000 men, 7,000 tanks and 2,350 BMP (infantry combat vehicles) supported by the powerful 16th Air Army capable of launching almost 1,000 aircraft. Northern Group in Poland (HQ Legnica) has the equivalent of three tank divisions and is supported by 37th Air Army. Central Group in Czechoslovakia has 5 to 6 divisions (60,000 to 70,000 men) and two air divisions. Southern Group in Hungary has four full strength divisions (two tank, two motor-

NATO/WARSAW PACT FORCES LOCATED IN EUROPE

In a general war situation, Warsaw Pact Forces committed against Nato might be allocated as follows:

Soviet Forces in the Leningrad Military District against Norway.

Soviet Ground and Naval and Air Forces from the Baltic Military District, plus Polish and East German airborne and amphibious forces against Denmark, the northern coast of West Germany and Holland.

Soviet Ground and Air Forces from the Group of Soviet Forces in Germany (GSFG) and the Soviet Northern Group of Forces (NGF) in Poland, and from the Moscow and Belorussian Military Districts, plus Ground Force elements of the East German and Polish armies, against North Germany (Hanover and the Ruhr); and (together with Czech army units and elements of the Soviet Central Group of Forces in Czechoslovakia (CGF) and Soviet troops from the Kiev Military District) against Central Germany (Frankfurt).

Soviet forces from GSFG, CGF and SGF (Soviet Southern Group of Forces in Hungary) plus elements of the East German, Czech and Hungarian Armies, and troops of the Kiev and Carpathian Military Districts, against Southern Germany (Stuttgart-Munich), Austria and Italy.

Against Southern Europe and Turkey Soviet troops of the Odessa and Causcasian Military Districts and elements of the Hungarian, Romanian and Bulgarian armies.

This would give a comparison of strengths as follows (Nato forces in parenthesis):
Warsaw Pact divisions 140-150(45) tanks 27,000 (10-11,000) artillery pieces 8-9,000 (6,000) men (under arms now) 1,240,000 (1,200,000).

Although the manpower under arms is approximately equal, the Warsaw Pact capacity for very rapid mobilisation would give them a 3-1 superiority in fighting troops after three weeks of mobilisation. Nato could only close the gap after a further month had elapsed.

To what extent the Soviet Union's Warsaw Pact allies can be relied upon depends, of course, on the political situation in which conflict occurs. The startling improvement in the quality and quantity of equipment with which the USSR has equipped the non-Soviet Warsaw Pact countries since 1970 would seem to indicate that these countries are increasingly being considered by the USSR as quite reliable allies. The German and Bulgarian Armies have particularly benefitted from this trend. The Poles, Czechs and Hungarian armies in addition use good quality domestically produced equipment. Only the Romanian army has failed to show a marked improvement since 1970. Presumably, due to Romania being the least controllable regime politically and having the least important position strategically, her army is accorded the lowest priority of resupply by the USSR.

It should be borne in mind that to ensure internal security in both peace and war, all Eastern European countries have very large forces under the control of their Ministries of the Interior or State Security organisations. These forces are, to all intents and purposes, military; being equipped with small warships, combat aircraft and armoured vehicles. To quote an example: A Polish conscript might find himself called up to do not two years national service in the army, but three years in the Border Troops of the Territorial Defence Force. Poland has 80,000 such troops, Romania 45,000, East Germany 80,-100,000, Hungary 20,000, Czechoslovakia 25,000 and Bulgaria 22,000. The USSR has in addition almost half a million such troops, many of whom would be used to ensure the stability of Eastern Europe in the event of war. In addition, all Eastern European countries have TA-style militia forces involving a very large percentage of their adult male populations.

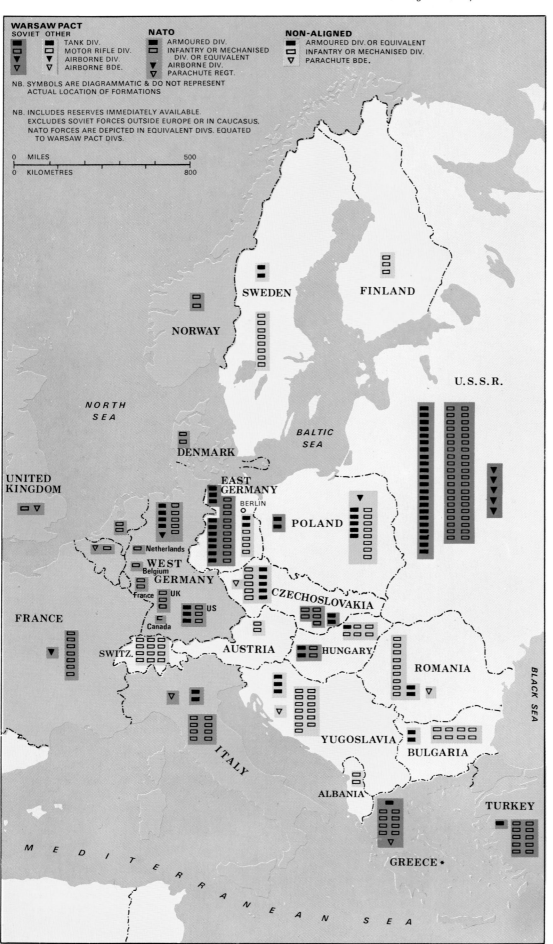

WARSAW PACT

SOVIET	OTHER	
		TANK DIV.
		MOTOR RIFLE DIV.
		AIRBORNE DIV.
		AIRBORNE BDE.

NATO

	ARMOURED DIV.
	INFANTRY OR MECHANISED DIV. OR EQUIVALENT
	AIRBORNE DIV.
	PARACHUTE REGT.

NON-ALIGNED

	ARMOURED DIV. OR EQUIVALENT
	INFANTRY OR MECHANISED DIV.
	PARACHUTE BDE.

NB. SYMBOLS ARE DIAGRAMMATIC & DO NOT REPRESENT ACTUAL LOCATION OF FORMATIONS

NB. INCLUDES RESERVES IMMEDIATELY AVAILABLE. EXCLUDES SOVIET FORCES OUTSIDE EUROPE OR IN CAUCASUS. NATO FORCES ARE DEPICTED IN EQUIVALENT DIVS. EQUATED TO WARSAW PACT DIVS.

* Greece's membership of NATO is in the balance.

rifle), some 80,000 men, 1,300 battle tanks and eight air regiments with 350 aircraft.

This force amounts to some 590,000 men, formed into 16 tank and 15 motor-rifle divisions all with their own tactical air support: of these 31 divisions, 27 are deployed within the confines of the major central sector of a potential European battlefront. In addition, immediate and substantial reinforcement is to hand from the westerly Military Districts of the Soviet Union proper (Baltic, Carpathian and Belorussian MDs), providing the equivalent of eight armies, that is, 400,000 men and 6,800 battle tanks, plus tactical air.

During the 1970s Soviet forces in general and those deployed forward, in particular, have undergone both expansion and modernisation: the overall manpower level of the Soviet military grew from 3.7 million to 4.8 million, with 15 per cent of this increase going to Soviet forces in eastern Europe (35 per cent to the internal MDs in European USSR, thus available for operations against NATO, with the remaining 50 per cent going to the Far East). Some 2,000 battle tanks have been added to the Groups of Forces, with many going to increase the tank strength of motor-rifle divisions (MR divisions now have 268 tanks) and quality has accompanied quantity, for the new T-64 has gone to Soviet divisions with GSFG and the equally modern T-72 to units in eastern Europe. New self-propelled guns (122mm and 512mm) are in service with regimental and divisional artillery, the BMP has been widely introduced and is used in a variety of roles (command vehicle, reconnaissance), holdings of the 40-barrel multiple rocket launcher (MRL) vastly increased and battlefield missiles (SCUD and FROG) modernised, not to mention continuing improvement in mobile battlefield air defence systems (SA-8,

SOVIET FORCES IN EAST GERMANY

(G)="Guards" division, a title of honour given to units/formations which distinguished themselves in the 1941-45 war

Left: Soviet radio detachment in East Germany. In the past 35 years the Soviet Army has put down uprisings in East Berlin, Poland, Hungary and Czechoslovakia: membership of the WP has its hazards.

SA-9, improved SA-7s). Not only has tactical aviation expanded numerically (with 25 per cent more aircraft per regiment) but major qualitative improvement has brought the MiG-23 (Flogger), the MiG-27 and the Su-19 (Fencer) into front-line service. Assault engineers, high-speed bridging capability and logistics have also received much attention, with the latest changes involving the combat support for the MR division (eliminating yet one more weakness).

The non-Soviet national forces of the Warsaw Pact, generally distinguished by a division into the "northern tier" (DDR, Poland, Czechoslovakia) and "southern tier" (Hungary, Bulgaria, Rumania) armies, add a nominal 55 divisions (29 in the northern tier, and 26 in the southern) to the Soviet/non-Soviet order of battle. Of all these states Poland maintains the largest military establishment—over 300,000 men, five tank divisions, eight MR divisions, one airborne and one amphibious division, 3,800 tanks and 750 aircraft together with the largest non-Soviet naval force (including four patrol submarines, one destroyer, 59 fast attack and patrol craft, 24 ocean minesweepers, over 40 landing craft, supported by a large mercantile marine and extensive shipbuilding capacity). The Polish Air Force also is alone in the Pact in operating fifty modern semi-VG Su-17/20 strike aircraft. Though smaller, the East German forces rival the Poles for the position of the leading non-Soviet military element: efficient, well equipped and well trained, the East German Army (NVA) can field two MR divisions and four tank divisions with over 2,500 battle tanks; the air force with 360 combat aircraft is equipped predominantly with MiG-21 and the navy contributes light coastal forces. The East German forces are, however, unique within the Warsaw Pact in being permanently and *directly subordinated* to the Soviet military command (GSFG). The Czechoslovak forces, much dispirited and disorganised by the 1968 Soviet invasion, have slowly recovered some of their place in the Pact order of battle, the army presently organised with ten divisions (five tank, five MR) and 3,500 tanks, one airborne regiment and over 600 aircraft in the air force. Taking the "northern tier" as a whole, with Soviet and non-Soviet forces, the overall order of battle (including some elements deployed further northwards) amounts to some 56 divisions, over 940,000 men and 20,000 battle tanks and more than 3,000 aircraft.

These gross figures, however, need some adjustment in the light of variations in manning, equipment and readiness, not to mention training. Recent Soviet practice in exercises and manoeuvres has demonstrated further interest in integrating joint combat groups (battle groups), which may be a method of selecting or "earmarking" specific non-Soviet formations for operations with Soviet first echelon (Polish airborne and amphibious forces, Czechoslovak motor-rifle units, East German air units and so on). With such selection, a first echelon force of some 48 Soviet and non-Soviet divisions could be assembled without major reinforcement, with up to 9,000 tanks and 1,750 tactical aircraft, while systematic reinforcement could rapidly augment this total with a further 50 divisions. It is conceivable that senior non-Soviet officers would command one sector (though not their own national forces) where, for example, a Polish general would command elements of the Soviet-Polish strike force designated for operations along the Baltic coastline, using also Polish airborne troops for deep penetration and possibly East German para-commando/sabotage battalions.

The relative importance assigned to these non-Soviet forces can be gauged to some degree by the respective modernisation within each army or air force. In general, Polish forces have received priority, due no doubt to their status in the eyes of the Soviet command and Polish willingness to pay for more advanced Soviet equipment: the Polish Army was the first to receive the new self-propelled guns and the air force the Su-17/20 (though the Polish economy evidently will not sustain any further increase in defence burdens). East Germany is presently embarking on a ten year modernisation programme, particularly command and control systems, while receiving up-rated MiG-21 aircraft and the formidable

Mil Mi-24 assault/"gun-ship" helicopter. It would appear that licensed production of the new Soviet T-72 main battle tank has already begun and, while even in "northern tier" armies the older T-54/55 tank predominates, with only a few T-62s, non-Soviet armies may "leap-frog" the process and obtain the T-72, thus bypassing the costly and somewhat inefficient T-62. Czechoslovakia has already acquired its first dozen advanced MiG-23 (which may also be on their way to East Germany) and the air forces of the "northern tier" now consist of about one-third modern combat aircraft capable of offensive air operations: it has been estimated that of the 6,000 fighters to be produced in the USSR over the next five years 25 per cent will be exported to the Warsaw Pact nations.

The "southern tier" (Hungary, Bulgaria and Rumania) presents a marked contrast in manning, equipment, training and modernisation. Hungary has an army of 90,000 organised into six divisions (one tank, five motor-rifle) though only two-thirds of this force are anywhere near operational fitness: the tank-park is in the order of 1,300, though older types predominate, while the 180 combat aircraft are committed almost exclusively to the air defence role. The stolid Bulgarians, hampered by economic difficulties, maintain eight motor-rifle divisions and the equivalent of two tank divisions (organised into five brigades with 2,000 tanks, again elderly machines) and just over 250 aircraft, plus four submarines and two escort vessels in the navy. While Bulgaria retains the closest links with the USSR, Rumania has worked hard to loosen these ties, refusing to remove Rumanian troops from tight national control and resisting all attempts at Soviet military integration, least of all having Soviet troops even on exercise on Rumanian territory. The Rumanian army, in urgent need of modern weapons, comprises two tank divisions and seven motor-rifle divisions, two Alpine brigades and an airborne brigade, with about 1,700 tanks: the air force, which has a small amount of western equipment and is developing a joint Rumanian-Yugoslav fighter, amounts to about 430 aircraft. The Rumanian navy is a light coastal defence force with six corvettes, minesweepers and fast patrol boats.

Integration, standardization, command and control

Essentially, the Warsaw Pact constitutes a military bloc which expedites the forward deployment and the stationing of Soviet ground, air and missiles forces on the territory of member states, thereby developing a major *place d'armes* within an extensive geographic zone formed by contiguous countries. This same zone also comprises a key theatre of operations, in which powerful "shock forces" equipped with the most modern weapons, trained to a common tactical doctrine and operated under common principles of command can be deployed, being kept at a high state of combat-readiness. To this must be added a significant, if not superior reinforcement and mobilization capability. The facility provided by the Warsaw Pact serves three vital Soviet purposes: defence, internal security (which includes securing the continued existence of

Above left: A column of Polish ZSU-23-4 self-propelled AA guns on the march. This combination of well-tried chassis, proven guns and a valve-equipped radar is a weapon feared by airmen everywhere.

Left: Non-WP Yugoslav Army engineers practise river-crossing. These men are well-drilled in Soviet tactics, and Soviet 'steamroller' invaders would have to fight for every hill, pass, river and bridge.

Above: This Polish Army nonour-guard looks smart, but the Soviet Union may well wonder whether they could be relied on in a war in which the Poles felt their own vital national interests were not at stake.

Below: Yugoslav mortar detachment kitted out for NBC warfare. The threat of Soviet invasion with the use of chemicals, especially in mountain regions, may seem more real following events in Afghanistan.

regimes acceptable to the Soviet Union) and a favourable stance for *pre-emption* in the event of major military operations in the European theatre. Finally, the Warsaw Pact is not the sole mechanism or military-political arrangement whereby the Soviet Union can maintain its present military disposition in east-central and south-eastern Europe, which is heavily under-pinned by bilateral treaties: it should be noted *inter alia* that the "status-of-forces agreement" concluded in 1968 with Czecho-slovakia subordinates Soviet troops in Central Group to the *Soviet high Command* and makes *no* reference to the Warsaw Pact.

In view of Soviet preponderance within the Warsaw Pact and its monopoly of senior posts, "integration" has been and must continue to be largely on Soviet terms. Soviet hegemony in nuclear matters is absolute and likely to remain so. At the same time, there have been and are still reserva-tions over Soviet plans for "closer integra-tion", which has stopped far short of the "supra-national" force once mooted by Moscow and resisted above all by Rumania, whose armed forces have been placed by special legislative enactment inalienably under Rumanian *national* command. Some regularisation has been introduced by standardizing separate east European national legislation on universal military service obligations on the Soviet model, but the economic burden of defence outlays has made itself increasingly felt. In spite of Moscow's demand for higher defence

expenditure at the end of 1978, Poland could not comply and Rumania refused to comply. The expense of modernization will obviously feature increasingly in the politics of the Warsaw Pact in the coming decade. The Soviet Union may emphasize its own burden in providing the nuclear shield which shelters the Warsaw Pact, while the separate Pact members point to the costs of maintaining large conventional forces which suck men and money for the common defence. For this and other reasons there seems to be common dislike of and resistance to any Soviet suggestion to "extend" the

Above right: Female soldiers working as plotters in a Warsaw Pact headquarters during a major exercise. Agitation for 'women's lib' does not occur in WP and there are no senior female officers.

Right: Polish troops of the United Nations on patrol in the Middle East. Alone of the Warsaw Pact nations the Polish Army has taken part in UN peacekeeping operations including those in Vietnam.

Far right: A fighter squadron of the Polish Air Force. The aircraft are MiG-21MF (Fishbed) fighters, except for that nearest the camera, which is a two-seat trainer version, designated MiG-21U (Mongol).

Below: A WP engineer reconnaissance party closes up to a river in preparation for a crossing. WP armies often practise assault river crossings, which would clearly feature in an advance across W. Europe.

Warsaw Pact militarily beyond the confines of Europe, least of all to the USSR's ally, Vietnam. However, East Germany has become more deeply involved in Africa, in support of its own aims and also Soviet purposes.

The pace of modernization obviously affects the integration of Soviet with non-Soviet forces and this could be seriously prejudiced if overall modernization lags appreciably. There are, nevertheless, quite considerable advantages in the present Soviet-dominated consolidation and standardization, above all, in matters of organization and doctrine: national armies, whatever their designation, are organized, equipped and trained along Soviet lines, thus implanting a common tactical doctrine and common battle drills. Since the main source of weapons and equipment is the Soviet Union, then a high degree of standardization is automatic: main battle tanks (T-54/55 and now the latest T-72) are Soviet, armoured personnel carriers and infantry combat vehicles (with the exception of a few non-Soviet designs such as the Hungarian D-442 FUG) are Soviet, artillery and mortars are Soviet, as is most assault engineering equipment. Ammunition of all calibres is standard and small arms are Soviet, though Czechoslovak industry produces highly effective indigenous designs. Individual nations produce their own motor vehicles (lorries, transporters) and in all instances the fact that most vehicles are common to the military and civilian sectors facilitates the rapid mobilization of "civilian resources". The Soviet Union has also succeeded in overwhelming the native aircraft industry, with the Poles and Czechs now confined to producing trainers and light

aeroplanes. Polish shipyards are also committed to producing amphibious assault ships for the Soviet Navy.

There are drawbacks, inevitably. Reliance on Soviet production can mean difficulties in enforcing deadlines, in acquiring spare parts and the admixture of old and new equipment presents maintenance problems, as well as reducing interchangeability (as with different types of artillery or new power-plants used in the BMP infantry combat vehicle and the newer battle tanks). Yet this cannot offset the fact that standardization within the Warsaw Pact is much in advance of the situation which prevails in NATO with its diversity of battle tanks, aircraft, ordnance and logistical procedures. Pact standardization, common tactical doctrine and uniformity of training lead inescapably to an acceptance of common principles of command and control, which is becoming increasingly important and an aspect presently receiving close attention from the Soviet command.

The Warsaw Pact as such is not, however, a wartime command organisation in its own right, for all the existence of the "Joint High Command": nor has it a logistics apparatus separate from that of the Soviet armed forces themselves. The Pact in its present form is essentially an administrative and training organisation, subordinated to Soviet operational interests and political objectives. For operational purposes the Soviet "Groups of Forces" would become wartime "Fronts" or Army Groups directly subordinated to the Soviet High Command and fighting under the highly centralised control exercised through the Soviet General Staff, whose shadow "battle staffs" exercise throughout east-central Europe and thus

emplace genuine "command staff" alongside the peacetime administrative structure. It is worth recalling that the troops involved in the invasion of Czechoslovakia came under the command of the Soviet Ground Forces rather than any "Warsaw Pact command", where the Warsaw Pact C-in-C did not take control while logistics did not come within the Pact's competence. We can assume, therefore, that *all* combat-ready forces within a given wartime Front would come under immediate and centralised Soviet command, to which individual senior eastern European commanders would also be responsible in the first instance.

By its existence in peacetime the Warsaw Pact is designed to serve primarily Soviet military commitments and to meet particular political ends. Ironically, by the very act of disappearing for all practical purposes under wartime conditions the Pact could render yet another service to the Soviet armed forces and to the Soviet state.

Notes:

1. The original signatories included the Soviet Union, Albania, Bulgaria, Czechoslovakia, East Germany (German Democratic Republic), Hungary, Poland and Rumania. Albania ceased to participate in the affairs of the Pact in 1962 and officially denounced its membership of the Pact in September 1968.

2. Mutual aid treaties have also been concluded and are presently maintained between the individual east European states. In addition, the Soviet Union has signed "status-of-forces agreements" with those countries in which Soviet troops are stationed: a specific "status-of-forces agreement" was duly concluded with Czechoslovakia on October 16, 1968—after the invasion—covering "the temporary presence of Soviet troops".

UNIFORMS OF THE SOVIET ARMED FORCES

ФОРМА ОДЕЖДЫ И ЗНАКИ РАЗЛИЧИЯ ОФИЦЕРОВ СОВЕТСКОЙ АРМИИ

Uniforms and Badges of Rank of Officers of the Soviet Army

1 Parade and Parade/Walking Out.
2 Shoulderboards for Parade/Walking Out uniforms:
3 Colonel.
4 Colonel-Engineer.
5 Lieutenant Colonel-Engineer (Airforce and Airborne).
6 Lieutenant Colonel (Intendant, Medical, Veterinary, Administration Services and Justice).
7 Captain-Engineer and Captain of Technical Services.
8 Captain.
9 Colonel (for greatcoat).
10 Summer parade dress when on parade (except Airforce and AB).
11 Summer parade dress (Airforce and AB).
12 Winter parade uniform when on parade (except Airforce and AB).
13 Winter parade uniform when on parade in Moscow, capitals of Republics and "hero-cities" (except Airforce and AB).
14 Winter parade uniform (Airforce and AB).
15 Summer parade/walking out dress (except Airforce and AB).
16 Summer parade/walking out dress (Airforce and AB).
17 Winter parade/walking out dress (except Airforce and AB).
18 Summer parade/walking out dress (shirt and shoulderboards).
19 Winter parade/walking out dress (Airforce and AB in blue).

20 Wearing of Orders, Medals and Chest Badges on the parade/walking out uniform.
20a Everyday and Field uniforms:
21 Shoulderboards for Everyday uniforms
22 Colonel (for open-necked jackets and greatcoat).
23 Captain (on shirt).
24 Shoulderboards for field dress (for buttoned up jacket).
25 Summer everyday uniform.
26 Summer everyday uniform off duty.
27 Summer everyday uniform off duty (shirt and shoulderboards).
28 Summer everyday dress off duty (in summer coat).

29 Winter everyday dress off duty.
30 Summer everyday dress off duty.
31 Winter everyday dress off duty.
32 Summer field dress.
33 Summer light dress (in warm climates).
34 Winter field dress.
35 Winter field dress (padded jacket).
36 Summer field dress.
37 Winter field dress.
38 Wearing of ribbons of Orders, Medals and Chest Badges on everyday uniforms.
38a Cockades and Emblems.
39 Parade/walking out peaked hat.
40 Everyday hat gear of the Airforce and AB as well as the parade/walking out beret of women officers.
41 Emblem for the crown of the parade/walking out peaked hat of officers of the Airforce and AB.
42 For everyday head gear of officers (except Airforce and AB).
43 Collar Patches:
44 For parade/walking out uniform.
45 For everyday dress and summer coat.
45a For field dress buttoned up jacket.
46 Insignia on Collar Patches and Shoulderboards:
Top Row (left to right):
Motor Rifle Troops—Artillery—Armoured Troops—Airforce—Airborne—Engineer Troops—Signal Troops and Radiotechnical Troops—Engineer Technical Services in the Airforce—Chemical Troops—Military Technical Schools (POL Supplies Services—Fire Brigades)—"all Arms" engineer technical personnel.
46 Bottom Row (left to right):
Pipe-laying Units—Construction and Aerodrome Engineer units—Motor Transport and Road Troops—Military Topographical Service—Railway Troops and VOSO—Intendant Services and Administrative Services—Military Bandmasters—Justice—Medical Services—Veterinary Services.

ПАРАДНАЯ И ПАРАДНО-ВЫХОДНАЯ

ПОВСЕДНЕВНАЯ И ПОЛЕВАЯ

ПЕТЛИЦЫ

КОКАРДЫ И ЭМБЛЕМЫ

ЭМБЛЕМЫ НА ПЕТЛИЦЫ И ПОГОНЫ

ПОГОНЫ И ПОЛЕВЫМ ОБМУНДИРОВАНИЕМ

Uniforms and Badges of Rank of Marshals and Generals of the Soviet Army

ФОРМА ОДЕЖДЫ И ЗНАКИ РАЗЛИЧИЯ МАРШАЛОВ И ГЕНЕРАЛОВ СОВЕТСКОЙ АРМИИ

1 **Shoulderboards—Parade and Parade/Walking Out and greatcoats.**
2 Marshal of the Soviet Union.
3 Chief Marshal of Armoured Troops (for greatcoats).
4 Chief Marshal of the Airforce.
5 Marshal of Artillery.
6 Marshal of Armoured Troops.
7 Marshal of Airforce.
8 Marshal of Engineer Troops.
9 **Parade and Parade/Walking Out.**
10 Summer parade uniform when on duty (except Airforce).
11 Summer parade uniform when off duty (except Airforce).
12 Winter parade uniform when on duty (except Airforce).
13 Winter parade uniform when off duty (except Airforce).
14 Winter parade uniform when on duty (except Airforce) to be worn on parades held in Moscow, capitals of Union Republics and "hero cities".
15 Summer uniform (Airforce).
16 Winter uniform (Airforce).
17 Summer Parade/walking out uniform.
18 **Shoulderboards for Parade and Walking Out uniforms.**
19 Army General.
20 Colonel General.
21 Colonel General of Justice.
22 Colonel General of the Airforce.
23 Lieutenant General (Engineer and Signal Troops, Technical Troops and Intendant Services).
24 Major General of Medical Services.
25 Major General of Veterinary Services.
26 **Shoulderboards for Everyday uniforms (except greatcoats).**
27 Marshal of the Soviet Union.
28 Chief Marshal of Artillery.
29 Marshal of the Airforce.
30 Colonel General of the Airforce.
31 **Shoulderboards for Field uniforms (except greatcoats).**
32 Marshal of the Soviet Union.
33 Chief Marshal of Artillery.
34 Colonel General.
35 **Everyday and Field uniforms.**
36 Summer everyday form of dress.
37 Winter everyday form of dress.
38 Summer everyday form of dress when off duty.
39 Summer everyday form of dress when off duty (with summer coat).
40 Summer everyday form of dress when off duty (in shirt and shoulderboards).
41 Winter everyday form of dress when off duty.
42 Summer field dress.
43 Winter field dress.
44 **Wearing of Orders, Medals and Chest Badges on Parade uniforms.**
45 Wearing of ribbons of Orders, Medals and Chest Badges on the Parade/Walking Out uniforms and on the open-necked jacket.
46 Cockade and embroidery on the parade peaked hat of a Marshal of the Soviet Union.
47 Cockade and embroidery on the parade peaked/walking out peaked hat of Chief Marshals, Marshals of Arms of Services and Generals (except the Airforce).
48 Cockade and embroidery on the parade peaked hat of Chief Marshals, Marshals and Generals of the Airforce.
49 **Embroidery on Parade uniforms of Marshals of the Soviet Union:**
   a. peak and chin-strap
   b. cuffs
   c. collar
50 Cockade and embroidery on the parade/walking out peaked hat of a Marshal of the Soviet Union.
51 Cockade and embroidery on the parade/walking out peaked hats of Chief Marshals, Marshals of Arms of Services and Generals.
52 **Embroidery on Parade uniforms of Chief Marshals, Marshals of Arms of Services and Generals:**
   a. peak and chin-strap
   b. collar
   c. cuffs
53 Embroidery on the collar and cuffs on the Parade/Walking Out uniform of a Marshal of the Soviet Union.
53a Embroidery on the collar and cuffs on the Parade/Walking Out uniforms of Chief Marshals, Marshals of Arms of Services and Generals.
54 Cockade for everyday peaked hats and fur hats of Marshals and Generals (except the Airforce).
55 Emblem for the crown of the peaked hat on the parade, parade/walking out and everyday hats of Marshals and Generals of the Airforce.
56 Cockade and emblem on the everyday fur hat and peaked hat of Marshals and Generals of Airforce.
57 **Embroidery on the collar of the Everyday jacket:**
58 Of a Marshal of the Soviet Union.
59 Of Chief Marshals, Marshals of Arms of Service and Generals.
60 **Embroidery on the Field Service uniform collar:**
61 Of a Marshal of the Soviet Union.
62 Of Chief Marshals, Marshals of Arms of Service and Generals.
63 **Collar patches for greatcoats and summer coats of Marshals of the Soviet Union and "All Arms Generals":**
64 Marshals of the Soviet Union.
65 "All Arms Generals".
65a Collar patches for greatcoats and summer coats of Chief Marshals, Marshals and Generals of Arms of Service (Services):
   Airforce.
66 Artillery and Armoured Troops.
67 Engineer and Signals Troops, Technical Troops, Intendant, Medical, Veterinary Services and Justice.
68

ФОРМА ОДЕЖДЫ И ЗНАКИ РАЗЛИЧИЯ ПРАПОРЩИКОВ СОВЕТСКОЙ АРМИИ И ЖЕНЩИН, ПРИНЯТЫХ НА ВОЕННУЮ СЛУЖБУ В СОВЕТСКУЮ АРМИЮ

① ПАРАДНАЯ И ПАРАДНО-ВЫХОДНАЯ

② ПОВСЕДНЕВНАЯ И ПОЛЕВАЯ

③ НАРУКАВНЫЕ ЗНАКИ С ЭМБЛЕМАМИ ПО РОДУ ВОЙСК ЧАСТИ

Uniforms and Badges of Rank of Ensigns of the Soviet Army and for Women Accepted into Service in the Soviet Army

1 Shoulderboards for the Parade/Walking Out uniform of Ensigns and for Parade/Walking Out uniform and Everyday and Field uniforms of women accepted for military service in the Soviet Army:

2 Ensign (Motor Rifle Troops).
3 Ensign (Artillery, Tank, Engineer and Technical Troops, Signals Troops, Road, Construction, Pipelaying Units, VOSO Services).
4 Ensign (Airforce and AB).
5 Starshina.
6 Senior Sergeant.
7 Sergeant.

8 **Parade and Parade/Walking Out:**
9 Summer parade dress when on duty (except Airforce and AB).
10 Summer parade dress (Airforce and AB).
11 Winter parade dress (except Airforce and AB).
12 Summer parade/walking out dress (in the Airforce and AB in blue).
13 Summer parade/walking out dress (in the airforce and AB in blue).
14 Winter parade/walking out dress.
15 Wearing of Orders, Medals and Chest Badges on the parade/walking out uniform.
16 Wearing of Ribbons of Orders, Medals and Chest Badges on the everyday jacket.
17 "Those accepted as Ensigns, coming from the ranks of extended servicemen, may wear the **Chest Badge for extended service on their uniforms and jackets"**.
18 Emblem on the crown of the parade/walking out peaked hat of Airforce and Airborne Ensigns.
19 Cockade and emblem on the parade/walking out peaked hat.
20 Star and emblem for the beret.
21 Collar patches for parade/walking out uniform.
22 Collar patches for everyday jacket.
23 Collar patches for field dress.
24 **Everyday and Field Uniforms:**
25 Shoulderboards for everyday and field uniforms.
26 Ensign (for everyday uniforms).

27 Ensign (for field dress).
28 Summer everyday dress.
29 Summer everyday dress off duty.
30 Winter everyday dress off duty.
31 Summer everyday dress off duty (shirt and shoulderboards).
32 Summer everyday dress off duty.
33 Summer everyday dress off duty (shirt and shoulderboards).
34 Winter everyday dress off duty.
35 Summer field dress.
36 Summer light form of dress (in hot regions).
37 Winter form of dress.
38 Summer form of dress.
39 Winter form of dress.

40 Cockade for everyday head gear of Ensigns (except Airforce and AB).
41 Cockade and emblem for everyday head gear of Ensigns of the Airforce and Airborne Troops.
42 Star for the beret (field uniform) and fur hat of women accepted for service in the Soviet Army.
43 **Sleeve Patches with Insignia of Arm of Service:**
(from left to right):
Motor Rifle Troops — Artillery — Armoured Troops — Airforce — Airborne — Engineer Troops — Chemical Troops — Signal and Radiotechnical Troops — Railway Troops — Motor Transport Troops — Pipe-laying Units — Military Construction and other construction units — Medical and Veterinary Services — Military Directors of Music and Bandsmen.
44 **Years of Service — Chevrons for Ensigns:**
(from left to right and down):
1st year — 2nd year — 3rd year — 4th year — 5th — 9th year — 10th year and over.
Note: The chart was "signed for printing" on 27th March 1971 — The new rank of Ensign (PRAPORShchIK) was only published officially at the end of 1971.

246

① ПАРАДНАЯ И ПАРАДНО-ВЫХОДНАЯ

② ПОВСЕДНЕВНАЯ

③ ПОЛЕВАЯ

④ РАБОЧАЯ

⑤ СУВОРОВЦЫ

⑥ ПОГОНЫ И ПЕТЛИЦЫ СУВОРОВЦЕВ

⑦ ПОГОНЫ КУРСАНТОВ ВОЕННЫХ УЧИЛИЩ

⑧ НАРУКАВНЫЕ ЗНАКИ С ЭМБЛЕМАМИ ПО РОДУ ВОЙСК ЧАСТИ

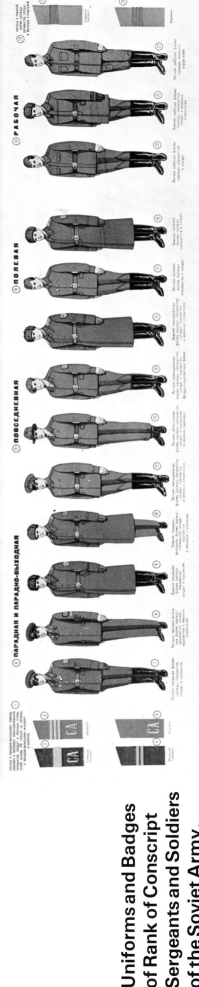

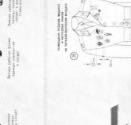
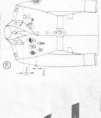
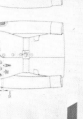

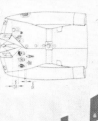

Uniforms and Badges of Rank of Conscript Sergeants and Soldiers of the Soviet Army, Cadets of Military Schools, Suvorov Cadets and Military Construction Troops

1 Shoulderboards for Parade/Walking Out, Everyday and Field uniforms of Sergeants, Soldiers, and Military Construction Troops (the letters SA (CA) are only worn on Parade/Walking Out uniforms and greatcoats):

2 Senior Sergeant.
3 Sergeant.
4 Junior Sergeant.
5 Private Soldier.
6 Parade and parade/walking out.
7 Summer parade dress of sergeants, soldiers and cadets.
8 Parade/walking out uniform of sergeants, soldiers, cadets and military construction troops (Summer).
9 Winter parade uniform of sergeants, soldiers, cadets and military construction troops.
10 Winter parade/walking out uniform of sergeants, soldiers, cadets and military construction troops.

11 **Everyday Uniforms:**
12 Summer everyday dress of sergeants, soldiers, cadets and military construction troops.
13 Summer light dress for sergeants, soldiers and cadets (in hot regions).
14 Everyday summer dress of sergeants, soldiers, and cadets of the Airborne Forces.
15 Everyday winter dress of sergeants, soldiers, cadets and military construction troops.

16 **Field Dress:**
17 Summer dress for sergeants and soldiers.
18 Winter field dress of sergeants and soldiers.

19 **Working Dress:**
20 Summer working dress of sergeants and soldiers.
21 Winter working dress of sergeants, soldiers and military construction troops.
22 Summer working dress of military construction troops.

23 **Shoulderboards for Working Dress of Sergeants, Soldiers and Military Construction Troops:**
24 Senior Sergeant.
25 Sergeant.
26 **Shoulderboards of Officer Cadets of Military Schools (left to right):** Cadet Starshina—Cadet Senior Sergeant

—Cadet Sergeant—Cadet Junior Sergeant—Cadet Lance Corporal—Cadet Private.

27 **Collar Patches for Parade/Walking Out Uniforms of Sergeants, Soldiers, Cadets and Military Construction Troops.**
28 Star and emblem for peaked hat.
29 Star for fur cap with ear-flaps.
30 Star for side cap and "panama".
31 **Suvorov School Cadets.**
32 Summer parade and parade/walking out uniform.
33 Winter parade, parade/walking out and everyday uniform.
34 Summer everyday No 1 dress.
35 Summer everyday No 2 dress.
36 Shoulderboards, and collar patches of Suvorov cadets.
37 Collar patches for the buttoned up jacket of sergeants, soldiers, cadets and military construction troops.
38 Collar patches for greatcoats and padded jackets of sergeants, soldiers, cadets and military construction troops.
39 Wearing of orders, medals and chest decorations on the parade/walking out uniform.
40 Wearing ribbons of orders, medals and chest decorations on the buttoned up tunic.
41 **Sleeve Patches with insignia of**

Arms of Service of the unit:
(left to right)—Motor Rifle Troops—Artillery—Armoured Troops—Airforce—Engineer Troops—Chemical Troops—Signals and Radiotechnical Troops—Railway Troops—Motor Transport Troops—Pipe-laying Units—Military Construction and other construction units—Medical and Veterinary Services—Military Band Masters and Bandsmen.
42 **Sleeve Chevrons for Officer Cadets of Military Schools to denote course years: (left to right and down)**—1st Course—2nd Course—3rd Course—4th Course—5th Course—6th Course.

247

Index to Modern Soviet Weapon Systems

Page numbers in bold type indicate illustrated references

A

AIRCRAFT

AIR DEFENCE WEAPONS

ARMOURED VEHICLES

ARTILLERY AND ANTI-TANK WEAPONS

E

ENGINEERING EQUIPMENT

M

MISSILES

Air-to-air tactical

Air-to-surface strategic

Air-to-surface tactical

Anti-satellite interception

Anti-tank missiles

Surface-to-air land

PRINTED IN BELGIUM BY

INTERNATIONAL BOOK PRODUCTION